SCHUBERT AND HIS WORLD
A BIOGRAPHICAL DICTIONARY

SCHUBERT AND HIS WORLD

A BIOGRAPHICAL DICTIONARY

PETER CLIVE

CLARENDON PRESS · OXFORD

1997

Oxford University Press, Great Clarendon Street, Oxford OX2 6DP

Oxford New York

Athens Auckland Bangkok Bogota Bombay
Buenos Aires Calcutta Cape Town Dar es Salaam
Delhi Florence Hong Kong Istanbul Karachi
Kuala Lumpur Madras Madrid Melbourne
Mexico City Nairobi Paris Singapore
Taipei Tokyo Toronto
and associated companies in
Berlin Ibadan

Oxford is a trade mark of Oxford University Press

Published in the United States
by Oxford University Press Inc., New York

© Peter Clive 1997

British Library Cataloguing in Publication Data
Data available

Library of Congress Cataloging-in-Publication Data
Clive. H. P.
Schubert and his world: a biographical dictionary/Peter Clive.
p.   cm.
Includes bibliographical references and index.
1. Schubert, Franz, 1797–1828–Friends and associates.
2. Schubert, Franz, 1797–1828–Dictionaries.
3. Composers–Austria–Biography.   I. Title.
ML410.S3C48   1996   780' 92–dc20   [B]   96–24977
ISBN 0–19–816582–X

1 3 5 7 9 10 8 6 4 2

Typeset by Pure Tech India Ltd., Pondicherry
Printed in Great Britain
on acid-free paper by
Biddles Ltd
Guildford & King's Lynn

For Megan

Preface

꒸ꙬꙮꙬ꒱

Franz Schubert's music is enjoyed by more people today than ever before. It is performed at countless concerts and recitals around the world, played on innumerable radio stations, and made available for private listening on a constantly growing number of recordings. A specialist can, moreover, enrich his knowledge and understanding of the compositions by consulting the new critical edition of Schubert's collected works which is in process of publication. At the same time, Otto Erich Deutsch's remarkable documentary biography is now being superseded by an even more comprehensive collection of printed and hand-written documents (accompanied by commentaries); at the time of writing, the first of the four planned volumes has already appeared.

In addition to these major research projects, a steady stream of publications dealing with biographical and musical matters testifies to the intense interest which scholars take in every aspect of Schubert's life and works. Indeed, certain aspects of his life have recently come under fresh scrutiny (*see* Bauernfeld*). The time therefore seems opportune for the publication of a book like the present one, which, it is hoped, will be of use and interest to the Schubert specialist as well as to the general music lover.

The dictionary provides information about more than 300 persons. It lists not only friends and acquaintances, and persons with whom Schubert was associated through his music (poets, librettists, publishers, patrons, musicians), but also a number of later 'Schubertians' who, in a variety of ways, were instrumental in promoting knowledge and appreciation of his music both in his own and in certain other countries, or who made a particularly significant contribution to the discovery and publication of important information about his life. Room has also been made for two persons whose names, it is true, evoke no great admiration or gratitude from modern Schubert scholars, but whose influence on the public perception of Schubert, both as a man and a composer, cannot be denied, and who therefore deserve to be mentioned in this context: the writer Rudolf Hans Bartsch and the composer Heinrich Berté. On the other hand, the catalogue does not list any of the distinguished modern interpreters of Schubert's music, since any choice among them would inevitably prove to be a highly personal one.

The amount of biographical particulars furnished in the different articles depends necessarily on the celebrity of the person in question. The better known a person is, the fewer are the facts which require to be mentioned, since the reader may be assumed to be already familiar with the broad outline of the subject's life. For such universally renowned persons as Beethoven, Goethe, and Shakespeare only the barest biographical data are provided. At the same time, in order not to clutter up the text with too many dates, information regarding the years of birth and death of persons other than the subjects of articles and their immediate family has been placed in the index.

As a rule, no attempt has been made to identify the precise edition which Schubert may be presumed to have used when setting the various poems, since in very many cases it is impossible to arrive at a firm conclusion. For information and suggestions on this matter, the reader is referred especially to *Franz Schubert: Die Texte seiner einstimmig komponierten Lieder und ihre Dichter* by M. and L. Schochow, and to L. Porhansl's series of articles in the journal *Schubert durch die Brille*. (Particulars of these publications will be found in the bibliographical section.)

SOURCES

The principal sources are cited in abbreviated form at the end of each article; full details are given in the Bibliography. In addition, the following books have been constantly consulted in the preparation of this dictionary: *Franz Schubert: Die Dokumente seines Lebens* by O. E. Deutsch (Kassel, 1964), *Franz Schubert: Dokumente 1817–1830*, vol. i, ed. T. G. Waidelich (Tutzing, 1993), *Franz Schubert: Die Erinnerungen seiner Freunde*, ed. O. E. Deutsch (Leipzig, 1957), and *Franz Schubert: Thematisches Verzeichnis seiner Werke in chronologischer Folge* (Kassel, 1978). These works have proved invaluable and deserve mention in countless entries, but to avoid tiresome repetition they are cited only in special cases.

VIENNESE ADDRESSES

Because the modern system of numbering houses in Vienna differs from that used in Schubert's day, no useful purpose would be served by citing the numbers which were assigned to them at that time. However, because readers may be interested to know just where in the city many of the buildings mentioned in the text stood (or still stand), their modern addresses are given within square brackets. It should be borne in mind, however, that the houses which occupy these sites today are not necessarily those which did so in the early nineteenth century. For the modern addresses, I am mainly indebted to Rudolf Klein's excellent *Schubert-Stätten* (Vienna, 1972). I have also consulted Felix Czeike's *Historisches Lexikon Wien* (5 vols., Vienna, 1992–7).

NAMES OF PERSONS

The original spelling of first names has normally been retained, but in the case of Joseph/Josef the latter form has been adopted throughout.

TITLES

Ranks of nobility have been rendered by the most closely corresponding titles in English, e.g. 'Graf' by 'Count'. Honorific titles such as 'Hofrat' have been left in German.

ASTERISK

An asterisk following a person's name at its first appearance in an article indicates that he or she is the subject of a separate dictionary entry. In addition, the asterisk is used in cross-references between articles (e.g. '*see* Beethoven*').

TRANSLATIONS

All translations from the German are my own.

I am indebted to a number of persons who have assisted me with information or advice or in other ways. I should particularly like to express my gratitude for the help I received in Vienna from Regierungsrat Clemens Höslinger, Walburga Litschauer (Neue Schubert-Ausgabe), Herbert Maska (Veterinärmedizinische Universität), Michael Nagy, Erich Wolfgang Partsch (Kommission für Musikforschung), Hubert Reitterer (*Österreichisches Biographisches Lexikon*), and Kurt Schuh (Wiener Männergesangverein); and elsewhere, from Werner Aderhold (Neue Schubert-Ausgabe, Tübingen), Mária Eckhardt and Imre Sulyok (Liszt Ferenc Memorial Museum, Budapest), Wolfgang Mayrhofer-Grüenbühl (Völkermarkt), Sr. M. Gratia Schneeweiss (Klagenfurt), Fridolin von Spaun (Dorfen), and Gerrit Waidelich (Berlin). Several parish priests in Austria have kindly supplied information concerning certain persons mentioned in this book. I wish to thank Peter Branscombe (St Andrews) for many extremely valuable comments on the typescript, and I am grateful to my friend Peter Zohar for reading the text and sharing the proof-reading. Last but not least, I wish to express my sincere thanks for the splendid assistance provided by Callista Kelly and her colleagues Jeet Atwal, Tina McKinnon-Cameron, Cicely Rayne, and Denize Tam of the Interlibrary Loans Section at Carleton University, Ottawa.

PETER CLIVE

Contents

✣

List of Illustrations

❧✳❧

Sources: Plates 1–15 are reproduced by courtesy of the Österreichische Nationalbibliothek, Vienna, and Plates 16–17 by courtesy of the Pierpont Morgan Library, New York.

A Chronicle of Schubert's Life[1]

1797   (31 January) Birth of Franz Peter Schubert, twelfth (and fourth surviving) child of the schoolmaster Franz Theodor Florian Schubert and his wife Maria Elisabeth Katharina Schubert, née Vietz, residing in the Himmelpfortgrund suburb of Vienna, in the parish of Lichtental [54 Nussdorferstrasse].
        (1 February) Schubert is baptized. His uncle Karl Schubert is named as godfather.

1801   The family moves to a house [3 Säulengasse] diagonally opposite the former one.

1805   From c.1805 Schubert is taught singing, counterpoint, and organ by Michael Holzer, choirmaster at Lichtental parish church.

1808   (Autumn) As a result of an examination held on 30 September, court Kapellmeister Antonio Salieri and Franz Innocenz Lang, the director of the Vienna Stadtkonvikt, recommend that Schubert be offered a place as choirboy in the court Kapelle and be simultaneously admitted as a pupil to the Konvikt. Schubert becomes a boarder at the Konvikt [1 Dr. Ignaz Seipelplatz], and, once there, joins the college orchestra, in which he plays among the second violins.
        (November) His musical ability attracts the attention of Josef von Spaun, who will become an enthusiastic and generous supporter and lifelong friend. (While at the Konvikt, Schubert will receive musical instruction from Wenzel Růžička and Antonio Salieri.)

1809   (September) Spaun leaves Vienna to join the civil service at Linz.

1810   *Compositions*: Fantasia in G major for piano duet (D1); [?1811] String Quartet in G minor (D18).

1811   (March) Spaun returns to Vienna, where he will be in close personal contact with Schubert during the next ten years.
        Compositions: Overture in C minor for string quintet (D8); Fantasia in G minor for piano duet (D9); the earliest surviving complete song, 'Hagars Klage' (D5),

---

[1] The biographical details are followed, where appropriate, by a selected list of compositions and publications.

also 'Der Vatermörder' (D10). Schubert begins work on his first stage work, *Der Spiegelritter* (D11), of which only a fragment survives.

1812   (28 May) Death of Schubert's mother.

Compositions: *Salve regina* in F major (D27); String Quartet in C major (D32); Trio in B flat major for piano, violin, and cello (D28); vocal settings of several texts by Metastasio, written as exercises for Salieri.

1813   (January) [?late 1812] Schubert, who has previously been taken by Spaun to hear operas by Josef Weigl and Spontini, accompanies him to a performance of Gluck's *Iphigénie en Tauride*, with Johann Michael Vogl and Anna Milder-Hauptmann in the leading roles. He is profoundly moved by the music and greatly impressed by the singers. After the performance, he is introduced to Theodor Körner.

(25 April) Schubert's father marries Anna Kleinböck [Kleyenböck].

(Autumn) Though having failed to attain the required standard in mathematics in the preceding school year, Schubert is conditionally granted a scholarship for 1813–14, but he declines the offer and leaves the Konvikt. He continues, however, to study with Salieri.

Compositions: Symphony No. 1 in D major (D82); Octet in F major for wind instruments (D72); several string quartets (D46, 68, 74, 87); a number of minuets and Deutsche for string quartet (D89); numerous partsongs to texts by Schiller, probably written as exercises for Salieri. Schubert begins work on the opera *Des Teufels Lustschloss* (D84).

1814   (Winter–spring) Schubert trains as a teacher at the St Anna Normal-hauptschule [3–3a Annagasse].

(Autumn) Schubert becomes an assistant teacher at his father's school. He regularly takes part in music sessions at his home.

(16 October) Performance of the Mass in F major (D105) at Lichtental parish church, under Schubert's direction. This is the first public perform-ance of any of his works.

(26 October) Another performance of the Mass, at St Augustine's Church in the city.

Compositions: the opera *Des Teufels Lustschloss* (D84), completed; Mass in F major (D105); String Quartet in B flat major (D112); thirteen songs to poems by Matthisson and several to texts by Goethe—among the latter: 'Gretchen am Spinnrade' (D118) and 'Schäfers Klagelied' (D121).

1815   Schubert makes the acquaintance of Anselm Hüttenbrenner (who is also studying with Salieri) and is introduced by Spaun to Franz von Schober.

(Spring) Performance of the Mass in G major (D167) at Lichtental parish church.

(Autumn) Otto Hatwig takes over the direction of the private concerts which have developed out of the music sessions at the Schubert home and which have more recently taken place at the house of the merchant Franz Frischling [1 Dorotheergasse]. Schubert plays the viola in the orchestra, which meets henceforth in Hatwig's rooms at the Schottenhof [Freyung].

Compositions: the Singspiels *Claudine von Villa Bella* (D239), *Der vierjährige Posten* (D190), *Die Freunde von Salamanka* (D326), and *Fernando* (D220); Masses in G major (D167) and B flat major (D324, begun November); Symphonies No. 2 in B flat major (D125) and No. 3 in D major (D200); some 150 songs, to poems by Goethe, Hölty, Klopstock, Körner, Kosegarten, and Schiller. The Goethe settings include 'Erlkönig' (D328), 'Heidenröslein' (D257), and 'Wandrers Nachtlied' (D224).

1816   (April) Schubert applies, unsuccessfully, for the post of music teacher at the teachers' training college at Laibach [Ljubljana]. Spaun seeks Goethe's permission for Schubert to dedicate to him several volumes of songs which Schubert intends to publish. With his letter (17 April), Spaun encloses the manuscript of the first volume, containing settings of Goethe poems; it is returned without comment.

(16 June) Schubert takes part in celebrations marking the fiftieth anniversary of Salieri's arrival in Vienna. He writes a congratulatory poem for the occasion, which he sets to music (D407). His studies with Salieri will cease later in the year.

(24 July) Schubert conducts his cantata *Prometheus* (D451) at Heinrich Josef Watteroth's house [17 Erdbergstrasse]. Among those taking part in the performance is Leopold von Sonnleithner, whose enthusiasm for Schubert's music will have significant consequences for his career.

(Autumn) Schubert moves to Schober's apartment [26 Tuchlauben], where he will stay until August 1817. First performance of the Symphony No. 5 (D485) at Otto Hatwig's.

Compositions: Mass in C major (D452); the cantata *Prometheus* (D451); Symphonies No. 4 in C minor (D417) and No. 5 in B flat major (D485); some 100 songs to poems by Claudius, Goethe, Hölty, Jacobi, Klopstock, Matthisson, Mayrhofer, Salis-Seewis, and Schmidt including 'Am Tage Aller Seelen' (D343), 'An die Nachtigall' (D497), 'An Schwager Kronos' (D369), 'Der Wanderer' (D489), 'Gesänge des Harfners aus *Wilhelm Meister*' (D478), 'Seligkeit' (D433), and 'Wiegenlied' (D498). Schubert also works on (but does not complete) the opera *Die Bürgschaft* (D435).

1817   (February–March) Schober presents Schubert to Johann Michael Vogl, who will become the foremost interpreter of his songs.

(Spring) Schubert, or Spaun, sends the manuscript of 'Erlkönig' (D328) to the Leipzig publishers Breitkopf & Härtel; they decline to publish the song.

(Autumn) Schubert returns to his father's house in Himmelpfortgrund. He resumes teaching at the school.

(27 September) Schlechta's poem 'An Herrn Franz Schubert (Als seine Kantate *Prometheus* aufgeführt ward)' is printed in the *Wiener allgemeine Theaterzeitung*. This is the first time that Schubert's name is mentioned in a periodical.

Compositions: two overtures in the Italian style (D590–1); several piano sonatas; the partsong 'Das Dörfchen' (D598); some sixty songs to poems by Claudius, Goethe, Mayrhofer, Schiller, Schober, and Schubart, including 'An die Musik' (D547), 'Der Tod und das Mädchen' (D531), 'Die Forelle' (550), 'Erlafsee' (D586), 'Ganymed' (D544), and 'Gruppe aus dem Tartarus' (D583). In October, Schubert begins work on the Symphony No. 6 in C major (D589).

1818   (Early 1818) Schubert's father having been transferred to a school in the Rossau suburb, the family moves there [11 Grünetorgasse]. First performance of the Symphony No. 6 (D589) at Otto Hatwig's.

'Erlafsee' (D586) is published, under the title 'Am Erlaf-See', in *Mahlerisches Taschenbuch für Freunde interessanter Gegenden, Natur- und Kunst-Merkwürdigkeiten der österreichischen Monarchie* (Vienna). It is the first of Schubert's songs to appear in print.

(1 March) An overture by Schubert (D590 or 591) is played at a concert at the 'Zum römischen Kaiser' inn. This is the first known performance of a work by Schubert at a public concert.

(5 March) Schubert applies, unsuccessfully, to become a member of the Gesellschaft der Musikfreunde.

(12 March) An overture by Schubert (probably the same as on 1 March) is played, in an arrangement for eight hands, at a private entertainment offered by the actor Karl Friedrich Müller at the 'Zum römischen Kaiser'. Schubert is among the four pianists participating.

(Spring) Hatwig moves from the Schottenhof to the Gundelhof [4 Bauernmarkt/5 Brandstätte], and the private orchestra now meets there. However, Hatwig falls ill shortly afterwards, and the concerts are moved to Anton von Pettenkoffer's apartment [11 Bauernmarkt].

(July–November) Schubert is employed as music teacher to Count Johann Karl Esterházy's two daughters at Zseliz [Želiezovce, Slovak Republic]. Through Esterházy, he meets Baron Schönstein. After his return to Vienna, he shares accommodation with Johann Mayrhofer [2 Wipplingerstrasse].

Compositions: Symphony No. 6 (D589), completed; Piano Sonatas in C major (D613) and F minor (D625), both incomplete; Rondo in D major (D608) and Sonata in B flat major (D617), both for piano duet; a few songs to texts by Petrarch (in translation), Friedrich von Schlegel, and Aloys Schreiber.

Publication: 'Erlafsee' (D586).

1819   (8 January) Another performance of *Prometheus* (D451), this time in Ignaz von Sonnleithner's apartment at the Gundelhof.

(28 February) First known public performance of a Schubert song: Franz Jäger sings 'Schäfers Klagelied' (D121) at a concert at the 'Zum römischen Kaiser'.

(July–September) Schubert spends the summer in Upper Austria with Vogl. He visits Steyr, where he stays with Albert Schellmann, and Linz, where he makes the acquaintance of Anton Ottenwalt.

(19 November) Performance of the quartet 'Das Dörfchen' (D598) at Ignaz von Sonnleithner's.

Compositions: the Singspiel *Die Zwillingsbrüder* (D647); Overture in E minor (D648); [probably] 'Trout' Quintet (D667); Piano sonata in A major (D664) [?1825]. Schubert begins the Mass in A flat major (D678) which will not be completed until 1822.

1820   (*c.*1820) Musical soirée at Matthäus von Collin's [7 Teinfaltstrasse], at which Schubert is introduced to some of the most influential and distinguished Viennese music lovers. Vogl sings several Schubert songs, including 'Der Wanderer' (D489), and Schubert and Anselm Hütten-brenner play the *Eight Variations on a French Song* (D624).

(March) Schubert is present when the police search Johann Senn's room. Although he is alleged to have behaved offensively, no action is taken against him.

(2 March) An overture by Schubert (probably D648) is played at Anton von Pettenkoffer's.

(4 April) Schubert conducts Haydn's 'Nelson' Mass at Alt-Lerchenfeld church.

(7 April) An overture by Schubert (perhaps again D648) is played at a concert at Graz. This is the first known public performance of a work by Schubert outside Vienna.

(14 June) Première of the Singspiel *Die Zwillingsbrüder* (D647) at the Kärntnertor-Theater.

(July) Schubert stays at Atzenbrugg Castle, near Tulln, as a guest of Schober and his uncle Josef Derffel. He will return there in the summers of 1821 and 1822.

(19 August) The melodrama *Die Zauberharfe*, for which Schubert has written the music (D644), is produced at the Theater an der Wien.

(21 November) Therese Grob, with whom Schubert is said to have been in love, marries Johann Bergmann.

(1 December) August von Gymnich sings 'Erlkönig' (D328) at Ignaz von Sonnleithner's.

(9 December) The song 'Die Forelle' (D550) is published as a supplement to the *Wiener Zeitschrift für Kunst, Literatur, Theater und Mode*.

Compositions: music for the melodrama *Die Zauberharfe* (D644), sketches for the opera *Sakuntala* (D701); the oratorio *Lazarus* (D689), Psalm 23 (D706); *Quartettsatz* in C minor (D703); settings of poems by Friedrich von Schlegel and Johann Mayrhofer (including 'Der zürnenden Diana', D707).

Publications: 'Die Forelle' (D550), 'Widerschein' (639).

1821   Schubert makes the acquaintance of Moritz von Schwind, who will become one of his closest friends.

(Early 1821) Schubert moves from Mayrhofer's room to new lodgings in the same street [21 Wipplingerstrasse].

(January) Schubert obtains testimonials from Count Dietrichstein, Ignaz Franz von Mosel, Salieri, and Josef Weigl, perhaps with the intention of seeking a post at the court theatre (see February below) or of soliciting a commission for an opera (see November below).

(19 January) Gymnich sings 'Der Wanderer' (D489) at Ignaz von Sonnleithner's.

(25 January) Gymnich sings 'Erlkönig' (D328) at an 'evening entertainment' of the Gesellschaft der Musikfreunde.

(26 January) Schubert sings a number of his songs at a party at Schober's.

(February) Schubert is briefly employed as répétiteur at the court theatre, where he coaches Karoline Unger in the part of Isabella [Dorabella] in Mozart's opera *Mädchentreue* [*Così fan tutte*].

(8 February) Josef Götz sings 'Sehnsucht' (D636) at an 'evening entertainment' of the Gesellschaft der Musikfreunde.

(2 March) Sophie Linhart sings 'Gretchen am Spinnrade' (D118) at Ignaz von Sonnleithner's.

(7 March) First public performance of 'Erlkönig' (D328), by Vogl at the Kärntnertor-Theater. Also on the programme: first public performances of the quartet 'Das Dörfchen' (D598) and the octet 'Gesang der Geister über den Wassern' (D714).

(April) Publication of 'Erlkönig' (D328) and 'Gretchen am Spinnrade' (D118), Schubert's Opp. 1 and 2, thanks to the generous support of Leopold von Sonnleithner and others who have agreed to cover publication costs for these and several further songs.

(8 April) Performance of 'Das Dörfchen' (D598) at a concert of the Gesellschaft der Musikfreunde in the Grosser Redoutensaal.

(22 April) First public performance of the quartet 'Die Nachtigall' (D724), at the Kärntnertor-Theater.

(20 June) Première at the Kärntnertor-Theater of L. J. F. Hérold's comic opera *Das Zauberglöckchen* (*La clochette, ou Le Diable page*), for which Schubert has written two additional numbers (D723).

(September) Spaun is transferred from Vienna to Linz.

(Mid-September to mid-October) Schubert and Schober spend some four weeks at St Pölten and at nearby Ochsenburg Castle, where they are guests of Schober's relative Johann Nepomuk von Dankesreither, bishop of St Pölten. Much of their time is devoted to the opera *Alfonso und Estrella* (D732), for which Schober is writing the libretto.

(November) Schubert is invited to write an opera for the court theatre. (However, for different reasons, none of his future operas will, in fact, be produced there.) On 18 November his Overture in E minor (D648) is played at a concert of the Gesellschaft der Musikfreunde. Moreover, by November at the latest, he has become a member of the Gesellschaft.

Compositions: the opera *Alfonso und Estrella* (D732), which will be completed in 1822; the octet 'Gesang der Geister über den Wassern' (D714); several Goethe songs, 'Suleika I–II' (D720, 717), and probably [?1822] 'Sei mir gegrüsst' (D741).

Publications: a collection of thirty-six dances (among them, the *Trauerwalzer*) for the piano (D365); twelve Goethe songs, including 'Der König in Thule' (D367), 'Erlkönig' (D328), 'Gretchen am Spinnrade' (D118), 'Heidenröslein' (D257), 'Schäfers Klagelied' (D121), and 'Wandrers Nachtlied' (D224); also 'Am Grabe Anselmos' (D504), 'Der Tod und das Mädchen' (D531), and 'Der Wanderer' (D489).

1822   Schubert once more moves in with Schober [9 Spiegelgasse]. He will remain there until summer 1823, except for a period between late 1822 and spring 1823, during which he will stay at his father's house in the Rossau suburb.

(21 January) Schubert sings some of his songs at a party given by Professor Vincentius Weintridt, to which he has accompanied Schwind. Eduard von Bauernfeld is also present, but he will not become a close friend until 1825.

(February) Schubert makes the acquaintance of Carl Maria von Weber.

(11 February) Performances, at the Theresian Academy, of 'Erlkönig' (D328) and of the cantata *Am Geburtstage des Kaisers* (D748).

(3 March) The quartet 'Geist der Liebe' (D747) is performed at a concert of the Gesellschaft der Musikfreunde.

(5 March) Schubert sings some of his songs at Karoline Pichler's.

(3 July) He writes the allegorical story *Mein Traum*.

(Winter) Frequent reading parties and Schubertiads at Schober's.

Compositions: the opera *Alfonso und Estrella* (D732) completed; Mass in A flat major (D678) completed (begun in 1819); the 'Unfinished' Symphony (D759); 'Wanderer' Fantasia (D760); the partsong 'Geist der Liebe' (D747) to a text by Matthisson; and some fifteen songs to texts by Bruchmann, Goethe, Mayrhofer, Schober, and Friedrich von Schlegel, including 'Der Musensohn' (D764) and 'Nachtviolen' (D752).

Publications: *Eight Variations on a French Song* for piano duet (D624); the
quartets 'Das Dörfchen' (D598), 'Die Nachtigall' (D724), 'Geist der Liebe'
(D747); the songs 'Der Alpenjäger' (D524), 'Die Rose' (D745), 'Geheimes'
(D719), 'Gesänge des Harfners aus *Wilhelm Meister*' (D478), 'Lob der Tränen'
(D711), and 'Suleika I' (D720).

1823   Both the Steiermärkischer Musikverein (Styrian Music Society) and the
Linz Gesellschaft der Musikfreunde confer honorary membership upon
Schubert.

(28 February) Schubert informs Ignaz Franz von Mosel that he is too ill
to leave his room. This is the earliest known reference to the disease,
believed to have been a venereal one, from which he suffers in 1823–4
(and possibly also in later years). He will probably be a patient at the
Vienna General Hospital in the autumn (the dates and circumstances of
his treatment there are not known).

(End July–mid-September) Trip to Linz and Steyr. At Linz, on 28 July,
Schubert is introduced by Spaun and Albert Stadler to Friedrich Ludwig
von Hartmann and his family, who will become fervent Schubertians. In
August he spends some time with Vogl at Steyr. During his return
journey to Vienna he again visits Linz.

(August) Schober leaves for Breslau [Wrocław]. He will be absent from
Vienna for two years.

(Autumn) Schubert moves into lodgings with Josef Huber [14 Stuben-
torbastei].

(25 October) Première of Weber's *Euryanthe* at the Kärntnertor-
Theater. Schubert is reported to have made critical remarks about
the opera, either before others at Steiner's music shop or directly to
Weber himself. As a result, relations between them are said to have
cooled.

(November) The reading parties, suspended since Schober's departure,
resume at Ludwig Mohn's.

(9 November) Schwind informs Schober that Schubert is well on the way
to recovery.

(11 November) Schubertiad at the Bruchmanns'.

(20 December) Première at the Theater an der Wien of Helmina von
Chézy's play *Rosamunde, Fürstin von Zypern*, with music by Schubert
(D797).

Compositions: for the stage, *Die Verschworenen* [*Der häusliche Krieg*] (D787),
Fierrabras (D796), and music for *Rosamunde* (D797); Piano Sonata in A minor
(D784); the songs 'Auf dem Wasser zu singen' (D774), 'Du bist die Ruh' (D776),
and the cycle *Die schöne Müllerin* (D795).

Publications: 'Wanderer' Fantasia (D760); Sonata in B flat major for piano duet
(D617); some fifteen songs, including 'Auf dem Wasser zu singen' (D774), 'Der

Zwerg' (D771), 'Frühlingsglaube' (D686), 'Gruppe aus dem Tartarus' (D583), and 'Sei mir gegrüsst' (D741).

1824   (19 January) Schubertiad at Mohn's.
(22 February) Schwind reports to Schober that Schubert has discarded his wig. (His head was shaved because of a rash caused by his illness.)
(14 March) The Schuppanzigh Quartet gives the first performance of the String Quartet in A minor (D804) at the Musikverein.
(Spring) First performance of the Octet in F major (D803) at Count Troyer's.
(31 March) In a letter to Leopold Kupelwieser (who is in Rome), Schubert describes himself as 'the most unhappy, the most wretched man in the world'.
(April) The reading parties at Mohn's are suspended.
(Late May to mid-October) Schubert, who has remained in contact with Count Esterházy's family in Vienna since 1818 (and appears to have conceived a deep affection for the younger daughter, Karoline), is once more engaged as music teacher at Zseliz. During his stay there he writes several pieces for piano duet. In October, he travels back to Vienna with Baron Schönstein. After his return, he stays at his father's house.

Compositions: String Quartets in A minor (D804) and D minor ('Death and the Maiden', D810); Octet in F major (D803); Sonata in C major (D812), *Divertissement à la hongroise* (D818), and *Eight Variations on an Original Theme* (D813), all for piano duet; a few songs, mostly to texts by Mayrhofer.

Publications: String Quartet in A minor (D804), the only one of Schubert's string quartets to be published in his lifetime; the vocal quartet 'Gondelfahrer' (D809); the song 'An den Tod' (D518), Axa's romance from *Rosamunde* (D797/3b), and the cycle *Die schöne Müllerin* (D795), which is issued in three parts (February, March, and August).

1825   (Early 1825) Frequent Schubertiads at Karl von Enderes's.
(February) Schubert takes a room in the suburb of Wieden [9 Technikerstrasse]. Beginning of his friendship with Bauernfeld.
(24 February) Schubert, with Vogl and Johann Baptist Jenger, is invited to lunch by the actress Sophie Müller, who is a great admirer of his songs. He will visit her on several further occasions in 1825 and 1826.
(March) Schubert turns against Franz von Bruchmann, who, with his parents, has prevailed on his sister Justina to break off her engagement to Schober.
(May) Spaun is transferred from Linz to Lemberg [Lvov].
(Early May) Wilhelm August Rieder paints Schubert's portrait.
(Mid-May to early October) Schubert undertakes a lengthy trip, during which he visits Steyr and Linz more than once, spends six weeks (4 June–

15 July) at Gmunden, and some three weeks (from 13/14 August) at Bad Gastein where he meets Johann Ladislaus Pyrker. During most of this time he is in Vogl's company.

(9 June) Anna Milder-Hauptmann sings 'Erlkönig' (D328) and 'Suleika II' (D717) at a concert in Berlin.

(July) Schober arrives back in Vienna.

(September) Schubert is elected a substitute representative (Ersatzmann) of the Gesellschaft der Musikfreunde.

Compositions: 'Great' C major Symphony (D944) begun; Piano Sonatas in A minor (D845), C major (D840, incomplete), and D major (D850); songs to texts by Craigher de Jachelutta, Pyrker, Schulze, and Scott, including 'Auf der Bruck' (D853), 'Die Allmacht' (D852), 'Die junge Nonne' (D828), and 'Ave Maria' ['Ellens Gesang III', D839].

Publications: Mass in C major (D452); numerous dances for the piano (D735, 779, 781, 783); *Eight Variations on an Original Theme* (D813), and six *Grandes marches* (D819), for piano duet; the songs 'An Mignon' (D161), 'An Schwager Kronos' (D369), 'Der Alpenjäger' (D588), 'Der zürnenden Diana' (D707), 'Die junge Nonne' (D828), 'Nachtstück' (D672), and 'Suleika II' (D717).

1826   During a large part of this year Schubert lives at Schober's (intermittently in the spring and summer at Währing, and during the autumn in the city [6 Bäckerstrasse]).

(?February) Performance of the Quartet in D minor ('Death and the Maiden', D810) at Franz Paul Lachner's.

(7 April) Schubert applies for the vacant post of deputy court Kapellmeister.

(31 May) Schubertiad at Enderes's.

(1 July) Spaun returns to Vienna, where he will remain in intimate contact with Schubert until the latter's death.

(9 October) The Gesellschaft der Musikfreunde, on learning that Schubert intends to present a new symphony to it in the very near future, awards him a sum of 100 florins. The award is not linked to the proposed gift, but is described as a token of appreciation of his past contributions to the society's activities.

(End November–December) Schubert presents the autograph of the 'Great' C major Symphony (D944) to the Gesellschaft.

(15 December) Big Schubertiad at Spaun's, at which Schubert plays duets with Josef von Gahy and Vogl sings some thirty of his songs.

Compositions: 'Great' C major Symphony (D944) completed by the autumn; String Quartet in G major (D887); Rondo for violin and piano (D895); Piano Sonata in G major (D894); three Shakespeare songs (D888–9, 891), 'Gesänge aus *Wilhelm Meister*' (D877), and settings of Schulze and Seidl.

Publications: Piano Sonatas in A minor (D845) and D major (D850); *Divertissement à la hongroise* (D818), *Divertissement en forme d'une marche brillante et raisonnée* (D823/1), *Grande marche funèbre* (D859), and *Grande marche héroïque* (D885), all for piano duet: the songs 'An den Mond' (D193), 'Ave Maria' ['Ellens Gesang III' D839], 'Dass sie hier gewesen' (D775), 'Dithyrambe' (D801), 'Du bist die Ruh' (D776), 'Hektors Abschied' (D312), 'Lachen und Weinen' (D777), 'Normans Gesang' (D846), and 'Sehnsucht' (D636).

1827   (January–February) Schubert lives alone near the Karolinentor (opposite the present Stadtpark).

(January) Josef Weigl is appointed deputy court Kapellmeister (*see* entry for 7 April 1826).

(Early 1827) Karl Maria von Bocklet and Josef Slavík play the Rondo for violin and piano (D895) at Domenico Artaria's.

(March) Schubert once more takes up residence at Schober's [18 Tuchlauben], where he has a music room and two other rooms at his disposal. Except for a short break (*see* May–June below), he will reside at this address until August 1828.

(March) At Katharina Lászny's, Vogl and Schubert perform some of the latter's songs in the presence of Johann Nepomuk Hummel, who is deeply moved by them.

(*c.*20 March) Schubert reportedly visits the dying Beethoven with Anselm Hüttenbrenner and others.

(29 March) Schubert acts as torch-bearer at Beethoven's funeral.

(16 April) First public performance of the Octet in F major (D803) by the Schuppanzigh Quartet and others at the Musikverein.

(21 April) Big Schubertiad at Spaun's.

(22 April) At a concert given at the Landhaus by the violinist Leopold Jansa, Schubert accompanies an unidentified singer in 'Normans Gesang' (D846). On the same day, the quartet 'Nachtgesang im Walde' (D913) is performed at Josef Lewy's concert at the Musikverein.

(May–June) Schubert stays for a few weeks, probably together with Schober, at the 'Zur Kaiserin von Österreich' inn in the Dornbach suburb.

(12 June) In a letter to the Gesellschaft der Musikfreunde, Schubert accepts the position of representative (Repräsentant), to which he has recently been elected.

(11 August) First performance of 'Ständchen' (D920), on Louise Gosmar's birthday.

(2–24 September) Schubert and Jenger travel to Graz where they are guests of Karl and Marie Leopoldine Pachler.

(26 December) Performance of a 'new' piano trio (perhaps D929) at the Musikverein.

Compositions: the opera *Der Graf von Gleichen* (D918) begun in June; Piano Trio in E flat major (D929), Fantasia in C major for violin and piano (D934); eight Impromptus for the piano (D899, 935); *Eight Variations on a Theme from Hérold's Opera 'Marie'* for piano duet (D908); 'Ständchen' (D920); *Winterreise* (D911), and songs to texts by Leitner, Metastasio, Rochlitz, and Schober.

Publications: Piano Sonata in G major (D894), two Impromptus (D899/1–2); *Eight Variations on a Theme from Hérold's Opera 'Marie'* (D908), *Andantino varié* (D823/2), and *Rondo brillant* (D823/3), all for piano duet; the partsongs 'Grab und Mond' (D893), 'Wein und Liebe' (D901); some twenty songs to texts by Goethe, Metastasio, Pyrker, Rochlitz, Schiller, Schober, and Seidl, including 'An die Musik' (D547), 'Das Heimweh' (D851), 'Das Zügenglöcklein' (D871), 'Der Wanderer an den Mond' (D870), 'Die Allmacht' (D852), 'Gesänge aus *Wilhelm Meister*' (D877), 'Wandrers Nachtlied' (D768).

1828   (January) The reading sessions, suspended since 1824, resume at Schober's. (20 January) Slavík and Bocklet give the first performance of the Fantasia for violin and piano (D934) at the Landhaus. (28 January) Schubertiad at Spaun's. Bocklet, Schuppanzigh, and Josef Linke perform a piano trio (?D929) by Schubert, who also plays one of his sets of variations for piano duet with Bocklet. (30 January) Schubertiad at Josef Wilhelm Witteczek's. (26 March) Schubert gives a concert (his only one) at the Musikverein. On the programme: the first movement of a 'new' string quartet (D810 or 887); a 'new' piano trio (D929); the partsongs 'Schlachtlied' (D912) and 'Ständchen' (D920); the songs 'Auf dem Strom' (D943), 'Der Kreuzzug' (D932), 'Die Allmacht' (D852), 'Die Sterne' (D939), 'Fischerweise' (D881), and 'Fragment aus dem Aeschylus' (D450). (14 April) Spaun marries Franziska Roner von Ehrenwerth. (10 May) Schubert sends his Piano Trio in E flat major (D929) to the Leipzig music publisher Heinrich Albert Probst. (After various delays, it will be published in October.) (3–4 June) Johann Schickh invites Schubert and Lachner to accompany him on an excursion to Baden and thence to Heiligenkreuz Monastery, where the two musicians play fugues they have specially written for the famous organ there. Schubert's Fugue in E minor for organ duet (D952) is his only composition for the organ alone. (1 September) On the advice of his doctor, Ernst Rinna von Sarenbach, Schubert moves to his brother Ferdinand's lodgings in the Neu-Wieden suburb [6 Kettenbrückengasse]. (6 September) Jenger informs Marie Leopoldine Pachler that Schubert hopes to visit her family in Graz in the near future. (Early October) Schubert and his brother Ferdinand, together with two friends (perhaps Josef Mayssen and Johann Rieder), make a three days' excursion, in part or entirely on foot, to Unter-Waltersdorf and Eisenstadt, where they visit Haydn's grave.

(31 October) Schubert is seized by nausea during a meal at the 'Zum roten Kreuz' restaurant [50 Nussdorferstrasse].

(3 November) He attends a performance, at Hernals parish church, of a Requiem composed by his brother Ferdinand.

(4 November) Schubert and Josef Lanz receive a joint lesson in fugal composition from Simon Sechter.

(11/14 November) Schubert takes permanently to his bed.

(12 November) In a note (his last) to Schober, Schubert writes that he has not eaten and drunk anything for eleven days.

(*c.*14 November) Beethoven's String Quartet in C sharp minor (Op. 131) is reportedly performed for Schubert, at his request, in Ferdinand's flat.

(*c.*15 November) Spaun visits Schubert for what will be their final meeting.

(16 November) Dr Josef von Vering, who has taken over from the indisposed Rinna von Sarenbach, confers at Schubert's bedside with Dr Johann Baptist Wisgrill.

(17 November) Bauernfeld and Lachner visit Schubert. In the evening, Schubert becomes violently delirious.

(19 November) Schubert dies at 3 o'clock in the afternoon. Cause of death: typhoid fever (according to some writers, tertiary syphilis).

Compositions: Mass in E flat major (D950); String Quintet in C major (D956); Piano Trio in B flat major (D898) [?1827]; Piano Sonatas in C minor (D958), A major (D959), and B flat major (D960); Fantasia in F minor for piano duet (D940); *Mirjams Siegesgesang* for solo soprano and mixed chorus (D942); songs to texts by Heine, Rellstab, and Seidl (published in 1829 as *Schwanengesang*, D957), and 'Der Hirt auf dem Felsen' (D965).

Publications: Piano Trio in E flat major (D929); Rondo in A major for piano duet (D951); some twenty songs to texts by Goethe, Leitner, Wilhelm Müller, Schulze, Scott, Seidl, and Shakespeare, including 'Auf der Bruck' (D853), 'Der Musensohn' (D764), 'Die Sterne' (D939), 'Gesang: Was ist Silvia' (D891), 'Im Walde' (D834), 'Lied der Anne Lyle' (D830), four Refrainlieder (D866), and the cycle *Winterreise* (D911) which is issued in two parts (January and December).

Some Further Notable Nineteenth-Century Dates

1828   (21 November) Schubert's funeral. Following services at St Josef's Church in the Margareten suburb and at the Church of St Lawrence and St Gertrude at Währing, he is interred at Währing district cemetery, close to Beethoven's grave.

(23 December) A memorial service is held at St Augustine's Church in the city, at which Anselm Hüttenbrenner's Requiem in C minor is performed. In the evening, there is a Schubert concert at Spaun's.

1829   (30 January and 5 March) Two private memorial concerts organized by Anna Fröhlich are held at the Musikverein; one half of the receipts are to be used for the erection of a funeral monument.
(23 February) Publication of Johann Mayrhofer's 'Erinnerungen an Franz Schubert' in *Neues Archiv für Geschichte, Staatenkunde, Literatur und Kunst* (Vienna).
(27 March, 30 March, and 3 April) Spaun's 'Über Franz Schubert' appears, anonymously, in *Österreichisches Bürgerblatt für Verstand, Herz und gute Laune* (Linz).
(9, 11, and 13 June) Bauernfeld's 'Über Franz Schubert' is published in the *Wiener Zeitschrift für Kunst, Literatur, Theater und Mode* (Vienna).

1830   (Summer) A funeral monument, reportedly designed by Schober with the help of Ludwig Förster, is erected at Schubert's grave. It contains a bust of the composer by Josef Alois Dialer.

1839   (21 March) First performance of the 'Great' C major Symphony (D944), by the Leipzig Gewandhaus Orchestra under Felix Mendelssohn.
(23 April–3 May) Ferdinand Schubert's 'Aus Franz Schuberts Leben' is published in *Neue Zeitschrift für Musik* (Leipzig).

1861   Heinrich Kreissle von Hellborn publishes *Aus Schuberts Leben*.

1863   (October) The Gesellschaft der Musikfreunde restores Schubert's grave. On this occasion his body is exhumed, examined, and reinterred in a stronger coffin for better preservation.

1865   Publication of *Franz Schubert*, Kreissle's second and far more substantial study of Schubert's life and works. (An English translation by Arthur Duke Coleridge will appear in London in 1869.)

1868   (12 October) The foundation stone of Karl Kundmann's Schubert statue is laid in the Stadtpark.

1872   (15 May) Unveiling of Kundmann's statue.

1884–97 A collected edition of Schubert's works is published by Breitkopf & Härtel in Leipzig.

1888   (23 September) Schubert's remains are transported to the Grove of Honour in the new central cemetery and interred in a grave near Beethoven's.

DICTIONARY

Adamberger, Antonie (b. Vienna, 31 December 1790; d. Vienna, 25 December 1867). Actress and singer. She was the daughter of the tenor Johann Valentin Adamberger (1740/3–1804), who created Belmonte in Mozart's *Die Entführung aus dem Serail*, and of the well-known actress and singer Maria Anna Adamberger, née Ja(c)quet (1752–1804). She first appeared at the Burgtheater on 22 February 1804 as Antonia in Heinrich von Collin's* *Der gestörte Abschied*. She was a full-time member of the company from 1807 to 1817, excelling in tragic roles. Among her early successes were Beatrice in Schiller's* *Die Braut von Messina* and Klärchen in Goethe's* *Egmont*; in the latter play she sang the songs 'Die Trommel gerühret' and 'Freudvoll und leidvoll', for which Beethoven* had written the music. In 1812 she became engaged to Theodor Körner,* in whose plays *Toni* (17 April 1812) and *Hedwig* (11 January 1813) she took the title roles. After his death (26 August 1813) in the German Wars of Liberation, she continued her acting career until June 1817, when, to the deep regret of Viennese theatre-goers who greatly admired her, she retired from the stage upon her marriage to the historian and numismatist Josef Cales von Arneth (1791–1863). He was appointed custodian of the imperial collections of coins and antiquities in 1840.

Antonie and her husband were well acquainted with Schubert and several members of his circle. They attended the Schubertiad at Josef von Spaun's* on 15 December 1826, and themselves entertained Spaun and others of the group on 20 April 1827. On the latter occasion, as Fritz von Hartmann* recorded in his diary, Antonie sang 'most charmingly' some songs by Friedrich Heinrich Himmel and Schubert. She was, indeed, known as a gifted interpreter of Schubert's Lieder. In October of the previous year, at St Florian's Monastery, near Linz, she had sung some of his Goethe* songs, as well as several from *Die schöne Müllerin* (D795) and 'Ave Maria' ['Ellens Gesang III', D839].

At the same monastery, Johann Michael Vogl* sang some Schubert songs on 4 June 1823, and Antonie's sister Mimi performed two of his songs there on 26 August 1829. The provost of St Florian at that time was Antonie's brother-in-law Michael Arneth who was on friendly terms with Josef and Anton von Spaun. He attended a Schubertiad at Josef von Spaun's on 28 January 1828.

(Arneth, Berger², *ÖBL*, Zimmer)

Aeschylus (b. Eleusis, Attica, 525/4 BC; d. Gela, Sicily, 456 BC). Tragic poet. In the song 'Fragment aus dem Aeschylus' Schubert set Johann Mayrhofer's* translation of a passage from the *Eumenides*, the third part of the *Oresteia*.

Setting: D450.

Arneth, Antonie von: *see* Adamberger.*

Artaria, Matthias (b. Mannheim, 1793; d. Vienna, 22 April 1835). Art dealer and music publisher; son of Domenico (II) Artaria (1765–1823). Having being initiated into business matters by his father, who directed the Mannheim branch of the firm, and having gathered useful experience while employed for some two years in a London bookshop, he settled in Vienna not later than 1818. There he became associated with the art dealer Daniel Julius Sprenger. After the latter's death, he married his widow Karolina [Charlotte] in 1821, and the following year obtained a licence to operate the business in his own name. In 1833 his firm was taken over by Anton Diabelli & Co.*

Among the composers on Matthias Artaria's list was Beethoven,* whom he met through Karl Holz* in 1826 and who entrusted him with the first publication of the String Quartet in B flat (Op. 130), the *Grosse Fuge* (Op. 133), and the arrangement of that fugue for piano duet (Op. 134). However, these compositions did not appear until after Beethoven's death, in May 1827. In April 1826 Matthias Artaria published first editions of Schubert's *Divertissement à la hongroise* for piano duet (D818), the Piano Sonata in D major (D850), and settings of seven texts from Walter Scott's* poem 'The Lady of the Lake' (D835–9, 843, 846).

First editions: D818, 835–9, 843, 846, 850.
(Slezak)

Artaria & Co. The famous Viennese branch of the Artaria firm was founded by the cousins Carlo Artaria (1747–1808) and Francesco Artaria (1744–1808), who arrived in the Austrian capital in the late 1760s. They started to deal in engravings in 1770, and in 1778 set up their own music publishing business. They ran the firm, at times together with Giovanni Cappi and Tranquillo Mollo, until the early years of the nineteenth century, when they retired to Blevio, in Lombardy, where the family came from. They were succeeded by Francesco's son Domenico (III) [Dominik] Artaria (1775–1842), who formed partnerships with Pietro Cappi and Carlo Boldrini before assuming sole proprietorship from 1824 until 1830, when his son August (1807–93) joined the business.

It was while he was sole owner of the firm that Domenico published the first editions of Schubert's Rondo in B minor for violin and piano (D895) in April 1827 and the Rondo in A major for piano duet (D951) in December 1828. The former work, composed in October 1826, was reportedly performed by Josef Slavík* and Karl Maria von Bocklet,* in Schubert's presence, at a party given by Domenico Artaria (perhaps in early 1827), while the latter work is said to have been written at Domenico's request. In 1840, Artaria & Co. published the first edition of the March in E major (D606).

First editions: D606, 895, 951.
(Kreissle, Slezak)

Assmayer [Assmayr], **Ignaz** (b. Salzburg, 11 February 1790; d. Vienna, 31 August 1862). Composer and organist. From 1808 until 1815 he was organist at St Peter's, Salzburg. He then moved to Vienna, where he studied with Antonio Salieri.* In 1825 he was appointed second court organist, in 1846 deputy court Kapellmeister, and later that same year Kapellmeister in succession to Josef Leopold von Eybler. His compositions include numerous settings of the Mass, several oratorios, operas, chamber music, quartets for male voices, and songs.

He became friendly with Schubert while both were pupils of Salieri. Anselm Hüttenbrenner* recalled that he himself, Schubert, Assmayer, and Josef Mozatti would meet at the latter's lodgings every Thursday evening to sing a quartet newly composed by one of them (Hüttenbrenner and Mozatti were also studying with Salieri at the time). In March 1818 Schubert wrote a humorous dedication in German and Latin to Assmayer on an autograph of the so-called *Trauerwalzer* (D365/2).

(Antonicek[1], Wurzbach[1])

Bacsányi, Gabriele: *see* Baumberg.*

Barbaia [Barbaja], **Domenico** (b. Milan, ?1778; d. Posillipo, near Naples, 19 October 1841). Impresario. In his youth he worked as a waiter, invented (or popularized) the 'barbaiata', a drink made with coffee or chocolate and cream, and operated the gambling tables in the foyer of La Scala, Milan. In 1809 he was appointed manager of the royal opera-houses in Naples, a position which he occupied almost uninterruptedly until 1840. His Neapolitan seasons became as celebrated for the brilliant singers he engaged (such as Isabella Colbran, Giovanni Davide, Manuel García, Andrea Nozzari, and Giovanni Battista Rubini) as for the works presented, which included a string of Rossini operas specially written for Naples, starting with *Elisabetta, regina d'Inghilterra* in 1815 and including *Otello* (1816), *Mosè in Egitto* (1818), and *La donna del lago* (1819).

In December 1821, Barbaia also took over the management of the Kärntnertor-Theater, Vienna, and at the same time he leased the Theater an der Wien from Count Ferdinand Pálffy* for several months. His initial tenure at the court theatre lasted until the end of March 1825, and it was followed by a further two-year period starting in April 1826.

His arrival in Vienna ensured that Italian opera, which had been steadily rising in popularity there for some years, would assume a still more dominant position in the musical life of that city. Local enthusiasm for it reached new heights when Rossini himself directed a season of his operas (April–June 1822). Later, Eduard von Bauernfeld* was to complain (in his obituary 'Über Franz Schubert', in the *Wiener Zeitschrift für Kunst, Literatur, Theater und Mode* in June 1829) that whatever hope Schubert might have had of developing his talent for German opera was dashed when the court theatre passed under Barbaia's direction. In fairness to the latter it should, however, be pointed out that while he naturally did his best to promote Italian opera and engaged outstanding singers like Lablache,* Davide, and Rubini to dazzle the Viennese audiences, German opera was not totally neglected. Indeed, one of the main functions assigned to the managing committee which was set up in July 1822 under the presidency of the composers Count Wenzel Robert Gallenberg and Josef Weigl* was to encourage the composition and production of German opera. Warmly welcoming this development, the Berlin journal *Der Gesellschafter* reported on 21 September that Weber,* Spontini, Michael Umlauf, Schubert, Baron Poissl, and Weigl himself had accepted commissions for new works. (In fact, at least Schubert and Weber had been invited to write operas for the court theatre as far back as November 1821.) Weigl's *Die eiserne Pforte* was premièred at the Kärntner-tor-Theater on 27 February 1823, and Weber's *Euryanthe* was produced there on 25 October 1823. In Schubert's case, it was reportedly Barbaia himself who commissioned the theatre's secretary, Josef Kupelwieser,* to write the libretto *Fierrabras* for him. None the less the management subsequently decided not to present the completed opera (D796), a decision which Schubert blamed on the poor quality of the text, but which may well have been prompted primarily by a certain reluctance to mount another grand romantic German opera after the mixed reception accorded to *Euryanthe*.

Barbaia was succeeded as lessee of the Kärntnertor-Theater by Count Gallenberg, who lost all his money in the venture. It is worth noting that Barbaia at one time directed simultaneously three of the most celebrated opera-houses of the period, for in addition to managing the Teatro San Carlo in Naples and the Kärntnertor-Theater in Vienna as mentioned above, he was in charge of La Scala, Milan, from 1826 to 1832.

(Bauer, Budden, Gualerzi)

Barth, Josef (b. Gross-Lippen [Lipno, Czech Republic], 29 December 1781; d. Vienna, 18 May 1865). Tenor. He sang in the court Kapelle and took part in many performances of Schubert's compositions at private, semi-public, and public concerts. He was in the employ of Prince Josef Johann Nepomuk Schwarzenberg; in the list of subscribers to *Schwanengesang* (D957) in 1829 he is identified as an accountant.

He sang in the first public performances of the quartet 'Das Dörfchen' (D598) and the octet 'Gesang der Geister über den Wassern' (D714) at the Kärntnertor-Theater on 7 March 1821. He also took part in several performances of the quartet 'Die Nachtigall' (D724)—including its first performance at the Kärntnertor-Theater on 22 April 1821—and of the quartet 'Geist der Liebe' (D747), probably again including the first performance at the Grosser Redoutensaal on 3 March 1822. At Ignaz von Sonnleithner's, on 18 April 1822, he sang in 'Geist der Liebe' and also performed the song 'Der Blumen Schmerz' (D731). When 'Das Dörfchen', 'Geist der Liebe', and 'Die Nachtigall' were published together in June 1822, the edition (Op. 11) bore a dedication to Barth 'by his friend Franz Schubert'.

On 1 February 1826, a private performance of the String Quartet in D minor ('Death and the Maiden', D810), took place in Barth's rooms at Prince Schwarzenberg's palace in Mehlmarkt [Neuer Markt]. The work did not receive its first public performance until 12 March 1833, in Berlin.

Barth's son Gustav (1811/12–97) was also a well-known musician who became the first choirmaster of the Wiener Männergesangverein in 1843 and was later appointed court Konzertmeister at Wiesbaden, then the capital of the duchy of Nassau. In 1840 he married the singer Anna Maria Wilhelmine von Hasselt.

(*ÖBL*, Wurzbach[1])

Bartsch, Rudolf Hans (b. Graz, 11 February 1873; d. Graz, 7 February 1952). Writer. The son of an army officer, he worked at the war office archives in Vienna from 1895 until 1911, when he retired with the rank of captain and returned to Graz. His first novel, *Als österreich zerfiel . . . 1848*, appeared in 1905 (it was reissued in 1913 under the title *Der letzte Student*), while his last, *Wenn Majestäten lieben*, was published in 1949. The sentimentality already present in his earlier novels became an increasingly dominant feature of the later ones, prompting a decline in his popularity and reputation. On the whole, his stories, of which he published several collections (*Vom sterbenden Rokoko, Bittersüsse Liebesgeschichten, Unerfüllte Geschichten*), have stood the test of time better.

His best-known work, the novel *Schwammerl: Ein Schubert-Roman*, was published in 1912. It offers a distorted and decidedly sentimentalized account of the composer's life. The story is mainly concerned with his unhappy love for Hedderl, Heiderl, and Hannerl, the three attractive daughters of the Viennese glazier Christian Tschöll. The girls are presumably based on the Fröhlich* sisters (or, at any rate, the three unmarried ones), but there is no evidence that Schubert ever felt deeply attracted to any of them. The family's residence is repeatedly referred to in the book as 'Das Dreimäderlhaus' ('The House of the Three Girls'), a term which was to achieve considerable celebrity thanks to Berté's* operetta of that title. To this day, a house in Vienna [10 Schreyvogelgasse] is popularly known as the 'Dreimäderlhaus'.

(Garland, Wilpert)

Bauernfeld, Eduard von (b. Vienna, 13 January 1802; d. Vienna, 9 August 1890). Dramatist. He was educated at the Schottengymnasium, where he formed a friendship with his fellow pupil Moritz von Schwind* which was to last until the latter's death in 1871. After studying philosophy and law at Vienna University, he reluctantly entered the civil service in September 1826; he left it with relief in 1848.

He was interested in literature and the theatre from an early age, and was commissioned by the lithographer and publisher Josef Trentsensky to contribute to the German Shakespeare* edition which appeared in Vienna in 1824–6. He translated *The Comedy of Errors, Two Gentlemen of Verona, King Henry VIII*, 'The Passionate Pilgrim', 'The Rape of Lucrece', and *Troilus and Cressida*, as well as *Antony and Cleopatra* together with Ferdinand Mayerhofer von Grünbühel,* and *Coriolanus* in collaboration with Josef Fick.

The first of his own plays to be performed at the Burgtheater, *Der Brautwerber* (5 September 1828), achieved only a modest *succès d'estime*, but the next one, *Leichtsinn aus Liebe, oder Täuschungen* (12 January 1831), won him wide recognition as a promising young dramatist. The successful productions of *Bürgerlich und romantisch* (7 September 1835) and *Der literarische Salon* (24 March 1836) firmly established him as a talented writer of comedies of manner, the genre which was to predominate in his vast dramatic output during the following decades. By 1889, the Burgtheater had presented more than 1,000 performances of forty-three plays by Bauernfeld. He also wrote poetry (*Gedichte*, 1852) and a novel (*Die Freigelassenen*, 1875). His memoirs, entitled *Aus Alt- und Neuwien*, provide information not only about his own ideas and activities, but also, more generally, about different aspects of Viennese intellectual life in his time. These memoirs were printed in the collected edition of his works (*Gesammelte Schriften*, 12 vols., 1871–3); certain parts had previously appeared in newspapers and other publications. One chapter is devoted to Schwind and Schubert.

Bauernfeld was fond of music, although it does not appear to have assumed as central a part in his life as it did in Schwind's. He was a competent pianist, having received tuition from the well-known composer and teacher Johann Baptist Schenk. He heard Schubert perform some of his songs at Professor Vincentius Weintridt's* apartment [8 Bankgasse] in January 1822 and subsequently at different musical soirées, but did not become personally acquainted with him until February 1825, when Schwind brought Schubert to his lodgings one evening. 'We were soon on friendly terms. At Schwind's insistence, I had to recite some of my crazy early poems, then we moved to the piano, Schubert sang, we played, also duets, and later repaired to the tavern where we stayed until long into the night. Our friendship was sealed there and then; from that day on we were inseparable'. By the following month he and Schubert were addressing each other with the familiar 'Du'. Later that year, he and Schwind suggested to Schubert that the three of them share lodgings, but nothing came of the idea. Bauernfeld remained an intimate friend of Schubert until the very end, frequently meeting him and other members of the circle at cafés and taverns, and attending Schubertiads hosted by Franz von Schober,* Josef von Spaun,* and others. He last saw Schubert two days before his death.

The diary which Bauernfeld kept during those years contains a number of references to Schubert. An entry made in August 1826, 'Schubert is not well (he needs "young peacocks" like Benv. Cellini)', has become the subject of conflicting interpretations, since M. Solomon argued in 'Franz Schubert and the Peacocks of Benvenuto Cellini', a paper presented to the American Musicological Society in

1988 (and published in the journal *19th Century Music* in 1989), that Bauernfeld's observation was among several strands of evidence which pointed to Schubert's probable homosexuality. His views have been accepted by some scholars, but firmly rejected by others (notably R. Steblin).

Schubert set poems by Bauernfeld in the songs 'Das Totenhemdchen' (D864, lost) and 'Der Vater mit dem Kind' (D906). In addition, he used Bauernfeld's translation of Shakespeare's *Two Gentlemen of Verona* in 'Gesang: Was ist Silvia' (D891), and Bauernfeld's and Mayerhofer's version of *Antony and Cleopatra* in 'Trinklied: Bacchus, feister Fürst des Weins' (D888). Bauernfeld furthermore wrote the libretto for the opera *Der Graf von Gleichen* (D918). That project was prohibited by the censor in October 1826, but Schubert nevertheless began to set the text in June 1827.

Schubert's death inspired a long poem by Bauernfeld which was not printed at the time, but the following year he published an obituary in the *Wiener Zeitschrift für Kunst, Literatur, Theater und Mode* (9, 11, and 13 June 1829). In 1851 he wrote a prologue for the opening of Spina's* Schubert Salon. On several later occasions he published recollections of Schubert, notably in *Die Presse* in April 1869 and in *Die neue freie Presse* in June of the same year.

Settings: D864, 888, 891, 906, 918.
(Bauernfeld[1,2], *ÖBL*, Porhansl[7], Solomon[1,2], Steblin[5])

Baumberg, Gabriele (Anna Maria Elisabeth Christine) von (b. Vienna, 24 March 1768; d. Linz, 24 July 1839). Poetess; daughter of a senior government official. In 1805 she married the Hungarian poet and scholar Janos Bacsányi [Batsányi] (1763–1845) who was employed in a Viennese bank. During the French occupation of Vienna in 1809 he agreed to translate into Hungarian Napoleon's proclamation of 15 May calling on his countrymen to rebel against the Austrians. As a result, he was subsequently obliged to flee the country; he settled in Paris, where Gabriele joined him. He was arrested there in 1815 and incarcerated at Brünn [Brno], but later allowed to reside at Linz. Gabriele lived with him for the rest of her life, in modest circumstances and largely forgotten by Viennese literary society, of which she had once been a popular and admired member. Among her friends had been Karoline Pichler,* who later paid tribute to her personal charm and literary talent. A collection of her poems, *Sämmtliche Gedichte*, appeared in 1800, followed by a second edition in 1805; in 1807 she published *Amor und Hymen: Ein Gedicht in 5 Gesängen*. She also contributed to different literary journals.

Schubert's first documented attempt at song-writing, which may date from 1810 or even earlier, took as its subject some lines from 'Lebenstraum', the prefatory poem to the 1805 edition of Baumberg's *Gedichte*. Only a long fragment (D39) has survived (*see also* D1A). In 1815 he composed five further songs inspired by poems by Baumberg: 'Abendständchen: An Lina' (D265), 'An die Sonne' (D270), 'Cora an die Sonne' (D263), 'Der Morgenkuss' (D264), and 'Lob des Tokayers' (D248). These songs have been dismissed by R. Capell as 'insignificant', and by D. Fischer-Dieskau as 'mere miniatures of little importance'.

Settings: ?DiA, 39, 248, 263–5, 270.

(Brown[2,5], Capell, Fischer-Dieskau, Hoorickx[2], Landon, Pichler, Wurzbach[1])

Beethoven, Ludwig van (baptized Bonn, 17 December 1770; d. Vienna, 26 March 1827). Composer. Schubert's profound admiration for his music is amply attested. He came to know some of it well at an early age, for, as a member of the student orchestra at the Stadtkonvikt, he took part in performances of the first two symphonies. According to an anecdote told by Moritz von Schwind* to Beethoven's biographer K. F. L. Nohl, Schubert sold his books so that he could buy a ticket to the première (of the third version) of *Fidelio* in 1814. And Anselm Hüttenbrenner* informed Ferdinand Luib* in 1858 that Beethoven's Fifth Symphony, his Mass in C, and the song 'Adelaïde' were among the compositions which Schubert loved best. In April 1822 he dedicated his *Eight Variations on a French Song* for piano duet (D624) to Beethoven 'with profound respect and admiration'.

On 29 March 1827, Schubert was among the torch-bearers at Beethoven's funeral at Währing district cemetery. The following year, as he lay on his sick-bed in his brother Ferdinand's flat, he is said to have expressed a fervent wish to hear Beethoven's String Quartet in C sharp minor (Op. 131), and the work was reportedly performed in the flat five days before he died by Karl Holz* and others. Finally, the very site of his grave was determined by his known veneration of the older composer, as is evident from Ferdinand's letter to their father on 21 November 1828: 'He said to me, half-deliriously: "I implore you, move me to my own room, don't leave me here in the earth—don't I deserve a place above ground?" I answered him: "Dear Franz, rest assured, believe your brother Ferdinand, whom you have always trusted and who loves you very dearly, you are in the room where you have always been until now, and are lying in your own bed." And Franz said: "No, that is not true. Beethoven does not lie here."—Should this not be regarded as an indication of his innermost wish to repose by the side of Beethoven, whom he revered so greatly?' As a result, Schubert was interred at Währing district cemetery, rather than at Matzleinsdorf cemetery, which was nearer. His grave there was very close to Beethoven's—as is his present one in the Grove of Honour (Group 32A) in the central cemetery where their remains were transferred in 1888.

Schubert's friends later made conflicting statements on whether or not he had ever met Beethoven, and what form such a meeting might have taken. Anton Schindler* stated in 1860 that Schubert had called in 1822, together with the publisher Anton Diabelli,* to present Beethoven with a copy of the above-mentioned, then newly published, *Variations*. According to Schindler's account, Schubert was overcome by shyness, completely lost his composure when Beethoven gently pointed out a mistake in harmony, and never again summoned up the courage to visit him.

On the other hand, Josef Hüttenbrenner* told Ferdinand Luib in *c*.1858 that Beethoven was out when Schubert called with the *Variations*, but that Schubert eventually visited Beethoven shortly before his death, together with himself, his brother Anselm Hüttenbrenner,* Schindler, and Josef Teltscher;* and he repeated the story in a letter to an unknown correspondent in 1868. Anselm likewise described this visit to Luib (though without mentioning Teltscher), dating it to about a week before Beethoven's death. There is thus a likelihood that the visit to the dying Beethoven really did take place. It is true that Josef von Spaun* commented, after reading Heinrich Kreissle's* Schubert biography, that 'Schubert frequently, and especially at the time of Beethoven's death, expressed his profound regret that Beethoven had been so unapproachable and that he had never spoken to him'. But this statement does not necessarily rule out the possibility of a visit to Beethoven's death-bed, for, at that very advanced stage of his fatal illness, Beethoven would have been incapable of conducting a meaningful conversation about music with Schubert. However, Spaun's statement does cast serious doubt on Schindler's previously mentioned account of a visit by Schubert in 1822, and lends weight to Schindler's reputation as an unreliable source.

Schindler also claimed credit for having brought Schubert's songs to Beethoven's attention. To keep the patient occupied and entertained during his long final illness, he later wrote, he had shown him a collection of some sixty Schubert Lieder and partsongs, many of them in manuscript. Beethoven, 'who until then did not know five songs by Schubert', is said by Schindler to have been astounded by the quality of the collection and to have repeatedly exclaimed: 'Truly, there is a divine spark in this Schubert'.

Given Schubert's well-documented veneration of Beethoven, his own compositions were bound to be influenced by the older composer, especially in the earlier years. The question of his unconscious or deliberate musical imitation of Beethoven has been repeatedly discussed—e.g. by E. Cone (1970) and N. Nettheim (1991) with regard to specific instances, and by W. Dürr (1988) within the more general context of Schubert's gradual abandonment of traditional forms in his pursuit of a more individual course. 'In some respects,' Dürr writes, 'this course runs parallel to Beethoven's, in others Schubert adopts a new direction—but at no time does he regard the older composer as a model to be imitated; he sees in him rather an authority who confirms that he has chosen the right path for himself.' In one way or another, Beethoven's titanic figure loomed large over Schubert's life, and by a curious coincidence his only concert took place on the first anniversary of Beethoven's death (the originally proposed date of 21 March having been changed to 26 March 1828).

(Cone, Dürr², Nettheim, Nohl)

Berchtold von Ungarschütz, Anton Maria, Count (b. Vienna, 18 November 1796; d. Vienna, 4 June 1875). Court chamberlain. Schubert dedicated to him the *Eight*

Variations on an Original Theme for piano duet (D813) in 1825. Nothing is known about any personal contacts between them.

Berg, Isak Albert (b. Stockholm, 22 August 1803; d. Stockholm, 1 December 1886). Baritone. After attending the University of Uppsala, he studied from 1825 to 1827 with the well-known Italian tenor and teacher Giuseppe Siboni in Copenhagen, and subsequently undertook an extensive concert tour through Germany and Italy. In 1827 he visited Vienna where he met the Fröhlich* sisters (Josefine had herself been a pupil of Siboni's). At their house he made the acquaintance of Schubert, who particularly enjoyed hearing him sing Swedish folk-songs. Berg, for his part, apparently took quite a liking to Schubert, for many years later he wrote of him to George Grove* 'with the clinging affection which such personal charm inspires' (according to Grove's article on Schubert in the *Dictionary of Music and Musicians*).

From 1830 until 1847 Berg was conductor of the Philharmonic Choir in Stockholm. In addition, he was a highly respected singing teacher at the Stockholm Opera (1831–50, and again 1862–9). Among his pupils were the future King Oscar II of Sweden and Norway, the coloratura soprano Matilda Gelhaar, the tenor Carl Oskar Arnoldson, and Jenny Lind. Berg composed a number of songs, one of which, 'Fjärran i skog' ('Far away in the forest'), Lind frequently sang at her concerts.

Leopold von Sonnleithner* told Ferdinand Luib* in 1857 that Schubert used in his Piano Trio in E flat major (D929) the best of the Swedish folk-songs which he had heard Berg sing. Later he told Kreissle,* more precisely, that the subject of the second movement was a Swedish national melody. Anna Fröhlich, however, believed that the Swedish melody was used by Schubert in the Andante of the String Quartet in G major (D887), but in this she was evidently mistaken, since that quartet was composed in June 1826, well before Berg's visit. On the other hand, the piano trio was not begun until November 1827, the month in which Berg is believed to have left Vienna. Other writers suggested that the melody in question did not come from a folk-song at all, but from one of Berg's own songs; according to G. Nottebohm,* the song in question opened with the words 'Se solen sjunker' ('Look, the sun is setting'). In 1978, M. Willfort confirmed in the *Österreichische Musik-zeitschrift* that the Andante of the piano trio was indeed inspired by this song, but he left open the question whether the latter had been composed by Berg.

(Kutsch-Riemens, Willfort)

Bernard, Karl Josef (b. Saaz [Žatec, Czech Republic], 1786; d. Vienna, 31 March 1850). Journalist. He moved to Vienna in 1800 and was subsequently associated with a number of periodicals devoted entirely, or in a significant degree, to literature and the arts, among them *Thalia* and *Friedensblätter*. He edited the *Wiener Zeitung* from 1819 to 1848.

Bernard was in close contact with Beethoven* who used his text 'Ihr weisen Gründer' in the *Chor auf die verbündeten Fürsten* in 1814. He also supplied, in 1823, a text for the oratorio *Der Sieg des Kreuzes* which Beethoven intended to write for the Gesellschaft der Musikfreunde, but the composer was apparently dissatisfied with the text and did not set it. Bernard was more successful with two opera librettos: Spohr used one in *Faust* (Prague, 1 September 1816) and Conradin Kreutzer the other in *Libussa* (Kärntnertor-Theater, 4 December 1822). In 1815 Schubert set a poem by Bernard in the song 'Vergebliche Liebe'.

Setting: D177.

(ÖBL)

Bernhardt, J. Physician. He treated Schubert in 1823–4, probably for syphilis, for a time together with Dr August von Schaeffer,* later apparently alone. His contacts with Schubert clearly transcended the doctor–patient relationship, for he was very frequently seen in Schubert's company and, in a more general way, became a member of his circle. In December 1823 he encouraged Schubert to hold a public concert. At a party given by Ludwig Mohn* at the end of that month, he and Moritz von Schwind* agreed to address each other with the familiar 'Du'. It therefore seems likely that he was on similarly intimate terms with others in the group, and quite possibly with Schubert himself.

He was an amateur writer. In May 1824, according to a letter from Schwind to Leopold Kupelwieser,* Schubert took with him to Zseliz an opera libretto by Bernhardt, based on Ernst Schulze's* poem 'Die bezauberte Rose'. Either the information was incorrect or Schubert was dissatisfied with the text, for in March of the following year he asked Eduard von Bauernfeld* to write a libretto on the same subject; however, nothing came of the project.

In 1825 Schubert dedicated his *Six grandes marches* for piano duet (D819) 'en marque de reconnaissance à son ami I. Bernhardt, docteur en médecine'.

Berté, Heinrich [Harry] (b. Galgócz, Hungary [Hlohovec, Slovak Republic], 8 May 1857; d. Perchtoldsdorf, near Vienna, 23 August 1924). Composer. After the death of his father, Dr Josef Berté, in 1867, he moved to Vienna where he studied with Josef Hellmesberger,* Robert Fuchs, and Anton Bruckner at the Conservatory. He became an excellent pianist.

Encouraged by the favourable reception of his second ballet, *Die goldene Märchenwelt*, at the Vienna Opera (2 April 1893), he composed at least four further ballets. He also wrote a number of undistinguished operettas, among them *Die Millionenbraut* (Theater an der Wien, 13 September 1904), *Kreolenblut* (Hamburg, 25 December 1910), and *Der Märchenprinz* (Hanover, 28 February 1914). It was, however, not until he was nearing 60 that he achieved a resounding success, and that with music of which only a minute part, if any, was of his own composition.

The operetta *Das Dreimäderlhaus* had its première at the Raimundtheater, Vienna, on 15 January 1916. The libretto by A. M. Willner and H. Reichert was adapted from R. H. Bartsch's* novel *Schwammerl: Ein Schubert-Roman* (1912) and focused on Schubert's unhappy love for Hannerl Tschöll. (The three sisters' names were as in Bartsch's book, except that the middle one's was now spelt 'Haiderl'.) The two principal parts were taken by Fritz Schrödter, who had already played Schubert in the 1886 revival of Suppé's* *Franz Schubert*, and Anny Rainer.

The original intention had apparently been to use only one composition by Schubert, the song 'Ungeduld' from *Die schöne Müllerin* (D795/7), with the rest of the score being furnished by Berté. However, his music was judged inadequate by Wilhelm Karczag, one of the joint managers of the Raimundtheater, and he was then asked to make up the score entirely from Schubert's own works. He chose from among a broad range of compositions, including orchestral pieces, chamber music, piano sonatas, dances, and songs. His arrangement was then orchestrated by Oskar Stalla. (However, Max Schönherr believes that at least one song, 'Geh' Alte, schau', was in fact written by Berté himself.) Berté has been frequently condemned as a desecrator and plunderer of Schubert's music, especially by critics unaware of the circumstances in which the operetta took shape. But he has also had his defenders, such as L. Kusche, who argues in his *Franz Schubert* (Munich, 1962) that Berté's arrangements in no way violated the character of the original compositions.

According to B. Grun (*Die leichte Muse*, Munich, 1961), *Das Dreimäderlhaus* had by 1961 been translated into twenty-two languages, presented in sixty countries, and probably performed some 85,000 times.

(Grun, Hilmar[9], Kusche, Schönherr, Traubner)

Bertrand, Friedrich Anton Franz (b. Könnern, near Halle an der Saale, 13 May 1757 [?17 July 1751]; d. [?Dessau], after 1829). Poet and essayist. After studying law at Halle he worked for some years at the tax office at Calbe an der Saale. He then returned to Könnern; from 1806 he lived at Köthen, and from 1829 at Dessau. Very little is known about his life. He contributed to *W. G. Beckers Taschenbuch zum geselligen Vergnügen* (Leipzig), and in 1813 a volume of his writings, *Gedichte und Prosaische Aufsätze*, appeared at Zerbst, near Magdeburg. In 1815, Schubert set two of his ballads in the songs 'Adelwold und Emma' (D211) and 'Minona' (D 152).

Settings: D152, 211.
(Bodendorff[2], Schochow)

Blahetka, (Maria) Leopoldine (b. Guntramsdorf, Lower Austria, 16 November 1809; d. Boulogne-sur-Mer, 17 January 1885). Pianist, physharmonika player, and composer. Daughter of Josef L. Blahetka, a journalist and poet, and his wife Babette, née Traeg. She studied the piano with Josef Czerny,* Frédéric Kalkbrenner, and Ignaz Moscheles, and composition with Simon Sechter.*

She attracted Beethoven's* attention when she was only 5, and at the age of 8 she was hailed as a 'Wunderkind' after her performance of Johann Nepomuk Hummel's *Variations on a Theme from Georg Josef Vogler's Opera 'Castor e Polluce'* at a concert given by the violinist Eduard Jaëll* at the 'Zum römischen Kaiser' inn on 1 March 1818. (The concert also featured an overture by Schubert, D590 or 591.) In October of the same year, while Schubert was staying at Zseliz, his friend Josef Doppler* transmitted to him a request from Josef Blahetka for a 'rondo brillant or whatever piece he preferred' for piano solo and orchestra, which his daughter could play at a concert that winter: 'You can put in all the difficulties, jumps, runs, and any other devilish complexities you like, except octave spans and similar features which do not suit the formation of her hands.' There is no evidence that Schubert responded to this request, nor is it known whether he ever received the text of the large-scale oratorio on a biblical subject which, according to Doppler, Blahetka had then almost completed and intended to send to him.

Leopoldine gave her own first public concert in Vienna on 28 March 1819. In 1821 she played in Prague and other Bohemian towns, and in 1825–6 toured extensively in Germany. The 19-year-old Chopin, who became well acquainted with her and her father during his stay in Vienna in August 1829, called her (in a letter to his friend Titus Woyciechowski on 12 September) the 'finest woman pianist in Vienna'. In later years she also performed in other European countries, including England.

Information about Leopoldine's contacts with Schubert is scarce, but she is likely to have known him quite well. She played at Otto Hatwig's* concerts, both their names appeared on the programmes of several 'evening entertainments' of the Gesellschaft der Musikfreunde, and on at least one occasion she presented a composition of his at one of her own concerts ('Erlkönig', sung by Ludwig Titze,* at the Landhaus in Vienna on 21 March 1824). She was, moreover, present at some social gatherings attended by Schubert and his friends, such as the ball given by Franz von Schober* in early February 1827. By then her reputation was well established. Both Franz von Hartmann* and his brother Fritz refer to her as the 'famous pianist' in their diary entries relating to this ball. Fritz adds: 'Three years ago I found her enchanting, but since then she has lost much of her beauty and still more of her charming behaviour, because she received too much adulation in Germany where she toured for eighteen months.'

Josef Blahetka published an obituary of Schubert in the *Allgemeine Wiener Theaterzeitung* on 27 December 1828, in which he paid tribute to the composer's unassuming and honest nature: 'He lived only for music and for a small circle of friends.'

By 1840—but probably already several years earlier—Leopoldine had settled at Boulogne-sur-Mer where she resided for the rest of her life and where she became a much admired teacher. Her compositions, some seventy in number, were mostly written for the piano. They included waltzes and other pieces which appeared in collections of dances published in Vienna in 1824–5, to which Schubert also contributed. Her opera *Die Räuber und der Sänger*, to a libretto by Georg von Hoffmann,* was produced at the Kärntnertor-Theater on 22 March 1830.

(Chopin, Gruber, Jancik¹, *ÖBL*)

Bobrik [pseud. 'B.b..k'], **Johann Friedrich Ludwig** (b. Marienburg, Prussia, 13 October 1781; d. Königsberg [Kaliningrad, Russia], 22 January 1844). Poet and translator. The son and grandson of Protestant ministers, he studied law at Königsberg and subsequently had a very successful career in that city, where he was appointed a judge at the regional court in 1810. At the same time, he was a prolific poet whose verse appeared in various periodicals and, after his death, was published in volume form at Leipzig in 1851. He furthermore prepared translations of Anacreon, Horace, Shakespeare,* Robert Burns, and Sir Walter Scott.*

In December 1815 Schubert set his poem 'Die drei Sänger' which had appeared earlier that year in Vienna in the collection *Dichtungen für Kunstredner* edited by J. L. Deinhardstein;* only a fragment of the song has survived.

Setting: D329.

(Schochow)

Bocklet, Karl Maria [Carolus, Charles Marie] **von** (b. Prague, 30 January 1801; d. Vienna, 15 July 1881). Pianist and violinist. He received his musical training in Prague, studying the piano with Franz Zawora, the violin with Friedrich Wilhelm Pixis, and composition with Bedřich Diviš Weber. He made his début in Vienna as a violinist in 1817; three years later he settled there. For a time he played first violin in the orchestra at the Theater an der Wien, but he soon concentrated entirely on the piano; he also became well known as a music teacher.

He was on friendly terms with Schubert and an enthusiastic and excellent interpreter of his works; in 1826 Schubert dedicated to him the Piano Sonata in D major (D850). Early in 1827 Bocklet and the violinist Josef Slavík* reportedly played Schubert's Rondo in B minor (D895), in his presence, at Domenico Artaria's. (The work, composed in 1826, was published by Artaria & Co.* in April 1827.) On 26 December 1827, Bocklet, together with Ignaz Schuppanzigh* and Josef Linke,* gave the first public performance of the Piano Trio in E flat (D929) at the Musikverein. Schubert described their rendition as 'excellent' in a letter to Anselm Hüttenbrenner* (18 January 1828). On 20 January 1828, Bocklet played the Fantasia in C major for violin and piano (D934) with Slavík at the Landhaus. A week later, on 28 January, at what turned out to be the final Schubertiad hosted by Josef von Spaun,* Bocklet, with Schuppanzigh and Linke, played a piano trio by Schubert (perhaps again D929), after which Bocklet and Schubert played piano duets— probably the *Eight Variations on an Original Theme* (D813)—so brilliantly that, as Spaun later recalled, 'everyone was enchanted and the highly delighted Bocklet embraced his friend'. The trio D929 was also performed at Schubert's concert at the Musikverein on 26 March 1828, this time by Bocklet, Josef Böhm,* and Linke. The same artists were to perform it again at the Schubert memorial concert at the Musikverein on 30 January 1829.

Bocklet was regarded as a virtuoso pianist and greatly admired for his skill at improvisation. Chopin, writing to his teacher Józef Elsner from Vienna in January 1831, ranked Bocklet among the most gifted musicians then performing in that city. Bocklet retired from the concert platform in the 1840s, but returned for a final appearance in 1866, when he introduced his son Heinrich, likewise a pianist, to the public. He composed some pieces for the piano and contributed to the *Diabelli* Variations*. He also founded a private school for piano-duet-playing.

(Chopin, Hellmann-Stojan[1])

Bogner, Ferdinand (b. Vienna, 1786; d. Vienna, 24 June 1846). Official at the court treasury; flautist. A pupil of the flautist Florian Heinemann, he regularly appeared as soloist and later as conductor at the 'evening entertainments' of the Gesellschaft der Musikfreunde; he also wrote some compositions for the flute. From 1821 he taught at the Conservatory.

Schubert must have known Bogner quite well, for apart from the fact that one or other of his works was performed at about a dozen concerts in which Bogner participated, the latter married, in 1825, Barbara Fröhlich,* one of the Fröhlich sisters with whom Schubert had such friendly relations. At the two memorial concerts on 30 January and 5 March 1829, Bogner played variations for the flute written by the Berlin flautist Johann Wilhelm Gabrielski.

Kreissle* suggested that Schubert probably composed his *Variations* for flute and piano (D802) for Bogner in 1824. The theme of the seven extremely virtuosic variations was taken from 'Trockne Blumen' (D795/18), one of the songs in the *Die schöne Müllerin* cycle. There is, however, no record of its having been performed by Bogner, or, for that matter, anyone else at that time.

(Kreissle)

Böhm, Josef (b. Pest [Budapest], 4 April 1795; d. Vienna, 28 March 1876). Violinist and composer. He was taught the violin and piano by his father and reportedly also received instruction from the famous French violinist Pierre Rode, perhaps when the latter visited Vienna in 1812.

Böhm made a very promising début in Vienna in 1816, playing works by Rodolphe Kreutzer and Franz Weiss. He won praise for his technical skill as well as for his artistic taste. According to Eduard Hanslick, he was one of the first violinists in Vienna to perform from memory. Later he toured with considerable success in Italy, Germany, and France. On 1 June 1819, at the age of 24, he was appointed the very first professor of violin at the Conservatory, and he remained on its faculty until 1848. His most brilliant pupils were Jakob Dont, Heinrich Wilhelm Ernst, Georg Hellmesberger, and Joachim.

He frequently played at concerts in Vienna and was, in particular, an enthusiastic champion of chamber music. In 1816 he arranged six concerts at the 'Zum römischen Kaiser' inn, which were mainly devoted to quartets by Beethoven* and Haydn. In 1821 he resumed chamber-music recitals with a quartet consisting, in addition to himself, of the violinist Karl Holz,* the violist Franz Weiss, and the cellist Josef Linke.* The excellence of their performances led one critic to declare approvingly: 'This is how Beethoven's and Mozart's quartets should be played.' Moreover, Böhm frequently appeared at the 'evening entertainments' of the Gesellschaft der Musikfreunde, usually in performances of chamber music.

There is no evidence that Böhm's contacts with Schubert were other than purely professional ones. He was invited to play at Schubert's concert on 26 March 1828, on which occasion he performed the first movement of a 'new string quartet' (D810 or 887) together with Holz, Weiss, and Linke, and a 'new trio' (D929) with Carl Maria von Bocklet* and Linke. He also took part in performances of the trio at the memorial concerts on 30 January and 5 March 1829.

In addition to his other engagements, Böhm was a member of the court Kapelle from 1821 until 1868. His own compositions were written mainly for the violin, but he also contributed to the collection of forty waltzes for the piano which was published by Thaddäus Weigl* in Vienna in December 1824 and which included a piece by Schubert.

(Hanslick, Moser¹, *ÖBL*, Wurzbach¹)

Brahms, Johannes (b. Hamburg, 7 May 1833; d. Vienna, 3 April 1897). Composer and pianist. Florence May, his pupil, friend, and biographer, states that he particularly loved Schubert's music, and quotes his statement that he did not regard even Schubert's longest works, with all their repeats, as too long. He may well have been made familiar with Schubert's music by his teacher Eduard Marxsen who had studied in Vienna with Karl Maria von Bocklet.* His understanding of Schubert's songs was subsequently greatly enriched as a result of his friendship with the baritone Julius Stockhausen,* whom he met in 1856 and whom he was to partner in numerous recitals, in Hamburg and elsewhere. In April 1861 they performed the complete *Die schöne Müllerin* (D795) in Hamburg and at nearby Altona. Brahms was afforded a further very important opportunity of extending his knowledge of Schubert's works when, during his first stay in Vienna (September 1862–May 1863), the publisher Carl Spina allowed him to make copies of as yet unprinted manuscripts and presented him with all the Schubert volumes so far brought out by his firm (C. A. Spina*). Brahms carefully scraped the writing sand used by Schubert from the autograph of the unfinished oratorio *Lazarus* (D689) and preserved it in a box. The oratorio later influenced his own cantata *Rinaldo*, Op. 50.

Brahms was associated with Schubert's music in different ways throughout his life. In addition to actually performing it, as solo pianist, accompanist, or conductor, he published a reduction for chorus and piano of the Mass in E flat major

(D950), and made arrangements (none of which he published) of the following songs: 'An Schwager Kronos' (D369), for voice or orchestra; 'Ellens Gesang II' (D838), for solo soprano, women's chorus, four horns, and two bassoons; 'Greisengesang' (D778), for voice and orchestra; 'Gruppe aus dem Tartarus' (D583), for voice or unison chorus and orchestra; and 'Nachtstück' (D672), for voice, piano or harp, and small orchestra. (A piano study based on the Impromptu in E flat major, D899/2, may not be authentic.) Brahms furthermore published editions of the *Quartettsatz* in C minor (D703), of the song 'Der Strom' (D565), and of various piano pieces (the twelve Deutsche D790 and the three *Klavierstücke* D946, both of them first editions, and an anthology of twenty Ländler). Finally, he was responsible for editing the two volumes of symphonies for the *Gesamtausgabe* published by Breitkopf & Härtel.*

His general attitude towards 'complete' editions appears to have been ambivalent, although he participated in several such projects. More specifically, he regarded the posthumous publication of previously unprinted compositions and especially fragments as unnecessary and even undesirable. When Oskar von Hase, one of the partners of Breitkopf & Härtel, visited Vienna in 1882 for a meeting with the prospective editors of the proposed Schubert *Gesamtausgabe*, Brahms tried to dissuade him from undertaking the project, contending that all the essential compositions had already been published and that all that was now needed was for Schubert's works to be examined by a competent musician and for one complete copy to be deposited in a library in Berlin or Vienna. When his reservations failed to sway Hase, he duly attended the meeting, which was held at Nikolaus Dumba's* house, and agreed to collaborate in the project. However, it was very probably due to his objections that a number of works which had figured in the original plan were omitted from the published volumes (a full list of the 'missing' items is given in O. E. Deutsch's* article 'Schubert: The Collected Works'). In the end, though, Brahms came to recognize the usefulness of complete editions, or at any rate of a complete edition of Schubert's songs. Meeting Hase again at Leipzig in February 1895, he told him: 'I was mistaken: one sees Schubert quite differently now, and Mandyczewski's* edition of all the songs, especially, gives us an entirely new insight into the character and progress of Schubert's creative activity. One can see how it built up momentum and then suddenly flowed forth in an irresistible stream. It really is a unique and great picture.'

Finally, the degree to which Brahms was influenced by Schubert in his own compositions has been frequently discussed, both with regard to particular works and to more general aspects of form and tonality. Some minor direct borrowings seem beyond dispute, such as the use of the melody of 'Der Leiermann' (D911/24) in 'Einförmig ist der Liebe Gram', the last of Brahms's *Thirteen Canons* for women's voices, Op. 113. The resemblance between one of the themes in his Piano Trio in B major, Op. 8, and Schubert's song 'Am Meer' (D957/12) is also likely to be more than accidental. Furthermore, some musicologists have recognized the influence of specific Schubert works on certain compositions by Brahms, e.g. of the 'Wanderer' Fantasia (D760) on Brahms's Piano Sonata in C, Op. 1, or of the String Quintet in C major (D956) on his Sextet in G major, Op. 36. In a wider sense, Donald Tovey concluded that in his tonal thinking Brahms owed far more to Schubert than to 'the combined influence of Bach and Beethoven*', and that 'the traces of Schubert amount to an integral part of Brahms's personal style'.

(Deutsch[9], La Mara, Macdonald, May, Tovey[1,2])

Breitkopf & Härtel. Leipzig firm of music printers and publishers founded in 1719 by Bernhard Christoph Breitkopf (1695–1777), and subsequently directed by his son Johann Gottlob Immanuel Breitkopf (1719–94) and then by his grandson Christoph Gottlob Breitkopf (1750–1800). The latter entered in 1795 into a partnership agreement with Gottfried Christoph Härtel (1763–1827). The following year, Härtel became sole owner of the firm, which retained, however, the name 'Breitkopf & Härtel'. After Härtel died, his nephew Florens ran the business until Härtel's sons Raymund (1810–88) and Hermann (1803–75) joined it in 1832 and 1835 respectively. Since both died without male issue, the firm then passed to their nephews Wilhelm Volkmann (1837–96) and Oskar von Hase (1846–1921). Its subsequent history, which has seen it maintain its prominent position in the publishing world even in very difficult political circumstances (after the Second World War it was divided into an East German and a West German section), is of no direct relevance to our subject.

Two attempts were made in Schubert's lifetime to induce Breitkopf & Härtel to publish some of his compositions. In the spring of 1817, either Josef von Spaun* or Schubert himself submitted 'Erlkönig' (D328) to the firm, but with no success. The song did, however, to the delight of later Schubertians, provoke an outburst from the Dresden composer Franz Anton Schubert,* to whom the publishers had sent the music by mistake and who, in a letter to the firm, vituperated against the wretch who had misused his name for such trash.

The second approach was made by Schubert on 12 August 1826, when he offered a choice of songs, chamber music, and compositions for the piano. (He sent an almost identical exploratory letter to Heinrich Albert Probst* that same day.) In their reply of 7 September, Breitkopf & Härtel (then still managed by Gottfried Christoph Härtel) declared themselves disposed to consider publishing some of Schubert's works, provided that he was prepared to accept a number of copies in lieu of a fee in respect of the first work or works thus printed, 'as we are as yet wholly unacquainted with the commercial profitability of your compositions and are therefore unable to offer you a fixed pecuniary remuneration at this stage'. As far as is known, Schubert did not respond to this letter.

The firm's interest was finally awakened by Schumann's* letter of 6 January 1839, in which he enthusiastically described the as yet unpublished Schubert treasures, including notably several symphonies and Masses, which he had discovered in

Ferdinand Schubert's* possession in Vienna. Even then the initial reaction was highly cautious: 'The fact that Schubert's songs were sensationally successful does not mean that his symphonies and Masses would be equally so, at any rate as far as their commercial success is concerned, as you well know. However, we would be most interested to examine these works and would be *glad* to consider the *possibility* of publishing them.' Informed of the encouraging tenor of this letter, Ferdinand wrote to the firm on 31 January, announcing the imminent dispatch of the autograph and copied parts of the Symphony No. 6 in C major (D589), and of a copy which he had himself made of the 'Symphony No. 7' (i.e. the 'Great' C major Symphony, D944). At the same time, he expressed the hope that the firm would arrange for the former work—which, he added, had already been successfully performed in Vienna in 1829 (actually, on 14 December 1828)—to be played in Leipzig under Felix Mendelssohn* later that year.

In the event, it was the 'Great' C major Symphony which was performed by the Gewandhaus Orchestra under Mendelssohn's direction on 21 March 1839. Its favourable reception led Breitkopf & Härtel to buy it from Ferdinand, for 100 gulden; the orchestral parts appeared in 1840, and the full score in 1849. The symphony was played by the Gewandhaus Orchestra again on 12 December 1839 and 26 October 1840. In *c.*1855, Breitkopf & Härtel published a reduction for piano duet made by the German pianist Karl Klindworth, a pupil of Franz Liszt.*

The firm eventually made generous amends for its earlier neglect of Schubert when it decided to issue a complete critical edition of his works. Oskar von Hase visited Vienna in 1882 to discuss the project with the prospective editors, who included Brahms,* at a meeting held at the house of Nikolaus Dumba.* The edition was arranged in twenty series and a supplement (Series XXI), and published in thirty-nine folio volumes under the overall title *Franz Schubert's Werke: Kritisch durchgesehene Gesammtausgabe* [*sic*] between 1884 and 1897, the centenary of Schubert's birth. (Notwithstanding its title, the edition did not include all of Schubert's works—*see* Brahms.*) The editors, apart from Brahms, were Ignaz Brüll, Anton Door, Julius Epstein, Johann Nepomuk Fuchs, Josef Gänsbacher, Josef Hellmesberger,* and Eusebius Mandyczewski,* who also acted as general secretary. In addition to the volumes of music, there was a series of editors' reports (*Revisionsberichte*) which were originally published in twelve parts and subsequently collected into one volume in 1897. The edition was reprinted in 1928 in forty-one volumes, the series IV, V, and VI, originally published in one volume, being issued separately. The edition is now being superseded by the *Neue Schubert-Ausgabe* published by Bärenreiter.

> *First editions*: D944, and various compositions first printed in the *Gesamtausgabe* (1884–97).
> (Deutsch⁹, Hase, Plesske)

Bruchmann, Franz Seraph Josef Vinzenz von (b. Vienna, 5 April 1798; d. Gars am Inn, Bavaria, 23 May 1867). Redemptorist. Son of Johann Christian Maria von

Bruchmann (1768–1849) and his wife Justine, née Weis (1774–1840). The couple also had three daughters: Sibylla Justina (1799–1820); Isabella Josefa (1801–36), who, in January 1826, became the wife of Josef Ludwig von Streinsberg;* and Justina Johanna Maria (1805–29), who married Rudolf von Smetana* in November 1828. The father, a native of Cologne, had settled in Vienna in 1788. He became a prosperous merchant and was for many years a director of the Nationalbank; he was ennobled in 1818. The Bruchmanns occupied a leading position in Viennese society, entertained generously, and were known for their interest in the arts.

As a young man, Franz von Bruchmann went through a lengthy period of profound intellectual disillusionment. Abandoning the Catholicism in which he had been raised, he was attracted by the pantheistic ideas of Friedrich Wilhelm Josef von Schelling, whom, together with Goethe,* he came to regard as the greatest Germans of the age; he also much admired the writings of August Wilhelm von Schlegel* and Friedrich von Schlegel.* In 1819 he met Johann Senn* and joined his circle. He was present when Senn's quarters were raided in March 1820, and was subsequently reprimanded for his insulting behaviour towards the officer conducting the search. (Regarding his later contacts with Senn, *see* the article on the latter.)

In January 1821 Bruchmann went to Erlangen to hear Schelling lecture at the university. During his stay there, which lasted until mid-April, he formed a friendship with Count August Platen-Hallermünde,* whose volume of poems *Ghaselen* appeared while he was there. They were to meet again later, at Erlangen (in 1823) and elsewhere, and they corresponded over several years. In one of his earliest letters (2 August 1821) to Platen, following his return to Vienna from his first journey to Erlangen, Bruchmann offered to send him 'some wonderful settings of Goethe poems by Schubert, which are certain to delight all your friends'. At the same time, he tried to interest Schubert in Platen's poems, two of which Schubert did, in fact, set the following year in 'Die Liebe hat gelogen' (D751) and 'Du liebst mich nicht' (D756).

It is not known when and in what circumstances Bruchmann and Schubert first met. They were evidently acquainted by early 1820, since Schubert was also present at the police search of Senn's lodgings, but, most likely, their acquaintance dated from several years earlier. If, as has been reported (but not confirmed), Bruchmann was educated at the Akademische Gymnasium, they may already have met during their schooldays, for the Gymnasium, which, like the Stadtkonvikt, was run by the Piarists, formed part of the same building complex and was attended by the pupils of the Konvikt. Their contacts were closest during the years 1822–4, when some Schubertiads were held at the Bruchmann home and Franz von Bruchmann attended others hosted by Franz von Schober.* It was in 1822 and 1823 that Schubert made musical settings of five poems written by Bruchmann: 'Am See' (D746), 'An die Leier' (D737), 'Der zürnende Barde' (D785), 'Im Haine' (D738), 'Schwestergruss' (D762). Furthermore, Schubert dedicated his Op. 20, which Sauer & Leidesdorf* published in April 1823, to Bruchmann's mother; it consisted of

'Frühlingsglaube' (D686), 'Hänflings Liebeswerbung' (D552), and 'Sei mir gegrüsst' (D741). Bruchmann also took part in some of the reading parties, and his two surviving sisters likewise joined the group.

However, his relations with Schubert changed after his sister Justina's secret engagement to Schober (who was then in Germany) was discovered in 1824 and she broke it off at her parents' insistence. Bruchmann himself appears to have played a major role in the termination of the engagement. Moritz von Schwind,* who had acted as go-between for Justina and Schober, turned against Bruchmann, as did Schubert. 'Schubert and Schwind live in open feud with Bruchmann,' Johanna Lutz* reported to her fiancé Leopold Kupelwieser,* who was in Italy, on 7 March 1825. 'They seem to me like children, and they also express their hatred in a childish manner. They do not associate any more at all, do not greet each other, and, if they chance to meet, behave like enemies. It is true that Justina has been weak and vacillating, and Franz has deliberately acted badly towards Schober...' There is no evidence of any contacts between Schubert and Bruchmann after this affair. (For some other details, *see* Schober.*)

Bruchmann, who was increasingly tormented by scepticism and despair (he was later to describe the years 1823–6 as the most terrible of his life), sank into an ever-deepening spiritual crisis, which was finally resolved in August 1826 when he recovered his religious faith. On 25 June 1827, some weeks after qualifying as a lawyer, he married Juliana Theresia von Weyrother, whose father, Maximilian von Weyrother, was an inspector at the court riding school. After his wife died in childbirth on 26 October 1830, Bruchmann joined the Redemptorist order, as his brother-in-law Rudolf von Smetana had done in 1829 in similar circumstances. Bruchmann was ordained at Graz on 28 July 1833, and thereafter he assumed an increasingly prominent role in the order. Finally, from 1862 until 1865, he was head of its Upper German province.

Settings: D737–8, 746, 762, 785.
(Bruchmann)

Bürger, Gottfried August (b. Molmerswende, near Halberstadt, 31 December 1747; d. Göttingen, 8 June 1794). Magistrate and teacher; poet. The son of a pastor, he studied theology at Halle and later law at Göttingen. In 1772 he was appointed a magistrate at nearby Altengleichen, a post he was to resign twelve years later. He then joined the faculty of Göttingen University, at first as an unpaid lecturer; in 1789 he became a professor.

He was associated with the group of young romanticists who founded the Göttinger Hainbund and who published their works in the *Göttinger Musenalmanach*. It was in that periodical that the ballad 'Lenore', the poem for which Bürger is best known, appeared in 1774; it was based on the Scottish ballad 'Sweet William's Ghost'. (Bürger's poem provided the subject for Anselm Hüttenbrenner's* opera of the same title.) In 1778 Bürger published a collection of his poems, *Gedichte*; a further, two-volume, edition was issued in 1789. Bürger is credited with having created the romantic ballad—apart from 'Lenore', his compositions in that genre include 'Das Lied vom braven Manne', 'Der Kaiser und der Abt', and 'Der wilde Jäger'. He is also regarded as a lyric poet of considerable accomplishment.

In December 1817 Schubert made a setting of Bürger's poem 'Das Dörfchen' (based on the poem 'Le Hameau' by Pierre Auguste Bernard, known as 'Gentil-Bernard'). The male-voice partsong (D598) became one of Schubert's most popular vocal quartets. The earliest known performance took place on 19 November 1819 at Ignaz von Sonnleithner's,* and the first public one at the Kärntnertor-Theater on 7 March 1821 (with the singers Josef Barth,* Josef Götz,* Wenzel Nejebse,* and Johann Baptist Carl Umlauff*). The quartet was again on the programme of a Gesellschaft der Musikfreunde concert on 8 April 1821. At both these public performances the composition was received so enthusiastically that it was encored. It was published by Cappi & Diabelli* in 1822.

Much uncertainty surrounds another Schubert composition which may have been inspired by Bürger and which has received the work-number D426. In 1858 Albert Stadler* informed Ferdinand Luib* that he had in his possession the original autograph of a vocal trio 'Herr Bacchus ist ein braver Mann' which Schubert had composed in May 1816. Unfortunately the autograph is lost and no other copy of the composition appears to have survived. It is likely that the author of the text used by Schubert was Bürger, who did indeed write a 'Trinklied: Herr Bacchus ist ein braver Mann' which was first published in the *Göttinger Musenalmanach* in 1771.

Settings: ?D426, 598.

(Häntzschel[1], Hettner, Hilmar[6], Little, Porhansl[4])

Cappi. Family of Viennese music publishers, with a commercial history no less involved than that of the Artarias,* with whom the Cappis had marital as well as business links. In 1765 Carlo Artaria married Maria Cappi, and in 1775 the latter's brother Giuseppe was married to Francesco Artaria's sister Rosa. Both families had their roots at Blevio, in the Brianza district of Lombardy.

In 1773, Maria's and Giuseppe's brother Giovanni Cappi (1765–1815) arrived in Vienna where he became an employee of Artaria & Co.* In 1793 he was made a partner in the firm. He left in 1801 to set up his own business under the name 'Johann Cappi', with the assistance of Giuseppe's son Pietro [Peter] who had himself been working for Artaria since 1793. However, Pietro returned to Artaria in 1803, and he remained with that firm until 1816, having been made a partner in 1805. In 1816 he founded his own firm under the name 'Peter Cappi'; when Anton Diabelli* joined it in late 1818, it was renamed 'Cappi & Diabelli'.* The partnership was dissolved in December 1823.

In September 1824 Pietro rejoined the firm he had left in 1803, which was now being run by Giovanni's son Carlo [Karl] Borromäus Cappi under the name 'Johann Cappi Sohn'; upon Pietro's arrival, the firm became 'Cappi & Co.'.*

This new association lasted only until the spring of 1826, when Pietro's half-share in the business was bought by Josef Czerny* and the firm was rechristened 'Cappi & Czerny'.* But this new partnership endured no longer than the preceding one, for in November 1827 Carlo Cappi turned in his licence, was bought out by Czerny, and entered government service.

The new firm 'Josef Czerny',* established in March 1828, survived until 1831, when it was sold to the lithographer Josef Trentsensky. He, in turn, was succeeded as proprietor later that same year by his brother Mathäus [Mathias]. The subsequent history of the business is of no interest to Schubertians; but the different firms of Cappi & Diabelli, Cappi & Co., Cappi & Czerny, and Josef Czerny most certainly are, for between them they published a considerable number of first editions of Schubert's works (for details, *see* the separate articles).

(Slezak, Weinmann[5,6])

Cappi & Co. Viennese firm of music publishers directed by the cousins Carlo [Karl] and Pietro [Peter] Cappi* from September 1824 until the spring of 1826. Between January and May 1825, it issued first editions of Schubert's Opp. 33–4 and 36–8. These comprised a number of pieces for the piano and the songs 'Der Alpenjäger' (D588), 'Der Liedler' (D209), 'Der Pilgrim' (D794), 'Der zürnenden Diana' (D707), and 'Nachtstück' (D672).

First editions: D209, 588, 672, 675, 707, 781, 783, 794.
(Slezak, Weinmann[5,6])

Cappi & Czerny. Viennese firm of music publishers directed by Carlo [Karl] Cappi and Josef Czerny* from the spring of 1826 until November 1827. Between June and November 1826, it issued first editions of Schubert's Opp. 60–1 and 65. These consisted of a set of six Polonaises for piano duet (D824) and the songs 'Der Wanderer' (D649), 'Dithyrambe' (D801), 'Greisengesang' (D778), 'Heliopolis I' (D753), and 'Lied eines Schiffers an die Dioskuren' (D360).

First editions: D360, 649, 753, 778, 801, 824.
(Slezak, Weinmann[5,6])

Cappi & Diabelli. Viennese firm of music publishers directed by Pietro Cappi and Anton Diabelli* from late 1818 until December 1823. Between April 1821 and October 1823 it issued first editions of Schubert's Opp. 1–18. In the case of Opp. 1–7 and 12–14, which consisted entirely of songs—among them 'Der Tod und das Mädchen' (D531), 'Der Wanderer' (489), 'Erlkönig' (D328), 'Gretchen am Spinnrade' (D118), 'Heidenröslein' (D257), 'Rastlose Liebe' (D138), and 'Wandrers Nachtlied' (D224)—the firm initially acted merely as agents receiving a commission on sales, but it subsequently acquired the future rights to the songs (for further details, *see* Leopold von Sonnleithner*). The other compositions first published by Cappi & Diabelli included several vocal quartets, notably 'Das Dörfchen' (D598), 'Die

Nachtigall' (D724), 'Frühlingsgesang' (D740), and 'Geist der Liebe' (D747), and, among the piano music, the 'Wanderer' Fantasia (D760).

In 1823 Schubert parted company with Cappi & Diabelli. On 21 February he wrote to Diabelli to express his dissatisfaction with the recent publication of the sets of waltzes, Ländler, and Écossaises (D145), which, he alleged, had not been in full accord with the agreed arrangements, so that he considered himself entitled to 'an appropriate compensation'; he evidently received none. Finally, on 10 April, he sent a letter full of complaints and grievances, in which he asked for the return of all published and as yet unpublished manuscripts. The publication of Op. 16, comprising the quartets 'Frühlingsgesang' (D740) and 'Naturgenuss' (D422), which Cappi & Diabelli issued in October 1823, had no doubt been arranged already prior to the dispatch of the second letter (*see also* Anton Diabelli & Co.*).

O. E. Deutsch* lays the responsibility for the quarrel with Schubert upon Pietro Cappi rather than Diabelli, since it was Cappi ('a hard man') who managed the financial affairs of the firm. It may, however, be of some significance that Schubert subsequently dealt with Cappi & Co.* (from early 1825) and Cappi & Czerny* (in 1826), before he resumed business contacts with Diabelli (in 1826/7).

   First editions: D118, 121, 138, 145/6, 162, 216, 224–6, 257, 328, 365, 367–8, 422, 478, 489, 504, 514–17, 524, 531, 539, 541–2, 586, 598, 624, 685, 697/5, 702, 711, 719–20, 724, 740, 747, 760, 983, 983A–C. (Deutsch[3], Slezak, Weinmann[5,6])

Castelli, Ignaz Franz [pseud. Bruder Fatalis, Kosmas, Rosenfeld, C. A. Stille] (b. Vienna, 6 March 1781; d. Vienna, 5 February 1862). Civil servant; dramatist, librettist, poet, and editor. He studied law at the University of Vienna, and in *c*.1800 entered the service of the Lower Austrian government, in whose employment he remained until his retirement in 1842. An ardent patriot, he attracted attention with his soldiers' songs, especially the 'Kriegslied für die österreichische Armee' (1809) which, on the instructions of Archduke Karl, the commander-in-chief of the Austrian army, was printed and distributed to the soldiers. It was eventually banned by the French invaders, and its author was forced to seek temporary refuge in Hungary.

Castelli not only frequently contributed to periodicals, he also edited some at different times, notably the *Allgemeiner musikalischer Anzeiger, Conversationsblatt, Der Sammler*, and *Thalia*. In his poetry and prose he generally favoured the shorter and lighter genres such as ballads, fables, anecdotes, proverbs, fairy-tales, and novellas; but he also wrote a vast number of plays, many in dialect (as were some of his most popular poems), and he was a prolific librettist.

For plays as well as librettos he frequently turned to French models. One of his librettos was set by Josef Weigl* in *Die Schweizerfamilie*, and the great success of that Singspiel (first produced on 14 March 1809) led to Castelli being appointed resident poet at the Kärntnertor-Theater in 1811, a position he held until 1814. Sometimes he prepared German versions of librettos which had already been set to music, as in the case of Adrien Boieldieu's *La Dame blanche* (*Die weisse Frau*) and Ferdinand Hérold's *Marie* (*Marie, oder Verborgene Liebe*). The Viennese production of the latter opera (18 December 1826) prompted Schubert to compose *Eight Variations* for piano duet (D908) on Lublin's aria 'Was einst vor Jahren'. Altogether, Castelli was a prolific, if rather facile, writer. His collected poems appeared in six volumes in 1835. A comprehensive edition of his works, published in 1843, ran to sixteen, and it was followed by six further volumes in 1858.

Although Castelli was, by all accounts, an extremely gregarious person who was a member of several artists' and writers' clubs, including the famous 'Ludlamshöhle', there is no evidence that he had any contacts with Schubert's circle. Indeed, in neither *Schubert: Dokumente* nor *Schubert: Erinnerungen* is there any mention of any meetings with Schubert, nor is there any reference to one in Castelli's own memoirs (*Memoiren meines Lebens*, 1861). It is therefore not altogether surprising that Castelli seems to have been only vaguely aware of the fact that Schubert had set his libretto *Die Verschworenen*, which had been printed in his *Dramatisches Sträusschen für das Jahr 1823*. Schubert hoped that his opera (D787), which he completed by April 1823, might be performed in Vienna, but any such expectations were squashed the following year by the news that a setting of the text by Georg Abraham Schneider had been produced at the Schauspielhaus, Berlin, on 6 January 1824. The title of Schubert's opera was subsequently changed to *Der häusliche Krieg*, perhaps at the demand of the censor. It had to wait for its first performance, and then only in a concert version under Johann von Herbeck,* until 1 March 1861; it received its first stage production in Frankfurt am Main on 29 August of that year. Castelli, who attended the concert performance, was reportedly pleasantly surprised by the quality of Schubert's music, having been previously given to understand that Schubert had made a rather uninspired setting of his libretto. Schubert also set three of Castelli's poems in 'Das Echo' (D990C), 'Frohsinn' (D520), and 'Trinklied: Brüder, unser Erdenwallen' (D148).

Among Castelli's other claims to fame is that of having founded the Austrian Society for the Protection of Animals in 1847.

Settings: D148, 520, 787, 990C.
(Antonicek[2], Fischer[1], *ÖBL*, Wurzbach[1])

Chézy, Helmina [Wilhelmina Christiane] **von**, née Klenke (b. Berlin, 26 January 1783; d. Geneva, 28 January 1856). Poetess and librettist; daughter of Karoline Luise von Klenke* and granddaughter of Anna Luise Karsch, both well-known writers. She led a rather turbulent life, both in and out of marriage. She married Baron K. G. Hastfer in 1799 and divorced him the following year; in 1805, while residing in Paris, she married the French orientalist Antoine Léonard de Chézy (1773–1832), but left him in 1810 and subsequently lived with their sons Maximilian and Wilhelm in Germany and Austria. She was acquainted with many prominent writers of the day. In Paris she became friendly with Adelbert von Chamisso and with Friedrich and

Dorothea von Schlegel;* in Dresden, where she settled in 1817, she was in contact with Friedrich Kind,* Ludwig Tieck,* and Weber.* At Weber's invitation she wrote the libretto for *Euryanthe*, and in the autumn of 1823 she went to Vienna for the première of that opera (Kärntnertor-Theater, 25 October). In 1830 she settled in Munich; towards the end of her life she moved to Geneva.

She wrote many poems (*Gedichte der Enkelin der Karschin*, 2 vols., Aschaffenburg, 1812; *Altschottische Romanzen*, Berlin, 1817), as well as some novellas and stage works. The Singspiel *Eginhard und Emma* was performed at Amorbach, Bavaria, in 1812, with music by Baron Hettersdorf. In Paris, her political views brought her into conflict with the authorities who confiscated copies of her *Leben und Kunst seit Napoleon I* (2 parts, Weimar, 1805–7). Her memoirs, dictated in old age, appeared posthumously at Leipzig in 1858, under the title *Unvergessenes*. Today she is remembered for the poem 'Ach, wie ist's möglich dann', and as the author of the extravagant *Euryanthe* and the no less bizarre *Rosamunde, Fürstin von Zypern*, mainly because Weber set the former and Schubert composed incidental music for the latter.

In her memoirs she relates that, while in Vienna in late 1823, she was asked by Josef Kupelwieser* to write a play for the benefit of a beautiful actress at the Theater an der Wien (Emilie Neumann*), with whom he was in love; Schubert would contribute a musical score. At its première on 20 December, *Rosamunde* was given an even more lukewarm reception than *Euryanthe* had been accorded eight weeks earlier, and there was only one other performance, on 21 December. The reviews focused predominantly on the improbable nature of the plot and the often precious style of the text, and several critics gleefully told the absurd story in some detail, thereby unwittingly rendering an important service to future Schubertians, for the original text was never printed and has not survived.

Chézy, who had already been blamed for some of the perceived shortcomings of *Euryanthe*, responded to the new attacks by alleging that she had been obliged to write *Rosamunde* in the space of five days (a complaint regarded with some scepticism by modern writers), and by contending that the under-rehearsed and inadequate production had not done justice to her work. She did, however, subsequently revise the text. She submitted the new version, still accompanied by Schubert's music, to theatres at Stuttgart and Karlsruhe, and even wrote to King Ludwig I of Bavaria in 1837 in the hope of securing a production at the Munich court theatre, but all to no avail.

Many years later, in her memoirs, she conceded that the libretto had been wrong for the occasion, 'since the Theater an der Wien had its own particular type of audience, for which I was unable to write, not knowing anything about it'. Some of her detractors would no doubt have regarded the libretto as inappropriate for any occasion. Some praise was, however, expressed by the critics for Schubert's music (D797), notably for the overture, which was encored on the first night. (This was not, in fact, a new composition, having been written for *Alfonso und Estrella* the previous year.) Chézy herself paid generous tribute to Schubert at the time, calling the music 'glorious', 'sublimely melodious', and 'indescribably moving and profound' (in a letter printed in the *Wiener Zeitschrift für Kunst, Literatur, Theater und Mode* on 13 January 1824). The sincerity of her remarks is proved by a reference, in a letter to a friend in Dresden on 2 February 1824, to 'the delightful melodies' devised by Schubert for Axa's romance (D797/3b). Later, in her memoirs, she again praised his 'glorious' score.

Schubert is also believed to have used a text by Chézy in bars 127–218 ('In tiefem Gram . . .') of the song 'Der Hirt auf dem Felsen' (D965).

Helmina's younger son Wilhelm Theodor von Chézy (1806–65) became a successful author of novels and novellas, and worked as a newspaper editor. In his memoirs, *Erinnerungen aus meinem Leben* (Schaffhausen, 1863–4), he described his contacts with Schubert's circle, to which he was introduced by Ernst von Feuchtersleben, later an eminent physician and well-known writer.

Settings: D797, ?965.
(Chézy, Daunicht, *ÖBL*, Riley, Wurzbach[1])

Cibber, Colley (b. London, 6 November 1671; d. London, 11 December 1757). Actor, dramatist, and poet; son of the Danish sculptor Caius Gabriel Cibber (1630–1700) who had settled in England. His first play, *Love's Last Shift* (1696), is generally regarded as having established a new form of English drama, the sentimental comedy. Among his other stage works are *The Careless Husband* (1704), *The Double Gallant* (1707), and *The Nonjuror* (1717), the latter being based on Molière's *Le Tartuffe*; altogether, he wrote or adapted some thirty plays. In 1710 he became joint manager of Drury Lane. Towards the end of his acting career, in 1740, he published *The Apology for the Life of Colley Cibber, Comedian*. Although successful in his various careers, he had his detractors, among them Alexander Pope* who, in 1743, made him the hero of his satirical poem *The Dunciad*.

Cibber's poem 'The Blind Boy', as translated by Jacob Nicolaus Craigher,* inspired Schubert's song 'Der blinde Knabe'.

Setting: D833.
(Ross)

Claudius, Matthias (b. Reinfeld, Holstein, 15 August 1740; d. Hamburg, 21 January 1815). German poet, journalist, and translator. The son of a Protestant clergyman, he read theology and law at the University of Jena (1759–62), but left without completing his studies. He was employed as a private secretary in Copenhagen (1764–5), worked on the *Adresscomptoir-Nachrichten* in Hamburg (1768–70), and then became editor of (and, under the pseudonym 'Asmus', chief contributor to) the newspaper *Der Wandsbecker Bothe* (1771–5) at Wandsbeck, near Hamburg. In 1785 he was awarded a Danish pension, and in 1788 he was given an appointment at a bank in Altona which left him largely free to devote himself to his writing.

His literary career opened in 1763 with *Tändeleyen und Erzählungen*, but it was the publication, in 1775, of *Asmus, omnia sua secum portans, oder Sämtliche Werke des Wandsbecker Botens*, a compilation of his prose and poetry, which established his reputation as a gifted writer. Further pieces appeared in seven more volumes, until 1812. His poems were characterized by piety, simplicity, and a delight in the pleasures of life and nature. At the same time, if the predominant tone of his writings was a profoundly religious one, he was the opposite of a bigot. The poems have inspired many composers apart from Schubert: among Claudius's contemporaries, notably Johann Anton André, Ferdinand Hiller, Johann Friedrich Reichardt, Johann Abraham Peter Schulz, and Carl Friedrich Zelter; among modern musicians, particularly Othmar Schoeck, whose *Das Wandsbecker Liederbuch* (1936) presents a cycle of seventeen songs to texts by Claudius. In his translations, Claudius concentrated on the spiritual writings of Fénélon, Pascal, André Michel de Ramsay, and Jean Terrasson.

Claudius's poems inspired the following Schubert songs: 'Abendlied' (D499), 'Am ersten Maimorgen' (D344), 'Am Grabe Anselmos' (D504), 'An die Nachtigall' (D497), 'An eine Quelle' (D530), 'Bei dem Grabe meines Vaters' (D496), 'Das Lied vom Reifen' (D532), 'Der Tod und das Mädchen' (D531), 'Klage um Ali Bey' (D496A), 'Philide' (D500), 'Täglich zu singen' (D533), and 'Zufriedenheit' (D362, 501). All the songs were written in 1816–17, with the possible exception of the first version of 'Zufriedenheit', which may date from 1815. In that year Schubert had also made a first setting of 'Klage um Ali Bey' as a trio (D140). The text of 'Wiegenlied' (D498), which was attributed to Claudius in the first edition of that song in 1829, has not been found among his published poems.

Settings: D140, 344, 362, 496, 496A, 497, ?498, 499–501, 504, 530–3.
(Brown[2], Fechner, Lorenzen, Roedl)

Clodi (family). The father, Florian Maximilian (1740–1828) had four children by his second wife Therese, an aunt of Josef von Spaun,* whom he had married in 1800: Therese (*c*.1801–after 1847), Max (1804–54), Josef (1806–49), and Franz (b. 1808). From 1802 the family lived at Eberzweier Castle, near Gmunden in Upper Austria. The mother died in March 1815 at the age of 46; the father eventually went blind. The daughter Therese assumed the responsibility of keeping house and managing the estate.

Schubert became acquainted with the family while staying at Gmunden together with Johann Michael Vogl* from early June to mid-July 1825. On 22 June Therese wrote to Max, who was studying law in Vienna, that Schubert and Vogl had called at Eberzweier and that she would very much like to invite them, but did not know yet how best to set about it (they were staying with Ferdinand Traweger*). She added: 'I have twice heard Vogl sing and Schubert play; it is and remains a divine pleasure to hear those two.' Moritz von Schwind* had visited Eberzweier already the previous year, and Eduard von Bauernfeld* would do so in July 1826. They both liked Therese who became known as 'Das Fräulein am See', no doubt mainly because the estate was situated on the shores of Lake Traun, but presumably also in reference to Walter Scott's* poem 'The Lady of the Lake'. (In 1825 Schubert drew on it for several compositions which were published the following year.) As for Max, his association with the Schubert circle in Vienna appears to have been especially close in 1827–8, when he is frequently mentioned in Franz von Hartmann's* diary, sometimes under the nickname 'Clax'.

Following Florian Clodi's death, his children sold Eberzweier Castle in 1830 to Archduke Maximilian Josef, a son of Archduke Ferdinand Karl Anton and grandson of Empress Maria Theresa. (He died at the castle in 1863.) The Clodis acquired a property at nearby Traunkirchen, but Therese soon moved to Vienna, where she supported herself with needlework; later she became headmistress of a girls' school at Penzing, near Vienna. Max occupied a senior position in the Upper Austrian administration, Josef died while serving as an officer at Venice, and Franz became head of an army dispensary in Transylvania.

Collin, Heinrich Josef von (b. Vienna, 26 December 1771; d. Vienna, 28 July 1811). Dramatist and poet; elder brother of Matthäus von Collin.* Both his father, also called Heinrich Josef (1731–81), and his uncle Matthäus (1739–1817) were well-known physicians. In 1803 his uncle was ennobled, as were Collin and his brother and sisters. He himself trained as a lawyer (1790–4) and became a distinguished civil servant. He devoted what spare time his duties left him to literary activities.

Several of his verse dramas, on subjects taken from ancient or modern history, glorify man's freedom and strength of will; not for nothing was he known as the 'Austrian Corneille'. The most successful of his plays was *Regulus* (Burgtheater, 3 October 1801); the others included *Coriolan* (1802), for which Beethoven* composed his famous overture in 1807, and *Polyxena* (1803), for which Abbé Maximilian Stadler* wrote several choruses. Schubert was almost certainly among the choirboys of the court Kapelle who sang some of these choruses at a 'celebration' in Collin's memory at the university on 15 December 1811, and again at a charity concert at the Burgtheater on 24 December 1811. As a poet, Collin is best remembered for his patriotic *Lieder österreichischer Wehrmänner* (1809). A volume of his poems was published posthumously in 1812, and his brother Matthäus brought out a six-volume edition of his collected works in 1812–14.

Schubert wrote two songs, 'Leiden der Trennung' (D509) and 'Kaiser Maximilian auf der Martinswand' (D990A), to texts by Collin, of which the first was a translation of Metastasio.*

Settings: D509, 990A.
(Skrine¹, Wurzbach¹)

Collin, Matthäus von (b. Vienna, 3 March 1779; d. Vienna, 23 November 1824). Dramatist, poet, and critic; younger brother of Heinrich Josef von Collin.* In 1804 he qualified as a lawyer at the University of Vienna. He taught aesthetics and philosophy, first at Cracow University (1808) and subsequently in Vienna (1810), where he was also employed as censor (1812–23) and worked in the ministry of finance. In 1816 he was appointed tutor to Napoleon's son, the duke of Reichstadt. He wrote numerous poems, which were gathered together by Baron Hammer-Purgstall in a posthumous edition (*Nachgelassene Gedichte*, 2 vols., 1827). He furthermore wrote a series of patriotic historical plays in verse which were published (1815–17), though never produced. But he made his greatest impact with his literary criticism which appeared in the periodicals *Archiv*, *Allgemeine Litteratur-Zeitung* (which he himself edited at one time), and *Jahrbücher der Litteratur* (which he founded in 1818).

Schubert was particularly indebted to Collin, for the latter, having heard him sing his songs at the house of Josef von Spaun* (who was Collin's cousin), asked Spaun to bring Schubert and Johann Michael Vogl* to a soirée at his apartment [7 Teinfaltstrasse], to which he invited a select group of Viennese music lovers. It was at this private concert, which took place in *c*.1820, that Schubert was introduced to Count Moritz Dietrichstein,* Baron Hammer-Purgstall, Ignaz Franz von Mosel,* Karoline Pichler,* and Johann Ladislaus Pyrker,* among others. All, Spaun later recalled, were most enthusiastic about the music they heard. According to the account of Schubert's life which Anselm Hüttenbrenner* prepared for Liszt* in 1854, the programme included the song 'Der Wanderer' (D489) and *Eight Variations on a French Song* for piano duet (D624); the latter composition was played by Schubert and Hüttenbrenner.

Schubert set poems by Collin in the duet 'Licht und Liebe' (D352) and the songs 'Der Zwerg' (D771), 'Herrn Josef Spaun, Assessor in Linz' (D749), 'Nacht und Träume' (D827), and 'Wehmut' (D772). The duet was probably composed in 1816 (the text is taken from the tragedy *Der Tod Friedrich des Streitbaren*); the four songs date from 1822–3. The songs 'Der Zwerg' and 'Wehmut' were published together in May 1823 as Op. 22, which was dedicated to Collin.

Settings: D352, 749, 771–2, 827.
(Collin, Skrine²)

Cowley, Abraham (b. London, 1618; d. Chertsey, 28 July 1667). English poet, dramatist, and essayist, who was a transitional literary figure between the metaphysical poets and the Augustan writers. He demonstrated his precocious literary talent by publishing in 1633, at the age of 15, a volume entitled *Poetical Blossoms*. It included the epic romance *Pyramus and Thisbe*, written when he was only 10 years old, and the epic *Constantia and Philetus*, composed two years later. The love-cycle *The Mistress* (1647) was strongly influenced by the poetry of John Donne. The *Miscellanies* (1656) include *Pindaric Odes*, as well as an unfinished epic in decasyllabic couplets, *The Davideis*, on the biblical story of David. The *Essays in Verse and Prose* (1668) reflect the evolution of Cowley's later work towards neo-classicism.

Schubert's song 'Der Weiberfreund' is based on a German translation by Josef Franz von Ratschky* of the poem 'The Inconstant' in *The Mistress*.

Setting: D271.

(Walton)

Craigher de Jachelutta, Jacob Nicolaus, Imperial Baron [pseud. Nicolaus] (b. Liposullo, Friuli, 17 December 1797; d. Cormons, near Görz [Gorizia], 17 May 1855). Merchant; poet and translator. In *c*.1820 he settled in Vienna where he joined the circle which had formed around Klemens Maria Hofbauer, the Redemptorist priest whose advocacy of religious reform evoked considerable support at the time. Craigher was in contact with Friedrich von Schlegel*, Zacharias Werner*, and Ludwig Schnorr von Carolsfeld;* he also became acquainted with Schubert.

His poetry reflected his religious and mystical tendencies. This aspect evidently attracted Schubert who, early in 1825, set two of Craigher's poems in 'Die junge Nonne' (D828) and 'Totengräbers Heimwehe' (D842). He also set 'Der blinde Knabe' (D833), Craigher's German version of Colley Cibber's* 'The Blind Boy'. On 23 October 1825, several months after the composition of the above-mentioned songs, Craigher noted in his diary: 'Today has truly been a day of joy for me. [Moritz von] Schwind* and Schubert came to breakfast and remained from nine until close to eleven o'clock ... Schubert has made an arrangement with me, under which I am to provide him with a number of poems by well-known English, Spanish, French, and Italian authors, together with German translations in the metre of the originals, which he will then set to music and have published with the original texts. I myself can only gain thereby, particularly as this may lead to a closer association between us, which ought to be in all respects beneficial to both of us. Besides, Schubert is such a splendid person that I should make every effort to draw him closer to us.—He also took some songs of mine away with him, which he will probably set to music.'

In fact, Schubert was to set no further original poems by Craigher. However, O. E. Deutsch* has suggested that Craigher may have been responsible for the German versions of Metastasio's* 'L'incanto degli occhi' and 'Il traditor deluso', and of the poem 'Il modo di prender moglie', three texts which Schubert set in 1827 (D902/1–3). The songs were published together in September of that year as Op. 83 by Tobias Haslinger,* with both the German and Italian words. Craigher may also be the author of the Italian translations which accompanied the German texts in certain editions of 'An die Leier' (D737), 'Der Wachtelschlag' (D742), 'Im Haine' (D738), and 'Willkommen und Abschied' (D767).

In 1828 Craigher published in Vienna a collection of verse, *Poetische Betrachtungen in freyen Stunden*. Later his growing prominence as a businessman led to his being appointed Belgian consul at Trieste, and to an invitation to undertake a study trip to the Orient on behalf of the Belgian government.

Settings: D828, 833, 842, ?902/1–3.

(Fischer², Wurzbach¹)

Czerny, Josef (bapt. Wrbno [Vrbno, near Melník, Czech Republic], 14 June 1785; d. Vienna, 22 September 1831). Composer, piano teacher, and music publisher. He was not related to the well-known pianist and composer Carl Czerny, but, like him, was at one time tutor to Beethoven's* nephew Karl. Among his other pupils was Maria Leopoldine Blahetka.* In the spring of 1826 he bought Pietro [Peter] Cappi's half-share in the firm Cappi & Co.,* thereby becoming the partner of Pietro's cousin Carlo [Karl] Borromäus Cappi. The new firm assumed the name 'Cappi & Czerny'.*

In November 1827 Carlo Cappi withdrew from the business and sold his part in it to Czerny, who registered his own firm 'Josef Czerny'* in March of the following year. In February 1831 it was acquired by the lithographer Josef Trentsensky.

While nothing is known about Czerny's personal contacts with Schubert, he is likely to have been acquainted with him before becoming his publisher. According to Leopold von Sonnleithner,* he used to attend the private concerts directed by Otto Hatwig,* at which Schubert played in the orchestra and where at least three of his early compositions were first performed. Furthermore, Czerny wrote variations on one of the Écossaises from Schubert's collection of dances for the piano (D145) which had been published by Cappi & Diabelli* early in 1823.

For a list of Schubert first editions issued by the firms 'Cappi & Czerny' and 'Josef Czerny', *see* the separate articles.

(Slezak)

Czerny, Josef (publishing firm). Viennese music publishing house owned by Josef Czerny* from March 1828 until February 1831. In addition to the publications with which he had been associated as a partner in Cappi & Czerny,* he was responsible for an even more considerable number of first editions of Schubert's works after he became sole owner of the firm. None of these appeared in Schubert's lifetime, but the four Seidl* songs making up Op. 105—'Am Fenster' (D878), 'Sehnsucht' (D879), 'Widerspruch' (D865), and 'Wiegenlied' (D867)—must have been acquired by Czerny some time before Schubert's death, since their publication was announced in the *Wiener Zeitung* on 21 November 1828, the day of the funeral. On 31 December, he inserted a further note in the *Wiener Zeitung* stating that he had bought eighteen vocal compositions and a string quartet in E major (D353) from Schubert's estate, all of which he proposed to publish in the course of the following year. In the event, some of them did not appear until 1830.

Czerny also published four other works by Schubert, between 1829 and 1831: the Piano Sonata in A major (D664), two further string quartets (D87, 810), and the 'Trout' Quintet (D667). Announcing the recent publication of the quintet, a writer in the *Wiener allgemeine Theaterzeitung* reported on 21 May 1829 that 'this quintet has already, at the publisher's instigation, received several private performances and has been declared to be a masterpiece by the musical connoisseurs present'. Czerny even made an arrangement of the quintet for piano duet, which he published at the same time as Schubert's composition.

First editions: D23, 87, 134, 141, 148–9, 189, 221, 232–4, 247–8, 270, 353, 391, 395, 594, 664, 667, 810, 865, 867, 878–9, 985–6.

(Slezak)

Dankesreither, Johann Nepomuk von (b. Vienna, 22 January 1750; d. St Pölten, Lower Austria, 10 June 1823). Ecclesiastic. He trained for the priesthood at the Benedictine Monastery in Vienna and later held various teaching posts. In 1779 he was appointed professor of dogmatics and polemics at the Lyzeum at Linz. After serving as assistant vice-rector of the general seminary in Vienna (1784) and as vice-rector of the seminary at Olmütz [Olomouc] (1785), he became a canon at Brünn [Brno] in 1786. In 1802 he was accorded the title Hofrat and made a member of the state council, with responsibility for ecclesiastic affairs. In 1806 he was named provost of St Stephen's Cathedral and chancellor of the University. From 1816 until his death he served as bishop of St Pölten.

Dankesreither was related to Franz von Schober,* and in September–October 1821 Schubert and Schober spent some five weeks at St Pölten and nearby Ochsenburg Castle, the summer residence of the bishops of St Pölten. In the town, they lodged either at the bishop's palace or at an inn. During their stay, they worked on the opera *Alfonso und Estrella* (D732), for which Schober was writing the libretto. Some private concerts were also arranged during their visit, at which Schubert's compositions were played. In a letter to Josef von Spaun* on 4 November 1821, Schober refers to these musical soirées as 'Schubertiaden'. This would appear to be the earliest known use of that term.

In December 1822 Schubert dedicated his Op. 12, the three 'Gesänge des Harfners aus *Wilhelm Meister*' (D478), to Dankesreither.

(*St Pölten*)

Deinhardstein, Johann Ludwig (Ferdinand) [pseud. Dr Röhmer] (b. Vienna, 21 June 1794; d. Vienna, 12 July 1859). Civil servant; playwright and poet. He studied law at the University of Vienna and subsequently entered government service. Later he taught aesthetics at the university and the Theresian Academy in Vienna. As a dramatist, he became most widely known as the author of light comedies (*Das Bild der Danae, Fürst und Dichter, Garrick in Bristol, Mädchenlist*), but he achieved his greatest success with the 'dramatic poem' *Hans Sachs*, produced at the Burgtheater on 4 October 1827. A collection of his poems appeared in Berlin in 1844, and his plays were published in seven volumes at Leipzig (1848–57). He was also chief editor from 1829 to 1849 of *Wiener Jahrbücher der Literatur*, the influential periodical founded by Friedrich Gentz in 1818. In addition, he held the posts of deputy director of the Burgtheater (1832–41) and censor of books (1829–48). He was thus, in several different ways, a very prominent figure in the Viennese cultural life of the period.

Schubert set two of Deinhardstein's poems in the song 'Skolie' (D306), composed in October 1815, and the cantata *Am Geburtstage des Kaisers* (D748). The latter was performed by pupils of the Theresian Academy on 11 February 1822, the eve of the birthday of Emperor Franz I, in whose honour the text and composition were written.

Settings: D306, 748.

(Fischer[3], Weinmann[3], Wurzbach[1])

Deutsch, Otto Erich (b. Vienna, 5 September 1883; d. Vienna, 23 November 1967). Biographer and bibliographer. After studying literature and art history at the universities of Vienna and Graz, he was employed as art critic on the Vienna daily *Die Zeit* (1908–9) and as assistant at the Kunsthistorisches Institut of the University of Vienna (1909–11). For some years, until 1926, he owned a bookshop; from 1926 until 1935 he was librarian of the music collection assembled in Vienna by Anthony van Hoboken. He lived at Cambridge in England from 1939 until 1951, when he returned to Vienna.

His name is principally associated with three composers: Handel, Mozart, and Schubert. Of all three he published documentary biographies which are mines of information and models of meticulous scholarship: *Handel: A Documentary Biography* was published in London in 1955; *Mozart: Die Dokumente seines Lebens* at Kassel in 1961 (in English, *Mozart: A Documentary Biography*, trans. E. Blom, P. Branscombe, and J. Noble, London, 1965); and *Schubert: Die Dokumente seines Lebens* in Munich in 1914, followed by a greatly expanded version in English, *Schubert: A Documentary Biography* (trans. E. Blom, London, 1946), and, finally, by a German edition of the latter book, with a few additions (Kassel, 1964, same title as in 1914).

Other publications on Mozart include a splendid pictorial record, *Mozart und seine Welt in zeitgenössischen Bildern* (Kassel, 1961), and an excellent edition, prepared in collaboration with W. A. Bauer, of the correspondence, *Mozart: Briefe und Aufzeichnungen* (Kassel, 1962–3). Deutsch also produced a fine pictorial record of Schubert's life, *Schubert: Sein Leben in Bildern* (Munich, 1913), and a valuable volume of recollections, *Franz Schubert: Die Erinnerungen seiner Freunde* (Leipzig, 1957; in English, *Schubert: Memoirs of his Friends*, trans. R. Ley and J. Nowell, London, 1958). Lastly, there is the monumental *Schubert: Thematic Catalogue of his Works* (with D. R. Wakeling, London, 1951), which was later issued in German in a revised and enlarged form (Kassel, 1978), as a supplement to the new collected edition of Schubert's works. It should be added that Deutsch also devoted some 150 articles to Schubert.

(King, Redlich)

Diabelli, Anton (b. Mattsee, near Salzburg, 6 September 1781; d. Vienna, 7 April 1858). Music publisher and composer. The son of a musician, he became a choirboy at Michaelbeuren Monastery at the age of 7. Two years later he moved to Salzburg, where he was taught by Michael Haydn. In 1798 he entered the Cistertian monastery at Raitenhaslach in Bavaria, but he left it in 1802 and moved to Vienna. There he earned his living primarily as a piano and guitar teacher, and as a composer. From 1815 he worked as proof-reader for the music publishing house S. A. Steiner & Co., which was directed by Sigmund Anton Steiner and Tobias Haslinger.* Through this work he became acquainted with Beethoven,* who called him 'Provost marshal and diabolus diabelli'.

In late 1818 he founded, together with Pietro Cappi,* the firm 'Cappi & Diabelli'.* Their association lasted until December 1823. Subsequently Diabelli obtained a new licence as an art and music dealer, and in June 1824 he formed a partnership with his lawyer Anton Spina. While the latter assumed responsibility for the management of the firm, Diabelli attended, in the main, to musical matters. They traded under the name 'Anton Diabelli & Co.'* very successfully for more than twenty-five years. In December 1850 Spina's son Carl joined the business, and in January 1851 Diabelli retired, to be followed at the end of that year by the elder Spina. The firm was henceforth known as 'C. A. Spina'.*

Diabelli published numerous compositions, both sacred (including Masses and cantatas) and secular (Singspiels, instrumental pieces, dance music, songs); he also made numerous arrangements of the works of other composers. But his enduring claim to fame rests on his having written the waltz which formed the basis of the so-called *Diabelli Variations*. Starting in 1819, he invited contributions from a host of musicians. Each provided one variation, with the exception of Beethoven who furnished thirty-three which Cappi & Diabelli brought out separately in 1823. The complete set was published the following year by the new firm Anton Diabelli & Co. (*see* the following article).

(Kahl, Kantner, Slezak, Weinmann/Warrack)

Diabelli & Co., Anton. Music publishing firm directed by Anton Diabelli* and Anton Spina from 1824 until 1851, in succession to Cappi & Diabelli.* The two partners' enterprise and success is strikingly illustrated by the fact that the plate numbers of published works rose from 1558 to about 9100 during that period. In the process, they took over several smaller firms, such as those of Thaddäus Weigl* in 1832, Matthias Artaria* in 1833, and Anton Berka & Co. in 1835. During the final year, they were joined by Spina's son Carl.

The firm Anton Diabelli & Co. launched its career with the publication of the *Diabelli Variations* in June 1824. These were issued in two parts, of which the first offered a further edition of the Beethoven* set already published by Cappi & Diabelli the previous year, while the second presented the contributions received from other musicians, which amounted to forty-nine variations and a coda. One of these variations was by Schubert (D718). This was presumably one of the compositions acquired by Cappi & Diabelli from Schubert before he quarrelled with the firm early in 1823; others were issued by Anton Diabelli & Co. at irregular intervals during the following years.

Not until 1826/7 does a reconciliation appear to have taken place between Schubert and Diabelli, of which the first important result was the publication in March 1827 of 'Gesänge aus *Wilhelm Meister*' (D877), composed as recently as January 1826. A few more compositions appeared between March 1827 and October 1828, some for the first time—e.g. the songs 'Gesang der Norna' (D831), 'Lied der Anne Lyle' (D830), und 'Romanze des Richard Löwenherz' (D907)—and others reprinted from the *Wiener Zeitschrift für Kunst, Literatur, Theater und Mode*, e.g. 'Auf dem Wasser zu singen' (D774), 'Der Wachtelschlag' (D742), and 'Drang in die Ferne' (D770). Publication of the last Schubert composition to be issued by the firm in his lifetime, the song 'Glaube, Hoffnung und Liebe' (D955), was announced on 6 October 1828.

In the course of the year 1829 Anton Diabelli & Co. brought out first editions of several more works, among them a number of songs, and two marches (D968B) and the Fantasia in F minor (D940), for piano duet. At the end of 1829 or early in 1830, following negotiations with Ferdinand Schubert,* the firm bought a significant part of Schubert's estate, thereby acquiring the rights to many already printed works, as well as to a large number of as yet unpublished compositions. It subsequently bought other works (some of which were eventually published by the firm's successor, C. A. Spina*), and it also came into possession of the catalogues of the firms it took over.

As a result, Anton Diabelli & Co. became by far the most important publisher of Schubert's works, and especially of Schubert first editions. In addition to various other publications, the firm brought out fifty fascicles ('Nachlass-Hefte') between 1830 and 1850, containing about 135 hitherto unpublished songs and partsongs. Among the notable piano and chamber-music works first published by the firm were the four Impromptus D935, the last three piano sonatas (D958–60), two piano trios (D897–8), and the String Quartet in G major (D887).

After Diabelli retired in January 1851 and Spina at the end of that year, the firm was run by the latter's son Carl under the name 'C. A. Spina'. One of the last actions taken by the old partnership had been to establish a 'Schubert-Salon' (*see* C. A. Spina*).

First editions: D37, 59, 75, 77, 95, 102, 115–16, 119–20, 123, 126, 136, 140, 143, 146, 150–1, 153, 161, 171, 174, 182, 184, 197, 210, 217–19, 223, 246, 255, 259, 261, 263–4, 269, 274, 278, 280–2, 286, 290–1, 293, 297, 300–1, 321–2, 343, 352, 358, 361, 369, 375, 384–6, 393, 397, 403, 408, 412, 432, 434, 436, 442, 444–5, 450, 452, 457, 472–4, 492, 497–8, 506, 508, 520, 526, 530, 534, 540, 544, 548, 551, 560, 564, 573–5, 578, 584–5, 599, 608, 611, 614, 616, 620–3, 626, 632, 639, 650–4, 666, 671, 674, 676–7, 684, 690, 694, 696, 698–700, 706, 708, 710, 712, 715–16, 718, 727, 732 (in part), 733–6, 739, 746, 749, 754, 757, 759A, 762–3, 779, 784–5, 788–9, 792, 799, 802, 805–7, 811–12, 815, 822, 830–2, 834, 842, 847–8, 853, 860–1, 869, 875–6, 877/1–4, 883, 887–90, 892, 897–8, 906–7, 910, 912, 920, 930, 933–5, 938, 940, 942, 947–8, 952, 955, 958–60, 968B.
(Kahl, Kantner, Slezak, Weinmann/Warrack)

Dialer, Josef Alois (b. Imst, Tyrol, 3 March 1797; d. Vienna, 5 December 1846). Sculptor. In 1815 he moved to Vienna, where he made the acquaintance of the Schubert family. Among his best-known works are the allegorical figures on the façade of the theatre at Ödenburg [Sopron], a plaster of Paris statuette called *The Spirit of the Year 1809* which commemorated the Tyrolean uprising against Napoleon (now at the Tiroler Landesmuseum Ferdinandeum at Innsbruck), the monument at Ferdinand Raimund's tomb at Gutenstein, and the bust of Schubert at his grave at Währing district cemetery. Dialer made the plaster cast free of charge; the bust itself was cast at ironworks at Blansko in Moravia. It constituted the centrepiece of the funeral monument erected in the summer of 1830, which is said to have been designed by Franz von Schober* with the help of the architect Ludwig Förster* and which bore an inscription composed by Grillparzer.*

George Grove* visited the cemetery with Arthur Sullivan* soon after their arrival in Vienna in October 1867: 'We went...to the Währinger Friedhof to see the tombs of Beethoven* and Schubert and it was very sweet and cheerful in the setting sun and we felt very nice and *ruhig*, and brought home our grass and ivy from the said graves,' he reported to his friend Olga von Glehn. He was delighted when the publisher Carl Spina presented him with a copy of the bust a few days later. (Plaster casts of the bust had been offered for sale by the music publisher Tobias Haslinger* as early as January 1829.) Grove later compared the bust favourably with the more stylized representation of Schubert in Kundmann's* statue in the Stadtpark, since the former frankly showed the composer's 'ugly' face, 'with every appearance of its being something of a likeness' (letter to *The Times* on 2 October 1889).

In 1888, Schubert's remains were moved to the musicians' Grove of Honour at the new central cemetery, but the first monument has been preserved on the original site in what has become the Schubert Park. Dialer's bust is now exhibited in the small museum set up in Ferdinand Schubert's* flat [6 Kettenbrückengasse] in which Schubert died.

(*ALBK*, Graves)

Dietrichstein von Proskau-Leslie, Moritz (**Josef Johann**), Count (b. Vienna, 19 February 1775; d. Vienna, 27 August 1864). Son of Prince Johann Karl Dietrichstein (1728–1808) and his wife Maria Christina, née Countess Thun (1738–88). He married Countess Therese Gilleis (1779–1860) in 1800. In 1815 he was given responsibility for the education of Napoleon's son, the duke of Reichstadt.

During several decades he played a highly important part in the cultural life of Vienna. In 1819 he was appointed Hofmusikgraf (count responsible for court music) in succession to Count Johann Ferdinand Kuefstein, a post for which he was well qualified since he had studied music with Abbé Maximilian Stadler* and was himself a composer. During his tenure, he established a music collection in the court library and strengthened the court Kapelle by engaging a number of younger musicians. In addition, he became director of the court theatres in 1821. He relinquished both offices when he was appointed director of the court library in 1826; he remained in charge of the library until 1845.

Schubert was introduced to Dietrichstein at a soirée given by Matthäus von Collin* in *c.*1820, at which several of his compositions were performed before a distinguished audience. In January 1821 Dietrichstein wrote out a testimonial certifying that Schubert had already provided eloquent evidence of his genius, thorough musical knowledge, and refined taste. The count sent it to his friend Johann Michael Vogl* with the following note: 'I request you, dear friend, to hand the enclosed to the worthy Schubert. May it prove of some benefit to him, for ever since I recognized the genius of this young, impressive, and extraordinarily promising composer, it has been one of my most deeply felt wishes to promote his career *sub umbra alarum tuarum,* so far as it is in my power.' Schubert showed his gratitude to Dietrichstein by dedicating 'Erlkönig' (D328) to him when the song was published in April of that year as his Op. 1.

Dietrichstein composed a certain amount of vocal music, both sacred and secular. He also wrote a number of dances and was among the musicians invited to contribute to the *Diabelli* Variations.* He passed on his musical talent to his illegitimate son Sigismond Thalberg who became a celebrated pianist and a fairly successful composer. His legitimate son Moritz (1801–52) had a successful career as a diplomat. From 1844 to 1848 he served as ambassador extraordinary in London.

(Antonicek[3], *ÖBL*, Wurzbach[1])

Doblhoff-Dier, Anton, Baron (b. Görz [Gorizia], 10 November 1800; d. Vienna, 16 April 1872). Politician. His grandfather Anton (1733–1810) and father Josef (1770–1831) were both senior government officials; his uncle Karl (1762–1837), a pupil of Johann Georg Albrechtsberger and Antonio Salieri,* was a composer of songs and church music.

Anton was a pupil of Johann Senn* and was himself regarded with some suspicion by the Vienna police in his student days, but, after qualifying as a lawyer, he was employed in the civil service from 1826 until 1836. Thereafter he devoted himself to the management of the family estate at Weikersdorf. Known for his liberal political views and his support of reforms, he was appointed minister of commerce in May 1848, and in July of that year became minister of the interior in Baron Johann Philipp Wessenberg's government, in which he played a leading role. He resigned his office in October, ostensibly for health reasons. He subsequently served as ambassador at The Hague (1849–58). In 1861 he was elected to the Reichstag, and in 1867 to the Herrenhaus.

He was a member of Schubert's circle throughout the 1820s, attended several Schubertiads, and participated in the reading parties. He may not have been one of Schubert's closest friends, but in the summer of 1823 he went to visit him at Steyr. Describing their meeting in a letter to Franz von Schober* on 12 November 1823, he referred to Schubert most affectionately as 'unser lieber Schwämmelein' ('our dear Tubby').

(*ÖBL*, Taddey, Wurzbach[1])

Doppler, Josef (1792–after 1867). In 1867 he told George Grove* and Arthur Sullivan* that he had been a pupil of Schubert's father* and had attended Schubert's baptism. He took the viola part in the quartet sessions arranged by Schubert's father from *c*.1814, and played the clarinet and bassoon in the private concerts held at Franz Frischling's and Otto Hatwig's.* An autograph of Schubert's Offertory in C major (D136), believed to have been composed in 1815, bears the indication 'Aria with clarinet solo for H[er]r Doppler'. Later he worked for Anton Diabelli & Co.* and subsequently became manager of that firm's successor, C. A. Spina.* It was at the latter publishing house that he spoke to George Grove and Arthur Sullivan in 1867.

While Schubert was at Zseliz in 1818, Doppler sent him a most affectionate letter (on 8 October), in which he addressed him as 'Herzensfreundchen' ('Most beloved friend') and informed him that he had arranged for the overture to the Singspiel *Claudine von Villa Bella* (D239) to be performed at a concert due to be given by the violinist Josef Scheidel in Vienna on 11 October. However, in the end, this attempt to secure a performance of the piece proved unsuccessful, as had an earlier one (for which Doppler may also have been responsible) to have it played at a concert by Eduard Jaëll* at Baden, near Vienna. Schubert was, perhaps understandably, not greatly impressed by Doppler's fervent enthusiasm. 'I can only marvel at the blind and foolish zeal of my rather clumsy friend Doppler, whose friendship does me more harm than good,' he wrote to his brother Ferdinand* on 29 October.

After Schubert's death Doppler remained in contact with Ferdinand, and when the latter agreed to sell his copy of the 'Great' C major Symphony (D944) to Breitkopf & Härtel* in April 1839, he authorized Doppler to collect the fee of 180 gulden on his behalf. While in Leipzig, Doppler also delivered a letter from Ferdinand to Mendelssohn,* who had recently conducted the first performance of the symphony.

(Krause)

Dumba, Nikolaus (b. Vienna, 24 July 1830; d. Budapest, 23 March 1900). Industrialist and politician; prominent patron of the arts. His father Sterio Dumba (1793–1870) was a Greek from Macedonia. From 1870 to 1896 Dumba was a member of the Lower Austrian parliament, and until 1885 also of the national parliament.

An extremely wealthy merchant, he was able to indulge his profound interest in the arts, and especially in music. His favourite composer was Schubert, and his palatial house [4 Parkring/12 Zedlitzgasse], which was decorated in the opulent style of the period, amply reflected that interest. On the ceiling of the music room a large round painting by Friedrich Schilcher symbolically depicted different aspects of Schubert's works, whilst the composer himself was portrayed, seated at the piano, in one of the two wall panels in which Gustav Klimt represented different functions of music.

Dumba was vice-president of the Gesellschaft der Musikfreunde and president of the Männergesangverein, as well as an honorary member of the Academy of Fine Arts. He was the principal speaker at the unveiling of Kundmann's* Schubert statue in 1872. He was, moreover, considered one of the finest Schubert singers in Vienna. He also collected Schubert manuscripts. Thus he bought from Johann von Herbeck* the autographs of the 'Unfinished' Symphony (D759) and of *Lazarus* (D689), and from Anna Fröhlich* those of Schubert's setting of Psalm 23 (D706) and of the original version, featuring a chorus for men's voices, of 'Ständchen' (D920). From Schubert's nephew Eduard Schneider, who possessed numerous autographs, Dumba purchased in May 1881, for 1,500 gulden, a batch which included the Mass in F major (D105), the Symphonies Nos. 1, 2, 3, and 6, various pieces of church and piano music, a large number of songs, and all the operas and opera-fragments except *Alfonso und Estrella* (D732) and *Die Verschworenen* (D787). Later, in 1883, he acquired almost all the manuscripts still owned by Schneider for a further 4,500 gulden. He made all the music in his possession available to the editors of the *Gesamtausgabe* published between 1884 and 1897 by Breitkopf & Härtel,* a project in the launching and realization of which he played a significant part. Shortly before his death, he presented his scores of Schubert symphonies to the library of the Gesellschaft der Musikfreunde. In his will he bequeathed his other Schubert manuscripts, amounting to some two hundred compositions, to the city of Vienna.

Dumba's son Konstantin Theodor (1856–1947) had a distinguished diplomatic career, culminating in his appointment as ambassador to the United States (1913–15). A pacifist, he later became president of the Austrian League of Nations Association.

(Brown[6], Hilmar[5], *ÖBL*, Wurzbach[1])

Ebner, Johann Leopold (b. Imst, Tyrol, 15 December 1791; d. Innsbruck, 1870). Civil servant. While a student, he lived at the Vienna Stadtkonvikt, at the same time as Schubert was a pupil there, but, being several years older, had no personal contact with him then. It was not until after Schubert had left the Konvikt that Ebner became acquainted with him, through their mutual friends Anton Holzapfel* and Albert Stadler,* on the frequent occasions when Schubert visited his old school in order to play his latest compositions to his former fellow pupils. Ebner left Vienna in August 1817 and never saw Schubert again, for he spent the rest of his life in his native province, where he reached a senior position in government service. In 1823 he married Seraphine (d. 1857), one of the daughters of the lawyer Albert Schellmann,* at whose house in Steyr Schubert had stayed in 1819.

Ebner's name is cherished by Schubert scholars because he was so greatly impressed by Schubert's early songs that he made copies of all he heard before his departure from Vienna. He gave the copies to his brother, Johann Ebner von Rofenstein. The latter subsequently lost most of them, but nevertheless still possessed a certain number in June 1858, at which time Ebner sent a (no longer extant) list of the surviving ones to Ferdinand Luib.* Like the copies made by Stadler, these were to constitute important sources for the editors of the *Gesamtausgabe*. They were eventually acquired by Consul Otto Taussig of Lund and are now in the library of that city's university.

Eckel, Georg Franz (b. Säusenstein, Lower Austria, 13 February 1797; d. 1869). Veterinarian. A fellow pupil of Schubert at the Stadtkonvikt, he played first flute in the school orchestra. He never saw Schubert again after the latter had left the Konvikt. He went on to study medicine at the University of Vienna, specializing in veterinary science. Having qualified in 1823, he taught epidemiology at Lemberg [Lvov] University from 1826. In 1834 he was appointed director of the Institute of Veterinary Medicine in Vienna. The author of several scientific studies, he founded his own journal, *Mittheilungen österreichischer Veterinäre*, in 1844, but its first issue turned out to be also its last. He retired in 1852, after the institute had been placed under the direct control of the war ministry.

His letter of 30 April 1858 to Ferdinand Luib,* who was then planning to write a biography of Schubert, is noteworthy for the sharp portrait of the young Schubert, which is by far the most detailed description we possess of his appearance and character, then or later. It is all the more remarkable for having being drawn forty-five years after they had last met.

(Schrader)

Ehrlich, Bernhard Ambros. A lawyer who became a government official and book censor in Prague. He was the author of the poem 'Als ich sie erröten sah', which appeared in Vol. I of the anthology *Erstlinge unserer einsamen Stunden* in Prague in 1791 and was set to music by Schubert in February 1815.

Setting: D153.

Enderes, Karl von (b. Teschen [Český Těšín, Czech Republic], 1787; d. Vienna, 1861). Civil servant; amateur botanist. He was introduced to Schubert by Josef von Spaun* and appears to have been a popular figure in Schubert's circle during the last years of the composer's life. He hosted several Schubertiads, was present at others, and frequently joined members of the group at taverns and restaurants. At one time he shared rooms with Josef Wilhelm Witteczek* and later with Spaun who thus described him in his memoirs: '[Enderes] was as conscientious, honest, and gentle a man as one can imagine. He was, like all his friends, a great admirer of

Schubert ... His gentle and considerate nature made him popular with everyone.'

His wife Kamilla, née Ellmaurer, whom he married after the death in 1834 of her first husband, Josef Gross, was an exceptionally fine pianist who had taken part in the musical evenings at Ignaz von Sonnleithner's.* She had also studied with Johann Michael Vogl,* whom Enderes knew well. After Vogl's death, Enderes became the guardian of his 12-year-old daughter Henriette.

Engelhardt, Karl August [pseud. Richard Roos] (b. Dresden, 4 February 1768; d. Dresden, 28 January 1834). Poet and narrative writer. After studying theology at Wittenberg (1786–90) he earned his living as a private tutor, but in 1794 decided to devote all his time to writing. From 1805 he worked as librarian or archivist in different government departments. His literary sympathies lay with Romantic writers such as Friedrich Kind* and Karl Gottlieb Theodor Winkler.*

Engelhardt's poem 'Ihr Grab' appeared in *W. G. Beckers Taschenbuch zum geselligen Vergnügen auf das Jahr 1822* (Leipzig). Schubert's setting may date from the same year.

Setting: D736.

Esterházy von Galánta, Johann Karl, Count (b. 23 December 1777; d. Zseliz [Želiezovce, Slovakia], 21 August 1834). Son of Count Johann Esterházy, of the Altsohl [Zvolen] branch of the family, and his wife Theresia, née Countess Erdödy. On 18 January 1802, at Penzing, near Vienna, he married Countess Rosina Franziska Festetics de Tolna (b. 2 January 1784; d. 2 August 1854), whom that noted connoisseur of female beauty, Tsar Alexander I, was later to rank among the six most beautiful women present in Vienna at the time of the Congress. The couple had six children, of whom only three—Marie (1802–37), Karoline* (1805–51), and Albert (1813–45)—were still alive in 1818, when Schubert was engaged to spend several months at Zseliz as music teacher to the two daughters whom he may already previously have taught in Vienna. The Esterházys used to spend the summer months on their estate at Zseliz, situated on the river Gran [Hron] to the north of Gran [Esztergom, Hungary], and the winter near or in Vienna, from 1802 to 1806/7 at Penzing [7–9 Penzingerstrasse], where they were guests of Rosina's mother, Countess Anna Festetics de Tolna, and subsequently at an apartment in the inner city [15 Herrengasse/Landhausgasse].

Schubert, who arrived at Zseliz in July 1818, had probably been recommended to Esterházy by Johann Karl Unger,* with whom the count had become acquainted while studying at the Theresian Academy in Vienna. In a letter addressed to Franz von Schober* and others on 8 September, Schubert briefly described the family: 'The count rather coarse, the countess haughty but more sensitive, the young countesses nice children.' He went on to complain that 'not a soul here, or at most the countess now and again (unless I am mistaken), possesses any true artistic feeling. I must rely wholly on myself. I have to be composer, author, audience, and heavens knows what else.' Yet Baron Schönstein,* who met Schubert that year through the Esterházys (either at Zseliz or, more probably, in Vienna), stated that they were extremely fond of music, and he himself frequently joined them in singing quartets, with the count singing bass, the countess contralto, and Marie, who had a particularly beautiful voice, soprano. By his account both girls were, moreover, very good pianists. (Marie, in particular, was later known as an excellent amateur performer on the piano.)

Schubert returned to Vienna in November 1818. According to Schönstein, he had become a great favourite with the family and continued to teach the daughters in Vienna. In May 1822 he dedicated his Op. 8, consisting of the songs 'Am Strome' (D539), 'Der Jüngling auf dem Hügel' (D702), 'Erlafsee' (D586), and 'Sehnsucht' (D516), to the count. He was once more engaged at Zseliz in 1824 and, on that occasion, spent four-and-a-half months there, arriving in late May and travelling back to Vienna with Schönstein in mid-October. It has been suggested that during this second visit to Zseliz Schubert formed a deep attachment for Countess Karoline, who celebrated her nineteenth birthday on 6 September 1824. (Schubert's relations with Karoline are discussed at some length in the article devoted to her.)

Countess Marie was married in December 1827 to Count August Ferdinand Paul Ludwig Breunner-Enkevoirth, a court chamberlain and senior official at the ministry of finance, and brother-in-law of Count Johann Nepomuk Weissenwolff.* Her brother Albert married Countess Marie Apponyi in September 1843; he died in Paris two years later. The mother thus survived not only her husband, but also all her six children.

(Weinmann[II], Wurzbach[I])

Esterházy von Galánta, Karoline, Countess (b. Penzing, near Vienna, 6 September 1805; d. Pressburg [Bratislava], 14 March 1851). Daughter of Count Johann Karl Esterházy von Galánta,* who engaged Schubert to give music lessons to her and her sister Marie at his summer residence at Zseliz in 1818, and again in 1824. According to Baron Schönstein,* a close friend of the Esterházys, the family became fond of Schubert during his first stay at Zseliz and the lessons resumed after their return to Vienna. Proof of Schubert's continued contact with the Esterházys between the two visits to Zseliz is, moreover, provided by the dedication of his Op. 8 to the count in 1822.

His feelings for Karoline appear to have deepened during the intervening years in Vienna, for in his first letter to Moritz von Schwind* from Zseliz in the summer of 1824, he wrote: 'I often feel a wretched longing for Vienna, in spite of a certain attractive *star* ('des anziehenden bewussten *Sternes*'). That he was indeed deeply attached to her is beyond doubt, though no document has as yet come to light which indicates that she returned his feelings. Schönstein told Ferdinand Luib* in 1857 that Schubert had loved Karoline until he died, but that she may not have appreciated the depth of his affection, although she could not have been altogether unaware of it, for when she reproached him one day in jest for not dedicating a single composition to her, he replied: 'What would be the point, since everything is in any case dedicated to you?'

Schönstein's statement about Schubert's love for Karoline is corroborated by another written source, all the more credible for being contemporary to the event. Eduard von Bauernfeld* notes in his diary in February 1828: 'Schubert really seems to be in love with the Countess E. I like him for that. He gives her lessons.' (A diary entry in 1825 had already indicated that Schubert was in love, but did not name the object of his affection.) The importance of the 1828 entry is threefold: it confirms that Schubert was in love with Karoline; it shows that he was regularly seeing her in the last year of his life; and it explains why, in his letter to B. Schott's Söhne on 21 February 1828, he should have mentioned, among the list of works available for publication, a fantasia for piano duet 'dedicated to the Countess Caroline Esterházy'. The work (D940), then only recently completed or perhaps even still unfinished, did not appear until March 1829, when it was published by Anton Diabelli & Co.,* with a dedication to Karoline. Further significant evidence of the important place which Karoline occupied in Schubert's heart, and possibly in his life, is surely provided by her inclusion in Schwind's group portrait *A Schubert Evening at Josef von Spaun's*,* in which Josef Teltscher's* portrait of her is reproduced in a central position, despite the fact that she is not known to have been present at any Schubertiads (in fact, Schwind had never met her).

Yet another pointer to what must, at the very least, have been a close friendship is the fact that Karoline had in her possession no fewer than fourteen Schubert autographs, as well as an impressive number of first editions, including some posthumous ones, of his works. Among the autographs, particular interest attaches to those of songs 9–11 from *Die schöne Müllerin* (D795), which are known to date from 1824 and in which the original keys have been transposed downwards. It has traditionally been thought that Schubert made these changes for Baron Schönstein's benefit, but already in the 1950s A. Orel speculated that they might have been due to Schubert's desire to render the songs suitable for Karoline's contralto voice. A more recent writer (E. Hilmar) has even speculated that, given their content, the very choice of 'Ungeduld', 'Morgengruss', and 'Des Müllers Blumen' may have constituted a 'secret programme', namely a declaration of love. Interestingly enough, a similar hypothesis, though based on quite different premisses, has been put forward by another scholar (R. Steblin) regarding the Fantasia in F minor (D940), which, as already indicated, Schubert dedicated to the countess. Steblin argues that, in the context of the intrinsic characters which were attributed to different tonalities at that time, a piece written in F minor may have been intended to convey a declaration of love. (This evidently presupposes that Karoline as well as Schubert were acquainted with these theories.)

Unlike her older sister Marie, who was married at the age of 25, Karoline remained single until she was nearly 40. Her marriage on 8 May 1844 to Count

Karl Folliot de Crenneville (1811–73), a retired army officer, proved an unhappy one and resulted in a separation. In 1853, two years after her death, he married Countess Anna Lazansky von Bukowa (1821–96), who bore him two sons.

(Clercq[2], Eder, Hilmar[8], Obermaier, Steblin[2,7])

Fellinger, Johann Georg (b. Peckau, Styria, 3 January 1781; d. Adelsberg [Postojna, Slovenia], 27 November 1816). Poet and dramatist (his play *Inguo*, on a subject from Carinthian history, was performed at Klagenfurt in 1817). After studying law at Graz he worked as tutor in an aristocratic household at Reiffenstein, near Cilli, Styria [Celje, Slovenia]. In 1809 he served as an infantry officer in the war against Napoleon, lost an eye in battle and was taken prisoner. After his release he held various military appointments, the last one, from 1815, at Adelsberg. In the end, unfit for active service and unable to secure suitable civilian employment, he committed suicide.

Schubert set two of his poems in April 1815 in 'Die erste Liebe' (D182) and 'Die Sterne' (D176). In addition, the song 'Die Sternenwelten' (D307), composed in October of the same year, was based on Fellinger's German translation of a poem written in Slovene by Urban Jarnik.*

Settings: D176, 182, 307.
(Wurzbach[1])

Förster, Ludwig (Christian Friedrich) (b. Ansbach, 8 October 1797; d. Gleichenberg, 16 June 1863). Architect. He attended school at Ansbach and subsequently studied in Munich (1816–18), after which he moved to Vienna. There he gained useful experience under the guidance of Peter Nobile, the director of the department of architecture at the Academy of Fine Arts, who also found him employment in the department (1820–6). Later he was himself on the academy's faculty (1843–6).

In 1836 he founded the *Allgemeine Bauzeitung* which became a highly influential journal among architects. His numerous public and private commissions included the construction of a Protestant church, a Jewish synagogue, the Elisabeth Bridge over the Wien, and houses for the Pereira family. Several of his proposals for the expansion of the inner city were incorporated in the officially approved scheme. In 1846 Theophil Hansen* joined him, and they worked together on several projects, such as the new arsenal complex.

The funeral monument, which was erected at Schubert's grave at Währing district cemetery in 1830, was reportedly designed by Franz von Schober* with Förster's help.

(*ÖBL*, Wurzbach[1])

Fouqué, Friedrich (Heinrich Carl), Baron de La Motte, (b. Brandenburg an der Havel, 12 February 1777; d. Berlin, 23 January 1843). Dramatist, novelist, and poet; descendant of a Huguenot family with roots in Normandy. The grandson of a

Prussian general, Henry August de La Motte Fouqué, he followed a military career until 1802. Thereafter he devoted himself entirely to his literary activities, except for the years 1813–15 during which he re-enlisted in the army and served with distinction against Napoleon's army. He lived mostly at Nennhausen, near Berlin, but from 1833 to 1841 he resided at Halle where he gave lectures on history and poetry.

He was a prolific writer. Among his most successful works are the novel *Der Zauberring*, the fairy-tale *Undine*, and the mythological dramatic trilogy *Der Held des Nordens: Sigurd der Schlangentöter, Sigurds Rache, Aslauga*. In addition, he made translations of Calderón and Thomas More, wrote poetry (*Gedichte*, 5 vols., 1816–27), and edited several periodicals and yearbooks, including *Die Jahreszeiten* (1811–14), *Frauentaschenbuch* (1815–31), and *Zeitung für den deutschen Adel* (1840–2), partly together with friends and with his second wife, Caroline, who was herself a well-known writer. (He married three times.)

Fouqué's works provided the text for the following five Schubert songs: 'Don Gayseros I–III' (D93), based on three songs sung by Don Hernandez in *Der Zauberring* and perhaps composed in 1815; 'Lied' (D373), based on a poem taken from *Undine* and perhaps composed in January 1816; and 'Der Schäfer und der Reiter' (D517), which dates from April 1817. In 1824 he set another Fouqué poem in the quartet 'Gebet' (D815).

Settings: D93, 373, 517, 815.
(Porhansl[4], Schmidt, Schulz)

Franck, Josefine von, née von Körber (b. Bielitz-Biala [Bielsko-Biala, Poland], 1789). She was married to Josef von Franck (d. 1827), a partner in the Viennese firm of wholesale dealers Franck & Co. (which was principally managed by Johann Jacob von Franck). He possessed an extensive collection of portraits of actors and actresses, most of which he had commissioned himself.

It may be an indication of the firm's prominence that when the Mainz music publishers B. Schott's Söhne wrote to Schubert on 9 February 1828 offering to acquire some of his compositions, they indicated that they would arrange for the fee to be paid to him in Vienna by Franck & Co. In the end, the offer did not lead to any publications. (Beethoven* also used the firm.)

In July 1828 Schubert dedicated to Josefine von Franck his Op. 87 (later renumbered 92) containing the Goethe* songs 'Auf dem See' (D543), 'Der Musensohn' (D764), and 'Geistes-Gruss' (D142).

Fries, Moritz (Christian), Count of the Realm (b. Vienna, 6 May 1777; d. Paris, 26 December 1826). Industralist and banker, of Swiss descent; prominent art collector and patron of the arts. Son of Count Johann Fries (1719–85), a successful industrialist who, together with Baron Johann Jakob Gontard, founded in 1766 the firm 'Fries & Co.' which became one of Vienna's leading financial establishments.

Johann Fries was ennobled in 1757, became a baron in 1762, and was created a count in 1783. In 1761 he acquired Vöslau Castle, near Vienna (now Vöslau town hall), and in 1783–4 he commissioned the architect Johann Ferdinand Hetzendorf von Hohenberg to build him an imposing residence in Vienna [5 Josefsplatz]. He married Anna d'Escherny (d. Paris, 1807) in 1764. Of their seven children, only four survived infancy, among them the two sons Josef Johann (1765–88) and Moritz, who is the subject of this article.

Moritz studied law at Leipzig from 1794 to 1797, before returning to Vienna to take charge of the family's business affairs which, apart from the bank, included important textile mills and extensive land holdings. He eventually accumulated an even greater fortune than his father had possessed and was considered the richest man in Austria. He was particularly famous for his magnificent art collection which comprised over 300 paintings by Anthony van Dyck, Albrecht Dürer, Raphael, Guido Reni, and other celebrated artists, and some 400,000 drawings and etchings, as well as sculptures and coins. He also owned a personal library of 16,000 books. In 1801 he was made an honorary member of the Academy of Fine Arts.

Fries and his wife Maria Theresia Josefa, née Princess Hohenlohe-Waldenburg-Schillingsfürst (d. 1819), were known for their lavish hospitality. Fries was also a great music lover and a generous patron, famous for his brilliant musical parties, at which Haydn and Beethoven,* among others, performed. In 1800 he arranged a contest between Beethoven and the German pianist Daniel Steibelt, which the former is said to have won handsomely. He reportedly paid Beethoven a regular subsidy for some years and furthermore commissioned his String Quintet Op. 29, and probably also the violin sonatas Opp. 23–4; all three works are dedicated to him, as is the Seventh Symphony. Haydn dedicated his last (uncompleted) string quartet (Op. 103) to him and also used the bank for personal transactions.

Schubert was among the musicians who sought Fries's patronage: in 1821 he dedicated his Op. 2, the song 'Gretchen am Spinnrade' (D118), to him. Schubert evidently had not met Fries at the time, for on 10 April Ignaz von Sonnleithner* provided him with a letter of introduction: 'I take the liberty of recommending the bearer of this letter, the talented composer Franz Schubert, to the patronage of your Honour...He will ask your Honour for permission to dedicate to you a small composition which he proposes to publish ... ' Fries rewarded Schubert with a gift of 20 ducats (about 86 gulden). There is no record of any further contacts between them.

In the end, Fries's extravagant life-style—in 1811, his household expenses alone amounted to the immense sum of 430,756 gulden—proved disastrous even for his enormous fortune, and by 1815 he was experiencing financial difficulties. In 1825 he was replaced in the management of the firm by his son Moritz (1804–87). The latter was, however, forced to declare bankruptcy in April 1826. At the end of that year, his father died in Paris, where he had moved with his second wife, the dancer Fanny Münzenberg, whom he had married the previous year.

The art collection was sold between 1823 and 1828, in part privately, in part at public auction in Vienna and Amsterdam. The estate at Vöslau was bought by Johann Heinrich Falkner-Geymüller, while the town residence was acquired by the banker Baron Georg Simon Sina. It was not until 1832 that all the firm's creditors were satisfied. Fries's dramatic fall from extreme wealth is believed to have inspired Ferdinand Raimund's well-known play *Der Verschwender* (1834).

(Fries, Hilmar/Brusatti, Mikoletzky[1,2], *ÖBL*, *StadtChronik*, Wurzbach[1])

Fröhlich (sisters). Daughters of Mathias Fröhlich (1756–1843) and his wife Barbara, née Mayr (1764–1841). Little is known about the father, who came from Pottenstein in Lower Austria, other than that he was a merchant who fell on hard times. In a letter to his friend Georg Altmüller in 1821, Franz Grillparzer* described the parents as 'very poor'. The four sisters made a remarkable contribution to Vienna's cultural life. All were exceptionally gifted musically and often participated in private and semi-public concerts. A writer in the *Allgemeine Wiener Musikzeitung* in 1841 speculated that 'the four Fröhlich sisters may well have done more for art, and particularly for singing, than many an Amazon of the throat celebrated throughout Europe'.

The oldest, (**Maria**) **Anna** [Nanette, Nettel, Netti] (b. Vienna, 19 September 1793; d. Vienna, 11 March 1880), was active as a soprano and a pianist. She studied singing with Giuseppe Siboni and the piano with Johann Nepomuk Hummel.* From 1819 until 1854—with an enforced break in 1848–51, when the school was closed owing to the unstable political conditions of that period—she taught an advanced singing class for female students at the Conservatory of the Gesellschaft der Musikfreunde. In 1854 the board of directors of the Gesellschaft, dissatisfied with the quality of her instruction, decided not to renew her contract and granted her a pension. She was replaced by Mathilde Marchesi, who later became a famous teacher in Paris (where her pupils included Emma Eames, Selma Kurz, Nellie Melba, Sibyl Sanderson, and her own daughter Blanche Marchesi). Anna does not appear to have borne a grudge for having her career thus terminated; in 1865 she presented two valuable violins to the Gesellschaft, one of which had reportedly been played by Haydn.

Anna's musical activities were not confined to her teaching at the Conservatory and her musical evenings. She also had a number of private pupils, and she performed at the semi-public 'evening entertainments' presented by the Gesellschaft and at soirées elsewhere. Thus, on 1 December 1820, she accompanied August von Gymnich* in the first performance of 'Erlkönig' (D328) at Ignaz von Sonnleithner's.* Many years later she described her first contacts with Schubert to Gerhard von Breuning, the son of Beethoven's* friend Stefan von Breuning: 'The lawyer Leopold [von] Sonnleithner* ... brought us some songs, which, he said, had been composed by a young man and were good. Kathi [Katharina Fröhlich] at once sat down at the piano and tried out the accompaniment. Hearing her, Gymnich ... pricked up his ears and asked: "What are you playing? Are you improvising?"—"No."—"But this is splendid, this is quite extraordinary. Do let me see." And then we spent the whole evening singing the songs. A few days later Sonnleithner brought Schubert to our house. We were then still living at 18 Singerstrasse and, after that, he often visited us there.' This first meeting with Schubert took place not later than 1820. Their house, which was called 'Zum roten Apfel', stood not far from St Stephen's Cathedral; in 1826—by which time they were probably reduced to three, since Barbara had married the flautist Ferdinand Bogner* the previous year—they moved to another house nearby [21 Spiegelgasse].

At Anna's suggestion, Schubert composed a number of partsongs, in most cases for her students. The setting of Psalm 23 (D706) was performed by four of her pupils at the Conservatory examinations on 30 August 1821; it turned up again as an examination piece in 1826, in which year it was also sung, once more by students, at the Gesellschaft's 'evening entertainment' of 16 November. The quartet 'Gott in der Natur' (D757) was sung by twelve students at an 'evening entertainment' on 8 March 1827; it reappeared at the Conservatory examinations that August, and was also performed at another 'evening entertainment' on 28 February 1828. The partsong 'Ständchen' (D920) was composed for the the birthday of one of Anna's students, Louise Gosmar,* while 'Des Tages Weihe' (D763) was written for the wife of Baron Geymüller,* again at Anna's request. Lastly, Anna told Gerhard von Breuning that *Mirjams Siegesgesang* (D942) was written principally for the Fröhlich sisters. In the score published by Anton Diabelli & Co.* in *c*.1839, the solo part is assigned to a soprano, but at the first public performance, at the memorial concert on 30 January 1829 (see below), it was taken by the tenor Ludwig Titze.* On that occasion, Anna herself played one of the two accompanying piano parts. (These were replaced in 1830 by an orchestral version made by Franz Lachner.*)

After Schubert's death, Anna organized a memorial concert, one half of the receipts of which were to be used for the erection of a funeral monument at his grave at Währing district cemetery. The concert took place on 30 January 1829; it was repeated on 5 March. The Schubert compositions performed were the Piano Trio in E flat major (D929); the songs 'Auf dem Strom' (D943), 'Die Allmacht' (D852), and 'Die Taubenpost' (D965A); and *Mirjams Siegesgesang*.

The second sister, **Barbara** [Babette, Betty], **Franziska** (b. Vienna, 30 August 1797; d. Vienna, 30 June 1879), was a contralto. On 9 January 1822 she took part in a performance of Schubert's setting of Psalm 23 at Ignaz von Sonnleithner's,* and she also sang at some 'evening entertainments' of the Gesellschaft der Musikfreunde. But she turned her attention increasingly to painting, studied with the well-known miniaturist Moritz Michael Daffinger, and was for many years his assistant. Later she taught drawing at the Institute for Officers' Daughters in the Hernals suburb. Among her works are a copy of Daffinger's miniature of Grillparzer* and two oil-paintings, *Medea* and *Amor Entering a Hut*. In 1825 she married the flautist Ferdinand Bogner; they had a son, Wilhelm (1826–48).

The third sister, **Katharina** [Kathi, Katti, Katty] (b. Vienna, 10 June 1800; d. Vienna, 3 March 1879), was a competent pianist and amateur singer, but Anna Fröhlich told Gerhard von Breuning that she had 'only a weak voice'. Franz Grillparzer wrote of her in his diary in 1822: 'As a drunkard becomes intoxicated with wine, so she does with music. She loses all power over herself when she hears good music'. He had met her in the winter of 1820–1 and was soon in love with her, a feeling she reciprocated. His poem 'Als sie, zuhörend, am Klavier sass' (believed to have been inspired by their second meeting, which probably took place at the house of Baron Geymüller) describes her listening entranced to a pianist whom tradition has identified as Schubert. The poem, written in March 1821, was published later that year in *Aglaja*, a yearbook edited by Josef Sonnleithner* and Josef Schreyvogel. Grillparzer and Katharina became engaged, but never married, apparently because his love, unlike hers, did not endure. Yet he remained deeply attached to her and to her sisters Anna and Josefine, and for some years he occupied an apartment located on the floor below theirs in Spiegelgasse. He finally vacated it in 1830, following a crisis in his relations with Katharina, but in 1849, when he was almost 60 years old, he returned to the house, this time installing himself in the sisters' apartment, where he had his own set of rooms. There he lived until his death in 1872, devotedly cared for by the three sisters, and especially by Katharina who is often referred to as his 'eternal bride'. He appointed her his sole heir and his literary executrix.

The youngest sister, **Josefine** [Pepi] (b. Vienna, 12 December 1803; d. Vienna, 7 May 1878), a soprano, studied from 1819 to 1821 at the Conservatory of the Gesellschaft der Musikfreunde, where Anna Fröhlich was one of her teachers. In 1821–2 she sang at the Kärntnertor-Theater, but her performances in Peter Winter's *Das unterbrochene Opferfest* and as Konstanze in Mozart's *Die Entführung aus dem Serail* were disappointing, at least partly owing to stage fright. She completed her training under Giuseppe Siboni at the Royal Conservatory in Copenhagen.

Subsequently she had a successful career as a concert singer in Scandinavia, and in 1829 she was appointed a Danish court chamber singer by King Frederik VI. On 5 and 8 June 1826 she gave recitals in Prague, in the intervals of theatrical performances, but with only mixed success. A critic in the Prague *Allgemeine Theaterzeitung* on 27 July praised her trill and portamento and found her voice pleasing in its lower and middle registers, but was less impressed by her upper range, which, he alleged, tended to be shrill. She was more successful at a concert in Berlin shortly afterwards. In 1829 she sang in opera at Venice, where her first appearance was as the page Isolier in Rossini's *Le Comte Ory*. There was talk of a contract for the following carnival season at La Fenice, but nothing came of it. Instead, she went to Milan in late 1830 to take part in rehearsals of *Il romito di Provenza*, a new opera by Pietro Generali. There she suffered weeks of frustration trying to persuade the composer to enlarge her role, which she considered inadequate for a singer of her standing. The opera met with a hostile reception at its première on 15 January 1831. Unwilling to accept further minor parts and with no prospect of better ones, Josefine was, at her request, released from her contract. She returned to Vienna with her sister Katharina, who had accompanied her to Milan. Eventually she became a teacher of singing and piano.

Schubert wrote the solo part in 'Ständchen' (D920) for her, and she sang it at the first private performance on Louise Gosmar's* birthday (11 August 1827) and subsequently at the first semi-public performance (24 January 1828), and again at Schubert's concert on 26 March 1828. According to her sister Anna, the solo part in *Mirjams Siegesgesang* (D942) was also written for her.

Theodor von Karajan, later a well-known philologist and historian, recorded his impressions of Anna, Katharina, and Josefine in his diary after meeting them in 1836. Of Anna he wrote: 'Nettel ... is absolutely charming, typically Italian in appearance and spirit. Short, stout, tremendously lively, wholly mercurial in temperament, warm-hearted, quarrelsome, readily moved to laughter and as easily to tears, you just cannot help liking her.' Josefine he considered to be 'not pretty and rather affected, but good-natured; her comportment suggests the Danish court chamber singer, she feels experienced, but is not conceited or overbearing'. Katharina, the most striking-looking of the sisters, appeared to him 'sensitive, highly intelligent, very lively, rather touchy, very well educated but never vaunting her knowledge, very beautiful in appearance, even if the beauty has a little faded ... and with a fine figure, a long oval face, and eyes that are limitless and wonderfully deep, almost unfathomable, and into which one would like to gaze forever, eyes of the blackest black'. He took her to be in her twenties, whereas she was, in fact, 36 years old.

Katharina long kept her attractive and youthful appearance, so that in 1859 the future poetess and novelist Marie von Najmájer, who had become Josefine's pupil, thought that Katharina looked more than ten years younger than Josefine (who, in reality, was her junior by three years). Najmájer particularly admired the 'natural gracefulness of her movements and the animated expression in her delicate face'. Josefine she described as 'if not ugly, at any rate anything but beautiful', but 'a person of the greatest kindness and sincerity'. As for Anna, she was a 'small, dear little old lady, with large black eyes and an intensely animated and intelligent face'.

On 13 October 1880, some months after Anna's death, Auguste von Littrow-Bischoff, who had published a book of reminiscences of Grillparzer in 1873, devoted an article, 'Von Vieren die Letzte', in the *Neue freie Presse* (Vienna) to the memory of Anna, Barbara, Josefine, and Katharina. The sisters (or, at any rate, the three unmarried ones) probably later served as models for the three Tschöll girls in R. H. Bartsch's* novel *Schwammerl* and in H. Berté's* operetta *Das Dreimäderlhaus*, though there is no historical basis for the incidents described in those works. It may also be noted that they never lived on the Kärntnerbastei, where Bartsch fancifully places their residence, nor in the house [10 Schreyvogelgasse] opposite the university, with which popular legend still links them today.

(Grillparzer[12], Kutsch/Riemens, Najmájer, *ÖBL*, Orel, Sauer[1,2])

Fuchs, Aloys [Alois] (b. Raase, Austrian Silesia [Razová , Czech Republic], 22 June 1799; d. Vienna, 20 March 1853). Civil servant; musicologist. He was educated at the Franciscan monastery at Troppau [Opava], where he received organ and cello lessons and sang in the choir. After studying philosophy and law at the University of Vienna (1816–23), he served at the war office as an assistant to Ralph Georg Kiesewetter.* He played the cello in the orchestra which performed at Ignaz von Sonnleithner's* soirées and later sang bass in the choir of the court Kapelle. He also took part in the first performance of Schubert's male-voice quartet 'Gondelfahrer'. (D809) at an 'evening entertainment' of the Gesellschaft der Musikfreunde on 17 November 1825.

In 1820 he began to form a music library which would ultimately contain a wealth of autographs and editions, and also an important number of portraits. The collection was particularly rich in works by Mozart and Gluck, but also covered numerous other German, as well as Italian, composers. In 1848, according to his own statement, he owned some 1,200 autographs. After his death, the bulk of the collection went to the Royal Library in Berlin.

Fuchs's work as a musicologist was of considerable distinction. Thus he published in the *Neue Berliner Musikzeitung*, in 1851, a comprehensive thematic catalogue of Gluck's compositions, and he furthermore prepared (but did not print) an important catalogue of Haydn's works. In addition, he wrote a number of valuable articles which dealt mainly with Mozart and Gluck, but also included biographical notes on certain other composers (Johann Anton André, Jan Václav Voříšek*), an examination of Beethoven* portraits, and a list of Viennese court Kapellmeisters, court composers, and court musicians during the preceding four centuries.

Anton Schindler* remarked in his 'Erinnerungen an Franz Schubert' (*Niederrheinische Musikzeitung für Kunstfreunde und Künstler*, 7 and 14 March 1857), that Fuchs 'had never paid sufficient attention' to Schubert. And indeed, he appears to have owned merely one autograph, that of the song 'Der Blumen Schmerz' (D731), and copies of only a few other compositions. None the less there can be no doubt that he was greatly interested in Schubert, for in the 1840s he was working on a thematic catalogue of his works; this was later printed by O. E. Deutsch* in *Schubert: Erinnerungen*. In July 1842 Fuchs published, apparently on behalf of Josef Wilhelm Witteczek,* an appeal for information about the lost cantata *Prometheus* (D451).

(Schaal, Wessely[3])

Gahy, Josef von (1793–1864). Civil servant; pianist. Born in Hungary, he moved to Vienna not later than 1818, for in a letter written at Zseliz on 8 September of that year Schubert asked to be remembered to 'H[err] Gahy'. The fact that Gahy was not among the seven Viennese friends to whom the letter was addressed, as well as the use of the word 'Herr', indicate that their relations were still at a formal stage. Later they were to become close friends and use the familiar 'Du'.

It was probably Josef von Spaun,* his colleague in the civil service, who introduced Gahy to Schubert. He became a regular member of the group, was present at many Schubertiads, and took part in the visits to Atzenbrugg Castle (*see* Schober*). He was highly musical and an excellent pianist. Schubert greatly enjoyed playing his own compositions and also arrangements of Beethoven* symphonies with him. Gahy was in great demand at balls; according to Spaun, his spirited rendition of Schubert waltzes, Écossaises, and Deutsche 'absolutely electrified' the dancers. He appears, indeed, to have had a special affinity for Schubert's music, which he continued to perform for his friends' pleasure after the composer's death.

In later life, he arranged some of Schubert's trios and quartets for piano duet, taking care not to assign to his right hand more than it could accomplish, for two of its fingers had by then become paralysed. He used to play these arrangements with Marie Stohl, a piano teacher and very competent pianist, whose sister Eleonore, a well-known Schubert singer, is believed to be portrayed—anachronistically, since she was not born until 1832—in Moritz von Schwind's* painting of 1868 *A Schubert Evening at Josef von Spaun's*. Gahy also prepared a version of the 'Trout' Quintet (D667) for four hands. None of these transcriptions was meant for publication, unlike the reduction, also for piano duet, of the same quintet which Josef Czerny* made and published in 1829.

Gahy told Kreissle,* when the latter was preparing his Schubert biography: 'I count the hours I spent playing duets with Schubert among the most enjoyable of my life, and I cannot think back on that period without being overcome by the most profound emotion … My friendship with Schubert remained untroubled until his death.'

Gerstenberg [Gerstenbergk; original name: Müller], **(Georg) Friedrich (Konrad Ludwig) von** (b. Ronneburg, Saxony, 1780; d. Rautenberg, Saxony, 1838). Civil servant; poet. He was adopted by his mother's brother and took his name. A lawyer by training, he was employed in that capacity, and also as archivist, in government service at Weimar. There he came into contact with Goethe* and his circle.

He is the author of the poems appearing in Johanna Schopenhauer's* novel *Gabriele* (1819–20). One of them inspired 'Hippolits Lied' (D890), composed by Schubert in 1826. When the song was first published by Anton Diabelli & Co.* in 1830, the text was mistakenly attributed to Johanna Schopenhauer herself, although she had correctly identified the author in the preface to her book.

Setting: D890.

Geymüller, Johann Heinrich, Baron (b. Basle, 17 May 1754; d. Vienna, 1 April 1824). Banker and industrialist of Swiss origin (his father was a city councillor at

Basle). He arrived in Vienna not later than 1772, in which year he entered a firm owned by another Swiss, Peter Ochs. In 1781 his brother Johann Jakob Geymüller (1760–1834) also joined the firm. It was renamed 'Ochs & Geymüller' in 1786, and after Ochs's death in 1804 'Geymüller & Co.'. During the final decade of the century the firm concentrated increasingly on banking activities. In 1805 it was instrumental in raising the sum of thirty-two million francs which the Austrian government was required to pay Napoleon after he had occupied Vienna. Both brothers, who, in addition to their banking interests, owned estates and factories in Lower Austria and Bohemia, were ennobled in 1810 and created barons in 1824. Johann Heinrich was among the founders of the Nationalbank in 1816, became a member of its first board of directors, and, in 1817, its deputy governor. The family's fortunes collapsed in 1841 and Johann Heinrich Falkner-Geymüller (1779–1848), a nephew of the aforementioned brothers who was then the owner of the firm, was forced to flee the country. He reportedly finished his days as a clerk in Basle.

Johann Heinrich Geymüller and his wife Barbara, née Schmidt (d. 1835), whom he had married in 1808, had ten children. Several of the daughters took music lessons with Anna Fröhlich.* Their town house [8 Wallnerstrasse] constituted an important focus for the city's cultural life and counted among its visitors the leading musicians, writers, and artists of the day. The Geymüllers were particularly fond of music and reportedly possessed no fewer than five pianos. Their soirées were justly renowned, for they featured such celebrated musicians as Rossini and Beethoven.* It seems likely that some of Schubert's compositions were performed there and that he himself was at least occasionally present (*see also* Katharina Fröhlich*). In November 1822, through Anna Fröhlich, Baroness Geymüller commissioned him to set a poem celebrating the recovery from illness of an acquaintance named Ritter. The result was the quartet 'Des Tages Weihe' (D763), for which Schubert was paid 50 gulden.

(Cloeter, Mikoletzky[1], *ÖBL*)

Goethe, Johann Wolfgang von (b. Frankfurt am Main, 28 August 1749; d. Weimar, 22 March 1832). No other poet provided Schubert with such a rich source of inspiration. Altogether he set more than sixty of Goethe's poems, mostly for single voice. Their composition extended from 1814 to 1826, with the vast majority being written during the first seven years of that period. Schubert set several of them more than once, and Mignon's 'Nur wer die Sehnsucht kennt' no fewer than six times (D310, 359, 481, 656, 877/1, 877/4). He furthermore used a libretto by Goethe in his Singspiel *Claudine von Villa Bella* (D239), begun in 1815. Lastly, a setting he had made many years previously of Goethe's poem 'Wonne der Wehmut' (D260) was incorporated by him in the opera *Der Graf von Gleichen* (D918), where it is sung by the countess. (In 1827, when Schubert began composing that opera, the song had not yet been published.)

Remarkably, the very first of his Goethe songs, 'Gretchen am Spinnrade' (D118), written on 19 October 1814, is also one of the most striking: 'It was Schubert's first masterpiece. There had been nothing at all like it in music before. The plan of the song . . . was as original as everything in the working-out was faultless' (R. Capell). It was an astonishing achievement for a 17-year-old composer. Four more songs, 'Nachtgesang' (D119), 'Schäfers Klagelied' (D121), 'Szene aus *Faust*' (D126), and 'Trost in Tränen' (D120) were composed that same year, and more than twenty-five others followed in 1815, among them 'Erlkönig' (D328), 'Erster Verlust' (D226), 'Heidenröslein' (D257), 'Meeres Stille' (D216), 'Rastlose Liebe' (D138), and 'Wandrers Nachtlied' (D224).

Leopold von Sonnleithner,* who did so much to further Schubert's early career, told Ferdinand Luib* in 1857 that it was the Goethe songs and, in particular, 'Erlkönig', which impressed him most among the Schubert songs he first encountered and copied for his own delight. In his enthusiasm, he decided to arrange performances of Schubert's songs at the private concerts regularly given by his father, Ignaz von Sonnleithner:* on 1 December 1820 August von Gymnich* sang 'Erlkönig', accompanied by Anna Fröhlich;* on 2 March 1821 Sophie Linhart sang 'Gretchen am Spinnrade'.

It was also 'Erlkönig' which was instrumental in making Schubert's name known to a wider audience. It was not the first of Schubert's songs to receive a public performance—another Goethe song, 'Schäfers Klagelied' (D121), had that distinction, having been sung by Franz Jäger at a concert at the 'Zum römischen Kaiser' inn on 28 February 1819. But the favourable reaction evoked by that song was surpassed by the great impact made by 'Erlkönig', which was sung by Gymnich at a semi-private 'evening entertainment' of the Gesellschaft der Musikfreunde on 25 January 1821, and subsequently performed by Johann Michael Vogl* at a public concert at the Kärntnertor-Theater on 7 March. On the second occasion, according to Anselm Hüttenbrenner* who accompanied Vogl, the song was encored. It was performed again on 25 March, by Franz Ruess at the Landhaus.

Yet Schubert had difficulty finding a publisher for the song. It had already been turned down by Breitkopf & Härtel* in 1817, and Sonnleithner's more recent efforts to interest Viennese music publishers such as Haslinger* and Diabelli* had proved equally unsuccessful. It was only after Sonnleithner and three of his friends had agreed to cover the production costs themselves that 'Erlkönig' and certain other Schubert songs were published, with Cappi & Diabelli* acting as agents (for further details, *see* the article on Sonnleithner).

Two attempts were made to bring Schubert's settings to Goethe's attention. In April 1816, Josef von Spaun* wrote to request permission for 'a 19-year-old composer by the name of Franz Schubert, whom nature has endowed from tenderest childhood with a most decided talent for composition' to dedicate to Goethe a proposed eight-volume edition of his German songs, the initial two volumes of which were to contain settings of poems by Goethe himself. Spaun enclosed a manuscript copy of the first of these volumes, which included 'Erlkönig', 'Gretchen am Spinnrade', 'Heidenröslein', 'Rastlose Liebe', and 'Schäfers Klagelied'. The manuscript was returned without comment.

In June 1825, Schubert sent Goethe two luxury copies of his newly published Op. 19, which was dedicated to the poet and comprised the three Goethe songs 'An Mignon' (D161), 'An Schwager Kronos' (D369), and 'Ganymed' (D544). A brief, respectful letter accompanied the gift. On 16 June, Goethe recorded the arrival of the music in his diary, but he sent no acknowledgement. His indifference to Schubert's settings has usually been attributed to his firm attachment to the regular strophic setting of poetry, which was the form generally preferred by his friends and favourite song-writers Johann Friedrich Reichardt and Carl Friedrich Zelter. Schubert's conception of the Lied as a potentially independent musical form was alien to his view of the proper relationship between words and music. He is, however, said to have been favourably impressed when he heard Wilhelmine Schröder-Devrient sing 'Erlkönig' in 1830.

> *Settings*: D118–21, 123, 126, 138, 142, 149, 160–2, 210, 215, 215A, 216, 224–6, 234, 239, 247, 254–61, 295–6, 310, 321, 325, 328, 359, 367–9, 440, 469, 478, 481, 484, 538, 543–4, 549, 558–60, 564, 656, 673–4, 705, 710, 714–16, 719, 721, 726–8, 764–8, 877, 918 (No. 13).
> (Moser[2])

Goldoni, Carlo (b. Venice, 25 February 1707; d. Paris, 6/7 February 1793). Playwright and librettist. Baldassare Galuppi used one of his librettos in the opera *Il filosofo di campagna* which was produced at the Teatro San Samuele, Venice, on 26 October 1754. The text was published there that same year. Schubert made two settings, under the title 'La pastorella al prato', of part of an arietta from the libretto: one for male-voice quartet (D513), the other for solo voice (D528).

> *Settings*: D513, 528.
> (Jackman[1,2])

Gosmar, Louise (b. ?Hamburg, 11 August 1803; d. Vienna, 1858). One of the four daughters of Wilhelm August (1773–1846) Gosmar, a merchant who moved from Hamburg to Vienna. She was a pupil of Anna Fröhlich.* On 6 May 1828 she married Leopold von Sonnleithner.*

She is of interest to Schubertians for having provided the reason for the composition of 'Ständchen' (D920) in July 1827. Many years later, Anna Fröhlich described the circumstances of its creation to Gerhard von Breuning, the son of Beethoven's* friend Stefan von Breuning. She had asked Franz Grillparzer* to write a poem for Louise's approaching birthday, and Grillparzer had obliged with 'Ständchen' ('Zögernd stille, | In des Dunkels nächt'ger Hülle | Sind wir hier ... '). At her request, Schubert had then set the poem for her sister Josefine* to sing with some of Anna's students. By mistake, Schubert initially set the text for contralto solo and male-voice quartet, and had to prepare a second version for solo voice and women's chorus. In Schubert's 'Ständchen', the word 'stille' in the opening line is replaced by 'leise'.

Louise and her family were living that summer in a house owned by Baron Josef Lang in Döbling, near Vienna [4 Silbergasse/2 Nusswaldgasse]. It was in their garden that 'Ständchen' was first performed, on 11 August 1827. The accompaniment was played by Anna Fröhlich, who had arranged for a piano to be secretly moved there from the house and who had arrived from Vienna by carriage with the other participants in the surprise performance. Schubert was invited, but forgot to come. The composition received its first semi-public performance at an 'evening entertainment' of the Gesellschaft der Musikfreunde on 24 January 1828, and it also appeared on the programme of Schubert's concert on 26 March of that year. Josefine Fröhlich sang the solo part on all three occasions.

Anna sold the autograph of the first version of 'Ständchen' to Nikolaus Dumba;* the manuscript is now in the Vienna Stadtbibliothek. The autograph of the second version she lent to Josef von Spaun* and, at the time of her conversations with Breuning, she believed that he had lost it. However, it turned up later and is now in the library of the Academy of Music (Musashino Ongaku Daigaku) in Tokyo. Breuning published an account of his conversations with Anna in the Vienna *Neue freie Presse* in November 1884.

This 'Ständchen' must not be confused with the two celebrated songs of the same title which open with the words 'Horch, horch! die Lerch im Ätherblau...' (D889) and 'Leise flehen meine Lieder...' (D957/4).

(*Schubert: Erinnerungen*)

Gotter, Friedrich Wilhelm (b. Gotha, 3 September 1746; d. Gotha, 18 March 1797). Poet, dramatist, and translator. After studying law at Göttingen (1763–6) he was employed for most of his life at the court of Sachsen-Gotha. In 1769 he founded the *Göttinger Musenalmanach* together with Heinrich Christian Boie. Many of his own poems first appeared there, as did, in 1771, his translation of Thomas Gray's 'Elegy in a Country Churchyard'.

He was the author of numerous plays, some of them adapted from French and Italian models, and also wrote several librettos for the composer Georg Benda, notably for the melodrama *Medea* and the Singspiels *Romeo und Julie* and *Walder*. A two-volume edition of his works appeared at Gotha in 1787 under the title *Gedichte*; a third volume was published there in 1802. In August 1816 Schubert set his poem 'Pflicht und Liebe'.

Setting: D467.
(Porhansl[8], Schimpf, Schlösser)

Gotthard, J. P. [original name: Bohumil Pazdírek] (b. Drahanowitz [Drahanovice, near Olomouc, Czech Republic], 18 January 1839; d. Vöslau, near Vienna, 17 May 1919). Publisher, composer, and teacher; son of Josef Pazdírek (1813–96), a tavern-keeper and later a music teacher. He arrived in Vienna in 1854/5, and, after completing his education, worked as a private tutor. He was subsequently employed as an assistant by the music publishers Ludwig Doblinger and Gustav Lewy. He also had some contact with C. A. Spina* and, in February 1863, arranged for the publication by that firm of Opp. 27 (Psalm 13) and 28 (four duets) of Johannes Brahms,* with whom he was on friendly terms. In March 1869 he officially changed his name to 'J. P. Gotthard'. (The death certificate of 26 May 1919 gives his Christian names as 'Josef Paul', whilst in H. Riemann's *Musiklexikon* (1904) and Z. Výborný's article in *Die Musik in Geschichte und Gegenwart* they appear as 'Johann Peter'. On the other hand, A. Weinmann believed that the initials 'J. P.' probably stood for 'Josef Pazdírek'.)

Also in 1869, Gotthard established a music publishing business under his new name in Vienna. His list included works by Brahms, Karl Goldmark, Mozart (first edition of the Offertory in D major K260/248a), Liszt,* and Schubert. The firm went bankrupt in 1873, but Gotthard did not entirely abandon his publishing activities. He continued to trade first under the name 'H. Jägermayer' and then under that of 'Jägermayer & Germ' (he had married Bertha Anna Josefa Jägermayer in 1870), until a further bankruptcy put an end to those ventures also in 1879. He subsequently taught music at the Theresian Academy (1882–1909) and also worked as a journalist. The publishing rights held by him were acquired in 1890 by the firm Ludwig Doblinger (Bernhard Herzmansky).

A considerable number of Schubert's compositions—mostly vocal music and dances—appeared under Gotthard's imprint; most of them were being published for the first time. The earliest of these first editions, issued in 1869, were of Ländler for two and four hands, edited (anonymously) by Brahms (in D366 and D814). Some more first editions appeared during the following two years, among them those of the *Deutsche Messe* (D872), the Sonata in A minor for arpeggione and piano (D821), a set of twelve Deutsche for piano (D420), and the Fantasia in C minor for piano duet (D48). The year 1872 was particularly rich in Schubert first editions; these were concentrated in two collections, one of forty songs, the other of nine partsongs. One major source of Schubert manuscripts for Gotthard was Albert Stadler,* from whom he purchased some thirty compositions in 1870–1. From manuscripts examined and described by A. Weinmann it is clear that Gotthard was preparing the publication of a number of other Schubert compositions when his firm went bankrupt; these works were afterwards issued by other publishers. He also arranged some of Schubert's Ländler for string quartet.

Gotthard, who studied musical theory with Simon Sechter,* composed five operas (*Iduna, Edita, Hermann und Dorothea, Gaudeamus, Rosenfest zu Clamercy*), some orchestral music, string quartets, songs, and sacred compositions. Together with his brother František Pazdírek (1848–1915), he published a catalogue of all music then in print, *Universal-Handbuch der Musikliteratur* (34 vols., Vienna, 1904–10). Another brother, Ludevít Raimund Pazdírek (1850–1914), founded a music publishing house at Obermoschtenitz [Horní Moštěnice, Czech Republic] in 1879. It subsequently moved to Butschowitz [Bučovice], Olmütz [Olomouc], and finally in 1911 to Brünn [Brno], where it remained in the family until it was nationalized in 1948.

> *First editions*: D48, 76, 122, 165, 168, 168A, 176, 179, 206, 237, 250–1, 264, 267–8, 272, 295, 309, 359, 366, 371, 377, 402, 409, 420, 439, 449, 454, 458, 466, 476, 494, 502, 509, 528–9, 545, 561, 572, 579, 592–3, 597, 609, 657, 659–62, 687–8, 692–3, 726, 752, 766, 808, 814, 821, 872, 915, 928, 937.
> (Tyrrell, Výborný[1], Weinmann[4,9])

Götz, Josef (b. Krumau [Český Krumlov, Czech Republic] 1784; d. Vienna, 9 March 1822). He arrived in Vienna in *c*.1812 and was employed by Prince Josef Johann Nepomuk Schwarzenberg. He had a fine bass voice and sang at numerous private and public concerts, sometimes together with his colleague Josef Barth.* In 1821 he left the prince's employment and was engaged at the Kärntnertor-Theater. His first role in what turned out to be a short-lived professional career was Bartolo in Rossini's *Il barbiere di Siviglia*. He was also an excellent pianist.

Götz probably took the title part at the private performance of the cantata *Prometheus* (D451) at Heinrich Josef Watteroth's* house on 24 July 1816. On 8 February 1821, at an 'evening entertainment' of the Gesellschaft der Musikfreunde, he gave the first performance of 'Sehnsucht' (D636), and he sang the song once more at another 'evening entertainment' on 29 April. He furthermore sang in the first public performances of the quartet 'Das Dörfchen' (D598) and the octet 'Gesang der Geister über den Wassern' (D714) at the Kärntnertor-Theater on 7 March 1821. He also took part in the first performance of the quartet 'Die Nachtigall' (D724) at the same theatre on 22 April of that year.

Gries, Johann Diederich (b. Hamburg, 7 February 1775; d. Hamburg, 9 February 1842). Translator and poet. The son of a wealthy merchant and senator, he acquired some commercial experience before commencing law studies at Jena in 1795; he qualified in 1801. In the course of a somewhat peripatetic existence—in addition to travelling in Italy and Switzerland, he spent periods at Heidelberg (1806–8) and Stuttgart (1824–7)—he became acquainted with many prominent writers of his day.

Among his major achievements as a translator were German versions of Torquato Tasso's *La Gerusalemme liberata* (1800–3), Ariosto's *Orlando furioso* (1804–8), and Calderón's plays (1815–42). He was also the author of the German version of sonnet CLXIV ('Or che'l ciel e la terra e'l vento tace') in Petrarch's* *Canzoniere*, which Schubert set in 1818 as 'Sonett: Nunmehr, da Himmel, Erde schweigt' (D630). Schubert mistakenly believed the original author to have been Dante. The error was repeated when the song was first published in Breitkopf & Härtel's* collected edition, where, moreover, the German text is wrongly attributed to August Wilhelm von Schlegel.* The latter mistake resulted from the fact that the poem had appeared, together with Schlegel's own versions of Petrarch's sonnets

XXXIV–XXXV (set by Schubert in D628–9), in Schlegel's *Blumensträusse italienischer, spanischer und portugiesischer Poesie* (Berlin, 1804). Schlegel's statement naming Gries as the translator of CLXIV had evidently been overlooked.

Setting: D630.

(Goldmann)

Grillparzer, Franz (b. Vienna, 15 January 1791; d. Vienna, 21 January 1872). Dramatist and poet; son of Wenzel Grillparzer (1762/3–1809), a lawyer, and his wife Anna Maria (1767–1819), a sister of Ignaz von Sonnleithner.* He studied law at the University of Vienna, graduating in 1811. His father's death having left the family in impoverished circumstances, he turned to private tutoring before joining the civil service in 1814 as a clerk in the finance department of the Lower Austrian government. In 1818 he transferred to the court treasury, and in 1832 he was appointed director of its archives. He retired in 1856.

He started writing plays while still in his teens. By the time he made Schubert's acquaintance, probably in 1819, he had become a prominent figure on the Viennese cultural scene. His tragedy *Die Ahnfrau* (Theater an der Wien, 31 January 1817) had made him famous overnight. The success of his next play, *Sappho*, produced at the Burgtheater on 21 April 1818, had earned him the appointment of resident poet at that theatre. Then came the trilogy *Das goldene Vliess* (Burgtheater, 26–7 March 1821). Two further new plays by Grillparzer were produced there in Schubert's lifetime: *König Ottokars Glück und Ende* on 19 February 1825, and *Ein treuer Diener seines Herrn* on 28 February 1828. Among his later works for the stage were the tragedies *Ein Bruderzwist in Habsburg* and *Die Jüdin von Toledo*, the 'dramatic fairytale' *Der Traum ein Leben*, and the comedy *Weh dem, der lügt!* His extensive literary output also included novellas and poetry. The edition of his collected works published by A. Sauer and R. Backmann between 1909 and 1948 ran to forty-three volumes.

Schubert was probably introduced to Grillparzer at Josef Sonnleithner's.* In February 1819 he composed the song 'Bertas Lied in der Nacht' (D653), taking the text from a poem which Grillparzer had written for insertion in *Die Ahnfrau* subsequent to the première and which had been published in 1818. Their friendship with the Fröhlich* sisters led to the composition of 'Ständchen' (D920), for which Grillparzer supplied the words and Schubert the music (for further details, *see* Gosmar*). Schubert set another poem by Grillparzer in *Mirjams Siegesgesang* (D942).

Music occupied a central position in Grillparzer's life. He may well have inherited his love for it, as well as his literary gifts, from his mother, for the Sonnleithners were a highly educated and intensely musical family. Grillparzer even studied for a time with Simon Sechter* (with whom Schubert took a lesson in 1828) and composed a few pieces himself. He was a great admirer of Mozart and had a high regard for Schubert's music. He is known to have attended several Schubertiads and is included in Moritz von Schwind's* group portrait *A Schubert*

*Evening at Josef von Spaun's.** When his opera libretto *Melusina* was not taken up by Beethoven,* Schubert seems to have hoped to be given an opportunity to set it himself, but Grillparzer told Schwind—who passed the news on to Schubert in a letter on 2 July 1825—that he could not help Schubert in that connection, since the matter was by then out of his hands. (The text was eventually used by Conradin Kreutzer in his opera *Melusine*, produced in Berlin on 27 February 1833.) However, Grillparzer also informed Schwind, on the same occasion, that he would try to arrange a commission for Schubert to write an opera for the Königstädtisches Theater in Berlin, whose manager Karl Friedrich Cerf was then looking for new works. Nothing came of his intervention, if indeed he ever contacted Cerf.

Schubert is assumed to be the unnamed pianist to whom Katharina Fröhlich listens entranced in Grillparzer's love poem 'Als sie, zuhörend, am Klavier sass', composed in March 1821. (On Grillparzer's relations with Katharina, *see* the article on the Fröhlich sisters.) Grillparzer's awareness of the originality of Schubert's music found expression in the short poem 'Franz Schubert' ('Schubert heiss' ich, Schubert bin ich'), which, although dated 1826 or 1827 in the collected edition of Grillparzer's works, is likely, according to O. E. Deutsch* (*Schubert: Erinnerungen*), to have actually been written after the composer's death. It was first printed in the *Wiener Zeitschrift für Kunst, Literatur, Theater und Mode* on 9 January 1841.

Schubert was present when, at Beethoven's funeral at Währing district cemetery on 29 March 1827, the actor Heinrich Anschütz read the speech written by Grillparzer for the ceremony. He did not rate a similar honour when he was himself buried in the same cemetery the following year. However, a committee was formed for the purpose of procuring the money required for the performance of a Requiem and for the erection of a funeral monument at Schubert's grave; Grillparzer served as one of the treasurers of this commmittee. The Requiem chosen was one composed by Anselm Hüttenbrenner;* it was sung at a memorial service at St Augustine's Church on 23 December 1828. As for the monument, on which was displayed Josef Dialer's* bust of Schubert, it was not placed in position until the summer of 1830. For this monument Grillparzer composed the following inscription: 'Die Tonkunst begrub hier einen reichen Besitz, aber noch viel schönere Hoffnungen...' ('The art of music has entombed here a rich treasure and still far richer promise...'—lit. 'but even far fairer hopes'). This text has been criticized as undervaluing Schubert's achievement. It should, however, be remembered that many of Schubert's greatest works were then still unknown, even to his friends. Moreover, Grillparzer's words need to be considered in the context of the over-powering impression left on his contemporaries by the titanic figure of Beethoven who had died only the previous year, at the age of 56—at which age he could well be regarded as having fulfilled his potential, whereas it was not unreasonable to suppose that Schubert, at 31, had not yet fully realized his.

Settings: ?D626, 653, 920, 942.

(Deutsch[8], Garland, Wurzbach[1])

Grob, Therese (b. Vienna, 15 November 1798; d. Vienna, 17 March 1875). Her parents Heinrich and Therese Grob owned a small silk factory in the parish of Lichtental and lived not far from the Schuberts. The father had emigrated to Austria from Switzerland and probably died before 1814; the mother lived on until 1826. Therese and her brother Heinrich (1800–55) were very musical. She had a beautiful soprano voice, and when Schubert's Mass in F major (D105) was performed at the Lichtental parish church on 16 October 1814, she sang the soprano solo. Heinrich was an accomplished violinist, cellist, and pianist; he played among the second violins in Otto Hatwig's* orchestra. Therese told Kreissle,* who spoke to her in the early 1860s while preparing his Schubert biography, that the *Adagio e Rondo concertante* (D487) had been written for Heinrich.

According to Anton Holzapfel,* who met her in *c*.1812, Therese 'was by no means a beauty, but had a fine, fairly full figure, a fresh complexion, and a wholesome face, plump like a child's'. Schubert, who was a frequent visitor to her house, fell in love with her, because, as he later told Anselm Hüttenbrenner,* she had a heart of gold. However, they did not marry, and on 21 November 1820 she became the wife of the baker Johann Bergmann. If the recollections which Hüttenbrenner set down for Franz Liszt* in 1854 are correct, Schubert had confided to him that he continued to love Therese even after her marriage to Bergmann and that no other woman had ever pleased him as well. When Kreissle met her, he found her to be 'a lively and cheerful woman'; she had then been a widow for over twenty years.

It is generally assumed that Schubert wrote some of his early songs for Therese, including 'Gretchen am Spinnrade' (D118), which he composed in October 1814, a few days after she had sung in the above-mentioned performance of the Mass D105, and 'Stimme der Liebe' (D187), which was composed in May 1815. Around November 1816 he wrote out for her a number of his songs and, at some later date, she had these manuscripts bound together. The album, which subsequently came into the possession of her great-niece Marianne Meangya, was eventually acquired by a Swiss collector. It remains a very precious document for musicologists, especially since some of the Lieder have not survived in other autographs.

There was another link between the Schubert and Grob families: in 1836 Franz's brother Ignaz married Therese's aunt Wilhelmine, a widow whose previous husband had been the coin engraver Leopold Hollpein. Her son Heinrich Hollpein became a very competent painter; he was responsible for the well-known portraits of Ignaz Schubert and Therese Grob.

(Brown[7], Kreissle)

Grove, Sir **George** (b. Clapham, London, 13 August 1820; d. Sydenham, London, 28 May 1900). Musicologist, educationist, and editor of the first edition of the *Dictionary of Music and Musicians* (4 vols., London, Macmillan, 1879–89), with which his name has ever since been closely associated and to which he contributed several articles, including one on Schubert. He was a man of astonishing versatility and wide-ranging intellectual curiosity. A civil engineer by training and early professional experience, he was, at different times, secretary of the Society of Arts (1850); secretary of the Crystal Palace Company (1852–73); an active participant in the organization of the Crystal Palace concerts, for which, in addition, he wrote analytical programme notes during more than forty seasons; a major contributor to a *Dictionary of the Bible* (1860–3) edited by William Smith; a moving spirit in the establishment of the Palestine Exploration Fund (1865); editor of *Macmillan's Magazine* (1868–83); author of a geography primer (1877); member (from 1881) and financial secretary (March–September 1882) of the council and organizing committee of the planned Royal College of Music; first director of the college (1883–94); and author of *Beethoven and his Nine Symphonies* (1896). He was knighted in 1883.

For Grove, whose knowledge of Schubert's music had been confined to a number of the songs, the first performance in England of the 'Great' C major Symphony (D944) at the Crystal Palace under August Manns in April 1856 came as a revelation: 'It was from that time that his enthusiasm for Franz Schubert's genius took root,' Manns wrote to the organist Frederick George Edwards (later editor of the *Musical Times*) on 1 December 1896. (The performance was spread over two weeks: movements 1–3 were played on 5 April, movements 2–4 on 12 April.) The publication in 1865 of Kreissle's* biography, with its detailed catalogue of published and unpublished music, further stimulated Grove's interest in Schubert's compositions. At his request, the Viennese publishing firm C. A. Spina* sent him printed and manuscript copies of certain works, and he promptly arranged to have these performed at the Crystal Palace concerts. Thus the score of the 'Unfinished' Symphony (D759), which had been published in Vienna in early 1867, reached Grove on 2 April of that year and was played the following Saturday, 6 April.

In the autumn of 1867 Grove travelled with Arthur Sullivan* to Vienna, where he stayed from 5 to 14 October; Sullivan left two days earlier. Grove gave accounts of this memorable journey in his appendix to Arthur Duke Coleridge's translation (1869) of Kreissle's book and in letters to Olga von Glehn, the daughter of his good friend Robert William von Glehn. His principal aim had been 'to obtain some of the great orchestral works of Franz Schubert, which I had reason to believe were lying neglected, or at least unperformed, there; and of these especially his Symphonies, and the completion of the incidental music to the Drama of *Rosamunde*'. In the fulfilment of this object he was to be spectacularly successful. Eduard Schneider, the son of Schubert's sister Maria Theresia, who possessed numerous manuscripts, permitted the visitors to consult those of symphonies Nos. 1–4 and 6, while Johann von Herbeck* showed them the orchestral parts of No. 5 and the autographs of the 'Unfinished' Symphony and of the opera *Fierrabras* (D796). In addition, they were allowed to peruse the autograph of the 'Great' C major Symphony at the Gesellschaft der Musikfreunde. They took notes and copied the openings of all movements, and Grove subsequently published these in the appendix to the English version of Kreissle's biography. Their most exciting experience, however, was the discovery in Schneider's store-cupboard of the missing *Rosamunde* (D797) music; of particular interest were the instrumental accompaniments to the choral numbers and Axa's romance. With Schneider's permission, they removed the sheets of music to their hotel room, and there, with the help of C. F. Pohl, the archivist and librarian of the Gesellschaft der Musikfreunde, they copied them, working until two o'clock in the morning. (For further details of this visit to Vienna, *see* Sullivan.*)

Grove spent three further periods in Vienna: 23 September–30 October 1880, 13–23 August 1889, and 6–20 August 1892. On the first occasion his interest still focused mainly on Schubert, since he was then preparing the article on him for the *Dictionary of Music and Musicians*. In 1889 he was more concerned with Beethoven,* for he was already working on his study of the latter's symphonies, but he found time to go and see the Schubert statue in the Stadtpark (had he really not seen it in 1880?). It failed to please him, for reasons which he set out in a letter to *The Times* on 2 October (*see* Kundmann*). In 1892, his principal purpose was to visit the international exhibition devoted to music and drama which was held in the Prater from 7 May to 9 October of that year. His contacts with Vienna thus covered many years and were extremely fruitful. He was on particularly friendly terms with Pohl and Eusebius Mandyczewski.*

(Brown[6], Graves, Young)

Gymnich, August von (b. 1786; d. 6 October 1821). Civil servant; tenor. He was employed as registrar at the court treasury. A great music lover, he took an active part in the 'evening entertainments' of the Gesellschaft der Musikfreunde, in which he frequently appeared as a singer and some of which he helped to organize.

He was acquainted with the Fröhlich* sisters, and it was in their drawing-room that he discovered Schubert's music (for details, *see* Fröhlich*). Leopold von Sonnleithner* later confirmed that Gymnich had been one of the first to recognize Schubert's genius.

Gymnich's name is associated with the first known performance of 'Erlkönig' (D328), which he gave at a musical soirée at Ignaz von Sonnleithner's* on 1 December 1820. He sang 'Erlkönig' again at an 'evening entertainment' of the Gesellschaft der Musikfreunde on 25 January 1821. On 19 January 1821 he sang 'Der Wanderer' (D489) at Sonnleithner's, and on 30 March he took part in a performance of the octet 'Gesang der Geister über den Wassern' (D714) there.

Haizinger [Haitzinger], **Anton** (b. Wilfersdorf, Lower Austria, 14 March 1796; d. Karlsruhe, 31 December 1869). Tenor. He was given his first singing and piano lessons by his father, a schoolmaster. He intended to become a teacher himself, but the exceptional quality of his voice soon attracted attention, and after further musical studies—his teachers included Josef Mozatti and Antonio Salieri*—and successful performances as an amateur, he was engaged as a leading tenor at the Theater an der Wien in 1821. He made his début as Giannetto in Rossini's *La gazza ladra*. Other early roles included Don Ottavio in Mozart's *Don Giovanni* and Florestan in Beethoven's* *Fidelio*; he created Adolar in Weber's* *Euryanthe* (25 October 1823). He also took part in the first performance of Beethoven's Ninth Symphony (7 May 1824). He furthermore made highly acclaimed guest appearances at Prague, Pressburg [Bratislava], and various towns in Germany, and in 1826 he accepted a long-term contract at Karlsruhe, where, the following year, he married the actress Amalie Neumann (1800–84). He sang in Paris in 1829 and 1830, in England in 1832, 1833, and 1841, and in St Petersburg in 1835. He retired from the Karlsruhe court theatre in 1850. The beauty of his voice and his splendid technique won him plaudits wherever he performed.

Haizinger took part in performances of Schubert's quartet 'Geist der Liebe' (D747) at the Landhaus in Vienna on 15 April 1822 and at the Kärntnertor-Theater on 24 September 1822; and on 9 May 1824 he sang in another quartet—perhaps 'Gondelfahrer' (D809)—at the Kleiner Redoutensaal. However, as a Schubert singer he was far outshone by his son, also named Anton (1827–91), who, although not a professional (he was an army officer and rose to the rank of Lieutenant-Field Marshal), was greatly admired for his rendition of Schubert's songs. 'He had, as a Schubert singer, a characteristic manner which he alone possessed, a kind of Vormärz [the period preceding the 1848 revolution] way of singing which has now completely disappeared and of which he was the last representative . . . ' the composer Karl Goldmark recalled in 1912. 'Whenever I heard Haizinger sing, I used to think: this may well be how the Schubert interpreter Vogl* sang Schubert's Lieder.'

(Hilmar[II], Kürschner, Kutsch/Riemens, Marshall/Warrack, *ÖBL*)

Hansen, Theophil Edvard, Baron (b. Copenhagen, 13 July 1813; d. Vienna, 17 February 1891). Architect. After spending eight years in Athens, he moved to Vienna in 1846 at the invitation of Ludwig Förster,* with whom he worked on several projects during the next five years. In 1851 he married Förster's daughter Sophie.

Later Hansen was responsible for the construction of many notable buildings in Vienna. For Baron Georg Simon Sina's town house in Hohe Markt Square (1860), the Heinrichshof apartment complex (1861–3), the splendid edifice he designed for the Gesellschaft der Musikfreunde which would house Vienna's most important concert hall, the Grosser Musikvereins-Saal (1867–9), the Academy of Fine Arts (1872–7), and the Stock Exchange (1874–7), he turned to Renaissance architecture as a source of inspiration. But for his most grandiose project, the Parliament (1873–83), he drew on the classical Greek style.

Hansen's association with Schubert arises from his collaboration with Karl Kundmann* in the construction of the monument which was put up at the composer's grave at the central cemetery in 1888.

(*ALBK*, *ÖBL*)

Harold, Edmund, Baron. Translator. He was born at Limerick, is said to have spoken Irish and English, and is described in the 1782 edition of his Ossian translations as a lieutenant-colonel in the Palatine army and an official at the Palatine court, as well as a member of several learned societies.

His German version of Macpherson's* Ossian poems appeared at Düsseldorf in 1775; a revised edition, published at Mannheim in 1782, provided the text which Schubert used when he composed his Ossian songs in 1815–17. In a letter to Ferdinand Luib* in 1858, Anton Holzapfel* recalled having lent Schubert a—as he later learned, 'wretched'—translation of Ossian which he had bought from a second-hand bookseller and 'on which [Schubert] unfortunately wasted several of his most inspired compositions'. In his 'Erinnerungen an Franz Schubert' (*Niederrheinische Musikzeitung für Kunstfreunde und Künstler*, March 1857), Anton Schindler* stated that the text was so bad and the German so unidiomatic that when Schubert sang his Ossian songs at private gatherings, they provoked laughter, whereupon Karl Pinterics* asked his friend Franz von Hummelauer to prepare a completely revised text which was substituted for the earlier one. It is impossible to say whether these recollections by Schindler, whose memory is notoriously unreliable, are correct. Certainly the first edition of the Ossian songs (Anton Diabelli & Co.,* 1830) presents a text which is in many instances different from that to be found in the extant autographs. (For a list of Schubert's settings, *see* Macpherson.*)

(Reed¹, Schochow)

Hartmann (family). Friends of Schubert and great admirers of his music. The family, which had left Würzburg for Salzburg in 1816, moved in 1820 to Linz where the father, Friedrich Ludwig von Hartmann (1773–1844), took up a senior administrative post with the Upper Austrian government. He and his wife Maria Anna (b. 1779) had five children: Anna (1800–81), Fritz (1805–50), Franz (1808–75), Ludwig [Louis] (1810–81), and Therese (b. 1812). There was much music-making at their home. The father was himself a competent pianist; Anna was an even better one, as well as being a very fine singer, and she performed at numerous amateur concerts (she was a member of the Linz Gesellschaft der Musikfreunde); Fritz played the flute; and the other children studied the piano. In Würzburg, Carl Maria von Weber* and Conradin Kreutzer had visited the family. In Salzburg, in February 1819, the Hartmanns met Albert Stadler* who, after he moved to Linz in 1821, frequently joined in their music-making and gave piano lessons to Therese.

Also at Linz, they became acquainted with Josef von Spaun* who started to work as a probationer in Hartmann's office in 1821 and was to become a close friend of the family. It was through Spaun and Stadler that they met Schubert. Franz von Hartmann later recorded the event in the family chronicle: 'On 28 July 1823 a new life began for me and surely for the entire family. That afternoon, Pepi Spaun and...Stadler brought to our apartment Franz Schubert, the Viennese composer who wrote those marvellous songs, and the retired court opera singer [Johann

Michael] Vogl,* and they performed some of Schubert's songs. I had previously only heard the so-called *Trauerwalzer* (D365/2) and, I think, "Lob der Tränen" (D711) ... Now, however, a stream of the most divine songs suddenly poured forth ... I believe that the first one was 'Erlkönig' (D328), then, if I remember rightly, 'Der Zwerg' (D771) by [Matthäus von] Collin,* 'Frühlingsglaube' (D686) by Uhland,* the "Miller" songs (D795) by Wilhelm Müller,* etc. etc. We all of us listened spellbound.' (Hartmann may have been mistaken about the last group, since the composition of the *Die schöne Müllerin* is now tentatively dated October–November 1823.) Schubert and Vogl visited the Hartmanns again two days later, and on 23 August the parents and Anna met them once more at the home of Anton Ottenwalt.*

If the Hartmanns' acquaintance with Schubert dated from 23 July 1823, Anna, at any rate, had met Vogl already earlier, for the latter wrote on 8 June from Steyr to his friend Franz Xaver Linder at Linz: 'My greetings and kisses to all my friends, above all Herr Spaun and his lady friends, and particularly to Fräulein von Hartmann, for whom I feel the greatest admiration, even if I was incapable of showing it adequately to her at our first meeting... Such a beautiful voice and such a beautiful manner of singing I had not previously encountered in an amateur. It is a thousand pities that this flower is rushing in such a mad frenzy towards her destruction in marriage.' This was a reference to Anna's recent engagement to Count Anton Revertera von Salandra (1786–1867); they were married on 20 April 1824.

Fritz and Franz, the two older brothers, frequently met Schubert during the following years in Vienna, where Fritz studied law at the university in 1823–7 and Franz in 1824–8; the third brother, Ludwig, was also there in 1827–8. When Anna contemplated buying a piano for her future home in early 1824, Schubert offered his advice, through Fritz, recommending her to acquire an instrument made by Wilhelm Leschen or Kaspar Pfaff. Anna finally bought one made by either Heinrich or Johann Krämer, which, in due course, was delivered to Przemysl [Przemyśl, Poland] where the newly-weds took up residence after their wedding, since Revertera's regiment was then stationed there.

Fritz and Franz Hartmann kept diaries during their stay in Vienna, which, especially from late 1826 on, provide a wealth of information about the social and musical activities of the members of Schubert's circle. Many years later Franz incorporated much of his diary in his family chronicle. Both brothers repeatedly expressed their profound admiration for Schubert's music in their diaries, as did their sister Anna in her correspondence. In a letter to Spaun on 15 December 1827, sent from Lemberg in Galicia [Lvov, Ukraine] where her husband's regiment had been transferred in August 1825, she expressed her delight with the parcel of 'wonderful songs' by Schubert which she had recently received from Spaun and confided that 'Das Zügenglöcklein' (D871), 'Der Wanderer an den Mond' (D870), and 'Hoffnung' (D637) were her 'dearest companions and friends'. The Reverteras had seen a great deal of Spaun at Lemberg where he was employed from mid–1825 until spring 1826; he was the godfather of their first child, Mathilde, born on 9 December 1825.

On 6 December 1828, the father wrote to Anna and her husband from Linz: 'On 22 November we learned of the death of the composer Schubert, news of which will doubtless also have reached you by now. His loss is irreparable.' That sentiment was shared by his daughter, who, in a letter dated 26 January 1829, thanked Spaun for sending her the second book of *Winterreise* (D911) 'of our immortal Schubert, whose death has deeply distressed me'.

Franz von Hartmann eventually became president of the district court at Graz, Fritz chief administrative officer at Braunau in Upper Austria, and Ludwig director of finance in Salzburg. Anna and her husband remained at Lemberg until the count retired from active service in 1846, when they moved to Upper Austria. He died at Linz in June 1867; his widow survived him by fourteen years. The various records left by the Hartmanns and their correspondence constitute documents of the utmost importance to Schubert scholars.

(Litschauer[3])

Haslinger, Tobias (Carl) (b. Zell, near Zellhof [Bad Zell], Upper Austria, 1 March 1787; d. Vienna, 18 June 1842). Art and music dealer. He was a boy chorister at Linz under Kapellmeister Franz Xaver Glöggl, and subsequently worked in the latter's music business; from 1807 to 1810 he was employed by the art and music dealer Friedrich Imanuel Eurich. In 1810 he moved to Vienna where he worked for the bookseller Katharina Gräffer, whose daughter Karoline (1789–1848) he married in 1815.

In 1813 he was engaged by Sigmund Anton Steiner as manager of his art and music business. Two years later he became Steiner's partner, and during the next decade the firm acquired an international reputation under its new name 'S. A. Steiner & Co.'. Its premises in Paternostergässchen [21 Graben] were renowned as a meeting-place for local and visiting musicians. It is therefore not surprising that in the (probably false) account of Schubert's public disparagement of the opera *Euryanthe*, the alleged incident was said to have taken place at Steiner's shop (*see* Weber*).

In 1826 Steiner withdrew from the firm, which henceforth traded under Haslinger's name. Haslinger was not only an enterprising publisher and excellent business-man, but also a person of considerable personal charm. His brother-in-law, Franz Gräffer, who met Haslinger when he was still living at Linz, described him as 'cordiality and amiability itself'. He enjoyed an almost unclouded and unusually warm relationship with Beethoven,* who delighted in devising amusing ways of addressing him in words ('Best of all Tobiases', etc.) and music (in the canon 'O Tobias!'). During the period when he was Steiner's partner, the firm published the first editions of Beethoven's Opp. 90–101, 112–18, and 121*a*. However, Beethoven's association with the firm more or less ended in 1823, after Steiner had threatened him with legal action to obtain repayment of loans.

Leopold von Sonnleithner* told Ferdinand Luib* in 1857 that he had originally offered 'Erlkönig' (D328) to both Anton Diabelli* and Haslinger (then still a partner of Steiner & Co.), but that they had declined to publish it, even if no fee was required, on the grounds that the composer was unknown and the piano accompaniment too difficult. (The song was eventually published in April 1821, after Sonnleithner and three of his friends had agreed to cover the costs themselves—for particulars, *see* Leopold von Sonnleithner.*) However, as Schubert's reputation grew, Steiner & Co. evinced greater interest in his music, and in April 1823, when his relations with Cappi & Diabelli* were becoming strained, he took satisfaction in informing Diabelli that Steiner had approached him with offers on several occasions. However, these contacts did not bear fruit until Haslinger had become sole proprietor of the firm.

The first of Schubert's works to appear under the imprint 'Tobias Haslinger' were the twelve waltzes D969, in January 1827, some six months after Haslinger had assumed full responsibility for the firm. The following year, he brought out an impressive number of further Schubert compositions. Altogether, the firm was responsible for issuing, in Schubert's lifetime, the first editions of Opp. 77–83, 89 (Part I), 90/1–2, and 91, which included the Piano Sonata in G major (D894) and the Impromptus D899/1–2, as well as the songs 'Das Heimweh' (D851), 'Das Zügenglöcklein' (D871), 'Der Wanderer an den Mond' (D870), and the first part (D911/1–12) of the *Winterreise* cycle. (The second part appeared in December 1828.) In addition, the two vocal quartets 'Grab und Mond' (D893) and 'Wein und Liebe' (D901) were printed, without opus numbers, in Haslinger's collection *Die deutschen Minnesänger* (1827).

In December 1828, Ferdinand Schubert* sold Haslinger three piano sonatas and thirteen songs (seven to poems by Rellstab* and six to texts by Heine*), all of them compositions written during the final months of Schubert's life. The songs, together with 'Die Taubenpost' (D965A), were published by subscription the following year under the collective title *Schwanengesang* (D957), but Haslinger must have had doubts about the commercial value of the sonatas (D958–60), for, although he announced in January 1829 that they were 'in the press', they never appeared under his imprint; they were eventually published by Anton Diabelli & Co.* in 1839. On the other hand, Haslinger was to publish, in addition to *Schwanengesang*, the first editions of the song 'Der Hirt auf dem Felsen' (D965), in June 1830, and of the Mass in B flat major (D324), in 1837.

The firm continued to flourish—already in 1827 a writer in the periodical *Der Sammler* had compared its presses to a *perpetuum mobile*—and eventually employed some fifty persons. Haslinger's list included works by Albrechtsberger, Eybler, Hummel,* Liszt,* Moscheles, Spohr, and Weber;* he furthermore published almost all the compositions of Johann Strauss the Elder and the later works of Josef

Lanner.* At his death in 1842 he left a fortune of more than 50,000 gulden. Thereafter the firm (which had moved to the nearby Trattnerhof on the Graben in 1835) was run by his widow and their only son Carl (1816–68) under the name 'Tobias Haslingers Witwe & Sohn', and, following Karoline's death in 1848, by the son alone as 'Carl Haslinger quondam Tobias'. Accordingly, three further Schubert first editions were to bear the name 'Haslinger' on their title-pages: the male-voice quartet 'Nachtgesang im Walde' (D913) in 1846, the Impromptus D899/3–4 in 1857, and the *Salve Regina* in F major (D379) in 1859.

> *First editions*: 324, 379 (Carl Haslinger), 851, 870–1, 880, 893–4, 899/1–2, 899/3–4 (Carl Haslinger), 901–3, 908, 911, 913 (Tobias Haslingers Witwe & Sohn), 924–5, 957, 965, 965A, 969.
> (Slezak, Weinmann[1,7])

Hatwig, Otto (b. Grulich [Králíky, Czech Republic], 18 May 1766; d. Vienna, 18 November 1834). Bassoonist, violinist, and conductor. He played in the Theater an der Wien and Burgtheater orchestras, and also gave piano and violin lessons. In late 1815, the private concerts which had their origin in the quartet sessions held at the Schubert home were transferred from Franz Frischling's rooms [1 Dorotheergasse] to Hatwig's apartment at the Schottenhof [Freyung], a complex of buildings attached to the Schottenstift. The orchestra grew sufficiently large and skilful to tackle the more demanding symphonies of Haydn and Mozart, as well as Beethoven's* first two symphonies. Schubert used to play the viola in the orchestra, while his brother Ferdinand* was among the violinists. It was at Hatwig's that the first performances of at least three of Schubert's orchestral works took place: the Symphony No. 5 (D485) was played there in the autumn of 1816, one of the two overtures in the Italian style (D590 or 591) in late 1817, and the Symphony No. 6 (D589) early in 1818. When, in the spring of 1818, Hatwig exchanged his apartment at the Schottenhof for one at the Gundelhof [4 Bauernmarkt/5 Brandstätte], the private orchestral society moved with him. By June of that year, however, Hatwig was in poor health and the concerts were moved to Anton von Pettenkoffer's* apartment.

Heine, Heinrich [Harry] (b. Düsseldorf, 13 December 1797; d. Paris, 17 February 1856). Poet and journalist. The son of a Jewish merchant, Samson Heine, he received some training in commerce at Frankfurt and later engaged in business at Hamburg, but he was bankrupted in 1819. He subsequently studied at Bonn, Göttingen, and Berlin, qualifying in law at the University of Göttingen in 1825. In that same year he was baptized and assumed the name 'Heinrich'. In 1831 he moved to Paris, where he was to spend the rest of his life, earning his living as a journalist.

Buch der Lieder, which appeared at Hamburg in 1827 and included most of the poems he had written up to that time, established him as a master of lyrical verse. His poems were set by numerous composers, among them Brahms,* Robert Franz,

Liszt,* Mendelssohn,* Schumann,* and Hugo Wolf. Schubert used Heine poems in the songs 'Am Meer', 'Das Fischermädchen', 'Der Atlas', 'Der Doppelgänger', 'Die Stadt', and 'Ihr Bild'. The poems had first appeared in Vol. I of Heine's *Reisebilder* (4 vols., 1826–31) and were reprinted in *Buch der Lieder*. Schubert's songs were written during the last period of his life, perhaps in September 1828; he probably owed his acquaintance with Heine's poetry to Franz von Schober.* The songs were published posthumously in *Schwanengesang* (D957) in 1829.

Settings: D957/8–13.
(Branscombe[1], Hilmar-Voit, Kramer)

Hellmesberger, Josef (b. Vienna, 3 November 1828; d. Vienna, 24 October 1893). Violinist, conductor, and teacher. Son of the violin virtuoso and conductor Georg Hellmesberger (1800–73), who was a professor at the Vienna Conservatory, Konzertmeister at the court Opera, and a founder and conductor of the concerts of the Gesellschaft der Musikfreunde. The father had himself some links with Schubert— he was among his fellow pupils at the Stadtkonvikt (1810–12)—and also with his music: his concert on 1 April 1824 included the vocal quartet 'Die Nachtigall' (D724), and at another concert on 20 March 1825 he presented the first performance of the quartet 'Flucht' (D825B).

Josef, who was taught by his father, had an even more brilliant career. He was conductor of the Gesellschaft der Musikfreunde concerts, professor and director of the Conservatory, Konzertmeister at the court Opera from 1860 and court Kapellmeister from 1877. But perhaps his greatest achievement was the creation of the Hellmesberger String Quartet, which he founded in 1849 and led until 1891; the other original members were Matthias Durst, Karl Heissler, and Karl Schlesinger. The exceptional quality of its performances secured for it a unique position in the musical life of Vienna. It was, in particular, instrumental in fostering public recognition of the excellence of Beethoven's* later string quartets and of Schubert's chamber music. The programme of its opening concert on 4 November 1849 consisted of Haydn's Quartet in C, Op. 76/3, Spohr's Piano Trio in A minor, Op. 124, and Beethoven's Quartet in F, Op. 59. Its second concert, on 11 November, included Schubert's Quartet in D minor ('Death and the Maiden', D810). Subsequently the Hellmesberger Quartet frequently played works by Schubert, and, notably, gave the first performances of the Quartet in G major (D887) on 8 December 1850, of the Quartet in B flat major (D112) on 23 February 1862, of the Quartet in G minor (D173) on 29 November 1863, and of the *Quartettsatz* (D703) on 1 March 1867. In addition, it gave the first public performance, with Josef Stransky, of the String Quintet (D956) on 17 November 1850. In his *Geschichte des Violinspiels*, A. Moser, who attended performances of the Hellmesberger Quartet in the 1870s and 1880s, describes its interpretation of the quintet as 'utterly unique', adding: 'Never has this work presented itself to my ear with such ravishing beauty of sound and such captivating verve as when it was played by these Viennese gentlemen.' The success of its Schubert performances was largely responsible for the publication of the G major Quartet in 1851, and of the Quintet and the Octet (D803) in 1853. Hellmesberger also conducted the first complete Viennese performance of the 'Great' C major Symphony (D944) on 1 December 1850.

According to R. M. Prosl, the biographer of the Hellmesberger musical dynasty, Josef so admired Schubert's compositions that, being blessed with an exceptionally retentive memory, he was able to play the accompaniment of every one of his songs without ever having to consult the music. True or not, there is no doubt that he venerated Schubert, as he did Beethoven. It was at his suggestion that their remains were exhumed at Währing district cemetery on 12 and 13 October 1863 and, in order to preserve them from further rapid deterioration, were placed in new zinc coffins before being reburied in the freshly restored tombs on 23 October. On that occasion, the caskets were carried by prominent members of the Gesellschaft der Musikfreunde; Josef Hellmesberger was among those supporting Schubert's coffin. The ceremony ended with a choral rendition of 'Am Tage Aller Seelen' (D343). Finally, Hellmesberger was among the editors of the *Gesamtausgabe* published by Breitkopf & Härtel* between 1884 and 1897; together with Eusebius Mandyczewski,* he was responsible for Vol. IV which contained the string quartets.

On 27 November 1851 Hellmesberger married the actress Rosa Johanna Wilhelmine Anschütz (1830–1909), a daughter of the actor Heinrich Anschütz. They had three sons, Georg (1852–72), Josef [Pepi] (1855–1907), and Ferdinand (1863–1940). Josef had a distinguished career as a violinist and Kapellmeister, until a scandal forced him to resign his official appointments in 1903. He wrote ballet music and also several operettas, one of the earliest of which, *Der Graf von Gleichen und seine Frauen* (1880), treated the same subject as Schubert had used in D918. Ferdinand became a cellist and conductor.

(Evidon, Moser¹, Prosl)

Herbeck, Johann von (b. Vienna, 25 December 1831; d. Vienna, 28 October 1877). Conductor and composer. He was largely an autodidact in musical matters, his formal training being confined to the instruction he received as a choirboy at the Cistertian monastery at Heiligenkreuz and to brief periods of study (in 1845 and 1846) with the well-known choirmaster, composer, and teacher Ludwig Rotter. Yet he obtained the most prestigious appointments available to a musician in the Vienna of his day.

He read philosophy and law at the University of Vienna, but did not complete his studies. In 1852 he was appointed choirmaster at the Piarists' Church. From 1856 until 1866 he was choirmaster of the Männergesangverein, and in 1858 he was furthermore appointed director of the Singverein, the newly-formed mixed choir of the Gesellschaft der Musikfreunde; he also taught at the Conservatory. In addition, he conducted the concerts of the Gesellschaft from 1859 to 1870, and again from 1875 until 1877. In the intervening period he served as director of the Vienna court

Opera. Lastly, he became deputy Kapellmeister of the court Kapelle in 1863, and succeeded Benedikt Randhartinger* as Kapellmeister in 1866. Twice, in 1859 and 1877, he turned down offers of important posts at Dresden. He wrote a number of sacred works (including seven Masses), as well as orchestral compositions (four symphonies) and chamber and piano music. To his chagrin, his compositions were not taken very seriously by his contemporaries.

Nowadays, he is best remembered for his veneration of the composer to whom, on more than one occasion, he referred as 'der einzige Schubert' ('the one and only Schubert'). He particularly admired Schubert's partsongs for male voices. Of some of them, for instance 'Der Entfernten' (D331), he gave the first public performances, in versions adapted for a large choir; others he rescued from the oblivion into which they had fallen for many years. Among the latter was the octet 'Gesang der Geister über den Wassern' (D714), which he presented at a concert on 31 December 1857, after discovering the autograph at the shop of the music publishing firm C. A. Spina.* The following year the firm brought out an edition of the original composition, as well as of an arrangement made by Herbeck for voices and piano duet. Other Schubert partsongs performed by the Männergesangverein under his direction include 'Die Nacht' (D983C), 'Sehnsucht' (D656), and 'Wein und Liebe' (D901). On 27 March 1863 he conducted *Lazarus* (D689), which had not been heard since 1830; in 1865 C. A. Spina published his arrangement for voices and piano of that oratorio. Moreover, his contacts with choral societies in the provinces as well as in Germany enabled him to extend Schubert's reputation well beyond the Austrian capital. As he wrote in 1865 in his preface to Spina's edition of Schubert's choral music: 'As one does not tire of pronouncing again and again names which one loves and holds dear, I am forever urging societies: Sing Schubert, more Schubert, and still more Schubert!'

As might be expected, Schubert's name figured regularly on the programmes of the Gesellschaft der Musikfreunde concerts for which Herbeck was responsible. During his first season as their conductor (1859–60), he directed performances of the 'Great' C major Symphony (D944), of the march D968B/1 as orchestrated by Liszt,* and of the 'Wanderer' Fantasia (D760) in Liszt's arrangement for piano and orchestra, with Hans von Bülow as soloist. (In a performance which Herbeck conducted of the same work on 11 January 1874, Liszt himself played the solo part.) Among the orchestral and dramatic works of which Herbeck directed first performances were *Die Verschworenen* [*Der häusliche Krieg*] (D787), in a concert version, on 1 March 1861; the 'Unfinished' Symphony (D759), on 17 December 1865 (on the background of this performance, *see* Anselm Hüttenbrenner*); and two numbers from *Adrast* (D137), on 13 December 1868. Lastly, Herbeck's work with the court Kapelle afforded him opportunities for presenting some of Schubert's forgotten sacred compositions. Thus he directed performances of the Mass in G major (D167) on 25 December 1865, of the Mass in E flat major (D950) on 12 August 1866, and of the Mass in A flat major (D678) on 18 April 1869.

Thanks to the exceptionally influential position which he occupied in the musical life of Vienna, Herbeck thus succeeded splendidly in his aim of making Schubert's works better known. His enthusiasm for Schubert's music led him furthermore to propose on 6 June 1862, jointly with the president of the Männergesangverein Franz Schierer, that the society should undertake the erection of a statue of the composer. The society thereupon established a fund for this purpose, to which it made an initial contribution of 500 gulden (eventually it was to bear the major part of the total costs of some 30,000 gulden). On 19 March 1865 Herbeck conducted a special Schubert concert for the benefit of the fund. The programme featured the 'Great' C major Symphony (D944), two entr'actes from *Rosamunde* (D797), and several songs performed by Karoline Bettelheim.

At the ceremony on 12 October 1868 at which the foundation stone was laid in the Stadtpark, the Männergesangverein sang compositions by Schubert and Herbeck. The statue was unveiled on 15 May 1872. (For details of the ceremony, *see* Kundmann.*) That same evening a Schubert concert was conducted by Herbeck at the Musikverein. The programme consisted of the 'Unfinished' Symphony; the Adagio from the String Quintet (D956), played by Josef Hellmesberger* and others; the Impromptu D899/1 and the Menuetto from the Piano Sonata in G major (D894), performed by Julius Epstein; the song 'Die Allmacht' (D852), sung by Marie Wilt; and the partsongs 'Gesang der Geister über den Wassern' (D714), 'Gondelfahrer' (D809), 'Grab und Mond' (D893), and 'Widerspruch' (D865), performed by the choir of the Männergesangverein. Herbeck's outstanding role in the realization of the project was formally recognized by the society, which presented him with a small bronze model of the Schubert statue.

It was doubtless as a final token of appreciation of Herbeck's lifelong devotion to Schubert that, at his funeral in 1877, his body was blessed, at the entrance to the central cemetery, by none other than the composer's half-brother Anton Eduard Schubert [Pater Hermann].

(Adametz, Herbeck, *ÖBL*, Perger/Hirschfeld, Wessely[4])

Herder, Johann Gottfried (b. Mohrungen, East Prussia, 25 August 1744; d. Weimar, 18 December 1803). Critic, philosopher, and preacher. His ideas made a profound impact in many areas; in literature, they played an important role in the formation of the 'Sturm und Drang' movement. He was himself greatly influenced by Johann Georg Hamann's view that 'poetry is the original language of the human race', and, as a result, came to attach paramount importance to folk-songs and to works such as those of Homer and Shakespeare* and the Ossian poems, which he considered to be particularly close to nature. Among his translations were German versions of numerous folk-songs from many countries, which he published in book form (*Volkslieder*, 2 vols., 1778–9); later the collection became better known under the title *Stimmen der Völker in Liedern*.

The translations which Herder made of Alexander Pope's* poem 'The Dying Christian to his Soul' and of Thomas Percy's* 'Edward, Edward' inspired Schubert's songs 'Verklärung' (D59), composed in 1813, and 'Eine altschottische Ballade' (D923) which dates from 1827.

Settings: D59, 923.
(Pross)

Hoffmann [Hofmann], **Georg von** (b. 1771; d. Vienna, 7 May 1845). Librettist and translator. He was associated with the Kärntnertor-Theater as secretary or resident poet in the 1820s, and provided librettos for a number of operas.

He wrote the text for Schubert's *Die Zwillingsbrüder* (D647), produced at the Kärntnertor-Theater on 4 June 1820, as well as that of *Die Zauberharfe* (Theater an der Wien, 19 August 1820), to which Schubert contributed musical numbers (D644). The former is apparently based on a French vaudeville, *Les Deux Valentins*, while the latter is likewise believed to have a French model, though it has not been identified. (*See also* Blahetka* and Schechner.*)

Settings: D644, 647.

Hohlfeld, Ch. Ch. His poem 'An Gott' appeared, accompanied by the note 'Music by Franz Schubert', in *Lieder für Blinde und von Blinden* (Vienna, 1827), a collection edited by Johann Wilhelm Klein, director of the School for the Blind in Vienna. Nothing is known about Hohlfeld; Schubert's setting is lost.

Setting: D863.

Hölty, Ludwig Christoph Heinrich (b. Mariensee, near Hanover, 21 December 1748; d. Mariensee, 1 September 1776). Poet. The son of a pastor, he studied theology at the University of Göttingen from 1769. He was a founder-member of the Göttinger Hainbund, a league of students and their friends who were united in their fervent admiration of the poetry of Friedrich Gottlob Klopstock;* he was also a contributor to the *Göttinger Musenalmanach*. In 1874 he returned to Mariensee where he earned his living as a translator and private tutor. He died two years later from tuberculosis.

In his poetry he experimented with a variety of genres, several imitated from classical literature. In the early years, he concentrated on neo-Anacreontic verse, idylls, elegies, and romances, whilst a more personal, bitter-sweet note characterizes the poems of the last period, which speak of the beauty of springtime, of unrequited love, and of approaching death. His poems did not appear in volume form during his lifetime. However, a posthumous collection was published in 1783 by Johann Heinrich Voss and Friedrich Leopold Stolberg,* with certain 'improvements' made in the original text by Voss; a further edition followed in 1804. It was not until a critical edition was published by Wilhelm Michael in the early twentieth century (2 vols., Weimar, 1914–18) that Hölty's work once more became available in its original form.

Schubert made more than thirty settings of poems by Hölty, mostly for single voice and almost all of them composed during the years 1815–16. They include 'An den Mond' (D468), 'An die Apfelbäume' (D197), 'An die Nachtigall' (D196), 'Der Liebende' (D207), 'Der Traum' (D213), 'Die Laube' (D214), 'Die Mainacht' (D194), and 'Seufzer' (D198).

> *Settings*: D38, 44, 129–30, 193–4, 196–9, 201–2, 204A, 207–8, 213–14, 242–4, 398–401, 427, 429–31, 433–4, 436, 468, 503, 988, 990D. In addition, in a contemporary copy (not an autograph), the text of 'Klage' (D371), which was composed in 1816, was attributed to Hölty. He is furthermore identified as the author of the text of 'Der Leidende' (D432) in autographs, copies, and the first edition (1850) of that song. However, neither text appears among Hölty's printed poems. His authorship is therefore extremely doubtful in both cases.
>
> (Kranefuss)

Holz, Karl (b. Vienna, 3 March 1799; d. Vienna, 9 November 1858). Official in the Lower Austrian chancellery; violinist and conductor. A pupil of Franz Xaver Glöggl at Linz, he played second violin in the quartet headed by Josef Böhm* and, from 1823, in that directed by Ignaz Schuppanzigh.* He also gave violin lessons and conducted at the Concerts spirituels which Franz Xaver Gebauer had founded in 1819; he became their regular conductor in 1829. He was a close friend of Beethoven,* whose acquaintance he probably made in 1824. From 1825, for about a year, he replaced Anton Schindler* as Beethoven's secretary and principal assistant. Beethoven wrote the two canons 'Das ist das Werk' and 'Wir irren allesamt' for Holz in 1826.

Holz did not belong to the circle of Schubert's intimates, but he knew him quite well and must have been familiar with several of his works as a member of the Schuppanzigh Quartet; he is said to have expressed admiration for Schubert's songs. He played the second violin part in the first performance of the String Quartet in A minor (D804) at the Musikverein on 14 March 1824, and probably in that of the Octet in F major (D803) at Count Ferdinand Troyer's* in the spring of the same year; he took the same part in the first public performance of the Octet under Schuppanzigh at the Musikverein on 16 April 1827. He furthermore participated in the performance, led by Böhm, of the first movement of a 'new' string quartet (either D810 or D887) at Schubert's concert at the Musikverein on 26 March 1828. Lastly, according to a statement made by Holz in 1858 and reported in K. F. L. Nohl's *Beethoven, Liszt, Wagner* (Vienna, 1874), he led a performance of Beethoven's String Quartet in C minor, Op. 131, which took place on 14 November 1828, at Schubert's request, at his brother Ferdinand's* apartment [6 Kettenbrückengasse] where he was then staying. Nohl underlined the exceptional circumstances of the occasion by stating that Beethoven's quartet was thus 'the last piece of music' heard by Schubert. However, O. E. Deutsch* (*Schubert: Die Dokumente*) expressed some doubt regarding the truth of Holz's story.

(Schmidt-Görg, Ullrich)

Holzapfel, Anton (1792–1868). He was accepted as a choirboy at the court Kapelle in 1806, and from then until 1817 was a boarder at the Stadtkonvikt. After the completion of his secondary education (1806–10) he studied law at the University (1811–17). He became friendly with Schubert in 1811–12. Their relations grew increasingly intimate later when Schubert, having left the Konvikt, returned there regularly to play over his recent compositions to his friends. It was, in fact, above all their common interest in music which drew the two young men together; another student, Johann Leopold Ebner,* described Holzapfel to Ferdinand Luib* in 1858 as 'an enthusiastic and knowledgeable music lover'. Holzapfel at first played with the second violins in the school orchestra, but subsequently switched to the cello, which thereafter remained his favourite instrument. According to his own statement, he became a very competent performer. Josef Kenner,* in a letter to Luib in 1858, recalled that Schubert, on his visits to the Konvikt, would usually sing and play his new songs to Holzapfel, Albert Stadler,* and himself, but that on some occasions he let Holzapfel sing them, with Stadler accompanying.

Once Holzapfel entered the legal service of the government in 1818, he and Schubert drifted apart. Eventually they met only very rarely, and then mainly by accident. Holzapfel enjoyed a successful career, from which he retired in 1850; he then moved with his family to Aistersheim, near Wels, in Upper Austria. His final years were marred by paralysis.

In 1858 he responded to Luib's enquiries with three letters which provided much interesting information, notably about the Stadtkonvikt orchestra, about Schubert's lessons with Salieri,* and about his love for Therese Grob.* Holzapfel also claimed to have awakened Schubert's interest in Ossian (*see* Harold*, Macpherson*).

Holzer, Michael (b. Vienna, 28 March 1772; d. Vienna, 23 April 1826). Schoolmaster and choirmaster. On the death of his father-in-law Carl Martinides (5 November 1794) he succeeded him as choirmaster at Lichtental parish church. He had studied with Johann Georg Albrechtsberger.

He was Schubert's first professional music teacher. He gave him instruction in singing, counterpoint, and organ from *c.*1805 until he was admitted to the Stadtkonvikt in 1808. Schubert's father* recalled in 1829 that Holzer had repeatedly assured him, with tears in his eyes, that he had never had such a pupil before: 'When I wished to teach him something new, he already knew it. Consequently I did not really give him any tuition, I merely conversed with him and marvelled silently at him.' Ferdinand Schubert* also studied singing, figured bass, composition, and organ with Holzer, who was later described by Schubert's friend Anton Holzapfel* as extremely fond of wine, but a competent contrapuntist.

In May–July 1814 Schubert wrote his Mass in F major (D105) for the centenary celebration of the first religious service at Lichtental church, which had been held on 25 September 1714. When the Mass was sung there on 16 October 1814, it was the first time that one of of Schubert's works was heard in public. Holzer conducted the choir, Ferdinand was at the organ, Josef Mayseder played among the first violins, and Therese Grob* sang the soprano part; Antonio Salieri* was present. (The Mass was again performed, under Schubert's direction, at St Augustine's Church in Vienna on 26 October 1814.) The Mass in G major (D 167), composed in March 1815, and that in B flat major (D324), which Schubert began writing in November 1815, were most probably also first sung at the Lichtental church. Schubert showed his gratitude to Holzer by dedicating the *Tantum ergo* in C major (D460) to him in August 1816. The dedication was inscribed on the autograph. The composition was not published in Schubert's lifetime; it was first printed in the *Gesamtausgabe*.

Schubert evidently remained in close contact with Holzer in later years, for when the Mass in C major (D452), composed in June–July 1816, was published in 1825, he dedicated it to Holzer. He moreover maintained a close friendship 'from his youth until his death' with Holzer's son Michael (b. 1803), according to the latter's brother Lorenz.

(Bodendorff[1], Hilmar/Brusatti)

Hönig, Anna [Nanette, Nettel, Netti] (b. Vienna, 27 August 1803; d. Klagenfurt, 10 October 1888). Daughter of Franz Hönig (1766–1852), a lawyer, and his wife Anna. The family lived at the Trienterhof [4 Domgasse], near St Stephen's Cathedral. Anna was a member of Schubert's circle, where she was known as 'die süsse Anne Page', evidently after the character in Shakespeare's *Merry Wives of Windsor* (Slender: 'Ah, sweet Anne Page' [III. i], etc.). She was described by Eduard von Bauernfeld* as 'not particularly pretty, but graceful and well educated, domesticated and middle-class rather than specially gifted'. And Franz von Hartmann,* writing in his diary about a ball at Franz von Schober's* in February 1827, observed that all the women present had been 'very beautiful, except Netti Hönig, who is, however, extraordinarily sweet'.

Schubert probably first visited the Hönigs in late 1824 or early 1825, but he had already met at least Anna's brother Karl before then. In a letter to Schober on 7 January 1825, Moritz von Schwind* mentions having taken Schubert to the Hönigs' a week earlier, after Schubert had previously accepted several similar invitations but failed to turn up. The visit was a success: 'Schubert enjoyed himself greatly and wants to go back soon, for he likes Netti very much,' Schwind wrote, adding: 'She really is a darling.' Schwind, in fact, was about to fall in love with her; by March 1826 he was, according to Bauernfeld, 'entirely in thrall to sweet Anne Page'. She returned his feelings, but their relationship was frequently strained, and though they eventually became engaged in the spring of 1828, the engagement was broken off in October of the following year. The trouble was that Anna was a far more fervent Catholic than Schwind, and while he made periodic attempts to live up to her expectations ('Schwind is in love and pious, to please his Netti,' Bauernfeld wrote in his diary in November 1825), he felt at other times exasperated by her reproaches. Many years later he observed, with reference to Anna: 'I can stand a good deal in the matter of Catholicism as a rule, but enough is enough.' However, after her marriage to Ferdinand Mayerhofer von Grünbühel* on 11 February 1832, he maintained friendly relations with both of them. The couple had two children. (For information about them and about the site of Anna's grave, *see* Mayerhofer.*)

On 16 April 1825 Schubert wrote a waltz in G major (D844), consisting of sixteen bars, in Anna's album; it was presumably composed for the occasion. A few weeks later he took umbrage at some remark or gesture she had made, and Schwind went to great pains to assure him in several letters that no offence had been intended: 'Netti Hönig ... shows her limitless devotion to you and your interests so frequently and naturally,' he wrote on 1 September, 'that, if I deserve some credence, I can vouch for the fact that you could not easily appear or sing before anyone who thinks more highly of you, or is capable of feeling more sincere sympathy and deeper pleasure.' Schubert resumed his visits. Moreover, in February 1826, he dedicated to her his arrangement for piano duet (D773) of the overture to *Alfonso und Estrella*.

Anna's brother Karl (d. 1836), who became a lawyer like his father, regularly attended gatherings of the Schubert circle by 1823 and took part in the reading parties. On 2 April 1824 Baron Doblhoff-Dier* told Schober that Karl was among the few friends who showed up every day at the Café Wasserburger [14 Seilerstätte/ 22 Weihburggasse], where he himself and Schubert were also regular customers.

(Litschauer[2], Steblin[5])

Huber, Josef (1794–1870), known in the Schubert circle as 'der lange Huber' ('tall Huber'). He was born at Aggsbach, Lower Austria, and educated at Kremsmünster. Later he became an official in the accounting office of the war department. In a letter to his fiancée Rosalie Kranzbichler on 30 January 1821, he gave an enthusiastic account of the party held at Franz von Schober's* on the preceding Friday (26 January): 'A lot of marvellous songs by Schubert were played and sung by himself. This went on until past ten o'clock, after which we drank punch, offered by one of the guests, and as it was excellent and plentiful, the company, which was already in high spirits, became even merrier, with the result that it was three o'clock in the morning before we separated.'

The following year he was among Schober's visitors at Atzenbrugg Castle. From autumn 1823 until the following spring, Schubert shared his lodgings at Stubentor Bastei [now Stubenbastei], as Johann Baptist Mayrhofer* was to do in 1826. Huber is known to have attended Schubertiads at Josef von Spaun's* on 15 December 1826 and 12 January 1827, and he was no doubt present at various other gatherings of the group. He was clearly a popular member of the group, but seems, at the same time, to have been regarded with some amusement by the others and on occasion served as butt of their jokes. When, one evening, Moritz von Schwind* drew his naked figure on a café table, Huber was so furious that he did not rejoin the group for several weeks. Schwind also portrayed him in the vignette which he drew for the cover of the first of three collections of dances by various composers, which Sauer &

Leidesdorf* published in 1824 (Schubert contributed to the second book); Huber is there shown playing the trumpet in the orchestra which accompanied the dancers. Franz von Hartmann* later recalled that Schwind was able to catch Huber's likeness brilliantly with just a few strokes of the pen. (When Hartmann first met Huber, he thought him the ugliest man he had ever seen.)

(Hilmar/Brusatti)

Hummel, Johann Nepomuk (b. Pressburg [Bratislava], 14 November 1778; d. Weimar, 17 October 1837). Composer, teacher, and one of the outstanding pianists of his time, especially famous for his improvisations. He studied with Mozart, Antonio Salieri,* Johann Georg Albrechtsberger, and Haydn in Vienna, and with Muzio Clementi in London. For some years he was Konzertmeister to Prince Nikolaus Esterházy at Eisenstadt. In 1816 he was appointed Kapellmeister at Stuttgart. Two years later he resigned and took up a similar post at Weimar, in which city he resided for the rest of his life. He also made several highly successful concert tours which took him as far as Russia.

Schubert was, of course, well acquainted with Hummel's compositions which were frequently performed in Vienna. Many concerts which featured works by Schubert also had one of Hummel's on their programme. Anselm Hüttenbrenner* informed Ferdinand Luib* in 1858 that Schubert greatly admired Hummel as a composer. When, in March 1827, Hummel came to Vienna with his pupil Ferdinand Hiller in order to visit the dying Beethoven,* they met Schubert at Katharina Lászny's* house, and on that occasion heard Johann Michael Vogl* sing some of Schubert's Lieder, accompanied by the composer himself. Hiller later recalled that Hummel 'said little, but large tears ran down his cheeks'. Among the songs performed by Vogl was 'Der blinde Knabe' (D833), and when Hummel was afterwards asked to improvise, he took that song as his theme, to Schubert's great delight.

In October 1828 Schubert offered to the Leipzig music publisher Heinrich Albert Probst* three piano sonatas 'which I should like to dedicate to Hummel'. However, Probst did not take the sonatas, which, as it turned out, were to be Schubert's last (D958–60). And although Tobias Haslinger,* in a statement dated 18 December 1828 and inserted in the *Wiener Zeitung* two days later, announced that he had acquired these sonatas and intended to publish them, they did not appear in print until 1839, when they were issued by Anton Diabelli & Co.,* with a dedication to Robert Schumann.*

Hüttenbrenner, Anselm (b. Graz, 13 October 1794; d. Ober-Andritz, near Graz, 5 June 1868). Composer and pianist; older brother of Heinrich Hüttenbrenner* and Josef Hüttenbrenner.* The son of a lawyer and landowner, he was educated at the Lyzeum in Graz and went on to study theology and semitic languages at Rein Monastery, near Graz, where he was a novice in 1812–13 (but which he left without taking his vows). Subsequently he enrolled as a law student at the University of Graz and also studied music with the Graz cathedral organist Matthäus Gell. While on a visit to Vienna, probably at the beginning of 1815, he became a pupil of Antonio Salieri,* thanks to the generous support of Count Moritz Fries* who had been greatly impressed when he had heard him play the piano at Deutschlandsberg (Styria) some months earlier. Henceforth Anselm attended law courses during the winter in Vienna and in the summer at Graz. After completing his studies in 1818 he worked in local government at Graz, before taking up a position in the civil service in Vienna the following year. However, his father having died in 1820, he was obliged to leave Vienna in 1821 in order to take charge of the family's estate in Styria. In November of that year he married Elise von Pichler (1800–48); they had nine children. During his married life he resided at Graz, where he served, for a time, as director of the Styrian Savings Bank. After his wife's death he withdrew increasingly from public life. He lived for a time at Radkersburg and Marburg an der Drau [Maribor, Slovenia], and eventually settled at Ober-Andritz.

Hüttenbrenner played an important role in the musical life of his native city, both as a composer and through his long and close association with the Steiermärkischer Musikverein (Styrian Music Society), whose director he was from 1825 to 1829, and again from 1831 until 1839. He was a prolific composer, especially of sacred and secular vocal music. He wrote ten Masses, four Requiems, over 250 male-voice quartets and choruses, and more than 200 songs (to texts by Bürger,* Goethe,* Leitner,* and Uhland,* among others). He also composed several operas, at least two of which were produced at Graz: *Armella, oder Die beiden Viceköniginnen* on 6 February 1827, and *Lenore*, based on Bürger's famous ballad, on 22 April 1835. He furthermore wrote a number of symphonies (the first of which was performed in Graz in September 1819), some chamber music, and various pieces for the piano; he was among the contributors to the *Diabelli* Variations*. In addition, he was a contributor to the Leipzig *Allgemeine musikalische Zeitung* and to the identically named Viennese journal, as well as to *Der Sammler* and Adolf Bäuerle's *Allgemeine Theaterzeitung*. In 1826 he was, like Schubert, among the unsuccessful applicants for the post of deputy court Kapellmeister.

He met Schubert in 1815 while they were both studying with Salieri; they were soon close friends. 'Between 1815 and 1821 we were together innumerable times,' Anselm told his brother Josef in 1842. Unfortunately, as he also informed him, he had the previous year burnt the diary he had kept for some twenty years 'in which Schubert must have been mentioned hundreds of times between 1815 and 1828'.

Schubert's affection for him is evident from the inscription on a copy which he made of his waltz D365/2 (the so-called *Trauerwalzer*) on 14 March 1818: 'Written down for my dear fellow coffee, wine, and punch drinker Anselm Hüttenbrenner, the world-famous composer'. They also collaborated in musical matters. Thus they both took part, at a concert at the 'Zum römischen Kaiser' inn on 12 March 1818, in a performance of an overture by Schubert (D590 or 591) which the latter had arranged for four pianists. Moreover, Anselm participated in at least two other events of considerable importance in Schubert's career: at a musical soirée hosted by Matthäus von Collin* in *c.*1820, which was attended by a distinguished company of Viennese music lovers, he accompanied Johann Michael Vogl* in a rendition of 'Der Wanderer' (D489), and, together with Schubert, played the *Eight Variations on a French Song* (D624); and at the Kärntnertor-Theater on 7 March 1821 he accompanied Vogl in the first public performance of 'Erlkönig' (D328). He is also known to have been the pianist in other performances of Schubert songs, in Vienna and in Graz.

Anselm and Schubert continued to meet, if at irregular intervals, even after 1821, for Anselm occasionally travelled up to Vienna and in September 1827 Schubert paid a visit to Graz, during which he was introduced to Anselm's wife and children. In March of that year, Anselm had gone to Vienna to visit the dying Beethoven.* He later claimed that he and one of Beethoven's sisters-in-law had been the only persons present at his death. It is likely that about a week earlier Schubert had accompanied him and others to Beethoven's apartment. (On this latter visit, *see* Beethoven.*)

Anselm's Requiem in C minor, which he had composed in 1825, was sung at the memorial service for Schubert held at St Augustine's Church on 23 December 1828. The Leipzig *Allgemeine musikalische Zeitung*, in its report on the service, described the Requiem 'as anything rather than a *Missa pro defunctis*, seeing that it treats these solemn words in far too merry a manner'. It had previously been performed in Graz in honour of Salieri and Beethoven, and it was to be sung there again in 1835 after the death of Emperor Franz I of Austria. In 1829 Anselm published a musical expression of the grief he felt at Schubert's death in *Nachruf an Schubert in Trauernstimmen am Pianoforte*. Many years later, in 1861, he set to music a four-line poem which Baron Schlechta* had written on the occasion of Schubert's death and which had been printed in the *Wiener Zeitschrift für Kunst, Literatur, Theater und Mode* on 9 December 1828. The music was published, together with Schlechta's text, in the periodical *Lyra* in Vienna on the centenary of Schubert's birth, 31 January 1897.

None of Schubert's works published in his lifetime was dedicated to Anselm, but the *Thirteen Variations* (D576) which he had composed in August 1817 on a theme from Anselm's String Quartet in E major, Op. 3, bore, in the posthumous first edition (C. A. Spina,* 1867), a dedication to 'my friend and fellow student Anselm Hüttenbrenner'. The same inscription appeared on a copy made of the variations by Anselm himself in 1853 and presented by him to Johann von Herbeck* in 1865, but not on Schubert's autograph which Anselm also had in his possession and later sent to Herbeck.

In 1854 Anselm set down some recollections of Schubert ('Bruchstücke aus dem Leben des Liederkomponisten Franz Schubert') for Liszt,* who was then planning to write a biography of the composer. (Liszt soon gave up the project.) Anselm kept a copy of his text, and this was published by O. E. Deutsch* in *Jahrbuch der Grillparzer-Gesellschaft* in 1906, and reprinted in *Schubert: Erinnerungen.*

Finally, a mystery surrounds Anselm's place in the history of Schubert's 'Unfinished' Symphony (D759). In a letter to Herbeck dated 8 March 1860, which was intended to persuade him to arrange performances of Anselm's works in Vienna, Josef Hüttenbrenner mentioned almost casually that Anselm possessed 'a treasure in Schubert's "B minor Symphony" which we consider the equal of the great C major Symphony, his instrumental swansong, and of any of Beethoven's symphonies'. The autograph, he explained, had been handed to him by Schubert for transmission to Anselm, as a mark of gratitude after Anselm had sent him, through Josef, the diploma conferring honorary membership of the Styrian Music Society in April 1823. (Elsewhere Josef claimed that Schubert had not merely sent the score to Anselm, but had, in fact, dedicated the work to him.)

In his biography of his father, Herbeck's son Ludwig drew a highly unfavourable portrait of Anselm and alleged that Herbeck had been forced to resort to trickery in order to obtain the loan of the score of the symphony during a visit he paid Anselm at Ober-Andritz on 1 May 1865. Some later writers likewise accused Anselm of having acted in bad faith in keeping the music, and it was even suggested that it had been Schubert's intention to dedicate the autograph to the Styrian Music Society (to which he had indeed promised, in a letter on 20 September 1823, to offer the score of one of his symphonies in appreciation of the distinction it had conferred upon him). It seems rather unlikely, however, that Schubert would have thought of dedicating an incomplete work to the society.

The full story will probably never be discovered now. Despite a spirited defence of Anselm by his descendant Felix Hüttenbrenner in the *Zeitschrift des historischen Vereines für Steiermark* in 1961, a cloud still hangs over Anselm's reputation. For the puzzling fact remains that he kept in a drawer, for some forty years, a work by Schubert which, even though incomplete, he regarded as a masterpiece. The 'Unfinished' Symphony received its first performance at the Musikverein on 17 December 1865 under Herbeck's direction. At the same concert the orchestra also played Anselm's Overture in C minor. The autograph of the symphony subsequently passed into the possession of the Gesellschaft der Musikfreunde.

A celebrated painting by their friend Josef Teltscher* shows Anselm together with Schubert and Johann Baptist Jenger.* The same artist also executed an individual portrait of Anselm.

(Deutsch[7], Federhofer, Herbeck, Hüttenbrenner)

Hüttenbrenner, Heinrich (b. Graz, 9 January 1799; d. Graz, 29 December 1830). Poet; brother of Anselm Hüttenbrenner* and Josef Hüttenbrenner.* He studied law at Graz, and from September 1819 at the University of Vienna; later he became professor of Roman and ecclesiastical law at Graz. He wrote some poetry and was a contributor to Adolf Bäuerle's *Allgemeine Theaterzeitung.*

In a note to Heinrich (written on the back of a letter from Schubert to Anselm, dated 19 May 1819) Josef Hüttenbrenner encouraged him and a friend, Karl Johann Nepomuk Schröckinger, to write opera librettos for Schubert: 'Your names will be known throughout Europe. Schubert, I am certain, will shine like a new Orion in the musical heavens.' Neither Heinrich nor his friend provided the desired libretto; but Schubert set poems by Heinrich in the song 'Der Jüngling auf dem Hügel' (D702), composed in 1820 and first performed at Ignaz von Sonnleithner's* on 30 March 1821, and in the partsong 'Wehmut' (D825), which he composed before the summer of 1826.

Settings: D702, 825.

(Suppan)

Hüttenbrenner, Josef (b. Graz, 17 February 1796; d. Vienna, 1882). Composer; brother of Anselm Hüttenbrenner* and Heinrich Hüttenbrenner.* Like Anselm, he studied with the Graz cathedral organist Matthäus Gell; like him, he later chose a career in the civil service. He was introduced to Schubert during a trip to Vienna in the summer of 1817 by Anselm who had made Schubert's acquaintance two years earlier. Schubert subsequently sent him copies of some of his songs, including 'Minona' (D152) and 'Rastlose Liebe' (D138), and on 21 February 1818 wrote out for him, in Anselm's room in Vienna, a copy of 'Die Forelle' (D550), 'as evidence of my profound friendship'. In December 1818 Josef arrived in Vienna to take up a probationary appointment at the court chancellery. (Eventually he rose to a senior position at the ministry of the interior.) He at first rented a room at the Bürger-spital, a large apartment complex near the Kärntnertor, but some time later took lodgings at the house [2 Wipplingerstrasse] where Schubert was sharing accommodation with Johann Mayrhofer* until the end of 1820, though on a different floor.

Josef was in frequent contact with Schubert in those early years, and he undertook various tasks for him. Thus he arranged the Symphony No. 1 (D82) for piano duet in 1819, and he made a similar arrangement of the overture to Act I of *Die Zauberharfe* (D644). By early 1821, he seems moreover to have assumed the functions of a secretary. He also tried to further Schubert's career by bringing his compositions to the attention of theatre directors and publishers; in a letter to the Leipzig publisher Carl Friedrich Peters on 14 August 1822 he did not hesitate to call him 'a second Beethoven*'. He rendered Schubert an even more signal service when, with three other persons, he agreed to cover the costs of publishing 'Erlkönig' (D328) and certain other songs (for further details, *see* Leopold von Sonnleithner*). And when 'Erlkönig' and 'Gretchen am Spinnrade' (D118) were published, he wrote glowing appreciations of the two songs in the Viennese journal *Der Sammler* (31 March and 1 May 1821).

Yet their personal relations remained rather cool. It is significant that in a note written in October 1822 (his last communication to Josef recorded in *Schubert: Die*

Dokumente), Schubert still used the formal 'Sie', whereas he had long before then adopted the familiar 'Du' in addressing Anselm. In fact, a person well acquainted with both (whom O. E. Deutsch* tentatively identified as Josef Doppler*) told Kreissle* that Schubert did not like Josef at all, was irritated by his fervent but quite uncritical admiration, and behaved so harshly towards him that others in their circle ironically nicknamed Josef 'the tyrant'. It is true that the first edition of the song 'Die Erwartung' (D159) was dedicated to Josef, but it did not appear until 1829 and it is not known whether the autograph, which is lost, was similarly inscribed.

After Schubert's death Josef made the arrangements for the performance of the Requiem which was sung at St Augustine's Church on 23 December 1828, and it was he who signed the printed invitations on behalf of Schubert's 'friends and admirers'. The Mass chosen for the occasion had been composed by Anselm in 1825; Josef, a tenor, took part in the solos. It was not his first association with Schubert as a singer, for on 12 May 1824 he had sung in a public performance of the partsong 'Die Nachtigall' (D724). (He had also sung in the choir at the first performance of Beethoven's Ninth Symphony on 7 May 1824.)

Josef possessed a number of autographs and copies of Schubert compositions. In particular, he owned the autograph scores of *Claudine von Villa Bella* (D239) and of the second version of *Des Teufels Lustschloss* (D84). Unfortunately, while he was away from Vienna in 1848, his servants disposed of the second act of the latter Singspiel and of the last two acts of the former by using them to stoke the fire.

In later years Josef became as enthusiastic—and, clearly, as uncritical—a supporter of Anselm's music as he was of Schubert's. On 8 October 1860, in a letter to the Beethoven scholar A. W. Thayer, he wrote: 'In the realm of the Lied, the romance, the song, and the ballad, and also of the men's chorus and the vocal quartet, Anselm's achievement is as great as Beethoven's and Schubert's. Indeed, he is superior to Schubert in his ballads...'

As a composer, Josef was no more than a dilettante. He made settings of Schiller's* 'Der Alpenjäger' and Georg Philipp Schmidt's* 'Der Wanderer' (which Schubert himself set in D588 and D489), and contributed to some collections of dance music.

(Suppan)

Jacobi, Johann Georg (b. Düsseldorf, 2 September 1740; d. Freiburg im Breisgau, 4 January 1814). Poet, translator, and editor; brother of the philosopher and novelist Friedrich Heinrich Jacobi (1743–1819). After studying theology, philosophy, law, and languages at Göttingen and Helmstedt, he was appointed professor of philosophy at Halle in 1766, and in 1768 became a lay canon at Halberstadt. In 1774 he moved to Düsseldorf, where, with Johann Jakob Wilhelm Heinse, he launched the literary quarterly *Iris* (1774–7). Finally, in 1784, he was made a professor at Freiburg im Breisgau, and there he spent the rest of his life. In 1795 he resumed his activity as a publisher of periodicals with *Taschenbücher*, which, renamed *Iris* in 1803, appeared until 1813.

His poetry, which was frequently mixed with rhythmic prose, was mainly in the pseudo-Anacreontic vein: *Poetische Versuche* (1764), *Abschied an den Amor* (1769), *Die Winterreise* (1769), *Die Sommerreise* (1770). His prose translation of Luis de Góngora (*Romanzen aus dem Spanischen des Gongora übersetzt*, 1767), by acquainting German writers with the subjects of the Spanish *romances*, contributed to the development of the eighteenth-century German literary ballad. Jacobi's collected works were published in eight volumes in Zurich between 1807 and 1822.

In August and September 1816 Schubert set poems by Jacobi in the songs 'Am Tage Aller Seelen', also known as 'Litanei auf das Fest Aller Seelen' (D343), 'An Chloen' (D462), 'Die Perle' (D466), 'Hochzeit-Lied' (D463), 'In der Mitternacht' (D464), 'Lied des Orpheus, als er in die Hölle ging' (D474), and 'Trauer der Liebe' (D465).

Settings: D343, 462–6, 474.
(Sauder, Schober)

Jaëll, Eduard (d. ? September 1849). Violinist. Styrian by birth, he became a well-known musician in Vienna (1818–30). In addition to being a member of the Theater an der Wien orchestra, he played in Otto Hatwig's* orchestra and performed at various concerts. In 1830 he moved to Trieste.

He was associated with a number of Schubert 'firsts'. The programme of his concert at the 'Zum römischen Kaiser' inn on 1 March 1818 included 'a completely new overture' by Schubert (no doubt D590 or 591). This was the first time that one of Schubert's compositions was heard in public. Franz Jäger's* rendition of 'Schäfers Klagelied' (D121) at another concert by Jaëll in the same hall on 28 February 1819 constituted the first public performance of any of Schubert's Lieder. Finally, when a 'new overture' by Schubert (presumably D648) was played at Jaëll's concert at Graz on 7 April 1820, it was the first time that one of his works was publicly performed outside Vienna.

Jaëll's son Alfred (1832–82) was a pianist of international renown. Alfred's wife Marie, née Trautmann (1846–1925), was likewise a brilliant and highly successful pianist, and also a composer and influential teacher.

(Kiener, *ÖBL*, Suppan)

Jäger, Franz (b. Vienna, 1796; d. Stuttgart, 10 May 1852). Tenor. He sang at the Theater an der Wien from 1817 until 1820, and subsequently at the Kärntnertor-Theater. In 1824 he left Vienna to join the company of the newly opened Königstädtisches Theater in Berlin; in 1828 he moved to Stuttgart. Later, when his voice failed, he turned to teaching.

At Eduard Jaëll's* concert at the 'Zum römischen Kaiser' inn on 28 February 1819, he sang Schubert's 'Schäfers Klagelied' (D121). This was the first public performance of any of Schubert's songs. 'The deeply felt and moving composition of this talented young man was performed in the same spirit by Herr Jäger,' the Leipzig *Allgemeine musikalische Zeitung* reported on 24 March. He sang 'Schäfers Klagelied' again at a concert at the Theater an der Wien on 25 March, and at a concert given by the Italian violinist Pietro Rovelli at the Landhaus on 12 April. He also took part in performances of the male-voice quartet 'Die Nachtigall' (D724) at the Theater an der Wien on 27 August 1822 and at Johann Gottfried Schunke's concert at the Landhaus on 5 December 1824.

Jäger's son Franz (1822–87), likewise a tenor, was a prominent member of the Stuttgart court Opera, where he sang for forty years (1843–83). Another son, Albert (d. 1914), also performed there as a tenor from 1855 to 1885.

(Kutsch-Riemens, Wurzbach[1])

Jarnik, Urban (b. Bach, near St Stefan an der Gail, Carinthia, 11 May 1774; d. Moosburg, Carinthia, 11 June 1844). Slovenian philologist and poet. He was ordained in 1806, and thereafter held ecclesiastic appointments in various parishes in Carinthia (from 1827, at Moosburg). He became an expert on the Slav languages, and in particular on the Slovene dialect spoken in Carinthia. He set some of his own poems to music.

Schubert's song 'Die Sternenwelten', composed in October 1815, is a setting of Johann Georg Fellinger's* German translation of Jarnik's poem 'Svésdishzhe'.

Setting. D307.
(*ÖBL*, Wurzbach[1])

Jenger, Johann Baptist (b. Kirchhofen, near Freiburg im Breisgau, 23 March 1793; d. Vienna, 30 March 1856). Civil servant; pianist. His father Anton Jenger (1760–1840), who came from nearby Riegel, had been a schoolmaster at Kirchhofen since 1783 and was also organist and choirmaster at the local church. Jenger learned to play the piano and organ at an early age. From 1810 he read philosophy at the University of Freiburg and then worked for a year in the local administration. In December 1813 Prince Karl Philipp Schwarzenberg, the commander-in-chief of the allied armies against Napoleon, took him under his wing while temporarily staying at Freiburg. Jenger was attached as quartermaster to a mobile field hospital throughout 1814, probably spending a part of that time in Vienna.

At the end of the year, no doubt thanks to his protector, he was promoted and posted to the regional military headquarters at Graz, where he remained for the next eleven years. During that period he became friendly with the Hüttenbrenner* family, Marie Pachler,* and Julius Schneller,* among others. He was also associated from its earliest days with the Steiermärkischer Musikverein (Styrian Music Society) which was founded in 1815; he was a member of the executive committee in 1819, and served as the society's secretary from 1820 to 1825. In addition, he appeared as pianist at some of its concerts.

On 4 July 1825 he informed the society that he was being transferred to Vienna, but he may not actually have moved there until later that year. On 6 December 1825 he visited the actress Sophie Müller,* together with Schubert. He had already been her guest at the beginning of that year, no doubt during a brief visit to Vienna, for her diary entry for 24 February recorded that 'Jenger, Vogel [i.e. Johann Michael Vogl*], and Schubert came to lunch here for the first time today'.

He was employed at the war office under Raphael Kiesewetter von Wiesen-brunn,* who promptly recruited him for his celebrated private concerts; in 1827 Jenger was to be given the responsibility of organizing them. He also soon became involved in the activities of the Gesellschaft der Musikfreunde, for on 20 February 1826 the society's vice-president, who was none other than Kiesewetter, invited him to serve on a new committee then being established for the purpose of gathering and writing up information on Austrian musicians and on the history of Austrian music. Each member was assigned certain composers. Jenger was asked to prepare biographies of Schubert and Anselm Hüttenbrenner,* but he does not appear to have got very far with the first and did not complete the second. However, his association with the society grew steadily closer: in 1829 he acted as deputy secretary, and he was to do so again after Josef Sonnleithner's* death (1835) and also in 1838. In 1840 he was placed in charge of the secretariat.

He thus came to assume an increasingly important place in Viennese musical circles, where he was also much in demand as a pianist, and especially as an accompanist. In particular, he frequently accompanied Baron Schönstein.* Some-times he played duets with Irene Kiesewetter;* on 26 October 1827 they performed Schubert's *Divertissement à la hongroise* (D818) at Sophie Müller's, and on 16 October 1830 they played arrangements of Beethoven's* 'Pastoral' Symphony and *Egmont* Overture at Dr Ignaz Menz's. Faust Pachler,* Marie Pachler's son, wrote about Jenger in 1866: 'The name of this man became inextricably interwoven with the history of music-making in Vienna. Although an amateur pianist of no more than average accomplishments, Jenger was drawn into all circles of society, includ-ing, eventually, the very highest, because he knew better than anyone else how to provide sensitive accompaniment for the singer's voice and how to transpose music, while playing, to any other key.'

It is not known when and in what circumstances Jenger made Schubert's acquaintance. It was at his suggestion that the Styrian Music Society conferred honorary membership upon Schubert in April 1823. Their first meeting, perhaps arranged by Anselm Hüttenbrenner, may have taken place some years earlier. In any case, as already indicated, he knew Schubert personally at the latest by Feb-ruary 1825, well before he moved to Vienna. Once he had settled there, he saw Schubert frequently; on several occasions in 1826 they were both among Sophie Müller's guests. Jenger was also on friendly terms with the painter Josef Teltscher,* who, in 1827 [?1828], painted the well-known triple portrait of Jenger, Anselm

Hüttenbrenner, and Schubert. (In 1837 Jenger was Teltscher's companion on the journey to Greece, during which the latter drowned.)

Jenger arranged for Schubert and himself to visit the Pachlers in Graz in September 1827. He had hoped to arrange such a trip already in 1826, and was to propose a further visit to the Pachlers in 1828, but Schubert lacked the necessary funds both times. It is clear that Jenger's relationship with Schubert remained an intimate one until the latter's death. Afterwards he was responsible, together with Grillparzer* and Franz von Schober,* for administering the funds collected to pay for the memorial service at St Augustine's Church on 23 December 1828 and for the funeral monument erected at Schubert's tomb in 1830.

Jenger was an honorary member of a number of Austrian and foreign music societies. He retired from the war office in 1853.

(Becker)

John, Saint, the Apostle. In 1818 Schubert set for single voice John 6: 55–8, in Martin Luther's* German translation.

Setting: D607.

Kalchberg, Johann (Nepomuk) von (b. Pichl Castle, Mürztal, Styria, 15 March 1765; d. Graz, 3 February 1827). Poet, dramatist, and historian; son of Josef Erhard von Kalchberg (d. 1779), a wealthy landowner. He studied literature, history, and law at Graz and was subsequently employed as a lawyer in the civil service (1785–8), but resigned in order to devote all his time to literary activities. He was also a representative member (Repräsentant) of the Steiermärkischer Musikverein (Styrian Music Society) and one of the three persons who signed the diploma conferring honorary membership on Schubert in April 1823 (the others being the president, Count Attems, and the secretary, Johann Baptist Jenger*). He died in straitened circumstances, having lost his considerable fortune as a result of injudicious investments in lead-mining.

He was the author of several historical plays, including *Agnes, Gräfin von Habsburg* (1786, later reworked as *Wülfing von Stubenberg*), *Die Tempelherren* (1788), and *Die Ritterempörung: Eine wahre Begebenheit der Vorzeit* (1792), and also wrote about Styrian history (*Historische Skizzen*). In 1788 he published a volume of poetry, *Lyrische Gedichte*. A collection of his writings was issued in 1816–17.

In October 1815 Schubert set one of his poems in 'Die Macht der Liebe'.

Setting: D308.
(Haefs, Wurzbach[1])

Kanne, Friedrich August (b. Delitzsch, Saxony, 8 March 1778; d. Vienna, 16 December 1833). Composer, poet, and writer on music. He studied medicine at Leipzig, theology at Wittenberg, and later music with the organist and composer

Christian Ehregott Weinlig at Dresden. In 1808 he settled in Vienna, where, supported by Beethoven's* great patron, Prince Josef Franz Maximilian Lobkowitz, he set about earning his living as a music teacher, poet, journalist, and composer. Fiercely independent, he refused permanent appointments and preferred to lead a precarious existence, in which alcohol played a notoriously prominent part.

He regularly contributed to several periodicals, among them the Vienna *Allgemeine musikalische Zeitung*, which he also edited from 1821 until it ceased publication in late 1824. His compositions include a dozen operas, instrumental works (symphonies, piano sonatas), and settings of poems by Matthisson,* Schiller,* and August Wilhelm von Schlegel.*

Kanne may be the author of several favourable discussions of Schubert's music which appeared, unsigned, in the *Allgemeine musikalische Zeitung* during the period of his editorship. It was in that journal that the first extensive appraisal of Schubert's songs was published, on 19 January 1822. The anonymous writer referred to him as 'der geniale Tonsetzer' ('the composer of genius'). The same adjective was applied to him in a later, similarly unsigned, article, on 11 June 1823 ('der geniale Schubert').

(Branscombe², Fellinger, *ÖBL*, Wurzbach¹)

Kenner, Josef (b. Vienna, 24 June 1794; d. Bad Ischl, Upper Austria, 20 January 1868). Civil servant; amateur painter and occasional poet. He was educated at Kremsmünster, Upper Austria, and, from 1806 to 1811, at the Vienna Stadtkonvikt. There Schubert became his fellow pupil in 1808, though they were, of course, at different levels of instruction. Kenner went on to study law at the University of Vienna (1811–16) and subsequently entered government service at Linz. He became chief administrative officer at Freistadt, Upper Austria, in 1850 and at Bad Ischl in 1854. He continued to reside in the latter town after his retirement in 1857. He wrote poetry and was a competent amateur painter; in April 1828 he gave Josef von Spaun* one of his water-colours as a wedding present. His poems appeared in various periodicals. (*See also* Ottenwalt.*)

Kenner's contacts with Schubert fell predominantly into the period of his university studies; according to his own statement, it was Spaun who introduced him to Schubert. After his departure from Vienna they saw each other only a few more times, on the occasion of Schubert's visits to Linz. Thus they are known to have met there in the summer of 1819, and probably did so again in 1825. They did not correspond, but Kenner had many opportunities to keep himself informed about Schubert's activities through mutual friends who either resided at Linz, such as Anton Ottenwalt,* Albert Stadler,* and Spaun, or occasionally visited that city, like Moritz von Schwind.*

Schubert set poems by Kenner in 'Der Liedler' (D209), in the ballad 'Ein Fräulein schaut vom hohen Turm' (D134), and in 'Grablied' (D218). The first and third of these songs are known to have been composed in 1815, and the second was probably also written in that year. In 1823 Schwind made twelve sepia illustrations for 'Der Liedler', which he showed to Kenner during a visit to Linz that autumn. Kenner was delighted with them, Schwind informed Franz von Schober* in a letter on 3 October, and 'could not stop looking at them'. Schwind evidently intended to publish his drawings, though not necessarily together with Schubert's music; but nothing came of the project, and only seven of the illustrations have survived. When Schubert published 'Der Liedler' in 1825, he dedicated it to Kenner.

In May 1858, in response to Ferdinand Luib's* request for his recollections of Schubert and his circle, Kenner wrote two long letters which were mainly remarkable for their violent attacks on Franz von Schober and their strong condemnation of his influence on Schubert. (For further particulars, *see* Schober.*)

In 1822 Kenner married Anna Kreil, whose brother Josef knew Schubert. Their son Anton (1833–1914) became a distinguished civil servant, and another son, Friedrich (1834–1922), a noted archaeologist and numismatist; both were ennobled.

Settings: D134, 209, 218.

(*ÖBL*, Porhansl[10], Wurzbach[1])

Keppen, Petr Ivanovich [Köppen, Peter Johann] (b. Kharkov, 19 February 1793; d. Alushta, Crimea, 23 May 1864). Scientist, statistician, and ethnographer; son of Ivan Ivanovich Keppen [Johann Friedrich Köppen] (1752–1808), a German-born physician who had settled in Russia, and his wife Karolina Ivanovna, née Caroline Friederike Schulz (1772–1851). A graduate of Kharkov University (1814), P. I. Keppen had a distinguished career and became a member of the Russian Academy of Sciences in 1839; he was also a co-founder of the Russian Geographical Society. His son F. P. Keppen published his biography in St Petersburg in 1911.

In 1821 Keppen was engaged by a young nobleman, Alexei Sergeevich Beresin (1801–24), as companion on a European tour which was expected to last between three to four years and was to be devoted to the study of the culture and scientific achievements of various European countries. They arrived in Vienna in early March 1822 and thereafter made it the centre of their activities, spending some time in the Austrian capital itself and undertaking journeys to Hungary, Transylvania, Bohemia, and Poland. These travels appear to have seriously depleted Beresin's funds, and he soon found it difficult to meet his contractual commitments towards Keppen, who was to receive an annual salary of 933 roubles and have his accommodation paid as well. Accordingly, the two men parted company in Vienna in the autumn of 1823. Beresin set out for Italy with Leopold Kupelwieser* in early November, while Keppen left some four weeks later for Germany, where he travelled by himself for several months before returning to Russia in April 1824. (Beresin died in Italy in December 1824.)

The notes made by Keppen during his travels in the West are preserved in the archives of the Russian Academy of Sciences in St Petersburg. A diary which he kept while he was in Vienna provides much interesting information about his activities there, and especially about his contacts with Josef Hönig von Henikstein, a wealthy merchant and prominent patron of music, and with Karoline Pichler.* At both their houses he heard performances of Schubert's music, and on one occasion he even heard the composer himself sing some of his songs ('with feeling but little voice') in Pichler's salon.

Among the last musical works which Keppen heard in Vienna was Weber's* *Euryanthe*, of which he attended not only the première on 25 October 1823, but also the second performance on 27 October. On the latter evening, according to his diary, he was seated next to Schubert, who voiced his displeasure at the lack of melody in the music ('Schubert, a German and a fervent admirer of German music—was bored'). Since it has always been stated that Schubert attended the première of *Euryanthe*, J. Chochlow, in an article on Keppen's diary, concludes that Schubert must have returned for a second hearing of the opera, because 'he was open-minded and wished to check the correctness of his initial impression'. While this assumption cannot be disproved, a more likely explanation might be that Schubert was in fact not present on the first night, but only on the second. (On his reactions to the opera, *see also* Weber.*)

(Chochlow, Keppen)

Kienreich, Johann [?Josef] **Nepomuk Andreas** (b. Graz, 2 May 1759; d. Graz, 6 April 1845). Publisher and printer at Graz. The son of a cheesemaker, he originally worked in the same trade, but later trained as a book printer. He was in partnership with the bookseller Christian Friedrich Trötscher until 1791, when he founded his own publishing house. In 1796 he set up his own printing works.

Schubert made Kienreich's acquaintance during his visit to Graz in 1827. The following year Kienreich published his Op. 90 (later changed to 93), consisting of the songs 'Auf der Bruck' (D853) and 'Im Walde' (D834).

First editions: D834, 853
(*ÖBL*, Suppan)

Kiesewetter von Wiesenbrunn, Irene (b. Vienna, 27 March 1811; d. Graz, 7 July 1872). Pianist. Daughter of Raphael Georg Kiesewetter von Wiesenbrunn* and his wife Jakobine, née Cavallo; on 25 November 1832 she married Anton Prokesch von Osten.* In a letter to Marie Pachler* on 29 January 1828, Johann Baptist Jenger* called her 'one of the foremost women pianists in Vienna'. She sometimes accompanied Schubert in performances of his songs, and later frequently partnered Baron Schönstein.* On 26 October 1827, at Sophie Müller's,* she played the *Divertissement à la hongroise* (D818) with Jenger.

Schubert's friendship with Irene and her father resulted in the composition of two occasional pieces, *Kantate für Irene Kiesewetter* (D936) and the quartet 'Der Tanz' (D826). The cantata, which dates from late December 1827, celebrated Irene's recovery from a serious illness; the author of the text is not known. In 'Der Tanz', which may have been written during the same period, Schubert set a text by

'Schnitzer'—perhaps the tenor Kolumban Schnitzer von Meerau who sang 'Der zürnenden Diana' (D707) at an 'evening entertainment' of the Gesellschaft der Musikfreunde on 22 November 1827 and participated in a performance of 'Gondelfahrer' (D809) in another 'evening entertainment' on 17 January 1828.

In his above-mentioned letter of 29 January 1828, Jenger told Marie Pachler that, Irene's doctor having recommended a change of air, she and her mother were contemplating a trip to Styria in the spring, on which they would be accompanied as 'tour guides' by Schubert and himself. However, the planned trip did not take place.

Irene was painted by Josef Teltscher* in 1830, and by Josef Kriehuber* in 1849. (ÖBL)

Kiesewetter von Wiesenbrunn, Raphael Georg (b. Holleschau [Holešov, Czech Republic], 29 August 1773; d. Baden, near Vienna, 1 January 1850). Civil servant; musicologist and singer. He was a son of the well-known physician Alois Ferdinand Kiesewetter (1739–93), and the father of Irene Kiesewetter von Wiesenbrunn.* After studying philosophy at Olmütz [Olomouc] and law in Vienna (though without taking a diploma), he was employed in the chancellery of the imperial army at Schwetzingen. In 1801 he became an official at the war office in Vienna and subsequently had a very successful career in that department. In 1807 he was accorded the title Hofrat, and he was ennobled in 1843; he retired two years later.

He was an accomplished musician, having been taught the piano and singing in his youth and having later learned to play the flute, bassoon, and guitar; he furthermore studied theory with Johann Georg Albrechtsberger. His great interest in early music led him not only to collect a large number of scores (which he eventually bequeathed to the court library), but also to hold, at his apartment [corner Salzgries/Heinrichsgasse], a series of concerts devoted to vocal compositions from the sixteenth to the eighteenth century. On 25 October 1829, for instance, he offered a programme made up entirely of works by Palestrina. The participants in these concerts were both amateur and professional musicians, and included, notably, the Fröhlich* sisters, Johann Baptist Jenger,* the bass Franz Sales Kandler, the Czech pianist and composer Jan Václav Voříšek,* and Franz Xaver Gebauer, choirmaster at St Augustine's Church and founder of the Concerts spirituels. At the same time, Kiesewetter also arranged numerous concerts featuring contemporary music, at which Schubert's compositions occupied an increasingly prominent place. Schubert himself was a frequent visitor. His music continued to be cherished at the Kiesewetters' after his death. In a letter to Friedrich von Gentz on 8 October 1830, Anton Prokesch von Osten* (Kiesewetter's future son-in-law) mentioned having spent the preceding evening at 'Hofrat Kiesewetter's, where Baron Schönstein* sang for us some twenty songs by Schubert in masterly fashion'.

Kiesewetter, who was an accomplished bass, himself took part in many public and private concerts. At an 'evening entertainment' of the Gesellschaft der Musikfreunde on 9 January 1823 he sang in a performance of Schubert's quartet 'Geist der

Liebe' (D747). He was vice-president of the Gesellschaft from 1821 to 1843. His importance as a musicologist derives from his studies of Greek, Egyptian, Arabic, Dutch, and medieval music.

(Kier, *ÖBL*, Wessely[1,5], Wurzbach[1])

Kind, (Johann) Friedrich (b. Leipzig, 4 March 1768; d. Dresden, 25 June 1843). Writer and editor. The son of a judge, Johann Christoph Kind (d. 1793), he studied law at Leipzig University (1786–90). After a spell in government service, he started to practise as a barrister at Dresden in 1793.

His literary output was extremely varied, comprising plays (*Dramatische Gemälde*, 1802), novels (*Natalia*, 1802–4), stories (*Erzählungen und kleine Romane*, 5 vols., 1820–7), poems (*Gedichte*, 5 vols., 1817–25), and librettos (notably, for Weber's* *Der Freischütz*). In addition, he edited *W. G. Beckers Taschenbuch zum geselligen Vergnügen* (Leipzig) from 1815 to 1832, and co-edited the *Abendzeitung* (Dresden) between 1816 and 1826. Schubert set one of his poems in 'Hänflings Liebeswerbung'.

Setting: D552.
(Huber, Pfannkuch, Porhansl[5], Warrack[1])

Kinsky, Karolina [Charlotte] **Maria**, Princess, née Baroness Kerpen (b. 4 March 1782; d. 2 November 1841). On 8 June 1801 she married Prince Ferdinand Johann Nepomuk Josef Kinsky von Wchinitz und Tettau (1781–1812); they had three sons. Her husband was a generous patron of Beethoven,* who dedicated his Mass in C major, Op. 86, to him. Beethoven furthermore dedicated to the princess his Op. 75 (containing the songs 'An den fernen Geliebten', 'Der Zufriedene', 'Es war einmal ein König', 'Gretels Warnung', 'Mignon', and 'Neue Liebe, neues Leben'), Op. 83 ('Mit einem gemalten Band', 'Sehnsucht', and 'Wonne der Wehmut'), and Op. 94 ('An die Hoffnung'). In a letter to Breitkopf & Härtel* on 28 January 1812, he referred to the princess as 'one of the prettiest and plumpest women in Vienna'. Later she became chief stewardess to Archduchess Sophie, the wife (since 1824) of Archduke Franz Karl and mother of the future Emperor Franz Josef.

In 1828 Schubert dedicated to the princess his Op. 96, which consisted of the songs 'Die Sterne' (D939), 'Fischerweise' (D881), 'Jägers Liebeslied' (D909), and 'Wandrers Nachtlied' (D768). On 7 July 1828 the princess made him a gift of money as a token of her appreciation. At the same time, she thanked him for participating, apparently together with Baron Schönstein,* in a concert which she had recently given at her house [4 Freyung]. It was perhaps on that occasion that the following incident later related by Josef von Spaun* occurred: when everyone loudly acclaimed Schönstein for his performance while taking no notice of the composer who had accompanied him, the princess sought to make amends by warmly praising Schubert and requesting his indulgence for the behaviour of her guests—whereupon Schubert remarked that he was quite accustomed to being ignored and, in fact, rather liked it, since he then felt less embarrassed. The anecdote was intended to illustrate Schubert's modesty, and also the shyness from which he tended to suffer in society.

(*Schubert: Erinnerungen*, Wurzbach[1])

Kleist, Ewald Christian von (b. Zeblin, near Köslin, Pomerania, 7 March 1715; d. Frankfurt an der Oder, 24 August 1759). Army officer; poet. He attended school at Danzig [Gdansk, Poland] and afterwards studied law at the University of Königs-berg [Kaliningrad, Russia]. Between 1736 and 1740 he served in the Danish army, and from 1740 in that of Prussia. During the Seven Years War, he was fatally wounded at the battle of Kunersdorf (12 August 1759), at which the Prussians were defeated by the Russian and Austrian forces; he died twelve days later.

He enjoyed friendly relations with several well-known writers, among them Johann Wilhelm Ludwig Gleim, Friedrich Nicolai, Karl Wilhelm Ramler, and especially Lessing who is believed to have portrayed him in the figure of Tellheim in *Minna von Barnhelm*. Kleist is best known for his nature poetry, especially *Der Frühling* (1749), a 400-line poem in hexameters inspired by James Thomson's *The Seasons*. He is further the author of a number of odes, idylls, and elegies, and also wrote some patriotic poetry, notably 'Ode an die preussische Armee' (1757) and the small epic *Cissides und Paches* (1759). He published a collection of his poems, *Gedichte*, in 1756, and a second in 1758. A two-volume edition of his works appeared in 1760.

In August 1822 Schubert set one of his poems in 'Gott in der Natur' (D757), a quartet for two sopranos and two contraltos. In the autograph and also in the first edition (Anton Diabelli & Co.,* 1839), the text is erroneously attributed to Gleim. The composition was performed for the first time at an 'evening entertainment' of the Gesellschaft der Musikfreunde on 8 March 1827, on which occasion it was sung by twelve female students of the Conservatory. (*See also* Anna Fröhlich.*)

Setting: D757.
(Joost[1], Porhansl[3], Schwarze)

Klenke [Klencke], Karoline Luise von, née Karsch (b. Fraustadt [Wschowa, Poland], 21 June 1754; d. Berlin, 21 September 1802). Poetess, playwright, and essayist; daughter of the poetess Anna Luise Karsch [Karschin] (1722–91) and mother of Helmina von Chézy.* She settled in Berlin in 1761.

Her play *Der ehrliche Schweizer* (1776) received numerous performances in Berlin. She published a volume of Anacreontic verse, *Gedichte*, in 1788, and further poems in the *Berliner Musenalmanach* (1791–5) and elsewhere. A selection of her poems appeared in a book printed shortly after her death, *Blumen auf's Grab der Frau C. L. von Klenke ... Aus ihren eigenen und ihrer Freunde Gedichten* (1802).

Her poem 'An Myrtill' was set by Schubert in September 1827 while he was staying with the Pachlers* in Graz. Faust Pachler later informed C. von Wurzbach that Schubert had been shown the poem by his mother, Marie Pachler, to whom her former teacher Julius Schneller* had sent it without mentioning the author's name and under a different title. This no doubt explains why Schubert's song (D922) was published as 'Heimliches Lieben' in 1828, without any indication of its author. However, since the other two songs in that edition were settings of poems by Karl Gottfried Leitner* and identified as such, it was generally assumed that 'Heimliches Lieben' had also been written by Leitner, until Faust Pachler eventually pointed out the error. It may be added that Klenke's 'An Myrtill' had already been set by Johann Friedrich Reichardt in 1780.

Setting: D922.
(Friedrichs, Riedl)

Klopstock, Friedrich Gottlieb (b. Quedlinburg, 2 July 1724; d. Hamburg, 14 March 1803). Poet and dramatist. He was educated at Schulpforta, near Naumburg (1739–45), and read theology and philosophy at Jena and Leipzig (1745–8). From 1751 until 1770 he lived mainly in Copenhagen. He subsequently settled at Hamburg.

The publication of the first three cantos of his religious epic *Der Messias* in 1748 established him as an outstandingly gifted poet. (The work, which eventually ran to some 20,000 lines, was not completed until 1773.) His reputation was further enhanced by the publication in 1771 of a collection of his odes, which made a great impact especially on the younger generation and, in particular, led to the formation of the so-called Göttinger Hainbund. The odes, often personal and emotional in tone and conveying an impression of considerable spontaneity, are to this day regarded as his most original achievement. On the other hand, his biblical and historical plays attracted far less attention. Schubert was familiar with the odes from an early age, for Anton Holzapfel* recalled, in a letter to Ferdinand Luib* in 1859, that he had himself long had in his possession a poem which Schubert had written in the style of Klopstock's odes in *c.*1811–12.

In addition to his literary activities, Klopstock took a great interest in music and he did his best to persuade contemporary composers to set his odes. In fact, his poetry has attracted a considerable number of well-known musicians, among them C. P. E. Bach, Beethoven,* Gluck, Mahler, Meyerbeer, Schubert, Schumann,* and Richard Strauss.

Schubert wrote thirteen songs to texts by Klopstock, nine in September–October 1815 and the remainder in June 1816. The first series consisted of 'An Sie' (D288), 'Das Rosenband' (D280), 'Dem Unendlichen' (D291), 'Die frühen Gräber' (D290), 'Die Sommernacht' (D289), 'Furcht der Geliebten' (D285), 'Hermann und Thusnelda' (D322), 'Selma und Selmar' (D286), and 'Vaterlandslied' (D287); the second of 'Das grosse Halleluja' (D442), 'Die Gestirne' (D444), 'Edone' (D445), and 'Schlachtlied' (D443). Of the latter composition, originally written for single voice or chorus, Schubert made a further setting (D912) for double chorus in February

1827 (*see also* Kundmann*). Schubert also set texts by Klopstock in the partsongs 'Nun lasst uns den Leib begraben' (D168) and 'Jesus Christus unser Heiland' (D168A), and in his German *Stabat Mater* (D383).

None of Schubert's Klopstock settings were published in his lifetime. The first to appear in print were 'Dem Unendlichen' and 'Die Gestirne' which were included by Anton Diabelli & Co.* in a collection of eight spiritual songs by Schubert published in April 1831. Thanks to Adolphe Nourrit,* 'Die Gestirne' was one of the songs which established Schubert's reputation in France.

Settings: D168, 168A, 280, 285–91, 322, 383, 442–5, 912.

(Branscombe[3], Sauder[2])

Koller, Josefa [Josefine] **von** (b. Steyr, 25 December 1801; d. Türnitz, Lower Austria, 8 July 1874). She was the daughter of Josef von Koller (1780–1864), a wealthy iron merchant, and his wife Therese, née von Horabek (1783–1853); Koller was ennobled in 1813. Schubert became acquainted with the family during his first visit to Steyr in 1819. 'The daughter of Herr von K., at whose house I dine with [Johann Michael] Vogl* each day, is very pretty, plays the piano well, and is going to sing several of my songs,' he reported to his brother Ferdinand* on 13 July. And Albert Stadler* recalled in 1858 that he, Schubert, Vogl, and the 'very talented' Josefine used to make music at the Kollers' house [11 Stadtplatz] most evenings.

On one occasion, they amused themselves by performing 'Erlkönig' (D328) as a trio, with Schubert as the father, Vogl as the Erlkönig, and Josefine as the child, while Stadler played the piano accompaniment. To mark Vogl's birthday on 10 August, Stadler wrote a cantata which Schubert set to music (D666) and which was sung by Josefine, a certain Bernhard Benedict, and Schubert himself, with Stadler again at the piano. According to Stadler, Schubert also wrote a piano sonata for Josefine during his stay at Steyr that year; it has been tentatively identified as the Sonata in A major (D664). Also at this time, or soon afterwards, Schubert set another text by Stadler in 'Namenstagslied' (D695), which Josefine is said to have sung on her father's name-day on 19 March 1820. In the latter year, Schubert inscribed an autograph of 'Morgenlied' (D685) to 'the singer P. [i.e. Pepi, for Josefine] and the pianist Stadler'. Presumably Schubert called on the Kollers again during his visits to Steyr in 1823 and 1825, but nothing is known about his contacts with the family on those occasions.

On 8 April 1828 Josefine married Franz Krackowizer, estate manager to Prince Karl Wilhelm Auersperg at Losensteinleithen Castle, near Steyr, and later chief steward at Wels Castle. Josefine survived her husband. In *Schubert: Erinnerungen*, O. E. Deutsch mistakenly states that the Ferdinand Krackowizer who served as mayor of Gmunden and published a history of that town (*Geschichte der Stadt Gmunden in Ober-Österreich*, 1898–1900), was a son of Josefine. In reality, the Ferdinand Krackowizer in question was not the son of Franz and Josefine

Krackowizer, but of the Gmunden physician Ferdinand Krackowizer and his wife Maria Josefa, née Margelik. He lived from 1851 to 1929, was himself a doctor, and mayor of the town from 1912 to 1914.

(Baumert/Grüll, *ÖBL*)

Köpken, Friedrich von (b. Magdeburg, 9 December 1737; d. Magdeburg, 4 October 1811). Poet and translator. He studied law at Halle (1756–9) and subsequently practised as a barrister at Magdeburg, where he later became a syndic. His interest in science and the arts led to his becoming a co-founder of the Gelehrten-Club (later known as 'Mittwochgesellschaft' and 'Literarische Gesellschaft') which was to assume an important role in the cultural life of the town.

In the 1760s he began to contribute poems and other short pieces to various periodicals. Later he published some volumes of verse, intended mainly for his friends: *Hymnus auf Gott, nebst andern vermischten Gedichten* (1792), *Skolien* (1794), *Episteln. Zum Anhange vermischte Gedichte* (1801). His preference was for elegant and charming poetry in the Anacreontic style. In July 1816 Schubert set one of his poems in 'Freude der Kinderjahre'.

Setting: D455.
(Riege)

Köppen: *see* Keppen.*

Korner [Karner], **Philipp Thaddäus** (b. Auersthal, Lower Austria, 4 May 1761; d. Vienna, 18 September 1831). Musician; son of a schoolteacher. In 1797 he joined the court Kapelle as a tenor. In addition, he was employed as singing master to the choirboys of the Kapelle, of whom Schubert became one in 1808. In a letter to Ferdinand Luib* in 1858, Anton Holzapfel* described him as 'a lean and dried-up man, with a long thin pigtail, who would often encourage us choirboys during singing lessons and rehearsals by cuffing us and pulling our ears', but he added that Korner was 'one of the best-known figures on the Viennese musical scene at the time'.

Korner was one of the first two teachers to be appointed at the newly established Conservatory of the Gesellschaft der Musikfreunde in 1817. The other one was Josef Frühwald, who sang Jacquino in Beethoven's* *Fidelio* in May 1814 and took part in the first performance of Schubert's octet 'Gesang der Geister über den Wassern' (D714) at the Kärntnertor-Theater on 7 March 1821. Korner taught at the Conservatory until 1822. He was succeeded by Frühwald as singing master to the choirboys after his death.

(*ÖBL*, Pohl¹)

Körner, (Karl) Theodor (b. Dresden, 23 November 1791; d. Gadebusch, Mecklenburg, 26 August 1813). Poet and dramatist; son of Christian Gottfried Körner (1756–

1831), a distinguished Saxon jurist and Friedrich Schiller's* closest friend. He studied geology at Freiberg (1808–10) and philosophy and law in Leipzig and Berlin (1810–11). In 1811 he went to Vienna, where he attracted favourable attention, first with his comedies (*Die Braut, Der grüne Domino, Der Nachtwächter*) and then with a series of tragedies (notably *Toni* and *Zriny*). As a result, he was appointed resident dramatist at the Burgtheater in January 1813 for a three-year period. However, he left Vienna in March 1813 and enlisted in Baron Adolf Lützow's Free Corps to fight against the French in the Wars of Liberation. He was wounded near Leipzig in June, rejoined his corps in mid-August, and was killed in battle two weeks later. While in Vienna, he had become engaged to the actress Antonie Adamberger.*

Körner published some early verse in *Knospen* (Leipzig, 1810), but he made his greatest impact as a poet posthumously with the patriotic poems he had written in the months preceding his death, which were published by his father under the title *Leyer und Schwerdt* (Berlin, 1814).

Schubert was introduced to Körner by Josef von Spaun,* in January 1813 or earlier, after a performance of Gluck's *Iphigénie en Tauride* (regarding the likely date, *see* Milder-Hauptmann*), and had supper with them at the Blumenstöckl restaurant [3 Ballgasse]. Like his father, Körner had a great love of music; he enjoyed improvising songs which he would accompany on the lute or guitar.

Between February and October 1815 Schubert wrote the following compositions, mostly for single voice, to poems by Körner, drawn both from his love poetry and his patriotic verse: 'Amphiaraos' (D166), 'Das gestörte Glück' (D309), 'Das war ich' (D174), 'Der Morgenstern' (D172, 203), 'Gebet während der Schlacht' (D171), 'Jägerlied' (D204), 'Liebesrausch' (D164, 179), 'Liebeständelei' (D206), 'Lützows wilde Jagd' (D205), 'Sängers Morgenlied' (D163, 165), 'Schwertlied' (D170), 'Sehnsucht der Liebe' (D180), 'Trinklied vor der Schlacht' (D169), and 'Wiegenlied' (D304). In March 1818 he returned to Körner for one more song, 'Auf der Riesenkoppe' (D611). None of these vocal compositions was published in Schubert's lifetime.

Schubert also used a text by Körner in the Singspiel *Der vierjährige Posten* (D190) which he composed in May 1815. The libretto, originally entitled *Die Vedette*, had been published in Vienna in 1813 and had already been set by Karl Steinacker, whose opera *Der vierjährige Posten* was produced at the Theater an der Wien on 19 August 1813. Schubert's Singspiel did not receive a performance until 23 September 1896, at Dresden.

Settings: D163–6, 169–72, 174, 179–80, 190, 203–6, 304, 309, 611.
(Berger[2], Branscombe[4], Haberland, Porhansl[2])

Kosegarten, Ludwig Gotthard [Theobul] (b. Grevesmühlen, Mecklenburg, 1 February 1758; d. Greifswald, 26 October 1818). Poet, prose writer, and translator. A pastor's son, he studied theology at Greifswald (1775–7). After taking holy orders, he worked as a private tutor before becoming headmaster of a school at Wolgast in

1785. From 1792 until 1808 he served as pastor at Altenkirchen, on the island of Rügen. In 1808 he became professor of history at the University of Greifswald; in 1817 he was appointed professor of theology. A prolific writer, he published a considerable number of poems, several novels, translations from English and French, and an autobiography, *Geschichte seines fünfzigsten Lebensjahres.*

Between June and October 1815 Schubert made twenty-one settings of poems by Kosegarten; on one day, 19 October, he composed no fewer than seven. Among the most successful are 'Alles um Liebe' (D241), 'Das Sehnen' (D231), 'Die Erscheinung' (D229), 'Die Mondnacht' (D238), and 'Nachtgesang' (D314). In May 1817, he composed 'An die untergehende Sonne' (D457). All the settings are for single voice, with the exception of the partsong 'Das Abendrot' (D236).

Settings: 219, 221, 227–31, 233, 235–8, 240–1, 313–19, 457.
(Heiderich)

Kotzebue, August von (b. Weimar, 3 May 1761; d. Mannheim, 23 March 1819). Dramatist. In the course of an extremely chequered career he worked, at different times, as a lawyer at Weimar, a theatre secretary in Vienna and St Petersburg, a high official in the Russian province of Estonia, a political journalist, and a magazine editor. In 1816 he was attached to the department of foreign affairs in St Petersburg. In 1817 he returned to Germany, where he probably acted as a political informant for Tsar Alexander I. The young German Liberals detested him for ridiculing their demands for greater freedom. In 1819 he was assassinated by a theology student named Karl Ludwig Sand.

In the course of his tumultuous life, he found time to write more than 200 plays, as well as several novels. Among the former, certain comedies, such as *Die beiden Klingsberg* and *Die deutschen Kleinstädter,* have best stood the test of time. Several composers found inspiration in his works. Some wrote music for the plays, as Beethoven* did for *Die Ruinen von Athen* and *König Stephan;* others based entire operas on them (e.g. Lortzing in *Der Wildschütz*).

Schubert composed, or set out to compose, at least two stage works to texts by Kotzebue: *Der Spiegelritter* (D11) in 1811–12 and *Des Teufels Lustschloss* (D84) in 1813–14. (The latter libretto was based on *Le Château du diable,* a comédie héroïque by Joseph-Marie Loaisel de Tréogate, first performed in Paris on 5 December 1792.) Both of Kotzebue's librettos had, in fact, been set before: *Der Spiegelritter* by Vincenc Mašek (produced Prague, 1784) and Ignaz Walter (Mainz, 1791), among others, and *Des Teufels Lustschloss* by Ignaz Walter (Bremen, 1801), Johann Friedrich Reichardt (Berlin, 1802), and Christian Ludwig Dieter (Stuttgart, 1802). But Schubert is hardly likely to have known these settings. Of his Singspiel *Der Spiegelritter* only fragments of Act I survive, and it is by no means certain that he ever completed the work; of *Des Teufels Lustschloss* he made two versions.

It is possible that he started setting a third text by Kotzebue. In an obituary published in February 1829, the usually reliable Leopold von Sonnleithner* stated that among Schubert's unfinished stage works was one called *Der Minnesänger*. No trace has survived of the fragment (it has been given the work-number D981). Kreissle,* who ascribed its composition to 1815–16, suggested that Schubert had most likely used a work by Kotzebue. The latter was, indeed, the author of a play entitled *Der arme Minnesänger* which had been produced in Munich in June 1811, with interpolated songs by Weber,* and performed at the Theater an der Wien thirteen times between 3 March 1812 and 5 September 1814 with music by Ignaz von Seyfried. Another source for Schubert's Singspiel, assuming that he did indeed ever work on it, could have been Christoph Kuffner's* *Die Minnesänger auf der Wartburg*, which was produced at the Theater an der Wien, with music by Seyfried, on 15 March 1819.

Settings: D11, 84, ?981.

(Bauer, Branscombe[5], Lorenz, MacKay, Waidelich[4], Wodtke[1])

Kreissle von Hellborn, Heinrich (b. Vienna, 19 January 1822; d. Vienna, 6 April 1869). Author of the first full-length biography of Schubert. A lawyer by training, he became a civil servant. He was married to Bertha von Pratobevera, a sister of Adolf Pratobevera von Wiesborn.*

In 1861, Kreissle published in Vienna an account of Schubert's life, *Aus Schuberts Leben*, of which five extracts were reprinted that same year in the Leipzig journal *Signale für die musikalische Welt* under the title 'Franz Schubert: Eine biographische Skizze'. Four years later, he published *Franz Schubert*, a far more substantial, two-volume biography. In it he drew on numerous personal recollections by individuals who had been friendly or acquainted with Schubert. (Some of the material had originally been collected by Ferdinand Luib* for his own projected life of the composer.) In addition, Kreissle's book presented much useful information on performances of Schubert's works in his lifetime and later, and contained a valuable catalogue of his published and unpublished works.

The first Schubert biography to appear in France, 'Franz Schubert: Sa vie, ses œuvres, son temps', which the composer and musicologist Hippolyte La Rochelle Barbedette published in the journal *Le Ménestrel* in 1864–5 (and in book form in 1866), owed a good deal to Kreissle. In England, Edward Wilberforce's *Franz Schubert: A Musical Biography* (London, 1866) was, as the author explained in his preface, no more than a condensation of Kreissle's book of 1865, prepared with the latter's blessing. Three years later, Arthur Duke Coleridge, a barrister and amateur musician, brought out a complete English version of Kreissle's study, under the title *The Life of Franz Schubert. Translated from the German of Kreissle von Hellborn* (2 vols., London, 1869). The interest of Coleridge's book was enhanced by an appendix contributed by George Grove,* in which he described his visit to Vienna in 1867 in search of Schubert manuscripts and also presented an annotated thematic catalogue of Schubert's symphonies.

(Brown[6], Jancik/Kahl)

Kriehuber, Josef (b. Vienna, 14 December 1800; d. Vienna, 30 May 1876). Painter and lithographer; son of a restaurant owner who dabbled in painting. After receiving some training in Vienna, he found employment as drawing teacher to the children of Prince Eustach Sanguszko at Slavuta, in Poland (1818–22). After his return to Vienna he completed his formal training (1824–5). He showed an early interest in lithography and, starting in the mid-1820s, concentrated increasingly on portraits, of which he lithographed some 3,000 during a brilliant career which reached its most productive period in 1830–45. He also produced about 200 water-colours (portraits and landscapes) and some twenty oil-paintings. The list of his sitters embraced almost everybody who was anybody in Vienna's social and cultural life, ranging from members of the imperial family and the nobility to musicians, painters, writers, actors, and scholars. It included, in addition to Schubert himself, many of the persons listed in this dictionary, e.g. Beethoven, Castelli, Diabelli, Haslinger, Lanner, Sophie Müller, Schönstein, and Sechter.

Kriehuber was in contact with Schubert's circle and is known to have attended several balls at Franz von Schober's,* especially in 1827. On 1 February of that year he married Marie Forstern; both were among the company invited by Schober on 4 March to hear Schubert's latest compositions. Marie's sister Louise (known, in tribute to her beauty, as 'The Flower of the Land') was also a regular member of the group; she was to marry the engraver Johann Nepomuk Passini in 1831.

Kriehuber's well-known lithographed portrait of Schubert was not drawn until after the composer's death. Based in some measure on Wilhelm August Rieder's* portrait of 1825, it exists in two versions, one of which shows him looking to his right, the other to his left. At least the former lithograph was executed and published in 1846; the history of the other one is less certain. According to Albert Stadler* and others, Kriehuber's portrait was an excellent likeness of Schubert. In Anton Schindler's* view, on the other hand, it was 'perhaps a successful representation of a celebrity closely related to the subject, but not of the composer Franz Schubert'.

Later Kriehuber taught drawing at the Theresian Academy (1865–71). He became a member of the Academy of Fine Arts in 1866. His sons Friedrich (1834–71) and Josef Franz (1839–1905) were also painters.

(*ALBK*, Jestremski², *ÖBL*)

Kuffner, Christoph (Johann Anton) (b. Vienna, 28 June 1777/80; d. Vienna, 7 November 1846). Civil servant; poet, dramatist, narrative writer, and translator. In 1803 he became an official at the war office, where he served until his death; he also occupied for a time the post of newspaper censor.

Kuffner was a prolific writer. He published poems and stories in journals, as well as in volume form (e.g. *Gedichte* in 1818, *Sämmtliche Erzählungen* in 1826–8, *Neuere Gedichte* in 1840). He also wrote novels, notably *Ahasver, der ewige Jude: Eine Wanderung durch Jahrhunderte* and *Artemidor im Reiche der Römer*, translated

Plautus's comedies, and was himself the author of numerous, mostly historical, plays.

In August 1828 Schubert set one of his poems in the song 'Glaube, Hoffnung und Liebe' (D955). This should not to be confused with the identically titled partsong D954 which is based on a poem by Johann Anton Friedrich Reil.* (*See also* Kotzebue.*)

Settings: D955, ?981.
(Badstüber, Fischer⁴)

Kumpf, Johann Gottfried [pseud. Ermin] (b. Klagenfurt, 9 December 1781; d. Klagenfurt, 21 February 1862). Physician, poet, and editor. After medical studies in Vienna and Pest [Budapest], he practised at Trieste before returning to Klagenfurt in 1811. He published a number of poems in various periodicals and collections, edited the periodical *Carinthia* (1811–13), and founded the *Kärntnerische Zeitschrift* in 1818.

Schubert set two of his poems, both in 1815, in 'Der Mondabend' (D141) and 'Mein Gruss an den Mai' (D305).

Settings: D141, 305.
(*ÖBL*, Schochow, Wurzbach¹)

Kundmann, Karl (b. Vienna, 15 June 1838; d. Vienna, 9 June 1919). Sculptor. After studying with Franz Bauer and Josef Cesar in Vienna and with Ernst Julius Hähnel in Dresden, he spent the years 1865–7 in Rome. Following his return to Vienna, he eventually made his mark with his Schubert monument in 1872, on the design of which Moritz von Schwind* reportedly had some influence. Among his other well-known monuments were two statues of Admiral Wilhelm von Tegetthoff, the victor of a famous naval battle against the Italians in 1866; the first statue was erected at Pola [Pula, Croatia] in 1877 and moved to Graz in 1935, the second, made in collaboration with Baron Karl Hasenauer, was unveiled in Vienna in 1886. He also created the seated figure of Franz Grillparzer* in the Volksgarten in Vienna (1889), and the statues of the poets Anastasius Grün [Count Anton Alexander Auersperg] and Robert Hamerling [Rupert Hammerling], which were erected in Graz in 1887 and 1904 respectively. He furthermore made several sculptures for the façades of the Naturhistorisches Museum, the Kunsthistorisches Museum, and the Burgtheater in Vienna, and was also mainly responsible for the Pallas Athene fountain in front of the parliament building.

Kundmann's Schubert monument in the Vienna Stadtpark owed its existence mainly to the persistent efforts of Johann von Herbeck.* The major part of the costs, amounting to some 30,000 gulden, was provided by the Wiener Männergesangverein. The city of Vienna contributed a mere 500 gulden (as compared with 10,000 gulden for the Mozart statue in 1896). The foundation stone was laid on 12 October 1868. On that occasion the Männergesangverein performed compositions by Schubert and Herbeck, Nikolaus Dumba* made a speech, and the well-known actor Ludwig Gabillon declaimed a poem specially written by Eduard von Bauernfeld.*

When the monument was unveiled on 15 May 1872, those present included Schubert's sister Maria Theresia, his half-brothers Andreas and Anton Eduard [Pater Hermann], and his friends Bauernfeld, Franz Paul Lachner,* Baron Schlechta,* Franz von Schober,* Leopold von Sonnleithner,* Baron Schönstein,* and the Fröhlich* sisters. The ceremony began with a performance of the Sanctus from Schubert's *Deutsche Messe* (D872) and ended with a rendering by the choir of the Männergesangverein of the 'Schlachtlied' (D912), sung to a new text by M. A. Grandjean. The principal oration was again delivered by Dumba. That evening, a special Schubert concert was conducted by Herbeck at the Musikverein (for details, *see* Herbeck*).

According to L. Scheewe (in *ALBK*), Kundmann's Schubert monument 'delightfully exemplified his particular talent for tempering the prevailing taste for classical realism with Viennese charm'. George Grove* was far less favourably impressed by what he termed 'this unhappy memorial', discerning in it little realism and even less charm. In a letter to *The Times* on 2 October 1889, he condemned Kundmann's representation of Schubert as the opposite of naturalistic, asserting that it was 'not only ideal, but incorrect in every detail'; as for the reliefs on the pedestal, they were 'allegorical in a most advanced and absurd style'.

In Vienna, however, there appears to have been both general and official approval, for Kundmann was offered a teaching appointment at the Academy of Fine Arts, a position he was to occupy until 1909. In addition, he served as principal of that institution in 1880–2 and 1895–7. And when it was subsequently decided to close Währing district cemetery and to remove Schubert's remains to the Grove of Honour at the central cemetery established in 1874, it was again Kundmann who was commissioned to build the funeral monument at the new grave, this time with the help of Theophil Hansen.* The reinterment took place on 23 September 1888. At the suggestion of the Wiener Männergesangverein, the ceremony was attended by all the choral societies of the city. It opened with a rendition of 'Der Tod und das Mädchen' (D531) by trombonists of the court Kapelle, after which Ludwig Gabillon declaimed a poem written for the occasion by L. A. Frankl. Following speeches by the president of the Männergesangverein, Carl von Olschbaur, and the deputy mayor of Vienna, Johann Nepomuk Prix, the coffin was lowered into the grave and the choir sang 'Am Tage Aller Seelen' (D343).

(*ALBK*, Herbeck, *Männergesangverein*[1,2], *ÖBL*)

Kupelwieser, Josef (b. Piesting, Lower Austria, 1792; d. Vienna, 2 February 1866). Theatre administrator; playwright, librettist, and translator. Son of Johann Baptist Georg Kilian Kupelwieser (1760–1813), co-owner of ironworks at Piesting, and his wife Maria Josefa Judith, née Gspan (1767–1831); brother of Leopold Kupelwieser.*

He was secretary of the Kärntnertor-Theater from 1821 to 1823, and during this period was reportedly commissioned by Domenico Barbaia* to write an operatic libretto for Schubert. However, *Fierrabras* (D796), which Schubert composed between May and October 1823 to Kupelwieser's text, was never produced at the court theatre. Schubert, rightly or wrongly, laid the blame entirely on Kupelwieser's shoulders: 'The opera written by your brother . . . has been declared to be unusable, and in consequence there has been no demand for my music,' he wrote to Leopold Kupelwieser on 31 March 1824. Schubert fared better with the music (D797) which he composed for Helmina von Chézy's* *Rosamunde, Fürstin von Zypern*. Chézy had been asked by Josef Kupelwieser to write a play for Emilie Neumann,* an actress at the Theater an der Wien with whom he was in love. While the play was not well received and only attained two performances (20 and 21 December 1823), there was some praise for Schubert's music. (On this point, *see also* Chézy.*)

Later Kupelwieser became secretary of the theatre at Graz—according to O. E. Deutsch* in 1824, according to K. Stekl not before 1827 (the date 1831 given in W. Kosch's *Deutsches Theater-Lexikon* is unlikely to be correct). For some time, probably between his engagements in Vienna and Graz, he was attached to the theatre at Pressburg [Bratislava]. Finally, he served for many years (?1836–62) as secretary of the Theater in der Josefstadt in Vienna.

He was the author of numerous plays and librettos, most of them adapted from French originals. Among the operas produced in Vienna and Graz with German texts provided by Kupelwieser were Balfe's *The Bohemian Girl* [*Die Zigeunerin*], Boïeldieu's *Les Voitures versées* [*Die umgeworfenen Kutschen*], Donizetti's *Les Martyrs* [*Die Römer in Melitone*] and *Maria di Rohan* [*Maria von Rohan*], Hérold's *Zampa*, Meyerbeer's *Il crociato in Egitto* [*Der Kreuzritter in Egypten*], and Rossini's *Le Siège de Corinthe* [*Die Belagerung von Corinth*] and *Matilde di Shabran* [*Mathilde von Chabran*].

Setting: D796.
(Denny, Kosch, Schöny², Stekl)

Kupelwieser, Leopold (b. Piesting, Lower Austria, 17 October 1796; d. Vienna, 17 November 1862). Painter and graphic artist. (For particulars of his parents, *see* his brother Josef Kupelwieser.*) He was accepted as a student at the Vienna Academy of Fine Arts in February 1809, when he was only 12. Once he began to paint professionally he quickly attracted attention, and in 1818 he executed the first of several portraits of Emperor Franz I of Austria.

Kupelwieser was reportedly introduced to Schubert by Josef von Spaun;* it is not known when their first meeting took place. A drawing in chalk now in the collection of the Prince of Liechtenstein at Vaduz was identified by Schubert's half-brothers Anton Eduard [Pater Hermann] and Andreas, probably some time between 1888 and 1891, as a portrait of Schubert executed by Kupelwieser in 1813. However, since Andreas was not born until 1823 and Anton Eduard not until 1826, these assertions have been treated with caution. Indeed, it has been forcefully argued (by E. Worgull in *Schubert durch die Brille* in 1996) that the sitter cannot possibly have been Schubert. Furthermore, neither the brothers' identification of the artist nor the date which they assign to the drawing can be accepted with certainty.

The earliest documented evidence of Schubert's association with Kupelwieser dates from 1820, in which year both were among Franz von Schober's* guests at Atzenbrugg Castle. It was there, in 1820 and 1821, that Kupelwieser painted his two famous water-colours of the group. One shows the friends during an excursion to nearby Aumühle Castle, the other while engaged in a game of charades, with Schubert seated at the piano. The two paintings were commissioned by Schober and remained in his possession until his death at Dresden in 1882. Kupelwieser also drew a separate portrait of Schubert on 10 July 1821, and, two days later, one of Schober. Other friends and acquaintances of Schubert of whom he executed portraits include Franz Seraph von Bruchmann,* Moritz von Schwind, Josef von Spaun, Johann Michael Vogl,* and Heinrich Josef Watteroth.*

In 1823 Kupelwieser executed a series of forty paintings of Hungarian national costumes for the visiting Russian nobleman Alexei Sergeevich Beresin (*see* Keppen*). They must have pleased Beresin, for he engaged Kupelwieser to accompany him to Italy, where he was to prepare illustrations for the account which Beresin intended to write of their journey. They left Vienna in early November 1823 and spent some time in Rome, from where Kupelwieser wrote to Schober on 8 March 1824: 'One hears no music here at all, but we Germans sing often and much, and now and again I also treat myself to a Schubertiad.' From Rome they travelled to Naples, and thence to Sicily. After Beresin suddenly died at Agrigento in late December 1824, Kupelwieser stayed on in Italy and did not return to Vienna until August of the following year. It was to Kupelwieser, then in Rome, that Schubert wrote on 31 March 1824 what is the most anguished of his extant letters: 'I feel myself to be the most unhappy, the most wretched man in the world... each night as I go to sleep I hope I will not wake again, and each morning merely proclaims the previous day's grief to me.'

Kupelwieser married Johanna Lutz* on 17 September 1826, and at a ball—which, according to his great-granddaughter, M. L. Kupelwieser de Brioni (*Une grande amitié: F. Schubert et L. Kupelwieser*), took place on the eve of the wedding— Schubert played music for the guests to dance to. Among other pieces, he is said to have played a waltz he had specially composed for the occasion (D. Anh. I, 14). Its melody was subsequently passed down from generation to generation in the Kupelwieser family, until Maria Mautner Markhof (née Kupelwieser) played it in Vienna on 4 January 1943 for Richard Strauss, who wrote it down. It was performed in public for the first time by Jörg Demus at the inauguration of the international association 'Pax et Ars' in Paris in 1956. Orchestrated by Gottfried von Einem, it was played at the Vienna Philharmonic Orchestra's ball on 21 January 1960.

Kupelwieser, who had first gained fame as a portraitist, later turned increasingly to religious art. In 1836 he was appointed a professor at the Academy of Fine Arts.

(*ALBK*, Feuchtmüller, Hilmar[4], Klein[1], Kupelwieser, *ÖBL*, Steblin[1,3], Worgull)

Lablache, Luigi (b. Naples, 6 December 1794; d. Naples, 23 January 1858). The most celebrated bass of his generation; his career lasted from 1812 until 1856. He appeared in Paris and London in 1830, and frequently returned to both cities. Among the roles he created were Giorgio in Bellini's *I puritani* (Paris, 24 January 1835) and the title roles in Donizetti's *Marino Faliero* (Paris, 12 March 1835) and *Don Pasquale* (Paris, 3 January 1843).

In 1824 Lablache went to Vienna where he became one of the leading singers of Domenico Barbaia's* company. Schubert, who reportedly met him at Raphael Georg Kiesewetter's* house, considered him a singer of the first rank. In 1827 he dedicated to Lablache his Op. 83, consisting of the songs 'L'incanto degli occhi', 'Il traditor deluso', and 'Il modo di prender moglie' (D902/1–3; on these texts, *see* Metastasio*). Dietrich Fischer-Dieskau has called the songs 'three marvellous studies for the bass voice'.

(Fischer-Dieskau, Robinson[2])

Lachner, Franz Paul (b. Rain am Lech, Bavaria, 2 April 1803; d. Munich, 20 January 1890). Composer and conductor; son of the organist Anton Lachner. After the death in 1822 of his father, who had taught him to play the piano and organ, he moved to Munich and not long afterwards to Vienna, where he became organist at the Lutheran church and received further instruction from Simon Sechter* and Abbé Maximilian Stadler.* In 1827 he was appointed deputy Kapellmeister at the Kärntnertor-Theater, advancing to Kapellmeister two years later. In 1834 he moved to Mannheim, and in 1836 he settled in Munich. He became conductor of the Munich court Opera and of the concerts of the Musikalische Akademie, and in 1852 was made Generalmusikdirektor. His compositions include sacred works, symphonies, chamber music, some 200 songs, and several operas.

According to an article ('Erinnerungen an Schubert und Beethoven') which he published in *Die Presse* (Vienna) on 1 November 1881, he had made Schubert's acquaintance at the Haidvogel restaurant [30 Graben], where both used to lunch. They soon became close friends; they would meet every day, show one another their new compositions, and take walks together in the surroundings of the city. Schubert, moreover, frequently visited Lachner at his lodgings in the Landstrasse suburb [12 Marxergasse]. Lachner states that it was there that the String Quartet in D minor ('Der Tod und das Mädchen', D810) and the Octet in F major (D803) were first performed (but he appears to be in error regarding the latter work which is believed to have been first played at Count Troyer's*). Furthermore, Schubert and Lachner played the newly composed Fantasia in F minor (D940) to Eduard von Bauernfeld* at Lachner's lodgings on 9 May 1828. A private performance of the Quartet in G major (D887) may also have taken place there on 7 March 1827.

Lachner and Schubert were clearly on very intimate terms. In his diary, which covers the last two years of Schubert's life, Franz von Hartmann* frequently mentions Lachner's presence at gatherings of the group at the 'Zum Anker' restaurant [10 Grünangergasse] and other establishments. On 12 January 1827 Lachner attended a Schubertiad at Josef von Spaun's.* In June 1828 he made an excursion to Baden and Heiligenkreuz with Schubert and Johann Schickh.* And when, in the autumn of 1828, he went to Pest [Budapest] where his first opera, *Die Bürgschaft*, was to be produced on 30 October, he and Anton Schindler* (who had moved there a year earlier) invited Schubert to travel down for the première, adding that he could take advantage of the occasion to give a concert there. As far as is known, Schubert did not reply, and by the time Lachner returned to Vienna, he was on his death-bed.

Later, in a letter to Kreissle* and also in the above-mentioned article in *Die Presse*, Lachner described his final visit to Schubert, which appears to have taken place on 17 November. Despite his weakness, Schubert had spoken to him at length of his plans for the future and, in particular, of his desire to complete the opera *Der Graf von Gleichen* (D918). (O. Kronseder, in an article on Lachner in the *Altbayrische Monatsschrift* in 1903, quotes Lachner as telling him that, apart from a brief moment of consciousness, Schubert had been wildly delirious during that visit; but Lachner's own earlier, written accounts are likely to be more reliable.)

Lachner left Vienna before Schubert died, for the purpose of recruiting new singers for the court theatre. News of Schubert's death reached him at Darmstadt. Sometime later he carried out the composer's intention of making an orchestral arrangement of the piano accompaniment to the cantata *Mirjams Siegesgesang* (D942). The work was first performed in this form in Vienna on 28 March 1830. In 1872 Lachner was present when Kundmann's* statue of Schubert was unveiled in the Stadtpark.

Among Schubert's friends, Lachner was especially attracted to Moritz von Schwind,* with whom he maintained an affectionate relationship until the latter's death. In 1862 Schwind drew the so-called 'Lachner-Rolle' which depicts various episodes in Lachner's life and includes scenes in which Schubert also appears.

Lachner's brothers Theodor (1788–1877) and Ignaz (1807–95) were likewise musicians, though less famous ones. Ignaz followed Franz to Vienna, where he studied with him and later succeeded him as organist at the Lutheran church. In 1828 he was appointed assistant Kapellmeister at the court Opera. He left Vienna three years later and spent his remaining career in Germany, except for a spell in Stockholm. While in Vienna, he sometimes accompanied his brother to gatherings of Schubert's circle.

(Leuchtmann[1], Würz[1])

Lang, Franz Innocenz (b. Marchegg, Lower Austria, 4 October 1752; d. Vienna, 10 April 1835). Piarist; teacher and educationist. After attending schools in Pressburg [Bratislava] and Vienna, he joined the Piarists at the age of 17 and was ordained in 1776. By then he had already embarked on his career as a teacher, which was spent mainly in Vienna. In 1791 he was appointed director of the Josefstädter Gymnasium, on whose staff he had been for the previous eight years. In 1794 Emperor Franz I of Austria asked him to teach Latin to his brothers, and later Lang also gave instruction in theology to one of them, Archduke Rudolf,* the future archbishop of Olmütz [Olomouc].

In 1803 he became director of the new Stadtkonvikt. (An earlier college at the same location had been closed down when the Jesuit order was abolished in 1773; the new college was run by the Piarists.) Lang remained director until 1817. The following year he was elected rector of the University of Vienna. In addition, he was responsible for many years for secondary education in Austria. He was accorded the title Regierungsrat in 1809 and that of Hofrat in 1816. He also served as head of the cathedral chapter at Grosswardein [Oradea, Romania].

A stern and high-minded individual, he was regarded by his pupils with profound respect rather than with affection, for, as Josef von Spaun* later explained, 'they could not feel any love for him, since he inspired too much fear in them.' After paying tribute to Lang's upright nature and his many other virtues, Spaun observed that he lacked only one quality, 'the ability to judge a pupil's character'.

Although, according to Anton Holzapfel,* Lang knew nothing about music, he took steps at an early stage to establish a students' orchestra at the Stadtkonvikt and to obtain the necessary musical instruments and scores. The orchestra undoubtedly played a significant part in Schubert's musical education, for, apart from providing him with regular practice on the violin, it made him familiar with numerous instrumental works and offered him invaluable experience of orchestral playing. It appears highly likely, moreover, that his Symphony No. 1 (D82) was played by the orchestra during the autumn of 1813. An extant manuscript copy of orchestral parts of the Symphony No. 2 (D125), which was composed between 10 December 1814 and 24 March 1815, bears a dedication to Lang.

(Deutsch², Wurzbach¹)

Lanner, Josef (Franz Karl) (b. Vienna, 12 April 1801; d. Oberdöbling, near Vienna, 14 April 1843). Composer of dance music and violinist. After playing for several years in the dance orchestra led by Michael Pamer, who was also a composer of Ländler and waltzes, he formed a trio (two violins and guitar) with Carl and Johann Alois Drahanek in 1818. The trio became a quartet the following year when Johann Strauss the Elder joined it as a violist, and a quintet in 1820 with the addition of a cellist. Schubert is said to have heard this quintet play on numerous occasions at the 'Zum goldenen Rebhuhn' café and tavern [6 Goldschmiedgasse], near St Stephen's

Cathedral. According to C. von Wurzbach, he even made a point of going there whenever Lanner was playing and encouraged him with applause and praise. There is, however, no firm evidence to support Wurzbach's statement, or, indeed, any which places Schubert at the 'Rebhuhn' before 1828, when it became a great favourite with his group. An account of a meeting between Lanner, Schubert, and Franz Paul Lachner* published in the Stuttgart *Neue Musikzeitung* on 27 June 1905 (and reprinted in *Schubert: Erinnerungen*) would, if true, indicate that Lanner and Schubert were well acquainted by 1823.

(Wurzbach[1])

Lanz, (Wolfgang) Josef (b. Michaelnbach, Upper Austria, 20 January 1797; d. after 1828). Pianist, violinist, and composer. He was employed as first violinist at St Peter's in Salzburg before he moved to Vienna. It is not known when he arrived there or how he made Schubert's acquaintance. His compositions include sacred as well as chamber music. Like Schubert, he also contributed to the collections of dances published by Pietro Mechetti in February 1825 and Sauer & Leidesdorf* in December 1826.

Lanz would no doubt have been forgotten long ago, were it not for the fact that in the autumn of 1828 he arranged to receive instruction in counterpoint and fugue from Simon Sechter,* together with Schubert. In the event, they had only one joint lesson, on 4 November.

(Wurzbach[1])

Lappe, Karl Gottlieb (b. Wusterhausen, near Wolgast, Pomerania, 24 April 1773; d. Stralsund, 28 October 1843). Poet. He was employed as a schoolmaster at Stralsund before turning to farming. In 1801 he published *Gedichte*, in 1836 his *Sämmtliche poetische Werke*, and in 1841 *Blüte des Alters*. In O. E. Deutsch's* judgement, he was 'an unimportant representative of the Romantic movement in Germany'; Kosch's *Deutsches Literaturlexikon* (Halle, 1830) described him as 'the most important Pomeranian lyric poet'.

Schubert set poems by Lappe in 'Der Einsame' (D800) and 'Im Abendrot' (D799). The former composition dates from early 1825, the latter either from the same period or shortly before. The first performance of 'Der Einsame' was given by Ludwig Titze* at the Musikverein on 23 November 1826. According to Franz von Hartmann,* 'Im Abendrot' ('a specially beautiful song') was performed twice by Johann Michael Vogl* at a Schubertiad at Josef von Spaun's* on 12 January 1827. During roughly the same period as he wrote the two above-named songs, Schubert set another of Lappe's poems, 'Flucht', for male-voice quartet (D825B). This composition was performed at a concert at the Landhaus on 20 March 1825.

Settings: D799, 800, 825B.
(Schochow)

Lászny von Folkusfálva, Katharina [Kathinka], née Buchwieser (b. Koblenz, 1789; d. Vienna, 9 July 1828). Singer and actress. She had a successful career in Vienna, first at the Theater an der Wien and later (1809–17) at the Kärntnertor-Theater, where her most important roles were Susanna in Mozart's *Le nozze di Figaro* and the Princess of Navarre in Boieldieu's *Jean de Paris*. The poet Theodor Körner* wrote in a letter in 1811 that she was 'almost unrivalled in integrating acting and singing'. Her father, Balthasar Buchwieser, was appointed third Kapellmeister at the Theater an der Wien in *c.*1815.

Her private life was the subject of much gossip. At the time of the Congress of Vienna she contributed to the gaiety of the occasion by conducting affairs with Prince Ghika and Prince Franz Seraph Rosenberg-Orsini. Her mother reportedly commented: 'My daughter has done a foolish thing in taking up with Prince Rosenberg. She should have stayed with Prince Ghika; he paid better.'

Katharina married twice: first a man by the name of Hrzon, and subsequently Ludwig Lászny von Folkusfálva, a wealthy Hungarian nobleman who managed Prince Josef Franz Pálffy's estates. She retained her ability to attract men well past her youth. 'What a woman!' the 21-year-old Moritz von Schwind* wrote to Franz von Schober* on 14 February 1825. 'If she were not nearly twice as old as I am and, regrettably, always ill, I would have to leave Vienna, for it would be more than I could stand. Schubert has known her for a long time, but I met her only recently. She takes pleasure in my work and likes me, more than anyone except yourself... I have not seen her lately, but we are to dine at her house tomorrow. Now I know what a woman looks like who is held in ill repute throughout the city, and what she does.'

She and her husband held musical soirées at their house in the Wieden suburb [7 Paniglstrasse]. Schubert, for whose music she had a very high regard, was a frequent visitor. He dedicated to her his Op. 36, comprising the songs 'Der zürnenden Diana' (D707) and 'Nachtstück' (D672), in 1825, and the *Divertissement à la hongroise* (D818) in 1826. (*See also* Hummel.*)

(Kutsch/Riemens, Spiel)

Leidesdorf, Marcus (Maximilian Josef) (b. Vienna, 5 July 1787; d. Florence, 27 September 1840). Pianist, composer, music publisher, and teacher; son of the wholesale merchant Josef Leidesdorf (1743–1805). He studied with Johann Georg Albrechtsberger, Emanuel Aloys Förster, and Antonio Salieri,* published his first composition at the age of 16, and later became a well-known piano virtuoso and a highly regarded piano and guitar teacher. Born into a Jewish family, he converted to Catholicism at Trieste on 6 December 1810, the day of his marriage to Elisabeth Cremes (1787–1845). The couple had nine children.

In July 1822 he became a partner in Ignaz Sauer's* art and music business, which henceforth traded under the name 'Sauer & Leidesdorf'.* The firm published first editions of a considerable number of Schubert's compositions and thus played a very significant role in his career. In addition, Schubert and Leidesdorf enjoyed, at least for a time, a close personal relationship, as is evident from letters written to Franz von Schober* by Moritz von Schwind* (24 December 1823) and Baron Doblhoff-Dier* (7 January 1824), in which Schubert is said to be frequently in Leidesdorf's company. Schubert himself wrote to Leopold Kupelwieser* on 31 March 1824: 'Leidesdorf, whom I have come to know quite well, is a most serious-minded and worthy fellow, but so deeply melancholy that I almost fear I may have been influenced by him more than I would wish in that respect.' Leidesdorf was also on friendly terms with Beethoven,* who, on one occasion, punningly addressed him as 'Dorf des Leidens' ['Village of sorrow'].

After Sauer withdrew from the business in 1826, Leidesdorf registered a new firm in his own name in May 1827. However, he was frequently away from Vienna during the following years, as he and his family travelled a great deal in Europe. In 1833 he settled more or less permanently in Florence where he had been appointed professor at the conservatory attached to the church of Santa Croce. In September of that year, the *Wiener Zeitung* announced the closing down of his Viennese publishing business.

Leidesdorf was a prolific composer whose output included three Masses, an oratorio, songs, orchestral and chamber music, and numerous works for the piano; among the latter were reductions of Rossini operas. He also contributed to the *Diabelli* Variations*. 'Leidesdorf was the typical nineteenth-century "fashionable composer", whose original works and piano arrangements of other composers' works were received enthusiastically by the public and as quickly forgotten' (Schmutzenhofer).

(*ÖBL*, Slezak, Schmutzenhofer)

Leidesdorf, M. J. (publishing firm). Music publishing house established by Marcus (Maximilian Josef) Leidesdorf* on 7 May 1827, following the dissolution of the firm Sauer & Leidesdorf.* He ceased trading in Vienna in September 1833. His stock was taken over by the firm Anton Berka & Co., which was itself acquired by Anton Diabelli & Co.* in 1835.

In January 1828, Leidesdorf published the first edition of Schubert's Waltz in C major (D980D) for the piano, and in July of the same year first editions of the following compositions: the songs 'Auf dem See' (D543), 'Der Musensohn' (D764), and 'Geistes-Gruss' (D142); three choruses from *Rosamunde* (D797/4,7–8); and *Moments musicaux* Nos. 1–2, 4–5 (D780/1–2, 4–5).

After Schubert's death, Leidesdorf published first editions of the following further songs, all in 1829: 'Auf dem Strom' (D943), 'Das Lied im Grünen' (D917), 'Die Erwartung' (D159), 'Sprache der Liebe' (D410), 'Todesmusik' (D758), 'Über Wildemann' (D884), and 'Wonne der Wehmut' (D260).

First editions: D142, 159, 260, 410, 543, 758, 764, 780, 797, 884, 917, 943, 980D.
(Slezak)

Leitermayer, Michael (1799–1867). Choirmaster, violinist, and conductor. Like Schubert, he was a pupil of Michael Holzer.* In 1827 he became choirmaster at Holy Trinity Church in the Alsergrund suburb. The following year Schubert composed the partsong 'Glaube, Hoffnung und Liebe' (D954) for the dedication of a new bell there on 2 September 1828. The Mass in E flat major (D950) was written for the same church, where it received its first performance on 4 October 1829 under Ferdinand Schubert's* direction. Leitermayer had been responsible for rehearsing the work with members of the Alsergrund Church Music Association, of which he was the founder and director.

He frequently included works by Schubert in the concerts which he conducted in Vienna. On 15 February 1835, he presented a concert at the Musikverein which consisted entirely of compositions by Schubert. On the programme were the overture to the Singspiel *Claudine von Villa Bella* (D239), the chorus 'In der Tiefe wohnt das Licht' from *Rosamunde* (D797/4), the partsong 'Die Nachtigall' (D724), and the songs 'Der Hirt auf dem Felsen' (D965), 'Sehnsucht' (D636), and 'Erl-könig' (D328), the latter in an arrangement by Ferdinand Schubert for three soloists, chorus, and orchestra. At a concert on 9 May 1835 at the Theater in der Josefstadt, where Leitermayer had been appointed singing master in 1834, he presented several vocal numbers from *Fierrabras* (D796). At the same theatre, he conducted the first public performance of the Symphony No. 5 (D485) on 17 October 1841.

Leitermayer's son Alexander (1826–98), a clarinettist by training, became an excellent conductor of military bands and wrote a considerable amount of music for them.

(Brusatti, Wurzbach[1])

Leitner, Karl Gottfried (Leopold) von (b. Graz, 18 November 1800; d. Graz, 20 June 1890). Poet and historian. He studied philosophy and law at the University of Graz (1818–24) and subsequently taught at schools in Cilli [Celje, Slovenia] and Graz. In 1835 he joined the Styrian administration, in which he served as first secretary from 1837 until his retirement in 1854. He played a prominent role in the cultural life of the province, both through his official activities and as the author of various literary works and historical studies; among the latter is a biography of 'the Styrian Prince', Archduke Johann (1782–1859). In 1880 he was awarded an honorary doctorate by his old university.

His literary output includes poetry, several novellas, and a tragedy, *König Tordo*, which was staged in Graz in 1830. He also wrote the major part of the libretto for Anselm Hüttenbrenner's* opera *Lenore*. His reputation as an important literary figure is primarily founded on his ballads and romances, written in the manner of Ludwig Uhland.* In fact, he has sometimes been called 'the Austrian Uhland'. He first made his mark with a collection of poems, *Gedichte* (Graz, 1825), which was reissued in a considerably augmented edition in Hanover in 1857. He is generally considered the outstanding Styrian poet of the 'Vormärz', the period preceding the 1848 revolution.

Schubert's attention was first drawn to Leitner by Johann Schickh* who invited him to set the poem 'Drang in die Ferne' and subsequently printed Schubert's song (D770) on 25 March 1823 in the *Wiener Zeitschrift für Kunst, Literatur, Theater und Mode* which he edited. When Schubert visited Graz in the summer of 1827, Marie Pachler* gave him a copy of *Gedichte*. During the following months, Schubert set seven of those poems in 'Das Weinen' (D926), 'Der Kreuzzug' (D932), 'Der Wallensteiner Lanzknecht beim Trunk' (D931), 'Der Winterabend' (D938) 'Des Fischers Liebesglück' (D933), 'Die Sterne' (D939), and 'Vor meiner Wiege' (D927). In addition, he left sketches for three other songs: 'Fröhliches Scheiden' (D896), 'Sie in jedem Liede' (D896A), and 'Wolke und Quelle' (D896B). The songs 'Der Kreuzzug' and 'Die Sterne' were first performed by Johann Michael Vogl* at Schubert's concert on 26 March 1828.

Schubert never met Leitner, for at the time of his visit to Graz in 1827 Leitner was teaching at Cilli. In a letter on 24 December 1881 to the composer's nephew Heinrich Schubert, Leitner wrote: 'As a layman in musical matters, I am not qualified to pass judgement on the musical merit of these works, but, quite apart from the reputation of their celebrated composer, I believe that their excellence is vouched for by the fact that, whenever I hear them performed, I experience exactly the same emotions as I did when writing the words of the text.'

Settings: D770, 896, 896A–B, 926–7, 931–3, 938–9.

(Fischer[5], *ÖBL*)

Leon, Gottlieb (b. Vienna, 17 April 1757; d. Vienna, 27 September 1830). Librarian; poet. After studying law and philology, he was employed from 1782 at the court library. He retired in 1827. In addition to publishing a volume of verse (*Gedichte*, 1788), he contributed to various literary periodicals, such as *Der teutsche Merkur* and the *Göttinger Musenalmanach*, and himself edited the *Wiener Musenalmanach* (1795–6) and *Apollonion* (1807–8) together with Josef Franz von Ratschky* in Vienna.

In 1817 Schubert set one of his poems in 'Die Liebe'.

Setting: D522.

(Czeike, *ÖBL*, Wallmoden, Wurzbach[1])

Lewy, Eduard Constantin (b. St Avolte, France, 3 March 1796; d. Vienna, 3 June 1846), and **Lewy, Josef Rudolf** (b. Nancy, 2 April 1802; d. Oberlössnitz, near Dresden, 19 February 1881). Virtuoso performers on the new valve horn. Both brothers studied in Paris under the celebrated French horn player and teacher Frédéric Nicolas Duvernoy and at one time played in an orchestra at Basle; both later joined the court theatre orchestra in Vienna, Eduard in 1822 and Josef in 1826. Both were associated with Schubert in their music-making.

For Josef's concert at the Kärntnertor-Theater on 22 April 1827 Schubert composed 'Nachtgesang im Walde' (D913), a male-voice quartet accompanied by four horns, two of which were were played by Josef and Eduard. At his own concert on 26 March 1828, Schubert presented a new song, 'Auf dem Strom' (D943), in which the voice is accompanied by the piano and horn. The latter instrument was played on that occasion by Josef, and the music had presumably been written for him; the singer was Ludwig Titze,* while Schubert himself played the piano part. This song was again on the programme of Josef's concert at the Kleiner Redoutensaal on 20 April 1828, with Schubert, and probably Titze, once more participating. (On the other hand, when 'Auf dem Strom' was sung by Titze at the Schubert memorial concerts on 30 January and 5 March 1829, the horn accompaniment was replaced by a cello obbligato played by Josef Linke.* It is not certain whether the alternative cello part had been written by Schubert himself; it was printed together with the horn part in the first edition of the song in October 1829.)

Josef Lewy left Vienna in the early 1830s. After numerous appearances as a virtuoso in several European countries, he was from 1837 until his retirement in 1851 first horn player in the royal Saxon orchestra at Dresden. Eduard, unlike his brother, continued to reside in Vienna, where he taught at the Conservatory and, in 1835, became a member of the court Kapelle.

(Fürstenau, *ÖBL*)

Liebenberg de Zsittin, Karl Emanuel von (b. Vienna, 15 November 1796; d. Vienna, 22 April 1856). Wealthy industrialist and landowner. Son of Ignaz von Liebenberg (1772–1844) who came from Temesvar in Hungary [now Timisoara, Romania], settled in Vienna in 1792, and established a thriving export business in wool. In 1817, the year in which Ignaz was ennobled for his services to Austrian industry, his sons Leopold and Karl Emanuel joined the firm.

The latter was a noted amateur pianist who had studied with Johann Nepomuk Hummel.* It was perhaps in part because of this that Schubert dedicated to him his 'Wanderer' Fantasia (D760), which Cappi & Diabelli* published in February 1823, although the main reason for the choice was no doubt a purely practical one. 'I have furthermore composed a fantasia for piano for two hands which is also to appear in print and is dedicated to a certain wealthy person,' Schubert wrote to Josef von Spaun* on 7 December 1822. The fantasia, composed in November 1822, was probably first played in public by Karl Maria von Bocklet* in 1832. Liebenberg was among the subscribers to *Schwanengesang* (D957) in 1829.

Liebenberg was greatly admired for his philanthropy, of which the principal beneficiaries were Vienna's children's hospitals and nurseries.

(Wurzbach[1])

Linke [Lincke], **Josef** (b. Trachenberg, Prussian Silesia [Żmigród, Poland], 8 June 1783; d. Vienna, 26 March 1837). Cellist and composer. Following the death of his father, a musician who had been his first music teacher, he became a choirboy at the Dominican monastery at Breslau [Wrocław] and, while there, studied the cello. He subsequently played in the theatre orchestra of that city.

In 1808 he arrived in Vienna, where he was chosen by Ignaz Schuppanzigh* to become a member of Count Razumovsky's private quartet. When the quartet was disbanded after the count's palace had burnt down in 1814, he was for a time attached to the household of Beethoven's* great patroness Countess Anna Marie Erdödy; in 1815, he accompanied her to her family's estate near Agram [Zagreb]. In 1818 he was appointed first cellist at the Theater an der Wien in Vienna. He also became a member of Josef Böhm's* Quartet and, following Schuppanzigh's return from St Petersburg in 1823, again appeared with him in various performances. In 1831 he joined the court Opera orchestra.

Linke was on friendly terms with Beethoven who called him 'Mylord' and wrote for him the two cello sonatas Op. 102. He was also well acquainted with Schubert and took part in numerous performances of his music. In particular, he played in the first public performances of the following works: the Quartet in A minor (D804), on 14 March 1824; the Octet in F major (D803), on 16 April 1827; the Piano Trio in E flat major (D929) on 26 December 1827; and the first movement of a 'new string quartet' (D810 or D887) at Schubert's concert on 26 March 1828. At that concert, he also once more took the cello part in the Piano Trio D929.

On 28 January 1828, Schubert took Linke, Schuppanzigh, and Karl Maria von Bocklet* to a Schubertiad hosted by Josef von Spaun;* the trio which they performed on that occasion was probably also D929. Linke played the same trio again at the two memorial concerts in 1829, at the first (30 January) with Böhm and Bocklet, at the second (5 March) with Böhm and Franziska Sallamon. In addition, he played the cello accompaniment for the song 'Auf dem Strom' (D943) at both concerts.

(*ÖBL*, Pohl²)

Liszt, Franz [Ferenc], (b. Raiding [Doborján] in Hungary [now in the Austrian province of Burgenland], 22 October 1811; d. Bayreuth, 31 July 1886). Composer, pianist, and teacher. In the early spring of 1822 the family moved to Vienna, where Franz studied the piano with Carl Czerny and composition with Antonio Salieri.* He played in public on 1 and 9 December 1822 and 13 April 1823, each time with the greatest success. The family left Vienna shortly after the last concert. During his stay in Vienna Liszt is known to have visited Beethoven,* but the frequently told story that he also met Schubert was later firmly denied by Liszt himself: 'I never met Schubert personally,' he told his pupil August Göllerich.

It was in France, where he lived for the next twelve years, that what was to become a life-long devotion to Schubert's music began and blossomed. His interest was probably partly stimulated by the composer and violist Chrétien Urhan, a warm admirer of Schubert's compositions, with whom he was on friendly terms. During his concert career Liszt frequently accompanied performances of Schubert's Lieder, in France and elsewhere (*see* e.g. Nourrit* and Titze*), but his love of Schubert's music was to find expression above all in his numerous piano transcriptions of the songs. Altogether, he was to publish some sixty such arrangements; the earliest, of 'Die Rose' (D745), appeared in 1833. The songs he transcribed included six from *Die schöne Müllerin* (D795), twelve from *Winterreise* (D911) and all fourteen of *Schwanengesang* (D957), as well as such celebrated Lieder as 'Auf dem Wasser zu singen' (D774), 'Die Forelle' (D550), 'Erlkönig' (D328), 'Gretchen am Spinnrade' (D118), 'Sei mir gegrüsst' (D741), and 'Ständchen' (D889). The paraphrase of 'Erlkönig' became particularly celebrated. After Liszt had played it in Vienna on 18 May 1838, H. Adami wrote in the *Wiener Theaterzeitung*: 'I do not believe that "Erlkönig" has ever, however brilliantly it may have been sung, made as deep and powerful an impression on the listener as in this arrangement, where the vocal line and the accompaniment emerge as a unified whole from an artist's inspired soul.' When he played the paraphrase in Leipzig in 1840, 'half the public stood up on their seats', Ferdinand Hiller recalled more than thirty years later. The 'Erlkönig' transcription also became a favourite with other virtuosos. The American pianist Amy Fay was thrilled by Anton Rubinstein's 'glorious' performance of it: 'Where the little child is so frightened, his hands flew all over the piano, and absolutely made it shriek with terror. It was enough to freeze you to hear it.'

In addition to these paraphrases for the piano, Liszt also arranged 'Erlkönig', 'Gretchen am Spinnrade', and a few other songs for voice and orchestra for the soprano Emilie Genast. He furthermore orchestrated some of Schubert's marches, wrote three *Mélodies hongroises* based on the *Divertissement à la hongroise* (D818), and made two arrangements of the 'Wanderer' Fantasia (D760), one for piano and orchestra, the other for two pianos.

In 1870 he published an edition of Schubert's piano sonatas, which, according to A. Walker, is 'a model of correct musicological practice'. While he was engaged on this project he wrote to the pianist and teacher Sigmund Lebert on 2 December 1868: 'Our pianists scarcely realize what a glorious treasure they can find in Schubert's piano compositions ... As a bird lives in the air, so he lived in music, and in so doing he sang melodies fit for angels.'

His devotion to Schubert also led Liszt to give the first performance of the opera *Alfonso und Estrella* (D732). He conceived the idea shortly after settling in February 1848 at Weimar where he had been director of music since 1842. He was doubtless encouraged in that project by the opera's librettist, Schubert's old friend Franz von Schober,* who had been on close terms with Liszt for many years and was then himself living at Weimar. However, once Liszt had received the score and begun piano rehearsals, he became convinced that, as he informed Breitkopf & Härtel* on 24 February 1850, 'Schubert's delicate and interesting music is virtually crushed by the weight of the text'. He intended to procure a fresh libretto and envisaged a production at the Opéra-Comique in Paris, using a French text. In the end, though, the work was produced at Weimar on 24 June 1854, essentially with Schober's text, but in a truncated form. In a brief study of the opera written shortly after that one and only Weimar performance and which appeared in the *Neue Zeitschrift für Musik* on 1 September, Liszt, while praising the beauty of much of the music, pointed out what he regarded as dramatic shortcomings in the work, and expressed the view that Schubert's genius was not well suited to the operatic genre.

Finally, Liszt at one time contemplated writing Schubert's life. In a letter dated 3 May 1851 he asked Princess Carolyne Sayn-Wittgenstein to draw up a questionnaire concerning essential biographical details, which he proposed to send to his friend Simon Löwy in Vienna. Some time later, Anselm Hüttenbrenner* was asked to write down his recollections of Schubert for Liszt, which he did, in a rather disjointed fashion, in 1854. He duly dispatched them to Weimar, but, as he informed Ferdinand Luib* in 1858, never received any acknowledgement. Presumably Liszt had quickly lost interest in the project.

(Liszt[1,2,4], Raabe, Searle, Waidelich[1,2], Walker[1,2])

Löwenthal, Max, Baron [pseud. Leo Walthen] (b. Vienna, 7 April 1799; d. Vienna, 12 July 1872). Civil servant; writer. After studying law in Vienna he travelled widely in Europe; in 1823 he entered government service. He joined the postal section in 1835 and was later to play an important part in the development of the Austrian postal and telegraph system, and in negotiations leading to international agreements. When a separate department for postal and telegraphic services was set up at the ministry for trade and national economy in 1866, he was appointed its director general. He retired the following year. He was ennobled in 1863 and created a baron in 1868.

He published some poetry and a number of plays (*Anna Lovell, Die beiden Schauspieler, Die Caledonier, Vater und Richter*), as well as an account of his travels, *Skizzen aus dem Tagebuch einer Reise durch Frankreich, Grossbritannien und Deutschland* (2 vols., 1825).

Löwenthal was a fellow pupil of Schubert at the Stadtkonvikt in 1812–13. He is believed to have remained in contact with the composer and may well have met him in later years at the house of Franz Joachim von Kleyle, an estate manager to Archduke Karl, who lived at Penzing, near Vienna [14 Beckmanngasse]. Schubert is known to have visited the family on several occasions in 1827. In 1829 Löwenthal married one of the daughters, Sophie (1810–89). Her sister Rosalie became the wife of Baron Schönstein.*

O. E. Deutsch* believed that Schubert may have been the subject of Löwenthal's poem 'Nemo profeta in patria' which appeared in a collection of his verse (*Gedichte*) in 1871.

(*ÖBL*)

Lubi, Michael (1757–*c.*1808). Poet. He was probably born at Tüffer, in Styria. He qualified as a lawyer at Graz, and there, in 1804, he published a volume of poetry, *Gedichte*. One of his poems was set by Schubert, in late 1814, in 'Ammenlied'.

Setting: D122.

Luib, Ferdinand (b. 1811). Civil servant; writer on music and editor. When, in July 1847, he succeeded August Schmidt as editor of the *Allgemeine Wiener Musikzeitung* (founded by Schmidt in 1841), he was, according to E. Hanslick's *Geschichte des Concertwesens in Wien*, 'a man totally unknown in the world of music'. This can scarcely be true, however, since he had been writing on musical events in *Der Wanderer*. His tenure as editor was a brief one, for the *Musikzeitung* ceased publication the following year. In 1856 he published a short book on the composer and piano manufacturer Karl Andreas Stein, and in 1858 an article 'Urteile und Meinungen berühmter Tonkünstler über Kunstgenossen und Leistungen derselben' in the *Neue Berliner Musikzeitung*.

In his concert reviews in *Der Wanderer* he had shown himself to be a great admirer of Schubert's music. Thus, in reporting a recital given by Liszt* in Vienna on 5 March 1846, he referred to the 'Wanderer' Fantasia (D760) as 'this magnificent musical painting' by the 'immortal composer'. However, he is best known to Schubertians for a book he never published. In 1857–8, when he was a minor official in the ministry of trade, he was busy gathering material for a biography of Schubert, and, in that connection, sent out letters and questionnaires to a large number of persons who had known him, or to their surviving relatives. Luib seems to have pursued this project even after the publication in 1861 of Kreissle's* *Aus Schuberts Leben*, for in 1862 the *Deutsche Musikzeitung* (Vienna) reported that he had completed his book. Yet shortly afterwards, the same journal stated that he had handed over to Kreissle all the material he had accumulated on Schubert. Curiously, Kreissle made no more than two glancing references to Luib in his comprehensive biography *Franz Schubert* (1865), even though he appears to have used much of Luib's documentation.

In *Schubert: Erinnerungen*, O. E. Deutsch* printed letters from almost forty persons who had replied to Luib's enquiries. Among the most interesting answers were those of Anton Holzapfel,* Anselm Hüttenbrenner,* Josef Hüttenbrenner,* Josef Kenner,* Baron Schönstein*, Leopold von Sonnleithner,* Albert Stadler,* Anton Steinbüchel von Rheinwall (a close friend of Johann Michael Vogl*), and Ferdinand Traweger's* son Eduard. Most of the letters received by Luib are preserved in the Stadtbibliothek in Vienna.

(Brusatti, Hanslick, *Schubert: Erinnerungen*)

Luther, Martin (b. Eisleben, 10 November 1483; d. Eisleben, 18 February 1546). Religious reformer. In 1818 Schubert set for single voice John* 6: 55–8, in Luther's German translation.

Setting: D607.

Lutz [Luz], **(Maria) Johanna (Evangelista Augustina Stephana Theodora)** (b. Vienna, 26 December 1803; d. Vienna, 1 March 1883). Daughter of Johann Adam Lutz (b. 1757), a senior official at the court treasury, and his wife Maria Regina, née Putz. Her aunt Anna Putz having married Ignaz von Sonnleithner,* Johanna was a cousin of Leopold von Sonnleithner.*

Her correspondence with her fiancé Leopold Kupelwieser* during the latter's travels in Italy (1823–5) contains much interesting information about the activities of Schubert and his friends and frequently offers perceptive observations on their characters. Thus she wrote on 15 November 1824, following Schubert's return from Zseliz: 'Schubert is back in Vienna. He is said to be very well and is often in [Moritz von] Schwind's* company. This is fine, for while they may not do each other much good, they do each other no harm, and that is already quite important in Schwind's case, since he is so easily influenced by those around him. He badly needs a male friend.' Above all, her letters reflect a deep affection for Schubert and great admiration for his music. 'Towards noon, when I am alone, I usually play some of Schubert's songs,' she wrote on 9 December 1823. 'They are so very beautiful. 'Der Schatzgräber' [i.e. 'Schatzgräbers Begehr' (D761)] and 'Lob der Tränen' (D711) are tremendously beautiful ... Schubert is now much better and already appears inclined to give up his strict regimen before long. If only he doesn't ruin his health.'

Johanna married Kupelwieser on 17 September 1826. At a ball which, according to M. L. Kupelwieser de Brioni, the great-granddaughter of the bridegroom, was given by Johanna's parents on the evening before the wedding, Schubert played dance music for the guests (*see also* Kupelwieser*). Johanna's sister Regina married the painter and scenic designer Hermann Neefe, the son of Beethoven's* teacher Christian Gottlob Neefe. He had moved from Bonn to Vienna by 1804 and worked at the Leopoldstädter-Theater and, from 1814, at the Theater an der Wien. He was partly responsible for Schubert being invited to write music for the melodrama *Die Zauberharfe* (D644) which was produced at the latter theatre on 19 August 1820 and for which Neefe designed the décor.

(Kupelwieser, Schöny')

MacDonald, Andrew [real name: Donald, Andrew; ps. Matthew Bramble] (b. Leith, *c*.1755; d. London, 22 August 1790). Dramatist and poet. He studied at Edinburgh University and in 1775 received deacon's orders in the Scottish episcopalian church, whereupon he adopted the name 'MacDonald'. He eventually resigned from his ecclesiastical duties and thereafter made his living as a writer in Edinburgh and later in London. His most successful work was the tragedy *Vimonda* which was produced at the Haymarket Theatre, London, in 1787. His publications include *Velina, a Poetical Fragment* (1782), and a novel, *The Independent* (1783). He died in poverty. A collection of his writings appeared in 1791 under the title *Miscellaneous Works*.

In his novel *A Legend of Montrose* (1819) Sir Walter Scott* incorporated a poem ('Wert thou, like me, in life's low vale ...') from MacDonald's opera libretto *Love and Loyalty*; the libretto had apparently never been set. Scott states that the poem (which is sung in chapter 21 of the novel by the principal female character, Annot Lyle) had been translated by MacDonald from the Gaelic.

In 1825 Schubert set the poem in his 'Lied der Anne Lyle'. According to O. E. Deutsch,* the German version he used was the work of Sophie May [pseud. of Sophie Mayer*]; but no translation of the novel by this writer has yet been found.

Setting: D830.

(Bayne)

Macpherson, James (b. Ruthven, near Kingussie, Scotland, 27 October 1736; d. Inverness-shire, 17 February 1796). Historian; 'translator' of the Ossianic poems. He studied at the universities of Aberdeen and Edinburgh. In 1860 he published *Fragments of Ancient Poetry collected in the Highlands of Scotland, and translated from the Gaelic or Erse Language*, which he followed with *Fingal, an Ancient Epic Poem* in 1762 and *Temora* in 1763, both allegedly translations from the Gaelic of works by a third-century poet named Ossian; a collected edition, *The Works of Ossian*, appeared in 1765. Of his historical writings, the most important was *The Secret History of Great Britain from the Restoration to the Accession of the House of Hanover* (1775). Macpherson served as secretary to Governor Johnstone at Pensacola, Florida (1764–6), and was later MP for Camelford (1780–6). He died at his estate, Belville, in Inverness-shire.

The Ossianic poems played a major part in the emergence of the Romantic movement in European literature, especially in Germany where Herder* and the young Goethe* were among their translators and most enthusiastic admirers. No fewer than ten German versions were published within the space of a few years, and among the composers inspired by the material were Karl Ditters von Dittersdorf, Carl Loewe, Johann Friedrich Reichardt, Schubert, Zumsteeg,* and, later, Brahms.* In France, Jean-François Le Sueur wrote the opera *Ossian, ou Les Bardes* (?1804). Although the authenticity of the poems was soon challenged, notably by Samuel Johnson, Macpherson managed to ward off exposure while he was alive. It was only after his death that a specially appointed committee reached the formal conclusion that he had in fact edited traditional Gaelic poems, into which he had interpolated passages of his own invention.

Anton Holzapfel* explained in a letter to Ferdinand Luib* in 1858 that he had been responsible for awakening Schubert's interest in the Ossianic poems by handing him a—as he later learned, 'wretched'—translation. This was presumably the version published by Baron Harold,* since that was the one used by Schubert. Between 1815 and early 1817 he set ten of Macpherson's Ossianic poems in 'Bardengesang' (D147), 'Cronnan' (D282), 'Das Mädchen von Inistore' (D281), 'Der Tod Oskars' (D375), 'Die Nacht' (D534), 'Kolmas Klage' (D217), 'Lodas Gespenst'

(D150), 'Lorma' (D327, 376), 'Ossians Lied nach dem Falle Nathos' (D278), and 'Shilric und Vinvela' (D293). Except for the first-named (a trio), these compositions were all written for single voice. None was published in Schubert's lifetime.

Settings: D147, 150, 217, 278, 281–2, 293, 327, 375–6, 534.

(*EB*, Kinsey)

Mailáth [Majláth] **von Székhely, János** [Johann], Count (b. Pest [Budapest], 5 October 1786; d. Lake Starnberg, Bavaria, 3 January 1855). Historian, poet, editor, and translator; son of Count József [Josef] Mailáth von Székhely (1737–1810) who held various important posts in the Austrian administration.

After studying political science, philosophy, and law at Erlau [Eger] and Raab [Gyor], Count Johann Mailáth entered government service in Hungary, but a serious eye malady forced him to retire after a few years. He moved to Vienna, where the disease was cured after prolonged treatment. Thereafter, Mailáth devoted himself entirely to literary activities. He published comprehensive histories of Hungary and Austria, prepared German translations of Hungarian folk poetry and of contemporary Hungarian literature, produced modern German versions of old German poetry, wrote the biography of the Viennese actress Sophie Müller,* and published a volume of his own verse (*Gedichte*, Vienna, 1824). In addition, he edited *Iris*, an influential literary almanach in German, which appeared at Pest (1840–8). Increasing financial difficulties led him to move to Munich in 1848, and eventually, in 1855, to commit suicide. His daughter Henriette chose to die with him.

Schubert was acquainted with Mailáth, but very little information is available concerning their contacts. In 1821 Schubert set Mailáth's poem 'Der Blumen Schmerz' (D731). The song was performed by Josef Barth* at Ignaz von Sonnleithner's* on 18 April 1822, and by Karl Maria Gross at an 'evening entertainment' of the Gesellschaft der Musikfreunde on 3 February 1825. After Schubert's death, a sketch by Mailáth for a libretto with the incomplete title *Die Salzbergwerke von . . .* was found among his papers.

Setting: D731.

(Fischer[6], *ÖBL*, Wurzbach[1])

Mandyczewski, Eusebius (b. Czernowitz [Chernovtsy, Ukraine], 18 August 1857; d. Sulz, Lower Austria, 13 July 1929). Musicologist, composer, and teacher. The son of a Greek Orthodox priest of Ukrainian origin and of a Romanian mother, he was educated at local German schools. In 1875 he enrolled at the University of Vienna, where he studied the history of music with Eduard Hanslick and musical theory with Gustav Nottebohm.* Later he became a close friend of Brahms* and of Nikolaus Dumba.* In 1887 he succeeded Carl Ferdinand Pohl as archivist of the Gesellschaft der Musikfreunde; he also conducted some of the society's concerts, and in 1896 he was appointed professor of music at the Conservatory. His compositions are predominantly religious in nature; they include twelve settings of the Mass. In 1903 he married the singer Albine von Vest (1860–1925).

Mandyczewski is now best remembered for his work on the complete editions of Beethoven,* Brahms, Haydn, and Schubert. His contribution to the Schubert *Gesamtausgabe* published by Breitkopf & Härtel* in 1884–97 was a particularly distinguished one. In the first place, he was solely responsible for the songs, which was in itself a tremendously exacting task entailing the collection and correlation of countless manuscripts (he printed the songs in chronological order, with all variants). In addition, he edited the Masses and smaller works of church music, the compositions for male chorus, the octets, the nonet, the string trio, and the string quintet. The supplementary volume, which consisted mostly of fragments, was also assigned to him. He furthermore collaborated in the editions of the string quartets, the works for women's and mixed chorus, and smaller works for three or two voices. Finally, he wrote many of the reports on the different volumes. In recognition of this extraordinary achievement he was awarded an honorary doctorate by the University of Leipzig in 1897.

Mandyczewski was, furthermore, involved in the preparation of various events connected with Schubert. Thus he organized the Schubert exhibition in Vienna in 1922 and also the International Schubert Congress which was held there from 25 to 29 November 1928. He seems to have been universally admired, as much for his personal qualities as for his exceptional scholarship. The composer and musicologist Hans Gál, who had been one of his students, wrote of him: 'He was for me more than my father: a teacher, a friend, and a model of the very best to be found among human beings; the only man I ever met who was totally free of the human frailties of ambition, selfishness, greed, or malevolence.'

(Brown[6], Cysarz, Deutsch[9])

Matiegka [Matejka], **Wenzel** [Václav] **Thomas** (baptized Chotzen [Choceň, Czech Republic], 6 July 1773; d. Vienna, 19 January 1830). Composer, pianist, and guitarist. He studied law at the University of Prague and music with Abbé Josef Gelinek. Subsequently he practised law, and he continued in that profession for some time after moving to Vienna in *c*.1800. But he soon established himself there as a virtuoso performer on the piano and guitar, and as a competent teacher of both instruments. His interest focused increasingly on the guitar, and his published compositions were written either for the solo guitar or for the guitar in combination with other instruments. In 1817 he was appointed choirmaster at St Leopold's Church and in 1821 also at St Josef's Church, both in the Leopoldstadt suburb.

In 1807 Artaria & Co.* published his Notturno for flute, viola, and guitar in G major, Op. 21. It was dedicated to Count Johann Karl Esterházy,* who was later to engage Schubert as music teacher for his daughters. In February 1814 Schubert turned the Notturno into a quartet by adding a cello part and, at the same time, thoroughly rearranged the music written for the other instruments; in addition, he introduced some new material. The surviving autograph of the quartet (D.Anh.II,2) is incomplete.

(Heck, Hoorickx[1], *ÖBL*)

Matthisson, Friedrich von (b. Hohendodeleben, near Magdeburg, 23 January 1761; d. Wörlitz, near Dessau, 12 March 1831). Poet; son of a Protestant clergyman. He studied theology and philosophy at Halle (1778–81), after which he taught at a school at Dessau (1781–3); later he earned his living as a private tutor. From 1795 until 1811 he was attached to the household of Princess Luise von Anhalt-Dessau, and thereafter entered the service of King Friedrich I of Württemberg. He was ennobled in 1809, was retained after Friedrich's death in 1816 by his successor Wilhelm I, and finally relinquished his duties at the Württemberg court in 1828.

He travelled extensively during his life, in and outside Germany, and these journeys inspired a considerable number of descriptive and anecdotal poems. His first volume of verse appeared in 1781 under the title *Lieder*, which he changed to *Gedichte* for a further edition in 1787; other editions followed. Matthisson's *Gesammelte Schriften* were published in eight volumes in Zurich in 1825–9, followed by the posthumous *Literarischer Nachlass* (4 vols., Berlin, 1832).

His poetry, elegant and tinged with a certain melancholy, was highly popular in his day, and attracted not only numerous readers, but also several composers, including Johann Friedrich Reichardt, Zumsteeg,* and Beethoven* ('Adelaide', 'Andenken', 'Opferlied'). Between c.1812 and 1823 Schubert set some thirty poems by Matthisson, most of them during the years 1814–16; the majority were written for single voice. In several cases he made more than one setting of a poem; of 'Der Geistertanz', he even made four (D15, 15A, 116, 494), the last one for a quintet of two tenors and three basses. Among Schubert's better known Matthisson songs are 'An Laura, als sie Klopstocks "Auferstehungslied" sang' (D115), 'Der Abend' (D108), 'Die Betende' (D102), 'Lebenslied' (D508), 'Lied aus der Ferne' (D107), 'Stimme der Liebe' (D187, 418), and 'Totenkranz für ein Kind' (D275).

Of all the Matthisson settings, only the quartets 'Geist der Liebe' (D747), 'Jünglingswonne' (D983), and 'Naturgenuss' (D422) were published in Schubert's lifetime. 'Geist der Liebe' was first performed in public at a concert of the Gesellschaft der Musikfreunde on 3 March 1822, and subsequently appeared on the programmes of several further concerts in Vienna that year (at the Landhaus, on 15 April 1822, it was so warmly received that it had to be repeated).

Settings: D15, 15A, 50, 95, 97–102, 107–9, 114–16, 186–8, 275, 357, 413–15, 537, 418–19, 422–4, ?425, 428, 494, 507–8, 579A–B, 747, 983, perhaps also D.Anh.I, 20–3.

(Heers, Joost[2], Wodtke[2])

May, Sophie: *see* Mayer.*

Mayer, Sophie Friederike Elisabeth [pseud. Sophie May] (b. Berlin, 4 November 1778; d. Berlin, 15 June/July 1827). Writer and painter; daughter of the physician Johann Andreas Mayer. According to O. E. Deutsch,* she was the author of the German text set by Schubert in 'Lied der Anne Lyle' (*see* under D830 in *Schubert: Thematisches Verzeichnis*). However, no translation by her of Sir Walter Scott's* novel *A Legend of Montrose*, in which the poem appears, has yet come to light. (On the poem, *see also* MacDonald.*)

Setting: D830.
(Friedrichs)

Mayerhofer von Grünbühel [Grünbühl], **Ferdinand (Franz Xaver Johann)** (b. Vienna, 18 [?16] May 1798; d. Klagenfurt, 26 March 1869). Son of Josef Mayerhofer von Grünbühel, a civil servant, and his wife Anna, née von Mitis. In 1808–9 he was a fellow pupil of Schubert at the Akademisches Gymnasium, and thereafter attended secondary schools at Wiener Neustadt, Lower Austria, and Graz. In 1816 he joined the navy, took part in an expedition to Brazil (1817–18), and was later employed in taking trigonometric, topographic, and hydrographic measurements along the shores of the Adriatic Sea (1819). Following several other postings, he became an instructor in mathematics at the military academy at Wiener Neustadt (1824–5). In 1828 he was stationed at Josefstadt [Josefov, Czech Republic], and later at Cracow (1832–40). He became district commander of Temesvar [Timisoara, Romania] in 1849 and subsequently served as governor of Voivodina and the Banat until 1851. He was created a baron in 1850 and retired from active service in 1856 with the rank of Lieutenant-Field Marshal.

It was probably during a leave spent in Vienna in 1820 that he came into contact with Schubert's circle, in which, because of his connection with the navy, he was given the nickname 'Sindbad'. He became a particularly intimate friend of Eduard von Bauernfeld* and collaborated with him in the translation of *Antony and Cleopatra* for the Vienna Shakespeare edition (1824–6), to which he also, on his own, contributed a German version of *Love's Labour's Lost*. Though frequently stationed outside Vienna, he remained in contact with several members of the group, mainly through Bauernfeld, but he also corresponded with Franz von Schober* and Moritz von Schwind,* and probably with others. He stayed, moreover, in Vienna at different times during the 1820s. Thus he was there in January–February 1826, and again from late April to mid-July 1828 (when he lodged with Bauernfeld). And while living at Wiener Neustadt in 1824–5, he no doubt paid periodic visits to the capital.

His engagement to Jeannette von Mitis was broken off in 1829. On 11 February 1832 he married Anna Hönig,* to whom Moritz von Schwind had paid court in vain. Schwind none the less maintained a friendly relationship with the couple and included both in his group portrait of 1868, *A Schubert Evening at Josef von Spaun's*.* Unlike Schwind, Mayerhofer was a fervent Catholic and thus able to live in religious harmony with the pious Anna; after his retirement, he became president of the Marian congregation in Vienna. They later moved to Klagenfurt, where Mayerhofer died in 1869 and his wife in 1888. They had two children: Maria (1835–1902) and Emil (1841–78), who became an army officer. Maria was mainly responsible for the foundation in 1890 of the Convent of the Sisters of the Good Shepherd at Harbach Castle, on the outskirts of Klagenfurt. Attached to the convent was a home for disadvantaged girls. In 1897, her parents' and her brother's remains were transferred from the municipal cemetery to the convent's burial ground, where she herself was also later interred.

In 1826 Schubert used the Bauernfeld-Mayerhofer translation of *Antony and Cleopatra* in 'Trinklied: Bacchus, feister Fürst des Weins'.

Setting: D888.

(Litschauer[2], Porhansl[7], Wurzbach[1])

Mayrhofer, Johann (Baptist) (b. Steyr, Upper Austria, 3 November 1787; d. Vienna, 5 February 1836). Civil servant; poet. Originally intended for the priesthood, he studied theology at St Florian's Monastery, near Linz (1806–10), but then enrolled as a law student at the University of Vienna. From 1815 until his death he was employed in the book censor's office, where, by all accounts, he performed his duties conscientiously, though with little enjoyment, since they were not in accord with his liberal political views. A volume of his poetry, *Gedichte*, was published in 1824; a further collection of his poems was printed in 1843. (*See also* Ottenwalt.*)

It was in 1814 that Josef von Spaun* (who, in 1858, was to describe Mayrhofer as his 'oldest friend') introduced him to Schubert. At Spaun's suggestion, Schubert had previously set Mayrhofer's poem 'Am See' (D124). Although Mayrhofer was over nine years older than Schubert, they were soon on very friendly terms. According to Spaun, Mayrhofer was not very handsome, but had an intelligent and attractive face. He was highly cultured, and particularly interested in classical literature. He was also a great music lover, liked to sing, and played the guitar; his favourite composers were Gluck and Mozart, both of whom Schubert revered. Though by no means averse to jokes, he possessed, on the whole, a gloomy character and contemplated the world increasingly from a melancholy, disillusioned, and misogynist viewpoint. It was probably no accident that after one of his visits to Mayerhofer Schubert should have expressed some decidedly pessimistic thoughts in his diary on life in general and marriage in particular (8 September 1816). Mayrhofer's mental attitude almost certainly exercised a considerable influence on Schubert's own ideas. Above all, though, Mayrhofer's poems struck a deep chord in his musical imagination. They inspired a larger number of settings than those of any other writer, with the exception of Goethe* and Schiller.* Most of these compositions date from the years 1816–17.

In the autumn of 1818, on his return from Zseliz, Schubert went to share lodgings with Mayrhofer [2 Wipplingerstrasse], and they lived together until the end of 1820.

During that period, they continued their artistic collaboration: 'I wrote poems, he composed what I had written,' Mayrhofer recalled in an obituary ('Erinnerungen an Franz Schubert') which he published in *Neues Archiv für Geschichte, Staatenkunde, Literatur und Kunst* (Vienna) on 23 February 1829.

In 1821 Schubert moved to another address in the same street [21 Wipplingerstrasse], but their friendship must have endured, at any rate for a time, since Schubert set further poems by Mayrhofer in 1822 and 1824, and in June 1823 dedicated to him his Op. 21, which consisted of the songs 'Auf der Donau' (D553), 'Der Schiffer' (D536), and 'Wie Ulfru fischt' (D525), all three composed to poems by Mayrhofer. On 2 December 1823 Mayrhofer was present at a Schubertiad at the Bruchmanns'.*

It has been suggested that Schubert's absence from the list of subscribers to Mayrhofer's *Gedichte* in 1824 may have reflected a certain coolness between them. Mayrhofer himself was to write in the above-mentioned obituary that 'the course of events, social attachments, illness, and changes in our attitudes to life kept us apart in later years'. For some time, he was rarely seen at gatherings of Schubert's circle, but his absences could also have been due in part to his real or imagined illnesses. He had, indeed, the reputation of being a hypochondriac; already in 1818 Schubert had written to him, from Zseliz: 'Stop feeling so sickly or, at least, stop dabbling in medicines.' Whatever the nature of their personal relations may have been during Schubert's final years, Mayrhofer's high opinion of Schubert's music remained undiminished. In June 1826, Anton von Spaun wrote to his wife from Karlsbad [Karlovy Vary, Czech Republic] that Mayrhofer, who was also staying there, 'sang many Schubert songs'; and he attended Josef von Spaun's Schubertiad on 15 December of that year. In his obituary of Schubert he expressed admiration for the man as well as the composer.

According to Adam Haller, an intimate friend of Mayrhofer during the period 1825–31, Schubert's death had a traumatic effect on his mental health, intensifying his melancholia and his dissatisfaction with the human condition. In 1831 he attempted suicide by jumping into the Danube, but was saved. He succeeded at his second attempt, in 1836, when he threw himself from a high window in the censorship office and died forty hours later.

Altogether, Schubert wrote, between 1814 and 1824, close to 50 songs and one vocal quartet ('Gondelfahrer', D809) to poems by Mayrhofer. Many of them treat classical subjects, e.g. 'Antigone und Oedip' (D542), 'Der entsühnte Orest' (D699), 'Der zürnenden Diana' (D707), 'Iphigenia' (D573), and 'Philoktet' (D540). Those with non-classical subjects include 'Der Alpenjäger' (D524), 'Der Schiffer' (D536), 'Erlafsee' (D586), 'Nachtstück' (D672), 'Nachtviolen' (D752), and 'Wie Ulfru fischt' (D525). 'Erlafsee' has the distinction of having been the first of Schubert's songs to appear in print. It was published in *Mahlerisches Taschenbuch für Freunde interessanter Gegenden, Natur- und Kunst-Merkwürdigkeiten der Österreichischen Monarchie*, in Vienna, in early 1818. (By then Schubert had composed almost 350 songs.)

Lastly, Mayrhofer provided the librettos (now lost) of Schubert's Singspiels *Die Freunde von Salamanka* (D326), composed in 1815, and *Adrast* (D137), which was probably written between 1817 and 1819 and survives only in incomplete form.

Settings: D124, 137, 297–8, 326, 360, 450, 473, 475–7, 490–2, 495, 516, 524–7, 536, 539–42, 548, 553–4, 561, 573, 585–6, 620, 654, 669–72, 682, 699, 700, 707, 752–4, 805–9.

(Litschauer¹, *ÖBL*, Porhansl¹, Wurzbach¹)

Mayssen, Josef (1790–1860). Schoolmaster and choirmaster in the Vienna suburb of Hernals. He was friendly with Schubert and, apparently, still more so with his brother Ferdinand.* On 16 August 1821, in Mayssen's rooms (or in his garden house), Schubert composed a *Tantum ergo* which he reportedly dedicated to Mayssen. This composition (D730) was not published until 1926.

In his letter of 3 July 1824 to Schubert, who was then staying at Zseliz, Ferdinand mentioned that he was arranging performances of Schubert's quartets at home, with himself playing first violin, their brother Ignaz second violin, Mayssen viola, and their brother-in-law Matthias Schneider cello. Mayssen may have been one of the two friends who accompanied Schubert and Ferdinand in early October 1828 on their excursion to Eisenstadt, where they visited Haydn's tomb; their other companion was probably Johann Rieder. (Regarding the latter, *see* Wilhelm August Rieder.*)

(Hilmar/Brusatti)

Mendelssohn(-Bartholdy), (Jakob Ludwig) Felix (b. Hamburg, 3 February 1809; d. Leipzig, 4 November 1847). Composer, pianist, and conductor. He is held in high regard by Schubertians for having given the first performance of the 'Great' C major Symphony (D944).

After Schumann* had awakened the interest of Breitkopf & Härtel* in the Schubert manuscripts which he had discovered in Vienna on New Year's Day 1839, Ferdinand Schubert* sent the scores of the two symphonies in C major (D589 and D944) to the Leipzig publishers. They passed them on to Mendelssohn, who had been conductor of the Gewandhaus Orchestra since 1835. Mendelssohn chose D944 over D589, because, as he explained to Ferdinand shortly after conducting the work at the Gewandhaus on 21 March 1839, it 'seemed to me quite exceptionally excellent, and I thought that it would appeal to our public more than the other one'. He added that it had been received with resounding applause, each separate movement being enthusiastically acclaimed, 'and, even more significantly, all the musicians in the orchestra were moved and delighted by the splendid work'. The *Leipziger allgemeine Musikzeitung* reported that the performance was 'as masterly as if the work had already been performed many times'. The success led to the publication of the instrumental parts of the symphony by Breitkopf & Härtel in 1840 (they did not issue the full score until 1849). The symphony was played again by the Gewandhaus Orchestra on 12 December 1839 and 26 October 1840. (An attempt to arrange a performance in Vienna on 15 December 1839 was only partially successful, reportedly because of the orchestra's refusal to give adequate time to rehearsals. As a result, only the first two movements were played. The complete symphony was not performed in Vienna until 1 December 1850, under Josef Hellmesberger.*)

Eager to secure a wider audience for the symphony, Mendelssohn, with the consent of Breitkopf & Härtel, sent the music on 23 April 1839 to the Philharmonic Society in London, with which he had enjoyed a close association for the past ten years. Describing the work as 'a very extraordinary composition, which has created an uncommon sensation amongst the musicians here', he nevertheless sounded a note of caution: 'I should strongly recommend you *not to repeat the first part* of the last movement, perhaps also not the first and the second part of the Scherzo.' This could be an indication of how he had himself dealt with the 'heavenly length' of the symphony, or he may simply be offering advice based on his experience of having played all the repeats. There is, however, no firm evidence to support the frequently made statement that the symphony had been performed by Mendelssohn in a 'considerably cut' version.

His hope of an immediate London performance was not fulfilled, and when he himself tried to rehearse the symphony with the Philharmonic in 1844, the musicians laughed so much at the repeated triplets in the last movement that he withdrew the work in disgust. He had to content himself with conducting the overture to *Fierrabras* (D796) at a concert on 10 June 1844, but that event cannot have brought him much joy either, for J. W. Davison, the editor of the *Musical Examiner* and the leading London critic of the day, dismissed the piece as 'literally beneath criticism'. But if Mendelssohn's efforts on Schubert's behalf fell on deaf ears in England, they were highly appreciated by Ferdinand Schubert, who, to Mendelssohn's delight, presented him in March 1845 with his brother's sketches for the Symphony in E major (D729). They are now in the possession of the Royal College of Music in London.

(Brown[4], Konold, Krause, Werner[2])

Mendelssohn, Moses (b. Dessau, 6 September 1729; d. Berlin, 4 January 1786). Jewish philosopher, champion of Jewish emancipation, and an influential figure in the German Enlightenment. In 1743 he moved to Berlin, where, in 1750, he became tutor to the children of the wealthy silk-merchant Isaak Bernhard. The latter appointed him his bookkeeper in 1754, and from 1761 left him virtually in charge of the business. After Bernhard's death in 1768, Mendelssohn ran the firm very successfully with the widow.

His life was enriched by a number of close friendships, notably with the mathematician and philosopher Thomas Abbt, with the Berlin bookseller and writer Friedrich Nicolai, and with Gotthold Ephraim Lessing (who may have had him in mind when writing *Nathan der Weise*). A man of very great erudition, he was able to extend his reading to several languages; for, in addition to fluency in Hebrew, Yiddish, and German, he possessed a competent knowledge of Greek, Latin, French, and English. His wide interests, which are reflected in his writings, encompassed aesthetics, literary criticism, Judaism, political theory, and metaphysics. His most important works are *Brief über die Empfindungen* (1755), *Abhandlungen über die Evidenz in den metaphysischen Wissenschaften* (1764), and *Phädon, oder Über die Unsterblichkeit der Seele* (1767). In 1783 he published a German translation of the psalms.

It was from this German version of the psalter that Schubert took the words for his setting of Psalm 13 (D663) in 1819, and he again resorted to it when setting Psalm 23 (D706) in 1820. Mendelssohn's name is furthermore associated with the setting of Psalm 92 (D953) which Schubert made in 1828 for Salomon Sulzer,* cantor at the Vienna synagogue. This time Schubert used the original Hebrew text, and it was in this form that the composition first appeared in Vienna in 1839[?]; but in 1870 it was republished by J. P. Gotthard* with Mendelssohn's German text.

Mendelssohn was married in 1762 to Fromet Gugenheim (1737–1812) who bore him three sons and three daughters. His son Abraham was the father of the composer Felix Mendelssohn(-Bartholdy).*

Settings: D663, 706.
(Hinske, Kupferberg, *ÖBL*)

Metastasio [real name: Trapassi, Antonio Domenico Bonaventura] (b. Rome, 3 January 1698; d. Vienna, 12 April 1782). Poet and librettist. His librettos were set more than 800 times in the eighteenth and early nineteenth centuries.

Schubert repeatedly turned to Metastasio for the text of his compositions. In his exercises for Antonio Salieri* in 1812–13 he used passages from the librettos for *Alcide al bivio* (D76), *Betulia liberata* (D34), *Demofoonte* (D42), *Gli orti esperidi* (D78), *Isacco figura del Redentore* (D17, 33), and *La clemenza di Tito* (D35). In December 1816 he set an aria from *Artaserse* (in the German translation by Heinrich von Collin*) in 'Leiden der Trennung' (D509), and also an aria from *Didone abbandonata*, 'Vedi quanto adoro' (D510). The text of two of the four 'Canzonen' (D688) which he composed in January 1820 ('Da quel sembiante appresi' and 'Mio ben ricordati') were taken from Metastasio's librettos *L'eroe cinese* and *Alessandro nell'Indie* respectively. The words of the two operatic numbers 'Durch der Ostsee wilde Wogen' and 'Ja, sie war's, der Frauen Krone' (D791/1–2), which he began to sketch out in May 1823, probably came from Ignaz Franz von Mosel's* (lost) libretto *Rüdiger*, itself modelled on Metastasio's *Ruggiero, ovvero L'eroica gratitudine*.

Finally, the first two of the 'Drei Gesänge' (D902), composed in 1827, were also settings of arias from Metastasio librettos: 'L'incanto degli occhi'/'Die Macht der Augen' from *Attilio regolo*, and 'Il traditor deluso'/ 'Der getäuschte Verräter' from *Gioas re di Giuda*. In *Schubert: Thematisches Verzeichnis* the numbers D990E and D990F were assigned to what were described as early versions of D902/1 and 902/2.

However, as E. Hilmar has since indicated (*Österreichische Musikzeitschrift*, 1989), D990F is not a setting of 'Il traditor deluso' at all, but of another text by Metastasio, 'Ombre amene' from his serenata *L'Angelica*. It thus represents a hitherto unknown composition by Schubert. (Hilmar confirms, on the other hand, that D990E is indeed an earlier version of D902/1.)

As for the text of the third 'Gesang', 'Il modo di prender moglie'/'Die Art ein Weib zu nehmen' (D902/3), which was likewise attributed to Metastasio in the first edition (Tobias Haslinger,* September 1827), it appears to be the work of a different, as yet unidentified, author. In fact, Schubert himself wrote 'Autore ignoto' on the manuscript used for that edition. (Regarding the German text of these songs, *see* Craigher de Jachelutta.*)

Settings: D17, 33–5, 42, 76, 78, 509–10, 688/3–4, 902/1–2, 990E–F.
(Hilmar³, Robinson¹)

Mikan, Johann Christian (b. Teplitz-Schönau [Teplice-Šanov, Czech Republic], 5 December 1769; d. Prague, 28 December 1844). Botanist and entomologist; occasional poet. The son of a well-known physician and chemist, Josef Gottfried Mikan (1742–1814), he qualified as a doctor at the University of Prague, but practised for only a short time before concentrating on botany and entomology. In 1800 he was appointed to the chair of natural history at the university, and from 1812 he taught botany to students of medicine and pharmacology. He was credited with having made significant botanical discoveries in Bohemia and elsewhere; in 1817–18 he took part in an expedition to Brazil. A climbing plant found in tropical South America and Africa was named 'Mikania' in his honour.

Schubert's song 'Die Befreier Europas in Paris', composed in May 1814, is a setting of a poem written by Mikan to celebrate the entry of Emperor Franz I of Austria, Tsar Alexander I, and King Friedrich Wilhelm III of Prussia into that city on 15 April 1814. (Paris had surrendered to the allies on 31 March.)

Setting: D104.
(Schochow)

Milder-Hauptmann, (Pauline) Anna (b. Constantinople, 13 December 1785; d. Berlin, 29 May 1838). Soprano. Her father Felix Milder earned his living as a confectioner in Constantinople, and was subsequently employed as an interpreter in Bucharest and as a government courier; in *c.*1800 he settled at Hütteldorf, near Vienna.

Anna Milder studied with Sigismund von Neukomm and Antonio Salieri.* She made a very successful début at the Theater an der Wien in 1803 as Juno in Süssmayr's comic opera *Der Spiegel von Arkadien*, and, at the same theatre, sang Leonore at the première of Beethoven's* *Fidelio* on 20 November 1805. Soon afterwards, at the Kärntnertor-Theater, she created the title role in Cherubini's *Faniska* (25 February 1806), which had been written for her, as was the part of

Emmeline in Josef Weigl's* *Die Schweizerfamilie* (14 March 1809). She also sang Leonore again in the final version of *Fidelio* (Kärntnertor-Theater, 23 May 1814). But she made her greatest impact with her interpretations of Gluck's heroines. Indeed, she was responsible for the Gluck revivals in Vienna and, later, in Berlin where she moved in 1816. She performed there with great distinction until 1829, and subsequently sang in Russia and Scandinavia, as well as in various German cities. At a concert in Vienna on 27 December 1835 she sang Schubert's 'Hermann and Thusnelda' (D322). She retired soon afterwards. Her marriage (1810) to the Viennese court jeweller Peter Hauptmann (1763–1858) had ended in separation.

Hearing Milder and Johann Michael Vogl* in Gluck's *Iphigenia in Tauris* [*Iphigénie en Tauride*] was one of the greatest musical experiences enjoyed by the young Schubert. 'He said that Milder's voice pierced his heart,' Josef von Spaun,* who had taken him to hear the opera, recalled in 1858. It has not been possible to determine the precise date of that performance, but since Spaun and Schubert afterwards had supper with Theodor Körner,* it evidently took place before 13 March 1813, the date of Körner's departure from Vienna. If O. E. Deutsch* is right to assign it to the beginning of that same year, then the date must have been either 5 or 23 January, for those were the only times when the opera was given at the court theatre in 1813. (There were seven performances in 1812, the last one on 2 November.) Spaun relates that at the supper, which they ate at the 'Zum Blumenstöckl' restaurant [3 Ballgasse], Schubert almost came to blows with a university professor at the next table who declared that Milder 'had crowed like a cock, did not know how to sing and was incapable of producing either runs or trills'. Curiously enough, Schubert later came to agree with the last criticism, for in a letter addressed to Franz von Schober* and others on 8 September 1818, he wrote: 'By the way, I am very glad that for you Milder is irreplaceable, for I feel just the same. She sings more beautifully than anyone else—and trills worse.'

Schubert never met Milder, but he exchanged some correspondence with her. It started with a flattering letter sent by Milder from Berlin on 12 December 1824, in which she expressed regret at not having made his acquaintance during a recent visit to Vienna (he had been away at Zseliz). She went on to praise his songs, and described the enthusiastic response they evoked wherever she sang them; she also offered to use her influence, should he wish to have an opera produced in Berlin. In reply, he sent her *Alfonso und Estrella* (D732), and also the song 'Ach um deine feuchten Schwingen' ('Suleika II', D717). She thought the latter 'heavenly' and 'indescribable', but did not consider the former work suitable for Berlin audiences, which 'were accustomed to grand tragic opera or French comic opera' (8 March 1825). At the same time, if she could not arrange a performance of his opera in Berlin, she managed to further his reputation as a composer of Lieder. She sang 'Die Forelle' (D550) at a concert on 13 January 1825; and on 9 June of the same year she sang 'Erlkönig' (D328) and gave the first public performance of 'Suleika II', which Schubert was to dedicate to her when it was published in August.

1. Ferdinand Schubert, portrait by his nephew Ferdinand Schubert

2. Therese Grob, portrait by Heinrich Hollpein

3. Josef von Spaun, copy by N. Reiter of a (lost) portrait by Leopold Kupelwieser

4. Franz von Schober, portrait by Leopold Kupelwieser

5. Moritz von Schwind, lithograph by Josef Kriehuber, 1827

6. Johann Baptist Jenger, Anselm Hüttenbrenner, and Schubert

7. Schubert (walking, second from left) and friends on an excursion from Atzenbrugg to Aumühle, water-colour by Leopold Kupelwieser, 1820

8. Schubert (seated at the piano) and friends engaged in a game of charades at Atzenbrugg, water-colour by Leopold Kupelwieser, 1821

9. Ignaz von Sonnleithner, lithograph by Josef Teltscher, 1827

10. Leopold von Sonnleithner, photograph taken in his later years by J. Székely & J. Gertinger, Vienna

11. Johann Michael Vogl, portrait by Julius Fargel, after the (lost) original by Leopold Kupelwieser

12. Baron Karl Schönstein, lithograph by Josef Kriehuber, 1841

13. Anton Diabelli, lithograph by Josef Kriehuber, 1841

14. Tobias Haslinger, lithograph by Josef Kriehuber, 1842

15. Marcus (Maximilian Josef) Leidesdorf, lithograph by Johann Stefan Decker

16. 'Erlkönig': autograph of the third version, presented by Schubert to Benedikt Randhartinger and given by the latter to Clara Wieck (later Clara Schumann), in 1838

17. 'Erlkönig': first edition, Vienna, 1821

Schubert did not comply with Milder's repeated requests that he set a Goethe*
poem for her (she suggested 'Verschiedene Empfindungen an einem Platz'). However, 'Der Hirt auf dem Felsen' (D965), which he composed in October 1828,
shortly before his death, is believed to have been written for her. Ferdinand
Schubert* made a copy which he sent to her, through Vogl, on 4 September 1829,
and she gave the first performance of the song at Riga in March 1830. She also sang
it in Berlin on 14 December of that year.

(Forbes[1], Kutsch/Riemens, *ÖBL*, Waidelich[3], Wurzbach[1])

Mohn, Ludwig (b. Halle an der Saale, Saxony, 3 August 1797; d. Vienna, 19 January
1857). Graphic artist and etcher. Both his father Samuel M. Mohn (1761–1815)
and his brother Gottlob Samuel Mohn (1789–1825) were well-known painters on
glass. The latter moved to Vienna in 1811; Ludwig followed him in *c.*1820 and
seems to have quickly joined Schubert's circle. In 1821 he was among the persons
invited by Franz von Schober* to Atzenbrugg Castle. He was partly responsible for
one of the pictorial representations of the different activities in which the friends
engaged there. The picture shows an outdoor game of ball. The landscape and
buildings were drawn by Schober, the human figures (which include Schubert) by
Moritz von Schwind,* and an etching of the complete drawing was made by Mohn
in 1823. (On the water-colours depicting an excursion and a game of charades, *see*
Kupelwieser.*)

Mohn assumed a leading role in the group after Schober's departure for Breslau
[Wrocław] in the summer of 1823, and his lodgings in Grasgasse in the Landstrasse
suburb [27 Neulinggasse/13 Linke Bahngasse] served for a time as a centre for its
activities. The New Year's Eve party was held there that year and a Schubertiad took
place on 19 January 1824. Mohn also helped to arrange and himself hosted several
reading parties. He had a rather prickly character: 'Mohn is a good enough fellow,'
Johanna Lutz* wrote to Leopold Kupelwieser on 25 January 1824, 'but he is
constantly upsetting conventional proprieties, and yet takes offence at the slightest
trifle.' In June 1824 he took temporary possession of the autographs of ten of
Schubert's songs, for reasons now unknown; O. E. Deutsch speculated that they
might have constituted a pledge for a debt.

Mohn later specialized in painting views of Vienna and its surroundings. He also
owned a lithographic printing press.

(*ÖBL*, Steblin[1,3])

Mosel, Ignaz Franz von (b. Vienna, 1 April 1772; d. Vienna, 8 April 1844).
Composer, conductor, and writer; son of a senior official in the court treasury.
During most of his adult life he played an important role in the cultural, and
especially the musical, life of Vienna. He himself showed musical talent at an early
age and became a proficient violinist, violist, and cellist. In 1788 he entered
government service, in which he was to hold several important appointments,

mainly due to his friendship with Count Moritz Dietrichstein* whose acquaintance he made in 1810. In 1821 he became deputy director of the two court theatres under Dietrichstein, and in 1826 succeeded him as director. In 1829 he was appointed principal curator of the court library, a post he held until his death. He was ennobled in 1818.

His publications include a life of Salieri* (*Ueber das Leben und die Werke des Anton Salieri*, 1827) and a book about the court library (*Geschichte der k.k. Hofbibliothek zu Wien*, 1835); he also wrote many articles on musical matters. His original compositions include Masses, psalms, and cantatas, as well as the Singspiel *Die Feuerprobe* (Kärntnertor-Theater, 28 April 1811) and the three-act heroic opera *Cyrus und Astyages* (13 June 1818). In addition, he wrote incidental music to numerous plays. For the production at the Burgtheater, on 18 December 1827, of the tragedy *Der Paria* (using his own translation of Casimir Delavigne's *Le Paria*), he adapted music by Mozart and also one of Schubert's marches for piano duet (D819/3). He furthermore made arrangements for string quartet of Haydn's oratorio *Die Schöpfung* and of several operas, notably Cherubini's *Medea* and Mozart's *Così fan tutte* and *Don Giovanni*. Lastly, he augmented the orchestration of a number of Handel's oratorios, which were then performed in these new versions and with German texts prepared by him. Mosel took an active part in the creation of the Gesellschaft der Musikfreunde and in the establishment of its Conservatory.

He was already familiar with Schubert's name when he made his acquaintance at Matthäus von Collin's* in *c.*1820, for in his capacity as secretary in the chief chamberlain's office he had received reports on Schubert's entrance test at the Stadtkonvikt and on his subsequent studies. He came to feel profound admiration for Schubert's music. Josef von Spaun* recalled in 1858 that after Mosel had heard Johann Michael Vogl* sing some of Schubert's songs at Collin's, he declared more than once that he had never heard anything comparable. Mosel regarded 'An die Türen will ich schleichen', one of the 'Gesänge des Harfners aus *Wilhelm Meister*' (D478/3), as 'a masterpiece which proved that Schubert was by no means just a prolific inventor of melodies, but a thorough musician'.

In 1821 Schubert dedicated to Mosel his Op. 3 which consisted of the four Goethe songs 'Heidenröslein' (D257), 'Jägers Abendlied' (D368), 'Meeres Stille' (D216), and 'Schäfers Klagelied' (D121). On 28 February 1823 he sent the overture and the third act of *Alfonso und Estrella* (D732) to Mosel, with an accompanying letter in which he asked for Mosel's opinion of the score and also for letters recommending the opera to Weber,* who was then director of music at Dresden, and to the administrator of the Dresden Opera, Hans Heinrich von Könneritz. It is not known what Mosel thought of the music, nor whether he wrote the letters in question; but Spaun later stated that he had warmly recommended the opera to Weber. However, the opera was not produced at Dresden. Also in 1823, Schubert may have set two texts by Mosel (*see* Metastasio*).

Mosel's profound regard for Schubert's music, and more specifically for his Lieder, is evident in his article 'Die Tonkunst in Wien während der letzten fünf Decennien', which appeared in *Jahrbücher des deutschen National-Vereins für Musik und ihre Wissenschaft* in 1841 and was reprinted in a revised form in the *Allgemeine Wiener Musikzeitung* on 9 November 1843.

The second of Mosel's three wives, Katharina Lambert (1789–1832), whom he married in 1808, was a writer and a fine musician, having studied the piano with Hummel.* She played at court and at various concerts in aid of charities, as well as at the musical parties which she and her husband gave at their residence at the Mölkerhof [3 Schottengasse]. Schubert is known to have attended at least one of them, in late 1822 or early 1823.

Settings: ?D791/1–2.

(Brusatti, Jancik², *ÖBL*, Wurzbach¹)

Müller, Karl Ludwig Methusalem (b. Schkeuditz, near Leipzig, 16 June 1771; d. Leipzig, 15 October 1837). Poet, novelist, and editor. He published several collections of poetry and novellas; his novels include *Nettchens 50 Franken* and *Henriette, Gräfin von Barnow*. From 1816 to 1832 he edited the *Zeitung für die elegante Welt* (Leipzig).

He was also the author of a German translation of Sir Walter Scott's* novel *Ivanhoe* (Leipzig, 1820). From it Schubert took the text for his 'Romanze des Richard Löwenherz', which he probably composed in March 1826. It was first performed in public by Ludwig Titze,* accompanied by Schubert himself, at a concert at the Landhaus in Vienna on 2 February 1828.

Setting: D907.

(Krüger)

Müller, Sophie (b. Mannheim, 19 January 1803; d. Vienna, 22 June 1830). Actress; daughter of Karl Müller (1763–1837), a horn player and actor, and of the singer Marie Boudet (1775–1824). Trained by her father, she performed on stage from early childhood. In 1820 she became a full-time member of the court theatre of the Grand Duchy of Baden at Mannheim. On the strength of a series of guest appearances at the Vienna Burgtheater in 1821, she was offered a permanent contract there the following year. Within a short time, she became one of the most admired and best loved members of the company. She achieved some of her greatest successes in plays by Friedrich Schiller* (Beatrice in *Die Braut von Messina*, Eboli in *Don Carlos*, Johanna in *Die Jungfrau von Orleans*) and Shakespeare* (Cordelia, Desdemona, Juliet, Ophelia). Her last stage appearance was on 11 April 1829 as Aurora in *Die Stimme des Blutes*, a German version by Alois Isidor Jeitteles of Agustín Moreto y Cabaña's comedy *La fuerza del sangre*. Her early death occasioned much public grief.

Her diary, which was discovered after her death, provides evidence of frequent contacts with Schubert during the years 1825–6, and of her great admiration for his songs. She herself had some musical training, played the piano and guitar, and was a fine singer. Anselm Hüttenbrenner,* writing in 1858, judged her to have been the most sensitive interpreter of Schubert's songs next to Baron Schönstein.*

On 24 February 1825 she wrote in her diary: 'Jenger,* Vogl,* and Schubert lunched with us for the first time to-day. Afterwards Vogl sang Schubert's settings of several poems by Schiller.' According to O. E. Deutsch,* she was living with her father at Hietzing, then still a village outside Vienna; but R. Klein, in *Schubert-Stätten*, places her residence in the inner city [28 Graben].

This first contact must have pleased Schubert, for he called on the Müllers no fewer than five more times over the next few weeks, on each occasion bringing different songs for Sophie to listen to or sing herself. 'Schubert came after lunch,' she noted on 2 March. 'I sang with him until nearly six o'clock, then drove to the theatre.' And on 3 March: 'Schubert came after lunch and brought a new song, 'Die junge Nonne' (D828). Later Vogl also called and I sang it for him. It is beautifully composed ... We made music until almost seven o'clock ...' Altogether, her diary records no fewer than thirteen visits by Schubert between February 1825 and November 1826.

Count Mailáth* published a biography of the actress (*Leben der Sophie Müller*) in 1832, in which he presented numerous extracts from her diary.

(Eisenberg, Klein², Mailáth, *ÖBL*, Wurzbach¹)

Müller, Wenzel (b. Tyrnau, [Trnava, Slovak Republic], 26 September 1767; d. Baden, near Vienna, 3 August 1835). Composer and conductor. His first engagement was at the theatre at Brünn [Brno], initially as violinist and later as conductor. In 1786 he became Kapellmeister at the Leopoldstädter-Theater in Vienna. He was associated with that theatre, as conductor and resident composer, for the remainder of his life, except for a six-year spell (1807–13) at the German Opera in Prague. He wrote many highly successful Singspiels, in which he amply demonstrated his talent for writing simple, catchy tunes. His total output of works for the stage ran to some 250 titles.

Schubert is known to have attended performances of at least two of his works, *Aline, oder Wien in einem andern Weltteil* (in October 1822) and *Herr Josef und Frau Baberl* (in 1826), and is almost certain to have known others. It is believed that Müller's fantastic operas and farces may have influenced Schubert's music for the stage, for instance in *Die Zauberharfe* (D644). In addition, H. Költzsch has suggested that the waltz theme in the scherzo section of the 'Wanderer' Fantasia (D760), which was composed in November 1822, i.e. during the month following his above-mentioned attendance of a performance of *Aline*, was inspired by the duet 'Was macht denn der Prater, sag', sung by Zilli and Bims in that opera.

Wenzel Müller was the father and grandfather of internationally known sopranos, Therese Müller [Grünbaum] (1791–1876), the original Eglantine in Weber's* *Euryanthe* (Vienna, 1823), and her daughter Caroline Grünbaum (1814–68), who created Anna in Heinrich August Marschner's *Hans Heiling* (Berlin, 1833). Wenzel's son Wilhelm (1800–82) was a composer.

(Branscombe[6], Költzsch, *ÖBL*, Raab, Würz[2])

Müller, Wilhelm (b. Dessau, 7 October 1794; d. Dessau, 30 September/1 October 1827). Poet. He studied philology, history, and English at the University of Berlin, served in the war against Napoleon, and in August 1817 set out for Greece in the company of a rich dilletante, Baron Sack. On the way, they stayed in Vienna in September and October, after which they abandoned their original travel plans and went to Italy instead. There, after parting from the baron, Müller spent an enjoyable year. There is no evidence of his having met Schubert during his visit to Vienna. In 1819 he became a schoolmaster at Dessau; he also served as ducal librarian.

He is best known for the *Gedichte aus den hinterlassenen Papieren eines reisenden Waldhornisten* (2 vols., 1821–4). The first volume contained the cycle *Die schöne Müllerin* and the second *Die Winterreise* (the latter cycle having previously appeared in the periodical *Urania* in 1823). A fervent philhellene, he also published *Lieder der Griechen* (1821–4) and a collection of translations of modern Greek folk-songs (*Neugriechische Volkslieder*, 1825). He was himself greatly influenced by folk poetry and his lyrics, though often rather superficial in ideas and feeling, appealed to a number of (mainly minor) contemporary composers by their simple charm, un-complicated emotions, and pleasing imagery. Many of these poems were, indeed, written to be sung, as their author himself indicated: 'In truth, my songs lead only half a life, a paper life, black on white ... until music imparts to them the breath of life, or calls it forth and awakens it, if it is already dormant in them', he wrote on 15 December 1822 to the composer Bernhard Josef Klein. However, Schubert alone felt moved to set entire cycles; the other composers rarely tackled more than one poem.

Müller's cycle *Die schöne Müllerin* consisted of twenty-three poems, with a prologue and epilogue. It had its origin in the Liederspiel *Rose, die Müllerin*, which was devised by a group of friends who, in 1815–16, met at the house of Staatsrat Friedrich August von Stägemann in Berlin. In addition to Müller, they included Stägemann's son August and daughter Hedwig, the future historian Friedrich Förster, Luise Hensel and her brother, the painter Wilhelm Hensel (who later married Fanny Mendelssohn-Bartholdy), and Ludwig Rellstab.* Also associated with the group was the somewhat older composer Ludwig Berger (the future teacher of Fanny's brother Felix*).

Schubert set twenty of the poems in the cycle in the autumn of 1823, and the songs (D795) were published in three parts between February and August 1824. His second Müller cycle, *Winterreise* (D911), was issued in two parts. The first twelve songs, which he began to compose in February 1827, were published in January 1828; the second twelve, which he started to write in October 1827, did not appear until after his death, in December 1828. In announcing publication of the second part, the publisher Tobias Haslinger* stated that the proof corrections had been 'the last pen strokes' made by Schubert.

Lastly, Schubert combined parts of two other Müller poems, 'Der Berghirt' and 'Liebesgedanken', in his song 'Der Hirt auf dem Felsen' (D965), which dates from October 1828 but was not published until 1830 (*see also* Chézy*).

Settings: D795, 911, 965.
(Baumann, Budde, Eisenhardt, Heim, Steblin[7], Warrack[2], Youens[2,3])

Nejebse, Wenzel (b. Budňan [Budňany, now part of Karlštejn, Czech Republic], 1796; d. Vienna, 19 April 1865). Civil servant; bass. He served in the censorship office, and later in the ministry of finance. He was presumably a relative (?brother) of the painter Johann Nejebse (1809–56) who came from the same Bohemian village and was a student at the Vienna Academy of Fine Arts by 1822.

Nejebse sang at numerous private and public concerts. He took part in a number of performances of Schubert's partsongs, notably the first public performances of the quartet 'Das Dörfchen' (D598) and the octet 'Gesang der Geister über den Wassern' (D714) at the Kärntnertor-Theater on 7 March 1821, and of the quartet 'Frühlingsgesang' (D740) at the same theatre on 7 April 1822. Other quartets in which he sang are 'Die Nachtigall' (D724), 'Geist der Liebe' (D747), and 'Gondelfahrer' (D809). On 20 November 1828, the day after Schubert's death, he sang 'Dithyrambe' (D801) at an 'evening entertainment' of the Gesellschaft der Musikfreunde. On 11 December 1828, at another 'evening entertainment', he sang 'Der Alpenjäger' (D588). He was also among the artists participating in the two memorial concerts on 30 January and 5 March 1829. However, on those two occasions he did not sing in any Schubert compositions, but in the Act I finale from Mozart's *Don Giovanni*.

Nejebse was a member of the Wiener Männergesangverein from its foundation in 1843 until his death.

(Adametz)

Nestroy, Johann Nepomuk (Eduard Ambrosius) (b. Vienna, 7 December 1801; d. Graz, 25 May 1862). Playwright, actor, and singer (bass); son of a Viennese lawyer. He studied law at the University of Vienna, but having appeared with some success in amateur dramatics and given a competent performance as solo bass in Handel's *Alexander's Feast*, he abandoned the law for the theatre. He sang at the Kärntnertor-Theater from August 1822 to August 1823, making his début as Sarastro in *Die Zauberflöte*. He subsequently appeared with the German Theatre company in Amsterdam (October 1823–August 1825) and at the National Theatre at Brünn [Brno] (October 1825–April 1826). During the following five years he performed mainly at Graz and Pressburg [Bratislava], in the double capacity of singer and actor.

By the time he was engaged by Karl Carl [Karl Bernbrunn] at the Theater an der Wien in 1831, he had not only become a highly accomplished performer, with an increasing predilection for comic parts, but had also discovered his great talent for writing popular comedies and farces. In 1845 he moved with Carl to the Leopold-städter-Theater, which, following Carl's death in 1854, he managed for six years before retiring in 1860. Altogether, he wrote more than eighty works for the stage. Music played a prominent part in his plays, especially the earlier ones, in the form of songs, ensembles, choruses, and instrumental pieces.

As a singer, Nestroy took part in performances of at least two of Schubert's vocal quartets: he sang in 'Das Dörfchen' (D598) at Ignaz von Sonnleithner's* on 19 November 1819 and at a concert of the Gesellschaft der Musikfreunde on 8 April 1821, and in 'Geist der Liebe' (D747) several times in 1822, including, perhaps, at its first performance at the Grosser Redoutensaal on 3 March.

There is a reference to another of Schubert's compositions in his farce *Die Familien Zwirn, Knieriem und Leim* (1835), where the opening phrase ('Ich wandre durch die halbe Welt') of Zwirn's song (I. 16) is set to the melody which accompanies the words 'Ich komme vom Gebirge her' in Schubert's 'Der Wanderer' (D489).

(Branscombe[7], Eisenberg, Wurzbach[1])

Neuhaus, Kajetan Franz (b. Krems, 20 April 1767; d. Linz, 15 May 1829). Ecclesiastic and academic. He taught theoretical and practical philosophy at the Lyzeum at Linz. A competent pianist, he played duets with Anna von Hartmann* and Albert Stadler.* He had a large collection of music for four hands.

In September 1827 Schubert dedicated to him the *Eight Variations on a Theme from Hérold's Opera 'Marie'* for piano duet (D908). The opera had been produced at the Kärntnertor-Theater on 18 December 1826, with a German text by Ignaz Franz Castelli.* Schubert took the theme from Lublin's third-act aria 'Was einst vor Jahren' ['Sur la rivière, comme mon père'].

Neumann, Emilie (b. Altona, near Hamburg, 1801; d. Vienna, 1872). Actress; daughter of the singer (Franz) Anton Neumann (1771–1827). Her sister Therese (1797/8–1876), a member of the court theatre ballet from 1804 to 1813, married the famous French dancer and choreographer Louis Duport, who was engaged as ballet-master in Vienna in 1812 and later leased the Kärntnertor-Theater.

In her posthumously published memoirs (Leipzig, 1858), Wilhelmina von Chézy* related that Josef Kupelwieser* had asked her to write a drama, in which Emilie Neumann—'a beautiful girl with whom he was in love'—would have the principal role and for which Schubert would compose the music. The result was *Rosamunde, Fürstin von Zypern* (D797), of which the première at the Theater an der Wien, on 20 December 1823, was given as a benefit performance for the actress. Contemporary reports indicate that she acquitted herself well. The critic of the *Wiener*

Zeitschrift für Kunst, Literatur, Theater und Mode reported on 3 January 1824 that she and Moritz Rott (in the role of Fulgentius) had been singled out for applause by the audience. Chézy herself spoke of the 'valiant acting of Mlle Neumann', but expressed the view that her talent was not yet fully developed.

Several years later, while appearing at a theatre at Pressburg [Bratislava], Emilie married the actor Carl Wilhelm Lucas (1803–57). In 1829 both were engaged at the Theater an der Wien, whose lessee was then Karl Carl [Karl Bernbrunn]. On 11 April 1833, 'Mad. Lucas' appeared as the fairy Fortuna at the première of Johann Nestroy's* *Der böse Geist Lumpacivagabundus, oder Das liederliche Kleeblatt.* The following year her husband joined the company at the Burgtheater, of which he remained one of the most widely admired members until his death.

The couple had two sons, one of whom became a physician and the other an army officer. Their grandson Moritz was a successful actor; at the opening of the Raimund-Theater in Vienna on 28 November 1893 he appeared as Apollo in Raimund's *Die gefesselte Phantasie.*

(Chézy, Eisenberg, Mansfeld, *ÖBL*, Ulrich)

Neumann, Johann Philipp (b. Trebitsch [Třebíč, Czech Republic], 27 December 1774; d. Vienna, 3 October 1849). Physicist and writer. He studied philosophy and law at the University of Vienna (1791–4). From 1801 he taught grammar and Greek at the Lyzeum at Laibach [Ljubljana], and, from 1803, also physics. In 1806 he was appointed professor of physics at the Lyzeum in Graz, and later taught astronomy at the Joanneum in that city. In 1816 he became secretary and librarian at the newly established Polytechnic Institute in Vienna, and the following year its first professor of physics. He retired in 1844.

He was the author of several scientific works and also dabbled in literature. Among his writings was the libretto *Sakuntala,* based on a play by the (c.fifth-century) Indian poet Kalidasa, of which several German versions had already been published. Schubert began to set the text in October 1820. Only sketches of the first two acts have survived. The music (D701) was first performed at a concert in Vienna on 12 June 1971.

Neumann was furthermore responsible for the composition, in 1827, of the *Deutsche Messe* (D872), for which he paid Schubert a fee of 100 gulden. For its text Schubert used a number of hymns written by Neumann himself. Ferdinand Schubert* later made several arrangements of the music for different vocal groups.

In the *Allgemeine Wiener Musikzeitung* on 15 January 1842, Neumann's son Ludwig Gottfried, who was then working on a biography of Schubert, invited readers to send him relevant manuscript and printed material. The book was never published.

Settings: D701, 872.

(Brusatti, Burkhart, *ÖBL*, Wurzbach¹)

Nottebohm, (Martin) Gustav (b. Lüdenscheid, Westphalia, 12 November 1817; d. Graz, 29 October 1882). Musicologist, teacher, and composer. After studying in Berlin and Leipzig, he settled in Vienna in 1845. There he was active as a teacher of musical theory and piano, as a composer of piano and chamber music, and, most notably, as a scholar. He is best known for his research on Beethoven.* He collaborated on the edition of Beethoven's works which Breitkopf & Härtel* issued in 1862–5, and published a series of seminal studies on his manuscripts. In addition, he prepared a thematic catalogue of Beethoven's compositions (Leipzig, 1865) which remained the standard reference source until Georg Ludwig Kinsky's catalogue appeared (posthumously, completed by Hans Halm) in 1955.

In 1874 Nottebohm's *Thematisches Verzeichnis der im Druck erschienenen Werke von Franz Schubert* was published in Vienna. It was for almost eighty years the authoritative source on the subject, until it was superseded by O. E. Deutsch's* thematic catalogue in 1951.

(Grasberger, Johnson)

Nourrit, Adolphe (b. Montpellier, 3 March 1802; d. Naples, 8 March 1839). Tenor; son of the tenor Louis Nourrit (1780–1831). After studying privately with the elder Manuel García, he made a successful début at the Paris Opéra on 10 September 1821 as Pylades in Gluck's *Iphigénie en Tauride*. His reputation increased steadily and upon his father's retirement in December 1826 he became the Opéra's principal tenor. He created several roles in Rossini operas: Néocles in *Le Siège de Corinthe* (9 October 1826), Aménophis in *Moïse et Pharaon* (26 March 1827), the title role in *Le Comte Ory* (20 August 1828), and Arnold in *Guillaume Tell* (3 August 1829). He was also the first Robert in Meyerbeer's *Robert le diable* (21 November 1831) and the original Raoul in *Les Huguenots* (29 February 1836). Yet, despite his great popularity, he felt insecure when Gilbert(-Louis) Duprez was engaged as joint leading tenor in 1836, and he resigned from the Opéra. Following his farewell appearance there on 1 April 1837, he performed in operas and concerts in the provinces before heading for Italy at the end of that year. Eventually he settled in Naples, where he studied with Donizetti in preparation for singing opera in Italian. He made some successful appearances at the Teatro San Carlo where he had been engaged by Domenico Barbaia,* notably as Pollione in Bellini's *Norma* (2 February 1839). Nevertheless, his mental and physical health, already impaired during his final period in France, deteriorated significantly, and a month later he committed suicide.

Nourrit is remembered by Schubertians as an important early French champion of the composer's songs. Hector Berlioz wrote in the *Journal des débats* on 22 March 1839: 'Without him, without his persistent efforts, without his profound love for these admirable Lieder and his ability to communicate it to others, without the translations he made of them, without the exquisite sensitiveness and supreme intelligence with which he sang them, our editors would not have dared to publish these songs by Schubert, who would probably still be appreciated only by a few artists, and the public would have been deprived of exquisite pleasures.' In actual fact, even though Nourrit was named as the translator when 'La Jeune Religieuse' ['Die junge Nonne', D828] was published in Paris in 1834, it is doubtful that he ever did more than refine French versions supplied by others or turn someone else's prose translations into verse, for he possessed little or no German. In 1835 he wrote to an unidentified friend: 'How fortunate you are to know German!... Teach me German and I will teach you to sing.'

According to Nourrit's biographer L. Quicherat, his enthusiasm for Schubert's songs was first aroused by hearing Liszt* play 'Le Roi des aulnes' ['Erlkönig', D328] at the house of a 'Hungarian banker, Monsieur Dessauer' (presumably the Bohemian composer Josef Dessauer) in Paris. Quichérat gives no date, but, assuming that his story has some factual basis, this momentous event in Nourrit's life probably took place in the summer of 1833. If Nourrit really heard Liszt play an arrangement of 'Erlkönig' at that time, this would indicate that Liszt worked on his transcription of that song earlier than is usually thought. It is, however, possible that what Nourrit actually heard on that occasion was a performance of the song by Marie d'Agoult, with Liszt accompanying. In a letter to her on 30 August 1833, Liszt wrote: 'You were *sublime* on Saturday morning, quite simply sublime... Never have Goethe and Schubert been understood so well.' In the same letter Liszt stated that Dessauer had greatly enjoyed a soirée given by Marie d'Agoult.

Having procured French versions, Nourrit soon began to perform certain Schubert songs in private as well as in public. Thus, at a concert given by the composer and singer Loïsa Puget on 21 December 1834, he sang 'Ave Maria' ['Ellens Gesang III', D839]. His performance at the Conservatoire on 18 January 1835 of 'La Jeune Religieuse' (with orchestral accompaniment) profoundly moved the audience and constituted an important event in the establishment of Schubert's reputation in France. 'It is difficult to imagine anything more poetic, more original or more dramatic than this composition', declared the critic of the *Gazette musicale de Paris* (25 January 1835). On 6 April 1835, at the Théâtre-Italien, Nourrit sang 'Le Roi des aulnes', again accompanied by an orchestra. He is also known to have performed several Schubert songs at the recitals given by Liszt in Paris in the spring of 1837.

At his provincial concerts later that same year he made a particularly strong impression with the songs 'Les Astres' ['Die Gestirne', D444] and 'Sois mes seules amours' ['Sei mir gegrüsst', D741]. At Marseilles, on 17 June 1837, he had to repeat part of 'Les Astres'. Charles Rouget declared in the *Sémaphore de Marseille* (20 June) that the nobility of the piece and of its interpretation 'makes one believe in God'. Nourrit again performed the two songs, together with 'Le Roi des aulnes', at a concert he gave jointly with Liszt at the Grand-Théâtre at Lyons on 3 August 1837; on that occasion, the whole of 'Les Astres' was encored. And on 12 August, at the Hôtel du Nord at Lyons, at what turned out to be his final concert appearance in France, he sang 'Les Astres' and 'La Jeune Religieuse'.

Following Nourrit's death, his coffin was transported from Naples to Paris, where he was interred at Montmartre cemetery. When the coffin reached Marseilles, a funeral service was held at the church of Notre-Dame-du-Mont on 24 April 1839, at which the organ was played by Chopin who had been well acquainted with Nourrit and happened to be staying in the city with George Sand. The newspaper *Le Sud* reported the next day: 'During the elevation of the Host the organ sounded its melancholy tones: M. Chopin, the celebrated pianist, was placing a memento on Nourrit's coffin. And what a memento: a simple melody by Schubert, but the one that moved us so profoundly when Nourrit sang it in Marseilles, the melody of "Les Astres".'

Nourrit's pupil Pierre François Wartel (1806–82) further helped to make Schubert's songs better known in France. He enjoyed an international career. At a concert in Vienna on 8 November 1842, at which he was accompanied by Benedikt Randhartinger,* he sang several Schubert songs—in French.

(Hascher, Legouvé, Liszt², Prod'homme, Quicherat, Robinson³)

Novalis [pseud. of Baron (Georg) Friedrich (Philipp) Hardenberg] (b. Oberwiederstedt, near Mansfeld, Saxony, 2 May 1772; d. Weissenfels, 25 March 1801). Poet and novelist. He studied law at Jena (where he made the acquaintance of Friedrich Schiller*), Leipzig (where he met Friedrich von Schlegel*), and Wittenberg; he qualified in 1794. In 1797 he enrolled at the school of mining at Freiberg, Saxony. He was, at different times, employed in local government and in the mining industry.

In November 1794, at Grüningen, he met and fell in love with the 12-year-old Sophie von Kühn; they became engaged four months later. Shortly afterwards, she was stricken with tuberculosis. The anguish which her illness and death (19 March 1797) caused him, together with his grief at losing his brother Erasmus, provoked a profound emotional and religious crisis which led to the composition in 1799 of the mystical *Hymnen an die Nacht*, in which night serves as a symbol for death. The same year he also wrote *Geistliche Lieder*, a collection of fifteen hymns.

Schubert used poems by Novalis in the four 'Hymnen' (D659–62), in 'Marie' (D658), and in 'Nachthymne' (D687). The first five texts, taken from *Geistliche Lieder*, were probably all set in May 1819, the sixth, from *Hymnen an die Nacht*, in January 1820. None of the songs was published in Schubert's lifetime.

Settings: D658–62, 687.
(Saul)

Ossian: *see* Macpherson.*

Ottenwalt, Anton (b. Linz, 5 November 1789; d. Vienna, 16 February 1845). Civil servant; dramatist and poet. He was employed in the Upper Austrian administration at Linz until, having qualified as a lawyer in 1828, he took up a senior legal post in the civil service in Vienna in 1830. He was later awarded the title Hofrat. Josef Kenner* described him as a man of the utmost probity, extremely hard-working, highly intelligent, and very cultivated. Together with Kenner, Anton von Spaun (Josef von Spaun's* brother) and Johann Mayrhofer,* he prepared the yearbook *Beyträge zur Bildung für Jünglinge* (Vienna, 1817–18), a publication prompted by a desire to enable young men to improve their mind and character through the study of edifying texts. In addition, Ottenwalt wrote some tragedies (*Caesar, Otto III*), as well as poetry. He was an intimate friend of the Spaun family; on 25 November 1819 he married Marie von Spaun (1795–1847), who had previously been courted by Franz von Schober.* Their only child, Karl, died in 1837 at the age of 8. (Before her marriage to Ottenwalt, Schubert had probably dedicated to Marie a set of Écossaises (D299) which he had composed in October 1815, and perhaps also six Écossaises (D421) written in 1816.)

In the autumn of 1817 Schubert set one of Ottenwalt's poems, which he may have been shown by Spaun, in the song 'Der Knabe in der Wiege' (D579). He did not make Ottenwalt's acquaintance, however, until he visited Linz in the summer of 1819. Schubert met him there again in 1823, and, in 1825, to the Ottenwalts' great delight, he stayed with them. 'Schubert looks so well and strong, he is so cheerful and at ease, so friendly and expansive that one cannot fail to feel greatly delighted about it ...' Ottenwalt wrote on 19 July 1825 to Spaun, who was then in Lemberg [Lvov]. And on 27 July, following Schubert's departure with Johann Michael Vogl* for Steyr, he wrote to Spaun: 'Of Schubert—I might almost write, of *our* Schubert—there is much I would still like to tell you ... [On Sunday] we sat together until almost midnight. I have never seen or heard him like that: serious, profound, and as though inspired ... This is why I am so glad that he too seemed to take much pleasure in being with me, and that he felt inclined to show us a side of himself such as one reveals only to kindred spirits.'

There was, of course, much music-making during Schubert's visits, and even at other times his compositions were frequently played at the Ottenwalts', as they were at the houses of other members of what J. Reed has called 'the Schubert supporters' club in Linz'. Thus, on 17 October 1826, Albert Stadler* and Josef von Gahy* played some of his marches and the overture to *Alfonso und Estrella* (D773) at the Hartmanns',* and three days later they performed Schubert duets at the Ottenwalts'.

Although Schubert did not visit Linz again, he met the Ottenwalts in Vienna in 1827 and 1828. On 28 January of the latter year, they attended a Schubertiad given by Spaun. After they left Vienna on 5 February, they did not see Schubert again.

Settings: ?D565, 579.
(Gramit[1,2])

Pachler. Family residing at Graz. **Karl** Pachler (b. Graz, 4 November 1789; d. Graz, 22 October 1850) was a lawyer and brewer. His wife, **Marie Leopoldine**, née Koschak (b. Graz, 2 February 1794; d. Graz, 10 April 1855), whom he had married in 1816, was a very cultured person and an exceptionally fine pianist. Beethoven,* whose acquaintance she made at Vöslau, Lower Austria, in 1817, wrote to her: 'I have not found anyone who performs my compositions as well as you do, and I am not excluding our famous pianonists [*sic*], who are merely technical automatons or show-offs. You are the true nurturer of my spiritual children.' She met him once more in 1823, on which occasion he wrote for her a two-bar farewell, 'Das Schöne zu dem Guten'.

At their house in Graz [corner Herrengasse/Pfarrgasse] the Pachlers received numerous visitors, including actors, writers, poets, and musicians. Among their guests were Heinrich Anschütz, Karl von Holtei, Anselm Hüttenbrenner,* Johann Baptist Jenger,* Karl Gottfried von Leitner,* and Sophie Müller.* Johann Baptist Jenger, who had become friendly with the couple during the years he spent at Graz (1815–25), arranged to visit them together with Schubert in 1827. They stayed with the Pachlers from 3 to 20 September. Schubert expressed his appreciation of their warm hospitality in a letter on 27 September: 'Above all, I shall never forget the welcoming house, with its charming hostess, the sturdy Pachleros [i.e. Karl] and little Faust, where I have spent the happiest days I have known for a long time.'

During his stay in Graz, Schubert composed the songs 'Eine altschottische Ballade' (D923) and 'Heimliches Lieben' (D922), and very probably also the *Graz Galop* (D925) and the set of *Graz Waltzes* (D924) for the piano. There was much music-making at the Pachlers', and Schubert also took part in a concert given by the Steiermärkischer Musikverein (Styrian Music Society), of which he was an honorary member, on 8 September. The programme included 'Normans Gesang' (D846), in which Schubert accompanied, and the two partsongs 'Geist der Liebe' (D747) and 'Gott in der Natur' (D757).

According to Karl Gottfried von Leitner, Marie brought his *Gedichte* (published in Graz in 1825) to Schubert's attention and even gave him a copy of the volume. The poet's name was not new to Schubert, since he had already set one of his texts, 'Drang in die Ferne' (D770), in 1823. Over the following months, he set seven of the poems from *Gedichte* (*see* Leitner*). In the spring of 1828 he dedicated to Marie his Op. 106, which contained two of the new Leitner songs, 'Das Weinen' (D926) and 'Vor meiner Wiege' (D927), as well as the above-mentioned 'Heimliches Lieben', and also 'Gesang: Was ist Silvia' (D891) which dated from July 1826, before he had met Marie, and which he apparently substituted at the last minute for 'Eine altschottische Ballade'.

At the time of Schubert's visit, the Pachlers' 7-year-old son **Faust** (b. Graz, 18 December 1819; d. Graz, 6 September 1891) was being taught to play the piano by his mother. She therefore asked Schubert to send her, after his return to Vienna, a short duet which she and Faust could play on her husband's name-day on 4 November. Schubert obliged by dispatching the *Kindermarsch* for piano duet (D928) on 12 October, but thought that it might not please the boy 'for I do not really feel that I am very good at this kind of composition'. When the piece was eventually published by J. P. Gotthard* in Vienna in 1870, it carried a preface by Faust describing the circumstances in which the composition came to be written and providing some details of Schubert's visit. He had already, some years previously, given an account of Schubert's stay at Graz to Kreissle,* who had incorporated it in his book on the composer.

Following his visit to Graz in September 1827, Schubert sent Karl Pachler the autograph score of the opera *Alfonso und Estrella* (D732), in the hope that it might be performed at the local theatre, whose director was apparently a friend of Pachler. His hope was, however, not fulfilled, and after Schubert's death the score lay forgotten in an iron chest for fourteen years until Pachler discovered it there one day. In October 1842 he forwarded it to Ferdinand Schubert,* who was hoping to have the opera produced at the court theatre in Vienna. This new plan likewise came to nothing, and it was not until 24 June 1854 that *Alfonso und Estrella* was first staged, though in an abbreviated version—and not in Vienna, but at Weimar, under Liszt's* direction.

The Pachlers invited Jenger and Schubert to visit them again in 1828. Jenger found it difficult to free himself from his office work that year, but as late as 6 September he informed Marie that his friend 'Schwammerl' intended to take up the invitation, if, as he hoped, his financial situation improved. It was not to be.

Faust Pachler later studied law at the University of Vienna and was subsequently employed in the court library from 1843 to 1886. He was also a writer [pseud. C. Paul], but his plays, novellas, and poems met with little success. C. von Wurzbach relates that in 1849 he submitted a printed copy of his tragedy *Begum Sumro* to the director of the court theatre, Franz Ignaz Holbein von Holbeinsberg, only to have it returned with the pages still uncut. In 1866 he published *Beethoven und Marie Pachler-Koschak: Beiträge und Berichtigungen*, a study of his mother's contacts with Beethoven, which had previously appeared in the *Neue Berliner Musikzeitung*.

(Feitzinger, Lohberger, *ÖBL*, Pachler, Wurzbach[1])

Pálffy von Erdöd, Ferdinand, Count (b. Vienna, 1 February 1774; d. Vienna, 4 February 1840). Mining engineer; theatre manager. Son of Count Leopold Pálffy von Erdöd (1739–99) and his wife Theresia, née Countess Daun. He attended the mining institute at Schemnitz [Banská Štiavnica, Slovak Republic] from 1794 to 1796 and was subsequently employed in government service in that town. In 1806 he returned to Vienna, where he worked in the department of mines.

He was a member of the Gesellschaft der Cavaliere [Association of Noblemen] which, in 1807, acquired the Theater an der Wien and, at the same time, leased the two court theatres, the Burgtheater and Kärntnertor-Theater. In 1810 Pálffy became fully responsible for the court theatres, and during most of the period between March 1814 and April 1817 he was the sole lessee of the two establishments. He furthermore bought the Theater an der Wien in 1813 and remained its proprietor until 1826. During that period he offered the public a wide range of entertainment, from opera to ballet and pantomime, and even variety acts featuring ventriloquists, acrobats, jugglers, and yodellers. In his efforts to attract a wide public by ever more lavish spectacles, he gradually lost his not inconsiderable private fortune. He was forced to sell the theatre at auction in 1826, and even had to sell his valuable collection of minerals. Fearing arrest, he fled to his estate at Pressburg [Bratislava]; he did not return to Vienna until 1830.

It was during Pálffy's ownership of the Theater an der Wien that Schubert's melodrama *Die Zauberharfe* (D644) and Helmina von Chézy's* play *Rosamunde, Fürstin von Zypern*, with Schubert's incidental music (D797), were produced there, on 19 August 1820 and 20 December 1823 respectively. Neither proved particularly successful, *Die Zauberharfe* achieving eight performances, *Rosamunde* only two. The fact that such figures were by no means untypical of Pálffy's productions no doubt helps to explain the increasingly precarious nature of his financial position.

In December 1823 Schubert dedicated to Pálffy the Sonata in B flat major for piano duet (D617).

(Bauer, *ÖBL*)

Paumgartner, Sylvester (b. Steyr, 6 September 1764; d. 23 November 1841). Assistant manager of iron mines at Steyr, Upper Austria. He was a great music lover and possessed a splendid collection of music and instruments. He also played the cello, though apparently not very well. There were two music rooms in his house, which was situated in the central square of the town [16 Stadtplatz] and served as a focus for music-making at Steyr. He was a good friend of Albert Stadler* and of Johann Michael Vogl,* both natives of the town. The latter, who liked to return there in the summer, repeatedly stayed with Paumgartner, who was a batchelor.

Schubert visited Steyr, together with Vogl, in 1819, 1823, and 1825. On the first occasion he lodged with Albert Schellmann,* but in 1825 both he and Vogl are known to have stayed with Paumgartner, and they may well have done so already in 1823. During Schubert's first stay at Steyr, Paumgartner commissioned him to compose a quintet; the result was the 'Trout' Quintet (D667). It carried no dedication when it was published by Josef Czerny* in May 1829, but a copy made by Albert Stadler indicates that Schubert had intended to dedicate it to Paumgartner. (The autograph is lost.)

In January 1838, Paumgartner arranged a concert at the municipal theatre at Steyr for the purpose of collecting a contribution to the costs of the Mozart statue which was to be erected in Salzburg. His reward was a letter of thanks from Mozart's widow, Constanze Nissen. The statue was unveiled on 4 September 1842. This was not Paumgartner's only link with Salzburg. His brother was the great-great-grandfather of the musicologist, conductor, and composer Bernhard Paumgartner, who was for many years director of the Salzburg Mozarteum (1917–38, 1945–59), and president of the Salzburg Festival from 1960 until his death in 1971.

(Angermüller[3])

Pazdírek, Bohumil: *see* Gotthard.*

Pennauer, Anton (b. Vienna, *c*.1784; d. Vienna, 20 October 1837). Music publisher; son of Kaspar Pennauer, a musician and music copyist. He set up as a music publisher in the Leopoldstadt suburb in 1822. After several refusals, he was finally granted permission on 1 March 1825 to open an art and music shop in the city centre, and he did so on 5 July of that year [1 Bräunerstrasse]; not very long afterwards he moved into an adjoining house on the Graben. In 1834 the publishing firm went bankrupt and its stock was acquired by Anton Diabelli & Co.* Pennauer died in utter poverty.

His publications, which were known for their elegant title-pages and neat graphical production, included works by Georg Hellmesberger, Conradin Kreutzer, Franz Paul Lachner,* Josef Mayseder, Benedikt Randhartinger,* and Schubert. Pennauer, or his manager Franz Hüther, must have been in contact with Schubert well before the end of May 1825, when Schubert left Vienna for a long holiday in Upper Austria, for the firm announced first editions of three of his songs during his subsequent absence: 'Die junge Nonne' (D828) and 'Nacht und Träume' (D827) on 25 July, and 'Suleika II' (D717) on 12 August.

Pennauer issued first editions of thirteen further compositions by Schubert in his lifetime: the songs 'An die Leier' (D737), 'Der Jüngling am Bache' (D638), 'Der Unglückliche' (D713), 'Hoffnung' (D637), 'Im Haine' (D738), 'Sehnsucht' (D636), and 'Willkommen und Abschied' (D767); the male-voice quartets 'Ewige Liebe' (D825A), 'Flucht' (D825B), and 'Wehmut' (D825); the Piano Sonata in A minor (D845); and the piano duets *Grande marche funèbre* (D859) and *Grande marche héroïque* (D885).

After Schubert's death, Pennauer brought out first editions in 1829–30 of the song 'Viola' (D786), of 'Zwei Szenen aus dem Schauspiel *Lacrimas*' (D857), and of the Piano Sonata in E flat major (D568).

First editions: D568, 636–8, 713, 717, 737–8, 767, 786, 825, 825A–B, 827–8, 845, 857, 859, 885.
(Weinmann²)

Percy, Thomas (b. Bridgnorth, Shropshire, 13 April 1729; d. Dromore, County Down, Northern Ireland, 30 September 1811). He was educated at Christ Church, Oxford. In 1753 he became vicar of Easton Maudit, Northamptonshire, and in 1756 rector of Wilby, Northamptonshire. He was appointed dean of Carlisle in 1778, and bishop of Dromore four years later. In 1765 he published *Reliques of Ancient English Poetry,* a collection of ballads, sonnets, historical songs, and metrical romances; subsequent editions in 1767, 1775, and 1794 added further material. One of the poems from *Reliques,* entitled 'Edward, Edward', was translated into German by Herder,* whose version was set to music by Schubert in 'Eine altschottische Ballade' in September 1827.

Setting: D923.
(*EB*)

Petrarch [Petrarca, Francesco] (b. Arezzo, 20 July 1304; d. Arquà, 18 July 1374). Poet. In 1818 Schubert set sonnets XXXIV–XXXV and CLXIV of his *Canzoniere*, in German versions by Johann Diederich Gries* and August Wilhelm von Schlegel.*

Settings: D628–30.

Pettenkoffer, Anton von (1788–1834). In 1818 he made his Viennese apartment [11 Bauernmarkt] available to the private orchestral society which had previously held its concerts at Otto Hatwig's.* For the next two years it regularly met at Pettenkoffer's on Thursday evenings; Schubert frequently took part, playing the viola. In addition to the usual fare of orchestral music, the society now tackled oratorios, including Handel's *Messiah* and Haydn's *Die Schöpfung* and *Die sieben letzten Worte unseres Erlösers am Kreuze*.

According to Leopold von Sonnleithner,* these concerts came to an end when Pettenkoffer, who was employed in the wholesale trade, won first prize in a lottery, acquired a country estate, and moved out of Vienna. Sonnleithner states that the concerts ceased in the autumn of 1820; but Matthias Franz Perth records in his diary a performance of 'Erlkönig' (D328) at Pettenkoffer's on 8 February 1821. Sonnleithner adds that Pettenkoffer did not manage his new fortune well, and died poor. His son August (1822–89), who went by the name 'von Pettenkofen', became a well-known painter.

Pfeffel, Gottlieb Conrad (b. Colmar, 28 June 1736; d. Colmar, 1 May 1809). Translator, dramatist, and poet. The son of a senior official in the French foreign ministry, he intended to follow a diplomatic career, but was unable to do so when an eye-disease left him blind in 1758. He played a prominent role in the Protestant community of his native city, where, in 1773, he founded a military academy for the sons of Protestant noblemen, which he ran until 1792.

In 1761 he published a three-volume collection of his poetry, *Poetische Versuche*. This was followed by three further, augmented, editions, the last of which appeared in ten volumes between 1802 and 1810. A companion ten-volume edition of his *Prosaische Versuche* was published posthumously (1810–12). His mastery of both French and German enabled him, moreover, to translate poems by Magnus Gottfried Lichtwer into French (*Nouvelles fables*, 1763, together with a certain d'Abquerbe), and a collection of French plays into German (*Theatralische Belustigungen nach französischen Mustern*, 5 vols., 1765–74).

In December 1811 Schubert set a poem by Pfeffel in 'Der Vatermörder'.

Setting: D10.

(Porhansl⁹, Rector)

Pichler, Karoline, née von Greiner (b. Vienna, 7 September 1769; d. Vienna, 9 July 1843). Novelist, playwright, poetess, and literary hostess; daughter of Franz Sales von Greiner (1730–98), a councillor in the Austro-Bohemian chancellery who was ennobled in 1771. The Greiners were very fond of music; Mozart was one of several well-known performers who regularly played in quartets at their house. From an early age, Karoline studied singing and the piano with Josef Anton Steffan; she eventually became an excellent pianist, guitarist, and singer. In 1796 she married Andreas Pichler (1764–1837), a civil servant.

She was a prolific writer and her complete works, published between 1828 and 1844, ran to sixty volumes; but she is remembered today almost solely for her memoirs (*Denkwürdigkeiten aus meinem Leben*) which appeared posthumously in 1844. Her salon in the Alserstadt suburb [8 Alserstrasse] was a favourite meeting-place for Vienna's intelligentsia.

She met Schubert at a soirée which Matthäus von Collin* gave in *c*.1820 to introduce the composer to distinguished Viennese music lovers. According to Anselm Hüttenbrenner,* she was very complimentary and encouraging. Her admiration for Schubert's music is confirmed by Petr Ivanovich Keppen* who, after conversing with her on 20 April 1822, wrote in his diary: 'She highly praised his talent as a composer.' Schubert's music was frequently played at her house. Thus Keppen heard Pichler's daughter Karoline sing several of the Goethe* songs when he visited them on 15 and 22 March 1822. Those performed on the second occasion included 'Erlkönig' (D328), 'Meeres Stille' (D216), and 'Wandrers Nachtlied' (D224). Schubert himself is known to have visited Pichler's salon repeatedly during this period. Count Prokesch von Osten* heard him sing some of his songs there on 5 March 1822 'with a wealth of feeling and profundity'; and on 24 April Keppen was present when Schubert himself turned the pages while mother and daughter played his *Eight Variations on a French Song* (D624). As Schubert stepped up to the piano, Karoline Pichler remarked: 'I feel as if Mozart had once more come to turn the pages while I played one of his sonatas.'

The following three Schubert songs are settings of texts by Pichler: 'Der Sänger am Felsen' (D482) and 'Lied' (D483), both composed in September 1816, i.e. before he had met their author; and 'Der Unglückliche' (D713), which he wrote in January 1821. The words are taken, respectively, from the idyll entitled 'Der Sänger am Felsen', from the idyll 'Der Sommerabend', and from the novel *Olivier, oder die Rache der Elfen*. Furthermore, K. Scheit and E. W. Partsch indicate in their article 'Ein unbekanntes Schubertlied in einer Sammlung aus dem Wiener Vormärz' (in *Schubert durch die Brille*, No. 2, 1989) that, in addition to making a through-composed setting of the third text in D713, Schubert may also be the composer of a strophic song composed to the same words.

Settings: D482–3, 713.
(Chochlow, *ÖBL*, Scheit/Partsch)

Pinterics, Karl (d. 6 March 1831). Private secretary of Prince Josef Franz Pálffy von Erdöd, and, after his death in 1827, of his son Prince Anton Karl. He had an office at the Pálffys' residence [6 Josefsplatz].

He was highly musical, played the piano very competently, and had a pleasing bass voice. He knew Beethoven* quite well. In 1821 he met Schubert, and he soon became a close friend and an ardent admirer of his music. He often received Schubert and members of his circle at his lodgings at the 'Zuckerbäckerhaus' near the Karlskirche. In August 1824, while Schubert was absent at Zseliz, Moritz von Schwind* informed Franz von Schober* that he frequently heard Schubert's music at Pinterics's, whom he described as 'an excellent and enterprising man, friendly, enthusiastic, and an avid collector of old German works of art'. In 1826 Schubert dedicated to him his Op. 56, consisting of the songs 'An die Leier' (D737), 'Im Haine' (D738), and 'Willkommen und Abschied' (D767).

In his 'Erinnerungen an Franz Schubert' (*Niederrheinische Musikzeitung für Kunstfreunde und Künstler*, 7 and 14 March 1857), Anton Schindler* stated that Pinterics had dissuaded Schubert in 1824 from studying counterpoint with Simon Sechter,* arguing that it would be inopportune for him to do so at a time when he was already a well-established composer. Schubert was eventually to take one lesson with Sechter on 4 November 1828. (*See also* Harold.*)

Pinterics was survived by his wife Franziska, née Moll (1780–1867). He left a very considerable collection of Schubert Lieder, which was acquired by Josef Wilhelm Witteczek.* A list which he had made of Schubert's songs ran to 505 items.

(Kreissle, Wurzbach[1])

Platen, August, Count [in full: Platen-Hallermünde, Karl August Georg Maximilian, Count] (b. Ansbach, 24 October 1796; d. Syracuse, Sicily, 5 December 1835). Poet and dramatist. Born into an impoverished Protestant aristocratic family (his father was a forestry official), he attended school in Munich and later served as an officer in the army (1814–18). Subsequently he studied literature and languages at Würzburg and Erlangen until 1826. In that year, vexed by his failure as a playwright and tormented by feelings of isolation occasioned by his homosexuality, he turned his back on Germany and went to Italy.

It was Platen's ambition to write monumental epic poems and imposing plays, but in the first genre he did not get beyond the rather modest *Die Abbassiden*, whilst his stage works, which included comedies in the manner of Aristophanes, met with little acclaim. On the other hand, he made a certain impact with his lyric poetry, which was notable for its virtuosic handling of a large variety of forms, including oriental ones in *Ghaselen* (1821) and *Neue Ghaselen* (1823). Another volume of poetry, *Lyrische Blätter*, also appeared in 1821, followed by *Vermischte Schriften* in 1822. An edition of his collected writings, published in Leipzig in 1910, ran to twelve volumes.

In 1820 Platen spent two weeks in Vienna, but he does not appear to have come into contact with any of the literary circles of the city. In early 1821 he became friendly at Erlangen with Franz von Bruchmann,* to whom he presented a copy of the newly published *Ghaselen*. After his return to Vienna, Bruchmann introduced

Schubert to Platen's poetry, and in 1822 Schubert set two of his poems in 'Die Liebe hat gelogen' (D751) and 'Du liebst mich nicht' (D756). These songs have been described as 'extraordinary—a perfect marriage of Platen's bitter laments of false or unreciprocated love to some of Schubert's most harmonically intense, tonally far-ranging music' (S. Youens).

Settings: D751, 756.
(Dove[1], Platen, Youens[1])

Platner, Anton or **Eduard,** (b. Zirl, near Innsbruck, 3 November 1787; d. Brixen [Bressanone], 27 January 1855). Priest; poet. He attended school at Hall, and later studied philosophy at Innsbruck. He took an active part in the 1809 rising against Bavaria, to which Tyrol had been attached by the treaty of Pressburg [Bratislava] in 1805. After the collapse of the rebellion he led an adventurous existence in Southern Germany, Bohemia, Vienna, and Hungary, before returning to Tyrol. In 1818 he was ordained, and he subsequently served in various parishes, but his increasingly bizarre behaviour repeatedly brought him into conflict both with his parishioners and with the religious authorities, and led to his being confined in lunatic asylums on more than one occasion.

He left a considerable number of poems, many of which were published after his death. He may be the author of 'Die Blumensprache', which appeared in *W. G. Beckers Taschenbuch zum geselligen Vergnügen* over the letters 'Pl' in 1805, and was set by Schubert, probably in 1817, in his identically titled song.

Setting: ?D519.
(Wurzbach[1])

Pollak, Aaron. He is named as the author of 'Frühlingslied' on the title-page of a copy (now in the possession of the Wiener Männergesangverein) of Schubert's setting of that poem for single voice (D919). Nothing else is known about him. This composition has been tentatively ascribed to the spring of 1827 and may have been written shortly after Schubert had set the same text for male-voice quartet (D914) in April of that year.

Settings: D914, 919.

Pope, Alexander (b. London, 21 May 1688; d. Twickenham, 30 May 1744). Poet. His poem 'The Dying Christian to His Soul' was translated by Herder* and published by him under the title 'Popens sterbender Christ an seine Seele'. This German version was set by Schubert in May 1813 in 'Verklärung'.

Setting: D59.

Prandstetter, Martin Josef (b. Vienna, 5 October 1760; d. Munkács, Hungary [Mukachevo, Ukraine], 25 June 1798). Viennese magistrate. Between 1782 and 1786 he was active in Masonic affairs, being a member successively of the 'Zum heiligen Josef', 'Zur wahren Eintracht', and 'Zur Wahrheit' Lodges. In August 1794 he was arrested on suspicion of involvement in the so-called 'Jacobin' conspiracy. On 25 July 1795 he was found guilty of treason and sentenced to thirty years' imprisonment in the fortress at Munkács. He died there three years later.

From 1779 onward he published ballads and Anacreontic verse in the *Wiener Musenalmanach*, which he himself edited during the year 1780. In August 1815 Schubert set his poem 'Die Fröhlichkeit'.

Setting: D262.
(Haderer, Reinalter, Wurzbach[1])

Pratobevera von Wiesborn, Adolf, Baron (b. Bielitz-Biala, Austrian Silesia [Bielsko-Biala, Poland], 12 June 1806; d. Vienna, 16 February 1875). Government official; son of Karl Josef Pratobevera von Wiesborn (1769–1853), a distinguished lawyer who was appointed vice-president of the Lower Austrian court of appeal in 1818, taught at Vienna University (of which he served as rector in 1824), was ennobled in 1829, and created a baron in 1838.

Adolf studied law at the University of Vienna (1824–8) and subsequently had a distinguished career in government service. In 1848 he became Ministerialrat in the ministry of justice, and in 1850 head of department; from 1851 he served on the high court of justice. In 1861 he was elected to the Lower Austrian assembly and chosen by the latter to sit in the lower chamber of the Reichsrat. That same year he became minister of justice, but was obliged to resign his post in 1862 because of an eye ailment. However, he was able to resume his political career two years later. From 1867 to 1870 he held the position of governor of Lower Austria; in 1869 he was appointed a life member of the Herrenhaus, the upper chamber of the Reichsrat.

He was the author of some occasional verse and of a number of stories. In 1825 he wrote a dramatic poem entitled 'Der Falke'. It concludes with an epilogue spoken by Mechthild as her father-in-law, Hugo (Ritter von Eicheck), is dying. Pratobevera asked Schubert to compose some pianoforte music to accompany Mechthild's speech. The epilogue thus constitutes an example of 'melodrama', the genre or technique perfected by the composer Georg Benda, in which a character speaks either during pauses in the accompaniment or, more usually, simultaneously with the music. Schubert had previously used melodrama in *Des Teufels Lustschloss* (D84), *Die Zauberharfe* (D644), and *Fierrabras* (D796). The title 'Abschied', under which Schubert's music for 'The Falke' is known, does not appear either in his autograph or in Pratobevera's manuscript. The composition (D829) was first published by A. Reissmann in his book *Franz Schubert: Sein Leben und seine Werke* (Berlin, 1873).

Pratobevera's 'Der Falke' was performed on the occasion of his father's birthday on 17 February 1826, in the family's flat at the Bürgerspital, a large apartment building near the Kärntnertor. It is not known whether Schubert participated in the performance, nor is any information available about his other contacts, if any, with

Pratobevera. In any case, a rather formal reference in the latter's diary in 1833 to 'the late composer Schubert' suggests that their relationship was never an intimate one.

Pratobevera had received some musical instruction from Jan Václav Voříšek,* but he was, in his own phrase, an 'unmusical music lover'. His diary none the less reveals an interest in music and shows, in particular, that he venerated Beethoven* ('an all-powerful magician') and had a very high regard for Mozart. On the other hand, he rated Schubert far less highly: 'Few of his numerous songs filled me with enthusiasm; many are very beautiful, but quite a few did not appeal to me at all, in fact revolted me with their frightful sentimentality (e.g. 'Gefrorne Tränen' in *Winterreise*, etc.).'

At least two of Pratobevera's sisters responded much more warmly to Schubert's compositions. 'On Twelfth Night my uncle [the barrister Kaspar Wagner] gave a small musical party,' Marie, the oldest, wrote to her fiancé Josef Bergmann on 10 January 1828. 'True, Schubert kept us waiting for him in vain, but, in his place, [Ludwig] Titze* sang many of his songs so touchingly and expressively that his absence did not weigh on us too heavily. I wished, dear friend, that I could, by magic, have transported you here, so beautiful and glorious was this concert.' Another sister, Franziska [Fanni], whom Marie called 'our little nightingale', greatly enjoyed singing Schubert's Lieder, to the delight of her fiancé Josef Tremier who brought her 'enormous quantities of sweet and touching songs by Schubert' (Marie to Bergmann, 31 May 1828). The youngest sister, Bertha, married the future Schubert biographer Heinrich Kreissle von Hellborn.*

Pratobevera's cousin Maria Mitterbacher, a daughter of the above-mentioned Kaspar Wagner, left an interesting account of her contacts with Schubert, who frequently visited her family in Obere Bäckerstrasse, and describes the overwhelming impression which his songs had made on her. Concerning his rendition of his own compositions, she wrote: 'I have heard all the famous Schubert singers... but no one sang them like Schubert, who had no voice.'

Setting: D829.
(Höslinger, *ÖBL*, Wurzbach[1])

Preisinger [Preysinger], **Josef** (b. Vienna, 24 January 1792; d. Prague, June 1865. Bass and composer; son of a wealthy merchant. He made his début at the Kärntnertor-Theater in 1823 as the Mayor in Rossini's *La gazza ladra*. During the next ten years he led a somewhat nomadic artistic existence, moving from Vienna to Graz in 1824 and thence to Pressburg [Bratislava], returning to the Viennese court theatre in 1826, appearing in Berlin in 1828, subsequently undertaking a tour of Germany and France, and thereafter accepting engagements in Graz (1828–32), at the Theater in der Josefstadt in Vienna (1832–4), and finally at the German Theatre in Prague in 1834. Among his most successful roles were Basilio in Rossini's *Il barbiere di Siviglia*, Oroe in the same composer's *Semiramide*, and Mephistofeles in Louis Spohr's *Faust*. He retired from the stage in 1862.

Preisinger gave the first performances of Schubert's songs 'Gruppe aus dem Tartarus' (D583) and 'Der Zwerg' (D771) at 'evening entertainments' of the Gesellschaft der Musikfreunde on 8 March 1821 and 13 November 1823 respectively. He also took part in the first performance of the quartet 'Nachtgesang im Walde' (D913) at Josef Rudolf Lewy's* concert at the Musikverein on 22 April 1827. In addition, he was one of the singers in 'Gesang der Geister über den Wassern' (D714) at Ignaz von Sonnleithner's* on 30 March 1821, and also sang 'Gruppe aus dem Tartarus' again at another 'evening entertainment' on 19 December 1822. He contributed waltzes to several collections of dances.

(Kutsch/Riemens)

Probst, Heinrich Albert (b. Dresden, 1791; d. Leipzig, 24 May 1846). Music publisher active in Leipzig and Paris. Son of the rope-maker and, later, schoolmaster Johann Gotthilf Probst (1759–1830) and his wife Johanna Eleonore, née Götz (1765–1829). He worked in the leather trade in Leipzig for several years before setting up a music publishing firm. He announced its existence in a circular dated 1 May 1823 and, at the same time, issued his first catalogue. He opened his career as a publisher with a Mass by Gottfried Weber. Whilst his list, over the next eight years, included the names of a large number of composers drawn from various countries, he gave pride of place to the works of Frédéric Kalkbrenner, of which more than one hundred were issued between 1823 and 1839 by himself and his successor, Carl Friedrich Kistner (1797–1844). On 28 May 1831 he sold the business (with effect from the beginning of that year) to Kistner, who at first ran it under the name 'H. A. Probst—F. Kistner', but, from 1836, traded entirely under his own name. Probst himself left Leipzig to join the Maison Pleyel in Paris, but later returned to Germany. The firm he had founded in Leipzig continued to prosper under different proprietors, and by 1943 had issued some 30,000 items.

Schubert first tried to interest Probst in his compositions on 12 August 1826. (On the same day he sent an almost identical letter to Breitkopf & Härtel.*) In his reply (26 August), Probst was cautiously encouraging, inviting Schubert to send him some songs and piano pieces for two or four hands through Robert Lähne, the bookkeeper of the Viennese firm Artaria & Co.,* for which Probst acted as agent. He stressed that the music should not be too difficult, for 'the distinctive, often ingenious but at times also rather unusual, nature of your mind's creations is not yet sufficiently and generally understood by our public'. On 15 January 1827 he acknowledged having received three compositions, but explained that he was not in a position to publish them just then since he was fully occupied with the edition of Kalkbrenner's works; moreover, he considered the fee of 80 florins, which Schubert was asking for each manuscript, to be rather high.

Later that same year Probst met Schubert in Vienna, and on that occasion invited him to submit further compositions. He repeated this invitation in a letter on 9 February 1828, again stressing that the songs ought not to be 'too difficult to comprehend' and that the piano pieces should be 'of a similar nature'. In his reply of 10 April, Schubert offered his new Piano Trio in E flat major (D929), which, he claimed, had been very well received at his recent concert [on 26 March]. Probst accepted by return of mail, but again asked for 'selected trifles' for the voice or piano duet, 'since a trio ... rarely brings in any money'. On 18 July Probst informed Schubert that he had only just received the trio, but promised publication within six weeks. On 2 October Schubert wrote to express his frustration at the delay ('I await its appearance with longing'), while at the same time offering further compositions, namely three piano sonatas (D958–60), several Heine* songs (which were later included in *Schwanengesang*, D957), and a string quintet (D956). The edition of the piano trio finally appeared in late October or early November; it is unlikely that Schubert ever saw it.

In December 1828 Probst published the four songs 'Der blinde Knabe' (D833), 'Im Frühling' (D882), 'Trost im Liede' (D546), and 'Wandrers Nachtlied' (D768). None was a first edition, since the songs had previously been printed in Schickh's* *Wiener Zeitschrift für Kunst, Literatur, Theater und Mode*.

First edition: D929.

(Linnemann, Neumann², Plesske)

Prokesch von Osten, Anton, Count (b. Graz, 10 December 1795; d. Vienna, 26 October 1876). General, diplomat, and writer. After his father, Maximilian Prokesch, had died in 1811, his mother Anna, née von Stadler, married the historian Julius Schneller* in 1815.

Prokesch volunteered in 1813 for service in the war against Napoleon, and thereafter made the army his career. Between 1815 and 1818 he was stationed at Mainz, Linz, and Olmütz [Olomuc], and in 1818 he was appointed adjutant to Field Marshal Prince Karl Philipp Schwarzenberg, who had commanded the allied armies at the Battle of Leipzig in 1813 and of whom Prokesch was to publish a biography in 1823. After Schwarzenberg's death in 1821, Prokesch was attached to the quarter-master-general's staff in Vienna. He remained there until 1823, when he was posted to Trieste. The years 1824–30 he spent in Greece and the Middle East, for the most part on military and diplomatic missions. From 1834 until 1871 he served with distinction in a series of diplomatic posts in Athens, Berlin, Frankfurt, and finally Constantinople. During that period he continued to receive military promotions. In addition, he was ennobled in 1830, became a baron in 1845, and was created a count in 1871. On 25 November 1832 he married Irene Kiesewetter von Wiesenbrunn.*

As a writer, he is best known for his travel books, notably *Erinnerungen aus Aegypten und Kleinasien* (3 vols., 1829–31), for the above-mentioned life of Prince Schwarzenberg, and for the historical study *Geschichte des Abfalls der Griechen vom türkischen Reiche* (6 vols., 1867).

It was in 1822, while a lieutenant on the quartermaster-general's staff, that he became friendly with Schubert. He himself later stated that they had met in

Karoline Pichler's* salon. Two entries in his diary in early 1822 record occasions when both were present there. The first, on 5 March, mentions that Schubert sang several of his songs 'with a wealth of feeling and eloquence'. The second, on 24 April, points to a closer acquaintance: 'At the Pichlers', where I meet Schubert, who sings some songs to me.' In fact, Prokesch indicates in some notes which he later wrote about this period that their relations became quite friendly: 'I was frequently together with Schubert, for, although he was not a cultured person, his frankness, sound judgement, and enthusiasm made him agreeable company. He sang most of his compositions to me. We spent many an evening in the most animated conversation at a beer-cellar near the Kärntnertor-Theater [Wichtl's tavern in Komödiengasse].' Yet a diary entry written on 6 August 1822 suggests that their contacts, while amicable enough, were never really intimate: 'Dined at an inn, where I met the composer Schubert. We discussed music. He walked back with me.' As already stated, Prokesch moved to Trieste in 1823.

(*ÖBL*, Wurzbach[1])

Pyrker [Pircher] von Felsö-Eör, Johann Ladislaus (b. Lángh, near Stuhlweissenburg [Székesfehérvár], Hungary, 2 November 1772; d. Vienna, 2 December 1847). Ecclesiastic, poet, and dramatist; member of an old aristocratic family. Son of Stefan Pircher von Felsö-Eör (1732–1814), estate manager of Count Johann Zichy von Vásonkeö. He was educated at Stuhlweissenburg and Fünfkirchen [Pécs] and then worked for a short time in the civil service at Ofen [Budapest]. In 1792 he was admitted to the Cistertian monastery at Lilienfeld in Lower Austria; he studied theology at St Pölten, and in 1796 took holy orders. Thereafter he exercised various functions at Lilienfeld, eventually becoming its abbot in 1812. In 1818 he was appointed bishop of Zips in Hungary [Spiš, Slovak Republic] and in 1820 patriarch (i.e. archbishop) of Venice; from 1826 he served as archbishop of Erlau [Eger]. During his final years, as his health was failing, he resided increasingly in Vienna. He was highly respected for his humanitarian and cultural activities. He established teachers' training colleges at Zips and Erlau, founded an art college at Erlau, and enlarged the Institute for the Blind in Vienna.

His literary output included several patriotic plays (*Die Korwinen*; *Karl der Kleine, König von Ungarn*; *Zrinis Tod*), the epic *Tunisias*, religious verse (*Perlen der heiligen Vorzeit, Bilder aus dem Leben Jesu und der Apostel*), and some more personal poems (*Lieder der Sehnsucht nach den Alpen*). He also left an autobiography, *Mein Leben*. His writings won the admiration of his contemporaries, a judgement not shared by modern critics.

In May 1821, Schubert dedicated to Pyrker his Op. 4, containing the first editions of the songs 'Der Wanderer' (D489), 'Morgenlied' (D685), and 'Wandrers Nachtlied' (D224). He had met Pyrker at a soirée at Matthäus von Collin's* in *c*.1820. Anselm Hüttenbrenner* later recalled that Schubert had, on that occasion, sung 'Der Wanderer', and Josef von Spaun* stated that Pyrker was particularly fond of the song. In authorizing Schubert to dedicate the three songs to him, Pyrker, writing from Venice on 18 May 1821, declared himself 'proud to belong to the same country as yourself'. In due course he showed his appreciation by sending a gift of 12 ducats (about 50 gulden).

In the summer of 1825 Schubert met Pyrker at Gastein, where the patriarch was in the habit of taking a cure each year. Schubert, who was travelling with Johann Michael Vogl,* stayed at the spa from 14 August to 4 September. During this time he set two passages from Pyrker's works: one from *Tunisias*, the other from 'Elisa', a poem in *Perlen der heiligen Vorzeit*. The songs, titled 'Das Heimweh' (D851) and 'Die Allmacht' (D852), were published as Schubert's Op. 79 in May 1827, with a dedication to Pyrker. The first performance of 'Die Allmacht' was given by Vogl at Schubert's concert on 26 March 1828; it was sung by Johann Karl Schoberlechner* at the memorial concerts on 30 January and 5 March 1829. Schubert set the same text once more in January 1826, this time for mixed voices (D875A).

The very high esteem in which Pyrker was universally held is evidenced by his membership of learned societies in Munich, Venice, Padua, Copenhagen, and elsewhere. In addition, he was an honorary member of the Hungarian Academy of Sciences, and a founder member of the Academy of Sciences in Vienna. On 4 September 1842 he was among the prominent guests present at the unveiling of the Mozart statue in Salzburg. He moreover wrote a special hymn, 'Oesterreich', for the festivities, which, in a choral setting by Sigismund von Neukomm, was performed that same evening in front of the statue by some three hundred singers, accompanied by the wind instruments of two regimental bands. It was later repeated before the house where Mozart was born and once more in the ceremonial hall of St Peter's. In his hymn, Pyrker pays tribute to Mozart, Haydn, and Schubert, Austria's outstanding composers ('Auch lasst uns Schubert preisen | Ob seiner Zauberweisen').

Settings: D851–2, 875A.
(Angermüller[3], Fischer[7], *ÖBL*, Pyrker)

Randhartinger, Benedikt (b. Ruprechtshofen, Lower Austria, 27 July 1802; d. Vienna, 23 December 1893). Composer, conductor, and singer. He was educated at the Stadtkonvikt, Vienna (1812–19), where he became acquainted with Schubert. He subsequently studied philosophy and law at the University of Vienna until 1825, and, at the same time, received instruction in composition from Antonio Salieri.* He worked as secretary to Count Louis Széchényi* from 1825 until 1832, when he was engaged as a tenor in the court Kapelle. From 1830 he conducted at court concerts, from 1840 at the court theatre. He became deputy court Kapellmeister in 1846, and, after the death of Ignaz Assmayer,* Kapellmeister (1862–6). A prolific composer whose output ran to more than 2,000 works, he wrote much church music (including some twenty Masses), as well as an opera (*König Enzio*), orchestral and chamber music, dances, and over 400 songs.

There is evidence, especially from Franz von Hartmann's* diary for the years 1826–7, that Randhartinger was a member of Schubert's circle. In 1830 he dedicated a vocal quartet, 'Ins stille Land', to Schubert's memory. Nevertheless, modern Schubertians (e.g. O. E. Deutsch* and M. J. E. Brown) are sceptical of his later claims that he had been among the composer's most intimate friends, and dismiss some of his stories about Schubert as unlikely or downright fanciful. For instance, he told Kreissle* that Schubert had composed the first songs of *Die schöne Müllerin* (D795) during the night which followed his discovery of a copy of the poems in Randhartinger's office at Széchényi's residence; yet the song cycle was written in late 1823 and published in 1824, before Randhartinger even entered the count's service. On the other hand, he may indeed, as he informed Albert B. Bach, have been the first to sing the newly composed 'Erlkönig' (D328) at the Stadtkonvikt, with Schubert accompanying. Schubert gave him an autograph copy (of the third version) in 1817, which Randhartinger presented to Clara Wieck in January 1838; it is now at the Pierpont Morgan Library in New York.

After Schubert's death, Randhartinger was associated with Schubert's songs on several occasions on the concert platform in Vienna, both as interpreter and pianist. To cite a few examples: on 5 February 1833, he sang 'Wohin' from *Die schöne Müllerin* (D795/2) at a concert given by the pianist Franziska Sallamon; on 14 May 1838 he sang 'Das Fischermädchen' (D957/10), 'Der Kreuzzug' (D932), and 'Die Forelle' (D550), accompanied by Liszt;* on 2 December 1839 he again sang 'Die Forelle' to Liszt's accompaniment; and on 8 November 1842 he accompanied Pierre François Wartel in 'Abschied' (D957/7), 'Die vier Weltalter' (D391), and 'Liebesbotschaft' (D957/1), all sung in French.

(Bach, Brown[8], Brusatti, *ÖBL*)

Ratschky, Josef Franz von (b. Vienna, 21 August 1757; d. Vienna, 31 May 1810). Poet, dramatist, and translator. In 1776, after studying philosophy at the University of Vienna, he entered the civil service, in which he had a very successful career.

In 1777 he founded the *Wienerischer* [from 1786: *Wiener*] *Musenalmanach*, an annual collection of poetry which played an important role in the literary life of Vienna until it ceased publication in 1796. Some of his own poems were printed in it, as well as in other anthologies such as *Der teutsche Merkur* and *Göttinger Musenalmanach*. His poetry appeared also in volume form: *Gedichte* in 1785 (with an augmented edition in 1791), and *Neuere Gedichte* in 1805. In addition, he wrote several works for the stage, including *Bekir und Gulroui*, adapted from a one-act play by Denis-Dominique Cardonne, and *Der verlogene Bediente*, based on David Garrick's *The Lying Valet*. Among the authors he translated were Horace, Lucan, Pope,* and Swift.

His poem 'Der Weiberfreund', a German version of the poem 'The Inconstant' from Abraham Cowley's* love-cycle *The Mistress*, appeared in *W. G. Beckers*

Taschenbuch zum geselligen Vergnügen in 1795. It was set by Schubert in August 1815.

Setting: D271.
(Kriegleder, Porhansl[9])

Reil, Johann Anton Friedrich (b. Ehrenbreitstein, near Koblenz, 2 February 1773; d. Penzing, near Vienna, 22 July 1843). Actor and writer. He first appeared on the stage at Brünn [Brno] in 1794, and subsequently performed at Laibach [Ljubljana], Innsbruck, and Regensburg, before joining the Burgtheater in Vienna, of which he was a member from 1800 to 1805 and again from 1809 to 1831. His most successful roles included Miller in Schiller's* *Kabale und Liebe*, and the title roles in Heinrich Josef von Collin's* *Regulus* and Lessing's *Nathan der Weise*.

He was himself the author of several plays, and of librettos set by Josef Weigl* (*Der Bergsturz*) and Conradin Kreutzer (*Fridolin, oder Der Gang nach dem Eisenhammer*). He furthermore wrote works of topographical and historical interest, and a number of poems. Among the latter was the poem 'Das Lied im Grünen' which Schubert set (D917) in June 1827, presumably from a manuscript supplied by the author, for the poem was not published in the *Wiener allgemeine Theaterzeitung* until 13 October of that year. For the first edition of Schubert's song, issued by M. J. Leidesdorf* in June 1829, Reil wrote several new stanzas 'as an expression of his grief at the composer's death'.

Reil also provided two additional stanzas for the edition of 'Ständchen: Horch, horch! die Lerch im Ätherblau' (D889) which Anton Diabelli & Co.* published in 1835. The German version which Schubert had taken from the Vienna Shakespeare* translation of 1825 consisted, like the original text of *Cymbeline*, of only one stanza, and neither the extant autograph nor the first edition of the song (1830, also by Anton Diabelli & Co.) contains the additions. Reil is probably also responsible for the further stanza printed in the first edition (Anton Diabelli & Co., 1850) of 'Trinklied: Bacchus, feister Fürst des Weins' (D888). There again, only one stanza appears in Shakespeare's *Antony and Cleopatra*, in the Vienna Shakespeare translation, and in Schubert's autograph. Finally, Reil was the author of the poem which Schubert used in the partsong 'Glaube, Hoffnung und Liebe' (D954).

Settings: D917, 954.
(*ÖBL*, Simmer, Wurzbach[1])

Reissig, Christian Ludwig (von) (b. Kassel, 24 July 1784; d. Steinamanger [Szombathely], Hungary, 5 December 1847). Poet. Arriving in Vienna in February 1809 while on his way to Italy, he volunteered to serve in the Austrian army against Napoleon. He was seriously wounded, but later fought in the Peninsular War. In 1822, finding himself in financial difficulties, he was obliged to sell his house at Hietzing, on the outskirts of Vienna, and moved with his family to Hungary. There his fortunes reportedly improved.

It is not known precisely how many poems Reissig wrote; between 1810 and 1826, some fifty of them were set to music by various composers, who included Beethoven,* Conradin Kreutzer, Wenzel Müller,* Salieri,* Josef Weigl,* and Karl Friedrich Zelter. It was Reissig's practice to request well-known musicians to set his poems, frequently without a fee. He would then publish the songs, sometimes without the composer's consent, and dedicate them to eminent persons who could be counted upon to express their appreciation in a suitable manner.

A collection of Reissig's poems was published in Vienna in 1809 under the title *Blümchen der Einsamkeit*; an augmented edition followed in 1815. In October of the latter year Schubert set one of the poems, 'Der Zufriedene'. Since the then 18-year-old Schubert was still unknown in Viennese musical circles, and in view of the fact that the song was not published in either his or Reissig's lifetime, it is likely that, for once, the composition had not been solicited by the poet.

Setting: D320.
(Deutsch[5,6])

Rellstab, (Heinrich Friedrich) Ludwig [pseud. Freimund Zuschauer] (b. Berlin, 13 April 1799; d. Berlin, 28 November 1860). Poet, novelist, and music critic; son of the music publisher and composer Johann Carl Friedrich Rellstab (1759–1813). Taught by his father, he performed piano concertos by Mozart while still a child. Later he studied the piano with Ludwig Berger and theory with Bernhard Klein. For some years he served in the army, but resigned in 1821. During the following years he studied classical languages at Frankfurt an der Oder and philosophy and philology at Heidelberg and Bonn, travelled to Switzerland and Italy, and in April 1825 visited Beethoven* in Vienna. There is no evidence that he met Schubert during his stay. In 1826 he was appointed music critic of the Berlin newspaper *Vossische Zeitung*, for which he wrote until his death. In addition, he founded his own musical journal, *Iris im Gebiet der Tonkunst* (1830–41). He was a prolific writer; his collected works, published in Leipzig in 1860–1, ran to twenty-four volumes. His output included novels (notably *1812*), plays (*Eugen Aram, Karl der Kühne*), and several volumes of poetry, among them *Gedichte* (1827).

In his posthumously published autobiography, *Aus meinem Leben* (1861), he states that he had sent Beethoven (evidently some time after his visit to Vienna in 1825) a copy of eight to ten of his poems; the copy was returned to him by Anton Schindler* after Beethoven's death. 'Some had pencil marks in Beethoven's own hand; those were the ones he liked best and which, at the time, he had passed on to Schubert to set, since he felt too unwell to do so himself.' Schindler, in his 'Erinnerungen an Franz Schubert' in the *Niederrheinische Musikzeitung für Kunstfreunde und Künstler* (March 1857), had already indicated that the poems had been in Beethoven's possession, only in his version of the events Schubert did not receive them until the summer of 1827, i.e. some months after Beethoven's death. In any case, by the time Schubert set them in 1828, they had been printed in *Gedichte*.

Altogether, Schubert composed the following ten songs to poems by Rellstab: 'Abschied' (D957/7), 'Auf dem Strom' (D943), 'Aufenthalt' (D957/5), 'Frühlings-sehnsucht' (D957/3), 'Herbst' (D945), 'In der Ferne' (D957/6), 'Kriegers Ahnung' (D957/2), 'Lebensmut' (D937), 'Liebesbotschaft' (D957/1), 'Ständchen' (D957/4). None of these songs was published in Schubert's lifetime, and only 'Auf dem Strom' is known to have been performed in public before his death. It was first sung by Ludwig Titze* at Schubert's concert on 26 March 1828. (For more on this song, *see* Lewy.*)

The seven Rellstab songs which now bear the work-number D957 were sold by Ferdinand Schubert* to Tobias Haslinger* in December 1828, at the same time as six Heine* songs. These thirteen songs, together with 'Die Taubenpost' (D965A), the setting of a poem by Johann Gabriel Seidl,* were published by Haslinger in May 1829 under the collective title *Schwanengesang* (D957).

'Leise flehen meine Lieder', the famous opening line of 'Ständchen', furnished the title for a very successful Austrian Schubert film (1933) directed by Willi Forst, with Hans Jaray as Schubert. An English version entitled *The Unfinished Symphony*, also starring Jaray and likewise made in Vienna, ran in London for a year.

Settings: D937, 943, 945, 957/1–7.
(Davis, Heussner, Hilmar-Voit, Janecka-Jary)

Rieder, Ambros Matthias (b. Döbling, near Vienna, 10 October 1771; d. Perch-toldsdorf, Lower Austria, 19 November 1855). Composer, organist, pianist, violinist, and theorist; father of Johann and Wilhelm August Rieder.* He was first taught by his grandfather Thomas Rieder who was choirmaster at Wilfersdorf, Lower Austria, and later studied with Carl Martinides, choirmaster at Lichtental parish church in Vienna, with Leopold Hofmann, Kapellmeister at St Stephen's Cathedral, and, after Hofmann's death, with his successor Johann Georg Albrechtsberger. By profession he was, like his father and his son Johann, a schoolteacher. After serving as an assistant to his father from 1787, he was employed as teacher and choirmaster at Perchtoldsdorf from 1802 until his death.

His musical output ran to 512 opus numbers, of which just under half appeared in print. Primarily a composer of liturgical music (twenty Masses, two Requiems, forty-one offertories, thirteen settings of *Tantum ergo*, in addition to numerous hymns and cantatas), he also wrote string quartets and pieces for the organ and the piano, as well as an opera, *Der Traum im Walde*. His works, in the words of E. Mandyczewski,* 'were without exception composed in the style of their period and accordingly vanished with it'. His theoretical writings include *Anleitung zum Fugieren auf der Orgel oder dem Pianoforte* (1826) and *Anleitung zum Präludieren auf der Orgel oder dem Pianoforte* (1828).

He came into contact with Haydn, Mozart (whose improvisations made a lasting impression on him), Beethoven,* and Simon Sechter,* was a personal friend of Johann Nepomuk Hummel,* participated as violist in some performances of the

Schuppanzigh* Quartet, and knew Schubert and his brother Ferdinand.* In July 1826 he dedicated his *Präludien und Fughetten für Orgel oder Pianoforte* 'respectfully to the esteemed composer, Herr Franz Schubert'. This is the only composition known to have been dedicated to Schubert by another musician. At the same time, Rieder dedicated a similar work to Ferdinand.

(Hilmar/Brusatti, Jancik[3], *ÖBL*, Wurzbach[1])

Rieder, Wilhelm August (b. Perchtoldsdorf, Lower Austria, 30 September 1796; d. Vienna, 8 September 1880). Painter and graphic artist; son of Ambros Matthias Rieder.* After studying at the Academy of Fine Arts in Vienna (1814–24), where one of his teachers was Hubert Maurer, he visited Florence and Rome in 1825. That same year he was appointed professor of drawing at the Institute of Engineering in Vienna, and in 1855 he took up a similar post at the military academy at Wiener Neustadt, Lower Austria. In 1848 he became a member of the Academy of Fine Arts. From 1857 until 1878 he was assistant curator of paintings at Belvedere Palace.

He met Schubert shortly before 1823 and was at times among his closest friends. According to an anonymous article published in the *Neue freie Presse* (Vienna) on 16 February 1897, Schubert, who did not always own a piano, at one time used to visit Rieder [at 32 Wiedner Hauptstrasse] in order to play on his piano. In May 1825 Rieder painted a portrait of Schubert in water-colours, based on a sketch which he had reportedly made one day while sheltering from a shower in Schubert's nearby lodgings [9 Technikerstrasse]. An etching made of this painting by Johann Nepomuk Passini was put on sale in December 1825 by Cappi & Co.,* who, in an announcement in the *Wiener Zeitung* on 9 December, described the portrait as 'an extremely good likeness'. (Rieder himself also made a lithograph of it.) Schubert's friends agreed that Rieder had well caught his subject's features. 'The portrait... is the most like him,' Leopold von Sonnleithner* stated in 1858; and Josef von Spaun,* writing in 1864, called it 'an extraordinarily good likeness'. The portrait is now at the Historisches Museum of the City of Vienna; a copy painted by Rieder in 1840 is preserved in the archives of the Gesellschaft der Musikfreunde. Rieder painted some further portraits of Schubert after the latter's death. One of these, executed some time after 1840, was described and reproduced by O. E. Deutsch* in the *Wiener Zeitung* on 18 November 1928; its present whereabouts are unknown. Another one, of considerable merit, which dates from 1875 (and is now also at the Historisches Museum) shows Schubert in the act of composing, and, behind him, a piano by Walter & Co. which is believed to be the one Schubert occasionally played in Rieder's room (see above). Rieder's other subjects include the Austrian Emperors Franz I and Franz Josef, Karoline Pichler,* and his own father, Ambros Rieder.

Rieder's brother Johann (1792–1876), a schoolteacher and choirmaster, was an intimate of Ferdinand Schubert,* who, in a letter to Schubert on 3 July 1824, described him as 'my only true friend'. He may have been one of their two companions on their excursion to Eisenstadt in October 1828. (The other was perhaps Josef Mayssen.*)

(Deutsch[10], Hilmar[7,10], Hilmar/Brusatti, *ÖBL*, Wurzbach[1])

Rinna von Sarenbach, Ernst (b. Görtz [Gorizia], 11 November 1793; d. ?Vienna, 23 May 1837); son of Johann Baptist Rinna von Sarenbach (1764–1846), a prominent physician ennobled in 1812. He himself qualified as a doctor in Vienna in 1816 and was appointed court physician in 1824. In 1830 he accompanied Crown Prince Ferdinand as attending physician to Pressburg [Bratislava] on the occasion of his coronation as king of Hungary, and in 1836 Rinna was again in attendance when Ferdinand, by then emperor of Austria, travelled to Prague to be crowned king of Bohemia. Between 1833 and 1836 he published a four-volume compendium of treatments, medicaments, and surgical procedures. Like his father, he was accorded the title Hofrat.

Rinna von Sarenbach knew Franz von Schober,* and his daughter Cäcilia attended several balls given by Schober. It was presumably through Schober that Schubert—who, except for a short period in May–June 1827, stayed at Schober's apartment [18 Tuchlauben] from March 1827 until August 1828—became Rinna's patient in 1828. On Rinna's advice he moved in September of that year to his brother Ferdinand's* lodgings in the Neu-Wieden suburb, where, it was hoped, the more salubrious air would be beneficial to his health. During the last days of Schubert's final illness, Rinna, having himself fallen ill, handed over the care of his patient to Dr Josef von Vering.*

(*Lexikon der Ärzte*, Wurzbach[1])

Rochlitz, (Johann) Friedrich (b. Leipzig, 12 February 1769; d. Leipzig, 16 December 1842). Writer, composer, music critic, and editor. In his time, he enjoyed some success with his comedies, novels, and stories, but today he is best remembered for having founded the Leipzig *Allgemeine musikalische Zeitung* in 1798; he remained its editor until 1818. A six-volume collection of his writings appeared in 1821–2 under the title *Auswahl des Besten aus Friedrich Rochlitz' sämmtlichen Schriften*.

His knowledge of music exceeded that of a simple amateur, for he had studied composition and counterpoint with Johann Friedrich Doles, Kantor of St Thomas's Church in Leipzig. In his youth he composed a number of works, including the cantata *Die Vollendung des Erlösers*; in 1838–40 he edited a comprehensive collection of vocal compositions (*Sammlung vorzüglicher Gesang-Stücke vom Ursprung gesetzmässiger Harmonie bis auf die Neuzeit*).

He stayed in Vienna from late May until the beginning of August 1822. In a letter addressed jointly to his wife and the publisher Gottfried Christoph Härtel on 9 July 1822, he described a chance meeting with Schubert. According to this account, he happened to see 'the young composer Franz Schubert' in the street one day, about a fortnight after his first meeting with Beethoven. Schubert, to whom Beethoven had spoken about him, took him to a restaurant where he was likely to find Beethoven dining 'in a relaxed and merry mood', and such was indeed the case. Rochlitz's letter was printed in the Leipzig *Allgemeine musikalische Zeitung* on 2 January 1828 and also in his book *Für ruhige Stunden* (September 1828), but without the 'young composer' being identified. Not until the letter was reprinted in the final volume of Rochlitz's *Für Freunde der Tonkunst* (4 vols., 1830–2) was Schubert named. Since modern critics are by no means convinced of the truthfulness of Rochlitz's accounts of his meetings with Beethoven and some even doubt that he met Beethoven at all, the story of his contacts with Schubert needs no doubt to be treated with similar caution. (On the question of Schubert's acquaintance with Beethoven, *see* Beethoven.*)

Rochlitz appears to have had a genuine admiration for Schubert's music, even if his appreciation of it was somewhat peculiar. On 30 April 1826 he wrote to Ignaz Franz von Mosel:* 'I consider some new compositions by your Schubert to be highly interesting and estimable. Perhaps this talented musician needs only a musically trained friend to enlighten him with affection about himself—about what he is, what he has, and what he aspires to. From which, it is to be hoped, he may then himself deduce what he should do.'

Schubert set four of Rochlitz's poems, the first one at the very beginning of his composing career, the others towards its end. In 1812 he composed 'Klaglied' (D23), and in January 1827 'Alinde' (D904), 'An die Laute' (D905), and 'Zur guten Nacht' (D903). The last three compositions were printed together in May 1827 in an edition dedicated to Rochlitz by the publisher, Tobias Haslinger.*

On 7 November 1827, Rochlitz addressed a long letter to Schubert, in which he wrote: 'Herr Haslinger has conveyed to you my thanks for your music to my three songs and also my desire that you embellish a longer poem [of mine] by your art, and he has informed me of your willingness to do so.' Rochlitz proposed 'Der erste Ton' as a suitable poem and went on to explain in some detail how the text might, in his view, best be set, adding: 'But I repeat that all this is merely a suggestion on my part; it will be for you to choose and decide.' The poem had been published in the *Allgemeine musikalische Zeitung* on 2 October 1805 and reprinted in *Auswahl des Besten* . . . It had already been set in 1808 by Weber,* and had been unsuccessfully offered by Rochlitz, through Haslinger, to Beethoven in 1822. Schubert sent a lukewarm reply, and that appears to have been the end of their contacts. Incidentally, neither Rochlitz's nor Schubert's letter made any reference to a past meeting between them.

Settings: D23, 903–5.
(Ehinger, Leuchtmann², Waidelich²)

Rückert, (Johann Michael) Friedrich (b. Schweinfurt, 16 May 1788; d. Neuses, near Coburg, 31 January 1866). Orientalist; poet, dramatist, and translator. He studied law, philology, and philosophy at the universities of Würzburg, Heidelberg, and

Göttingen, and taught philology at the University of Jena (1811). Subsequently he was employed as a schoolmaster at Hanau and later as editor of the Stuttgart *Morgenblatt für gebildete Stände*. In 1818, while in Vienna, he turned to the study of oriental languages under the influence of Josef Hammer-Purgstall. He became a distinguished scholar in this field and translated several important works, especially from Persian and Arabic. In 1826 he was appointed to a chair at Erlangen University, and in 1841 to one at the University of Berlin. He retired in 1848 in order to devote himself entirely to scholarship.

As a poet he was extraordinarily prolific, turning out more than 10,000 poems. Inevitably, his output was uneven in quality, and the sentimentality and banal language which frequently occur in it may not always be to the taste of the modern public. But his lyrical verse—in particular the more than 400 poems which celebrate his courtship of Luise Wiethaus-Fischer (whom he married in 1821) and which make up *Liebesfrühling* (1823)—contains many gems which have lost none of the charm they exercised on his contemporaries, and not least on musicians. Among his other volumes of poetry are *Deutsche Gedichte* (1814), *Kranz der Zeit* (1817), *Östliche Rosen* (1822), and *Gesammelte Gedichte* (1834–8); the poignant *Kindertotenlieder*, which express his grief over the early deaths of his children Luise and Ernst, were published posthumously. Composers who have set Rückert poems include Brahms,* Robert Franz, Liszt,* Carl Loewe, Mahler, Pfitzner, Reger, Schubert, Clara and Robert Schumann,* Richard Strauss, and Hugo Wolf. Unlike his poems, Rückert's stage works (a comic trilogy *Napoleon*, several plays on biblical and historical subjects) met with little success.

The following five Schubert Lieder, composed sometime in 1822–3, were inspired by poems from *Östliche Rosen*: 'Dass sie hier gewesen' (D775), 'Du bist die Ruh' (D776), 'Greisengesang' (D778), 'Lachen und Weinen' (D777), and 'Sei mir gegrüsst' (D741). In addition, fragments of two other songs have survived: 'Die Wallfahrt' (D778A), likewise using a poem from *Östliche Rosen*, and 'Ich hab in mich gesogen' (D778B), based on a poem published in the yearbook *Urania* (Leipzig) in 1823.

Settings: D741, 775–8, 778A–B.
(Branscombe[8], Dove[2], Ottich)

Rudolf (**Johann Josef Rainer**), Archduke (b. Florence, 8 January 1788; d. Baden, near Vienna, 24 July 1831). Composer and patron of music. Youngest son of Leopold (1747–92), Grand Duke of Tuscany, and his wife Maria Luisa (1745–92). He moved to Vienna in 1790 when his father became emperor. In 1805 he was appointed co-adjutor of Olmütz [Olomouc]; in 1819 he became archbishop of Olmütz, and that same year was created a cardinal.

A great admirer of Beethoven's* music, he received instruction from him in composition, piano, and theory for more than twenty years, beginning in 1803. At the same time, he became his close friend and very generous patron. Among the works which the grateful Beethoven dedicated to him were the *Missa solemnis*, the Fourth and Fifth Piano Concertos, the 'Hammerklavier' Piano Sonata, the Violin Sonata, Op. 96, and the 'Archduke' Piano Trio. The archduke's own compositions included a set of forty variations on a theme set by Beethoven.

In 1826 Schubert dedicated his Piano Sonata in A minor (D845) to the archduke.

(Forbes[2], *ÖBL*)

Růžička, Wenzel (b. Jaromeritz [Jaroměřice, Czech Republic], 8 September 1757; d. Vienna, 21 June 1823). Organist and music teacher. He arrived in Vienna in 1771 to complete his musical training, and subsequently taught singing, violin, and piano. In 1783 he joined the court theatre orchestra as a violist; from 1793 until his death he was court organist. In addition, he gave instruction in thoroughbass, piano, and other instruments at the Stadtkonvikt and helped to establish the students' orchestra there.

He was instructed by Antonio Salieri* to give the young Schubert tuition in thoroughbass, but Josef von Spaun* recalled in 1858 that, at the end of the second lesson, Růžička had said to him, greatly moved, and in Schubert's presence: 'I cannot teach this boy anything, he has learned it all from our good Lord.' Spaun also stated that Růžička had played Schubert's 'Erlkönig' (D328) through on the piano very soon after the song had been composed and had expressed great admiration for it.

(*ÖBL*, Wurzbach[1])

Salieri, Antonio (b. Legnago, 18 August 1750; d. Vienna, 7 May 1825). Composer and teacher. In 1766, as a young orphan, he was taken to Vienna by the composer Florian Leopold Gassmann, who supervised his education and whom he succeeded in 1774 as court composer. In 1788, on the death of Guiseppe Bonno, he became court Kapellmeister. He composed more than forty comic and serious operas, most of which were first produced in Vienna. His pupils included Beethoven,* Hummel,* Liszt,* Anna Milder-Hauptmann,* Karoline Unger,* and Josef Weigl,* among many other outstanding future composers and singers.

As court Kapellmeister, he was responsible for examining candidates for places as choirboys at the court Kapelle. As a result of an examination held on 30 September 1808, he and the director of the Stadtkonvikt, Franz Innocenz Lang,* recommended Schubert for one of the three vacancies. While at the Konvikt, Schubert was taught thoroughbass by Wenzel Růžička,* and from 1812 was given twice-weekly lessons in composition by Salieri at his apartment [1 Göttweihergasse/12 Seilergasse/11 Spiegelgasse]. This instruction continued even after Schubert had left the Konvikt until 1816. A considerable number of the exercises done by Schubert under Salieri's supervision in 1812–13 (fugues, settings of Metastasio* and Schiller,* etc.) have survived; some of them bear Salieri's corrections.

Doubt was later cast on the quality of Salieri's teaching by certain of Schubert's friends and acquaintances, notably Anton Schindler* who argued that if the instruction had been sufficiently comprehensive and competent, Schubert would not have had to turn to Simon Sechter* for tuition in counterpoint in 1828. However, Schindler's criticism has been rejected by M. J. E. Brown, for one. Salieri, Brown maintains, 'was not Schubert's master in any close, systematic or continuous sense of the word, but neither was his instruction so casual or so carelessly received as would seem from some accounts'. It has been generally accepted, however, that Salieri, not surprisingly, set out to train Schubert solely or almost exclusively in the Italian musical idiom. This view draws support from the notes left by Josef von Spaun,* normally a very level-headed and reliable witness. 'Schubert often spoke of Salieri with gratitude and his instruction was undoubtedly useful,' he wrote in 1858. 'However, when Salieri again and again strongly reproached Schubert for occupying himself with poems in the barbaric German tongue and demanded that he compose no more in the German language and instead set to music trite Italian poems, Schubert lost his patience and followed with redoubled enthusiasm the path condemned by his teacher, but which assuredly was the right one for him.'

It was at Salieri's apartment that Schubert participated on 16 June 1816 in the concert celebrating the fiftieth anniversary of his teacher's arrival in Vienna. Like other past and present students attending, he had brought a dedicatory composition; it consisted of a quartet for male voices, a tenor aria, and a canon for three voices (*Beitrag zur fünfzigjährigen Jubelfeier des Herrn von Salieri*, D407). In July 1821 Schubert dedicated to Salieri his Op. 5, which contained settings of the five Goethe* poems 'Der Fischer' (D225), 'Der König in Thule' (D367), 'Erster Verlust' (D226), 'Nähe des Geliebten' (D162), and 'Rastlose Liebe' (D138).

(Brown[4])

Salis-Seewis, Johann Gaudenz, Baron (b. Bothmar Castle, near Malans, Grisons, 26 December 1762; d. Bothmar Castle, 29 January 1834). Poet. Born into a wealthy Swiss aristocratic family, he was mainly educated by private tutors. In 1779 he went to Paris, where, for the next ten years, he was an officer in the Swiss Guard. He served in the republican army until 1793, when he resigned his commission and returned to Switzerland. He held various senior positions in the Swiss army, became a member of the Legislative Council (1801) and of the Supreme Court (1803), and was later active in an administrative capacity in the Grisons. He resigned his various offices in 1817.

He began to contribute poems to various literary publications (*Göttinger Musenalmanach, Schweizerischer Musenalmanach*) in 1788. During a journey through Germany in 1788–9 he met Goethe,* Herder,* Schiller,* and Wieland at Weimar. A collection of his poems, *Gedichte*, was published by Friedrich von Matthisson* at Zurich in 1793; it was subsequently reissued in several augmented editions.

Schubert's songs to texts by Salis-Seewis, which were for the most part composed in 1816–17, include 'Der Entfernten' (D350), 'Der Herbstabend' (D405), 'Der

Jüngling an der Quelle' (D300), 'Die Einsiedelei' (D393, 563), 'Fischerlied' (D351, 562), 'Lied: Ins stille Land' (D403), and 'Pflügerlied' (D392). In addition, Schubert set a number of Salis-Seewis's poems for several voices, some more than once—'Das Grab' no fewer than five times (D329A, 330, 377, 569, 643A).

> *Settings*: D300, 329A, 330–1, 337, 350–1, 364, 377, 392–4, 403–6, 502, 562–3, 569, 572, 643A, 983B, Anh.I,18 and 19.
> (Porhansl[3], Weber)

Sauer, Ignaz (b. Triebsch [Třebušín Czech Republic], 1 April 1759; d. Vienna, 2 December 1833). Choirmaster, music publisher, and composer. From 1780 he was employed as a schoolmaster at Bad Hall, Upper Austria, and in Vienna. In 1795 he was appointed choirmaster and organist at the imperial orphanage in the Alsergrund suburb, a position he occupied until his death. In 1796 he became a partner in Josef Eder's art and music business, and in 1800 he was granted a licence to set up his own firm, to which he gave the name 'Zu den sieben Schwestern'. It flourished for several years, publishing works by Clementi, Eybler, and Johann Baptist Vanhal, among others. But later it suffered a decline, perhaps as a result of the unfavourable conditions created by the wars against the French, or owing to Sauer's preoccupation with other matters; in 1813 he gave his stock-in-trade in commission to Heinrich Friedrich Müller. In July 1822 he concluded a partnership agreement with Marcus (Maximilian Josef) Leidesdorf* providing for the establishment of the firm 'Sauer & Leidesdorf' (*see* separate entry). The partnership was dissolved in February 1826 and Leidesdorf became the firm's sole proprietor. Sauer died in extreme poverty.

His compositions include sacred songs for the children at the orphanage, an oratorio (*Der grosse Tag des Vaterlandes*), and some dances and marches for the piano. His interests were not, however, confined to music; in 1812 he published a book on the guinea-fowl.

According to O. E. Deutsch,* Schubert made Sauer's acquaintance 'at the latest in *c*.1818' at the orphanage, where his brother Ferdinand* had been teaching since 1810.

(Deutsch[3], *ÖBL*, Slezak, Weinmann[8])

Sauer & Leidesdorf. Viennese firm of art dealers and music publishers established by Ignaz Sauer* and Marcus (Maximilian Josef) Leidesdorf* on 27 July 1822. From the outset, the business was almost entirely run by Leidesdorf, who alone had signatory powers and to whom was undoubtedly due the rapid development of the firm which soon attracted attention by its extremely well-produced publications. Unfortunately, its artistic success was not reflected in the financial returns, and it was chronically short of money. The partnership, renewed in 1824, was dissolved on 6 February 1826; but several Schubert compositions issued later that year still bore the imprint 'Sauer & Leidesdorf'. A new firm was registered in Leidesdorf's sole name on 7 May 1827.

Despite Leidesdorf's acquaintance with Beethoven,* the firm did not publish first editions of any of his works, although it did issue later editions of some of them, including the last two piano sonatas. On the other hand, it was responsible for bringing out first editions of a considerable number of Schubert's compositions, and Leidesdorf published yet more after Sauer's withdrawal from the business (*see* M. J. Leidesdorf*). Among the works of which Sauer & Leidesdorf issued first editions were the String Quartet in A minor (D804); *Moments musicaux* Nos. 3 and 6 (D780/3 and 6) for the piano; *Eight Variations on an Original Theme* (D813) and the Sonata in B flat major (D617) for piano duet; the songs 'Der Zwerg' (D771), 'Du bist die Ruh' (D776), 'Frühlingsglaube' (D686), 'Gruppe aus dem Tartarus' (D583), 'Hänflings Liebeswerbung' (D552), 'Lachen und Weinen' (D777), 'Sei mir gegrüsst' (D741), Axa's romance from *Rosamunde* (D797/3b), and the cycle *Die schöne Müllerin* (D795); and the quartet 'Gondelfahrer' (D809).

The earliest evidence of Schubert's dealings with the firm is provided by a note from Schubert to Josef Hüttenbrenner* on 31 October 1822, in which he stated his intention of making 'very important' alterations to some songs due to be delivered (or which perhaps had already been delivered) to Leidesdorf. The reference is presumably to the three songs which Sauer & Leidesdorf were to publish as his Op. 20 in April 1823 ('Frühlingsglaube', 'Hänflings Liebeswerbung', 'Sei mir gegrüsst'). Already prior to the publication of these songs, Schubert had contributed to a collection of German dances issued by Sauer & Leidesdorf in January 1823. Thus he must have been in negotiation with the firm almost from its establishment in July 1822, or at any rate for several months before he broke with Cappi & Diabelli* in April 1823. It is therefore evident that his decision to deal with Sauer & Leidesdorf was not precipitated by the dissatisfaction which he expressed in his letters of 21 February and 10 April 1823 to Cappi & Diabelli* and which led him to break with those publishers. Josef Hüttenbrenner informed Ferdinand Luib* in c.1858 that Schubert contracted to supply Leidesdorf with songs over a two-year period, for an annual payment of 1200 gulden.

First editions: D146, 229, 366, 525, 527, 536, 552–3, 583, 602, 617, 686, 741, 743–4, 751, 756, 761, 769, 771, 773, 775–7, 780–2, 795, 797, 804, 809, 813, 819, 971, 976, 978–80.

(Deutsch³, Slezak, Weinmann⁸)

Sauter, Ferdinand (b. Werfen, near Salzburg, 6 May 1804; d. Vienna, 30 October 1854). Poet. Son of Anton Sauter (d. 1807), a judge and an accomplished amateur singer and violinist. He attended school at Salzburg, and subsequently found employment at Wels (1819–25). In 1825 he settled in Vienna, where he worked at a paper-mill and later for an insurance company.

He was introduced to Schubert's circle by Franz von Hartmann,* whom he may have known before his arrival in Vienna. He probably first met Schubert in November 1826 at the 'Zum Anker' restaurant [10 Grünangergasse]. There are several references to him in the diaries of Franz and Fritz von Hartmann between late 1826 and the summer of 1828, from which it is evident that he was frequently in their company during that period and also repeatedly met Schubert. A typical entry occurs in Fritz's diary on 21 August 1827: 'Spaun,* [Max] Clodi,* Sauter and I went to the tavern, as is now our daily practice; Schober* and Schubert arrived later. We amused ourselves splendidly until midnight.' Later that year Franz von Hartmann notes: 'Dinand Sauter is very melancholy most of the time, but occasionally in a boisterous mood. In consequence, he is an unsatisfactory companion. Unfortunately Schober has taken a strong dislike to him, which I regret all the more since I was the one who introduced them to each other and encouraged Dinand, who is now well aware that his presence is unwelcome.' On a later occasion (4 May 1828), Sauter is said to have behaved 'oddly' and to have been soundly told off. However, he remained a member of the group and is again mentioned by Franz von Hartmann on 28 June (this time approvingly) and 19 July 1828.

In the 1830s Sauter joined a group of artists and writers, of which the poet Johann Nepomuk Vogl was the leading figure. Sauter himself gradually attained a certain celebrity through his poems, especially those in which he expressed the sentiments and aspirations of the ordinary people, sometimes in a melancholy but more often in a satirical manner. His 'Gassenlied', because of its political overtones, was particularly popular. The poems, mostly occasional pieces, appeared in periodicals and were not printed in book form until 1855. While the high quality of his verse has been fully recognized by modern critics, the manner of his life has often drawn harsh comments, for much of it was spent in the taverns of suburban Hernals and Neu-Lerchenfeld. Thus O. E. Deutsch* refers to him as 'a degenerate genius, addicted to drink'; but W. Häusler and E. Lebensaft (in *ÖBL*) call him, more charitably, 'a Bohemian of genius'.

Moritz von Schwind,* who was a close friend during Sauter's early days in Vienna, painted his portrait in 1828. But he did not include him in the later group portrait *A Schubert Evening at Josef von Spaun's*, which could indicate that Sauter was mainly a dining and drinking companion.

(Deissinger, *ÖBL*, Porhansl[7])

Sauter, Samuel Friedrich (b. Flehingen, Baden (Germany), 10 November 1766; d. Flehingen, 14 July 1846). Poet; son of a baker and innkeeper. He earned his living as a schoolmaster at Flehingen (1786–1816) and at nearby Zaisenhausen (1816–41). At the same time, he became known for his charming if rather naïve poems, such as 'Das arme Dorfschulmeisterlein', 'Der Wachtelschlag', 'Kartoffellied', and 'Krämer-michelslied'. In 1811 he published *Volkslieder und andere Reime* at Heidelberg, and in 1845 his collected poems at Karlsruhe.

He was, posthumously, associated with the coining of the term 'Biedermeier' and its pejorative connotations, after some of his unintentionally comical poems were presented by L. Eichrodt and A. Kussmaul in the Munich weekly *Fliegende Blätter* (together with others deliberately written in a similar vein by Eichrodt himself) as the work of 'the Swabian schoolmaster Gottlieb Biedermaier [*sic*] and his friend Horatius Treuherz'. (In 1869 these poems were collectively reprinted under the title *Biedermaiers Lebenslust.*)

Sauter's poem 'Der Wachtelschlag' first appeared in C. Lang's *Almanach und Taschenbuch für häusliche und gesellschaftliche Freuden* at Heilbronn in 1799. It was set to music in 1803 by Beethoven* whose song was published in Vienna the following year. Schubert made his own setting of it which was printed in the *Wiener Zeitschrift für Kunst, Literatur, Theater und Mode* on 30 July 1822.

Setting: D742.

(Siegert)

Schaeffer, August von (1790–1865). Physician. He was educated at the Stadtkonvikt in Vienna and qualified as a doctor in 1816.

He treated Schubert in 1823, apparently for syphilis. Schubert remained in contact with him even while absent from Vienna in the summer of that year. 'I am in constant correspondence with Schaeffer and am feeling quite well,' he wrote to Franz von Schober* from Steyr on 14 August. On 9 November Moritz von Schwind* informed Schober that three days earlier he and other members of their group had dined at the 'Zur ungarischen Krone' restaurant, 'except Schubert who stayed in bed that day. Schaeffer and Bernard [i.e. Dr Bernhardt*], who visited him, are confident that he is well on the road to recovery and believe that he may be fully restored to health within four weeks.' This prognosis turned out to have been decidedly optimistic.

(Franken, Neumayr)

Schechner [Schechner-Waagen], **Nanette** [Anna] (b. Munich, 1806; d. ?Munich, 29 April 1860). Soprano. After studying at Munich and in Italy, she quickly established herself as a leading singer in both the Italian and German repertories at the Munich Opera. In 1825 she sang her first Leonore in Beethoven's* *Fidelio*. In 1826 she went to Vienna where she made a splendid début on 22 May as Emmeline in Josef Weigl's* *Die Schweizerfamilie*. 'Mlle Schechner has ... pleased very greatly. Since her singing shows many similarities with that of [Pauline Anna] Milder,* she may well be suitable for our opera,' Schubert wrote to Eduard von Bauernfeld,* who was then working on the libretto *Der Graf von Gleichen* while staying in Carinthia. Franz von Schober* sent an even more enthusiastic account to Bauernfeld: 'Regarding theatrical matters, I can only report that a certain Mlle Schechner has created a sensation in our town by her marvellous singing in *German* opera. Not since Milder, it is claimed, has such a voice set the air vibrating. She is, moreover, still young, pretty, and vivacious. Schubert has heard her and joins in the hymn of praise. If only he would write an opera for her—perhaps yours may be suitable.'

It was not to be. In any case, Schubert did not begin composing the music of *Der Graf von Gleichen* (D918) until June 1827, by which time Schechner had left Vienna.

He met her at least once during her stay in Vienna, for Anselm Hüttenbrenner*
recalled in a letter to Ferdinand Luib* (7 March 1858) having dined at her lodgings
with Schubert and the bass Felice Santini. There is no firm evidence of any other
contacts between them, although Anton Schindler* made her the central figure in
what, if true, would have been a crucial episode in Schubert's career. According to
his 'Erinnerungen an Franz Schubert' (*Niederrheinische Musikzeitung für Kunstfreunde und Künstler*, 7 and 14 March 1857), Schubert was required to compose and
conduct a short operatic work to prove his suitability for the post of assistant
conductor at the Kärntnertor-Theater, for which he is said to have applied. The
score, composed to a libretto by Georg von Hoffmann,* included an important
number for solo soprano and chorus. At rehearsal, Schechner reportedly found the
sustained effort needed to make her voice heard above what she and others present
considered an unduly heavy orchestration extremely exhausting, and she requested
some cuts and alterations. Schubert refused, however, to allow more than a few
minor changes, grew increasingly angry, and finally picked up his score and ran out
of the theatre, thus putting an end to whatever prospects he may have had of
obtaining the position.

Schindler's story has been treated with scepticism by Schubert scholars, notably
Kreissle* and O. E. Deutsch,* since it seemed to them incompatible with the
almost universal accounts of Schubert's good temper. Moreover, other witnesses
produced conflicting recollections of the occasion, and Schindler's testimony is, in
any case, notoriously unreliable. It should nevertheless be emphasized that none of
the reservations expressed constitutes a conclusive argument against attaching some
credence to Schindler's remarks.

Schechner, who appeared with considerable success as Ninetta in Rossini's *La
gazza ladra* and in other roles during her Viennese engagement, scored even greater
triumphs in Berlin in May–September 1827. She was subsequently appointed a
court singer in Munich. But her career was to span barely ten years, for a persistent
chest disease increasingly impaired her voice and eventually obliged her to retire in
1835. During the final years she sang under the name 'Schechner-Waagen', following
her marriage in 1832 to the painter Karl Waagen. The poet and music critic Ludwig
Rellstab* wrote of her: 'I have never known a greater singer. She remains the most
wonderful artist in my memory.'

(Kutsch/Riemens, Schletterer, Warrack³)

Schellmann, Albert (b. Steinbach, Upper Austria, 14 November 1759; d. Steyr, 14
March 1844). Lawyer. He lived at Steyr with his wife Barbara, née Reutter (1770–
1845), a maternal aunt of Albert Stadler.* One of their numerous children, Albert
(1798–1854), a lawyer like his father, was an excellent pianist; he often accompanied
Johann Michael Vogl,* who was a friend of the family.

Schubert stayed at the Schellmanns' house [34 Stadtplatz] during his visit to Steyr
in the summer of 1819. At that time five of their daughters were living there (one of

them, Seraphine, later married Johann Leopold Ebner*). Stadler was then living in the same house with his mother and sister, as was district commissioner Weilnböck, one of whose three daughters, Antonie, later became Stadler's wife. 'At the house where I lodge there are eight girls, nearly all of them pretty,' Schubert reported to his brother Ferdinand* on 13 July. 'As you can see, there is plenty to keep me occupied.'

On 28 November 1822 Schubert made an entry in the younger Albert's album, and the following year he wrote out a dance (D145, Écossaise No. 8) in Seraphine's.

Schickh, Johann Valentin (b. Vienna, 6 January 1770; d. Badgastein, 1 August 1835). Merchant and newspaper publisher. After working for many years in the textile industry at Linz, he opened a haberdashery store in Vienna in 1814 together with Jakob Regenhart, but soon took sole charge of it. In 1816 he founded the *Wiener-Moden-Zeitung und Zeitschrift für Kunst, schöne Literatur und Theater* (renamed *Wiener Zeitschrift für Kunst, Literatur, Theater und Mode* in July 1817), of which he was, from 1820, the sole publisher and editor. It appeared three times a week and covered a wide range of cultural subjects. One noteworthy feature was the publication, in the form of supplements, of engraved fashion-plates and new music, generally songs.

Schubert was among the composers who benefited from this arrangement. The following of his songs appeared first in the *Wiener Zeitschrift für Kunst* ..., between 1820 and 1828: 'Die Forelle' (D550), 9 December 1820; 'An Emma' (D113), 30 June 1821; 'Der Blumen Schmerz' (D731), 8 December 1821; 'Die Rose' (D745), 7 May 1822; 'Der Wachtelschlag' (D742), 30 July 1822; 'Drang in die Ferne' (D770), 25 March 1823; 'Auf dem Wasser zu singen' (D774), 30 December 1823; 'Der Einsame' (D800), 12 March 1825; 'Trost im Liede' (D546) and 'Wandrers Nachtlied' (D768), both 23 June 1827; 'Der blinde Knabe' (D833), 25 September 1827; 'Im Frühling' (D882), 16 September 1828. The periodical also published Julius Schneller's* poem 'An Franz Schubert vom Rheinstrome' on 7 October 1826, and, after Schubert's death, commemorative poems by Johann Gabriel Seidl* (6 December 1828) and Baron Schlechta* (9 December 1828), as well as a biographical sketch by Eduard von Bauernfeld* (9, 11, and 13 June 1829). In addition, it carried a very warm, unsigned, tribute on 11 December 1828, which began: 'Franz Schubert, that enchanting composer, the pride of his country and an object of love and veneration for his friends and numerous admirers, is dead.'

Schubert probably had a fair measure of social contact with Schickh, even though only one such occasion is documented. In June 1828 Schickh took Schubert and Franz Paul Lachner* on an excursion to Baden, the famous spa near Vienna. After they had arrived there, he suggested that they should, on the following day, visit nearby Heiligenkreuz Monastery which possessed a celebrated organ, and he invited the two composers to write short pieces of music to perform on it. Each thereupon composed a fugue for four hands, which they duly played the next day in the presence of several monks. In November 1828 Schubert used the theme of his fugue (D952) in some of the contrapuntal exercises (D965B) which he wrote out for Simon Sechter.*

Schubert was also acquainted with Schickh's nephew Josef Kilian Schickh (1799–1851) who had been a fellow pupil at the Stadtkonvikt and later became a successful author of popular comedies.

(*ÖBL*)

Schiedermayr, Johann Baptist (b. Pfaffenmünster, Bavaria, 23 June 1779; d. Linz, 6 January 1840). Composer and organist. He received his musical training at the monasteries at Windberg and Oberaltaich, and at Straubing. He started his professional career as bass and organist at Passau. In 1804 he arrived in Linz, where he was entrusted by Kapellmeister Franz Xaver Glöggl with the direction of various musical performances. In 1810 he became organist of both the cathedral and the city church. In addition, he served from 1812 (with some interruptions) as Kapellmeister at the theatre and conducted for balls held at the Redoutensaal; he also taught singing at the Linz Gesellschaft der Musikfreunde from 1823. Following Glöggl's death in 1839, he was appointed temporary Kapellmeister at the cathedral and the city church. He composed much sacred music, as well as symphonies, chamber music, dances, and music for the stage. Altogether, he made a considerable contribution to musical life in Linz.

On 11 March 1825 the *Österreichisches Bürgerblatt für Verstand, Herz und Gute Laune* (Linz) reported that the cotillion had once again been the most popular dance at recent balls, and that 'the uncommonly beautiful German dances composed by that composer of genius, Franz Schubert, and arranged as cotillions by Herr Schiedermayr, had raised this graceful dance to a more noble entertainment'. The dances could have been taken from the collection of Deutsche and Écossaises by Schubert which Cappi & Co.* had published in January of that year (D783). It should, however, be pointed out that if Schiedermayr is the first musician known to have orchestrated Schubert dances, the winter of 1824/5 was not the first time when such arrangements were played. On 17 February 1824 Anna von Hartmann,* writing from Linz to her fiancé Count Anton Revertera, mentioned that the music at a recent ball had included waltzes by Schubert.

(Litschauer³, *ÖBL*, Wurzbach¹)

Schiller, Franz Ferdinand, Baron (b. Pontebba [now in Friuli-Venezia Giulia], 15 July 1773; d. Graz, 25 August 1861). The son of an official employed in the mining industry, he studied from 1793 to 1796 at the academy of mining at Schemnitz [Banská Štiavnica, Slovak Republic]. Subsequently he occupied various posts in the Austrian civil service, both in Vienna and the provinces, before being appointed secretary of the department of coins and mines in 1811. In 1824 he was placed in charge of salt mining in the Salzkammergut and posted to Gmunden, Upper

Austria, which was then a major centre for the processing of the extracted salt. He filled this position with great distinction until his retirement in 1844. During that period he reorganized the whole industry and introduced important new techniques. He was accorded the title Hofrat in 1815, was ennobled in 1823, and made a baron in 1840; he also became an honorary citizen of Gmunden. After retiring, he lived first in Vienna and later at Graz. In 1803 he had married the widowed Theresia Hasenbauer, née von Franken, who died in 1858.

Schiller was known for his generous hospitality and love of music. According to F. Krackowizer's *Geschichte der Stadt Gmunden in Ober-Österreich* (1898–1900), he used to provide entertainment, including music, dancing, and games, on each Sunday and holiday for the benefit of residents and visitors. During his stay at Gmunden in June–July 1825, Schubert benefited from Schiller's generous hospitality. 'I lived at Traweger's* very free and easy, like one of the family,' he wrote to his father* and stepmother on 25 [?28] July, from Steyr. 'Later, when Hofrat Schiller, who is monarch of the whole Salzkammergut, was there, we (Vogl* and myself) dined every day at his house and spent much time making music, as we also did at Traweger's. My new songs from Walter Scott's* 'The Lady of the Lake' were particularly appreciated.' He sometimes played duets with Anna [Nanette] Rosina Wolf* at Schiller's, and on at least one occasion she sang one of his new songs, accompanying herself on the piano. Most probably, these Schubertiads took place at the Kammerhof [corner An der Traunbrücke/Kammerhofgasse], a large building in which were located both Schiller's office and his service flat. Some of the music-making may have taken place in a pavilion situated on the Guglberg, a hill dominating the town, which was also available to Schiller for private entertaining.

(Klein², Krackowizer, *ÖBL*)

Schiller, (Johann Christoph) Friedrich (b. Marbach am Neckar, 10 November 1759; d. Weimar, 9 May 1805). Poet, dramatist, and philosopher. After Goethe,* he was the poet whose verse was most frequently set by Schubert. Altogether, Schubert composed songs to more than thirty of Schiller's poems. He was, moreover, so fascinated by the texts, and presumably dissatisfied with his efforts to realize their musical potential, that he made more than one setting of a third of them. In addition, he used a number of the same poems, as well as some others, in his partsongs. The total number of settings thus exceeds sixty.

The composition of the Schiller songs extends from 1811/12 to the early 1820s, but is concentrated in the period 1814–17. The earliest appear to have been 'Der Jüngling am Bache' (D30)' 'Des Mädchens Klage' (D6), and 'Leichenfantasie' (D7); however, the precise dates of composition of these three songs are not known. In 1813, in what are generally regarded as exercises undertaken for his teacher Antonio Salieri,* he set sixteen Schiller texts for three male voices (usually two tenors and one bass). In most of these cases, he used only parts of a particular poem.

Thus D51, 53–4, 57–8, and 60 are all settings of stanzas of the poem 'Elysium', which he was to set in its entirety for single voice in 1817 (D584).

The Schiller poems chosen by Schubert range from long narrative works such as 'Der Taucher' (D77) and 'Die Bürgschaft' (D248) to short, more lyrical pieces like 'An den Frühling' (D283, 338, 587) and 'Der Jüngling am Bache' (D30, 192, 638). But since even the latter type of poem rarely carries a truly personal note or conveys any profoundly felt emotion, critics have been puzzled by Schubert's repeated recourse to Schiller. Thus, in his book *Schubert's Songs*, R. Capell, while acknowledging that 'Gruppe aus dem Tartarus' (D583) is 'Schubert at his very best' and that 'other Schiller songs have characteristic beauties', observes that 'certain ones are relatively dull, and between them, as a collection, and the Goethe songs there is hardly a comparison ... On the whole the association was disappointing ... And again and again we see the musician returning to the charge—only to be put off by something in Schiller that was prosaic and frigid.' Probably the very great interest which Schubert took in Schiller's poetry owed something to the importance which Josef von Spaun* and his circle attached to Schiller's writings and aesthetic ideas.

Settings: D6, 7, 30, 47, 51–5, 57–8, 60–5, 67, 70–1, 73, 77, 113, 117, 159, 189, 191–2, 195, 232, 246, 249–53, 277, 283, ?284, 312, 323, 338, 387–91, 396–7, 402, 577, 583–4, 587–8, 594–5, 636–8, 677, 793–4, 801, 983A, 990–1.
(Capell, Gramit¹, Thomas)

Schimon, Ferdinand (b. Pest [Budapest], 6 April 1797; d. Munich, 29 August 1852). Painter and tenor. Schubert reportedly advised him to take up singing professionally. He took the part of the troubadour Palmerin at the première of *Die Zauberharfe* (D644) on 19 August 1820, but failed to do justice to his great aria 'Was belebt die schöne Welt?'. Baron Schlechta,* in his review in the Vienna *Conversationsblatt* on 29 August, warmly praised the music of the romance but regretted that 'the singer only let us guess at the composer's intentions'. He conceded, however, as a tribute to Schubert rather than to Schimon, that 'even the hapless Palmerin could not completely spoil his part'. The romance was omitted during subsequent performances of the melodrama; later Schubert made a concert version of it. In 1821 Schimon was engaged at the Munich court theatre, and on 1 July of that year he appeared there as Jacquino in the first Munich production of Beethoven's* *Fidelio*. He subsequently sang various secondary roles in Munich, such as Basilio in Mozart's *Le nozze di Figaro*, Harras [Rodolphe] in Rossini's *Guillaume Tell*, and Lorenzo in Auber's *La Muette de Portici*.

Schimon, who had studied with Johann Baptist Lampi (1775–1837), turned out to be a better painter than a singer, and after his retirement from the operatic stage in 1840 he devoted all his time to that art. His portraits of Beethoven (1818/19, now at the Beethoven-Haus, Bonn) and Weber* (1825, now at the Carl-Maria-von-Weber-Gedenkstätte, Dresden-Hosterwitz) were judged particularly good likenesses. He furthermore executed a number of portraits of royal and aristocratic persons, as well as of such well-known actors as Ferdinand Esslair and Josef Koberwein; he also excelled at painting female subjects. His brother Maximilian (1805–59) was likewise a painter.

Schimon's son Adolf (1820–87) was a highly regarded pianist, composer, and teacher. Adolf's wife Anna, née Regan (1841–1902), was a soprano who became a well-known Schubert singer.

(*ÖBL*, Wurzbach[1], Zenger)

Schindler, Anton Felix (b. Meedl [Medlov, Czech Republic], 13 June 1795; d. Bockenheim, near Frankfurt am Main, 16 January 1864). Conductor, writer on music, and biographer of Beethoven.* As a child, he was taught to play the violin by his father, Josef Schindler (1758–1835). He was educated at Olmütz [Olomouc] (1811–13), and at the University of Vienna where he studied philosophy and perhaps also law. He was employed by a Viennese lawyer from 1817 until 1822, after which he switched to a career in music, becoming leader of the violins and conductor at the Theater in der Josefstadt. From 1825 he conducted at the Kärntnertor-Theater.

He met Beethoven in 1814, but it was not until after the departure of Beethoven's secretary Franz Oliva in late 1820 that he came to play a significant role in Beethoven's life. He soon assumed the functions of an (unpaid) general factotum, carrying out his numerous tasks with efficiency and devotion. But when Beethoven accused him of cheating over the receipts of the 'grand musical concert' of 7 May 1824 (at which the Ninth Symphony and parts of the *Missa solemnis* were first performed), relations temporarily ceased between them. Karl Holz* became Beethoven's secretary in 1825, and it was not until late in 1826 that Schindler resumed his earlier position. Therafter he was in close attendance on Beethoven until the end. After his death, Schindler took possession of the conversation books and of a quantity of letters and manuscripts. In 1846 he sold most of this material (to the ownership of which he had a rather dubious claim) to the Royal Prussian Library in Berlin, in exchange for a lump payment and a life annuity. The library eventually received the remainder from his sister Marie.

In September 1827 Schindler moved to Pest [Budapest] where Marie, a professional singer, had been engaged at the local theatre. In October 1828 he invited Schubert, in his own and Franz Paul Lachner's* name, to travel to Pest in order to attend the première of the latter's opera *Die Bürgschaft*. At the same time, they proposed that he should give a concert during his stay. Schubert does not appear to have replied. In 1829 Schindler returned to Vienna to teach aesthetics at the singing school attached to the Kärntnertor-Theater. Later he was appointed director of music, first at Münster (1831) and then at Aachen (1835), and after a further spell at Münster (from 1842) he settled in 1848 at Frankfurt, where he was active as a teacher and writer. In 1840 he published his *Biographie von Ludwig van Beethoven* at Münster; a second edition appeared in 1845, and a completely revised and much improved third edition in 1860.

Already in his lifetime, his character and the position he arrogated to himself as the supreme authority on Beethoven's life and on the performance of his works aroused hostility. Nevertheless his credibility, though somewhat eroded by the detection of numerous inaccuracies in the biography, survived largely intact until the 1970s, when it was dealt a fatal blow by the discovery that more than 150 of his entries in Beethoven's conversation books had in fact not been made until after Beethoven's death. The falsifications have been shown to be largely self-serving. As a result, scholars are now wary of accepting any of his statements about Beethoven unless these are supported by other evidence. Similar caution needs clearly to be observed in respect of his remarks about other contemporaries, including Schubert.

Schindler wrote about Schubert on several occasions, most comprehensively in his article 'Erinnerungen an Franz Schubert', published in the *Niederrheinische Musikzeitung für Kunstfreunde und Künstler* (Cologne) on 7 and 14 March 1857 (extensively reproduced in O. E. Deutsch's* *Schubert: Erinnerungen*). Schindler is the principal or sole source for such stories as that Karl Pinterics* procured for Schubert a better German text of the Ossianic poems than that which he had previously set; that Schubert spoke with Beethoven in 1822 (for details of the alleged meeting, *see* Beethoven*); that he proposed to study with Simon Sechter* already in 1824, but was dissuaded from doing so by Pinterics; that he quarrelled with the singer Nanette Schechner*; that, in order to keep Beethoven occupied and entertained during his long final illness, he, Schindler, had shown him a collection of some sixty songs and partsongs by Schubert, many of them still in manuscript; that Beethoven, 'who, until then, did not know five songs by Schubert', had been astounded by the quality of the settings and would have liked to see Schubert's operas and compositions for the piano, and that he had repeatedly exclaimed 'Truly, there is a divine spark in this Schubert' and prophesied that Schubert would one day become celebrated; and that Schubert, grateful to Schindler for having enabled Beethoven to form such a high opinion of his talent, had called on him several times during the summer of 1827, 'chatting with me pleasantly *à la Beethoven*'.

In the same article, Schindler printed a chronological catalogue of Schubert's compositions, partly based on a list supplied to him by Ferdinand Schubert* in 1841, at a time when Schindler had contemplated writing Schubert's biography; he later abandoned the project for lack of material.

(Badura-Skoda, Klein[3], MacArdle[1], *ÖBL*, Stadlen[1,2])

Schlechta von Wschehrd [Wssehrd] [Šlechta ze Všehrd], **Franz Xaver,** Baron (b. Pisek [Písek, Czech Republic], 20 October 1796; d. Vienna, 23 August 1875). Civil servant; poet and playwright. Son of Franz Xaver Vinzenz Schlechta von Wschehrd (1765–1831), an army officer who was created a baron in 1819. Franz Xaver was educated at Kremsmünster School and in 1813 became a boarder at the Stadtkonvikt, Vienna. He studied philosophy and then law at the University of Vienna (1813–18). In 1818 he entered government service, in which he rose steadily through the ranks, until, in 1862, he was made an under-secretary of state; two years later he retired. Starting in 1817, Schlechta contributed poems and theatre reviews to a number of periodicals, and he also wrote some plays (*Cimburga von Masovien, Der Grünmantel von Venedig*). Most of the poems later appeared in *Dichtungen* (Vienna, 1824). This literary activity was largely confined to his youth. His marriage to Katharina Gutherz produced two sons: Kamill Franz Karl Adam (1822–80) who became a well-known writer [pseud. Camillo Hell), and Ottokar Maria (1825–94) who had a distinguished career as an orientalist and diplomat.

Schlechta arrived at the Stadtkonvikt in the autumn of 1813, shortly before Schubert officially withdrew from it. The two young men appear to have established friendly relations during the following years, and in February 1815 Schubert set one of Schlechta's poems in 'Auf einen Kirchhof' (D151). Schlechta was among the law students who took part in the performance of the cantata *Prometheus* (D451) on 24 July 1816 at Heinrich Josef Watteroth's* house, and he commemorated the event in the poem 'An Herrn Franz Schubert (Als seine Kantate *Prometheus* aufgeführt ward)' which appeared in the *Wiener allgemeine Theaterzeitung* on 27 September 1817. It was the first time that Schubert's name was mentioned in a periodical.

In 1818, in a review in the same journal of a 'private entertainment' offered by the actor Karl Friedrich Müller at the 'Zum römischen Kaiser' inn on 12 March and which had featured a performance by four pianists of an overture (D590 or 591) by Schubert, Schlechta drew attention to the exceptional musical talents of the still largely unknown composer: 'Each of his shorter or longer compositions is characterized by profound feeling, spontaneous but controlled force, and appealing charm . . .' Schlechta was no less generous and supportive in his reviews of the stage works *Die Zwillingsbrüder* (D647) and *Die Zauberharfe* (D644) (in the *Conversationsblatt* on 20 June and 29 August 1820). He particularly praised Schubert's contribution to *Die Zauberharfe*, while condemning the generally nonsensical nature of that melodrama: 'What a pity that Schubert's wonderful music did not find a worthier subject. This artist has now, after a very short interval, presented a second musical work on the stage and has brilliantly demonstrated his genius to those who found cause to doubt it at the performance of the first one.'

Schlechta remained a member of Schubert's circle until the latter's death. On that occasion, he published a short poem ('Die Muse weint . . .') in the *Wiener Zeitschrift für Kunst, Literatur, Theater und Mode* on 9 December 1828. It was set to music by Anselm Hüttenbrenner* in 1861; text and music were printed in the Viennese periodical *Lyra* on the centenary of Schubert's birth, 31 January 1897. Schlechta reportedly wrote a longer poem about Schubert in *c*.1840.

Schubert composed the following seven songs to poems by Schlechta between 1815 and 1826: 'Auf einen Kirchhof' (D151), 'Aus *Diego Manazares*' (D458), 'Des

Fräuleins Liebeslauschen' (D698), 'Des Sängers Habe' (D832), 'Fischerweise' (D881), 'Totengräber-Weise' (D869), and 'Widerschein' (D639).

Settings: D151, 458, 639, 698, 832, 869, 881.
(Fischer[8], Hilmar/Brusatti, *ÖBL*, Steblin[8])

Schlegel, August Wilhelm von (b. Hanover, 8 September 1767; d. Bonn, 12 May 1845). Poet, translator, and critic; older brother of Friedrich von Schlegel.* After studying theology and philology at Göttingen University and spending four years at Amsterdam as a private tutor, he settled at Jena in 1795. He and Friedrich became leaders of the Romantic movement and jointly edited its principal journal, *Das Athenaeum* (Berlin, 1798–1800); they also published a volume of essays, *Charakteristiken und Kritiken* (1801). Schlegel expounded his ideas in lectures given in Berlin between 1801 and 1804 and in Vienna in 1808. (The former were eventually published under the title *Vorlesungen über schöne Literatur und in Kunst* in 1884, the latter as *Vorlesungen über dramatische Kunst und Literatur* in 1809–11.) After the death in 1817 of Mme de Staël, with whom, in the course of a close friendship, Schlegel had travelled throughout Europe, he took up a chair in oriental languages at Bonn University. Like Friedrich, he was ennobled in 1815.

Apart from his critical writings, he is best known for his verse translation of seventeen plays by Shakespeare* (1797–1810), but he also produced excellent translations from the Romance languages in his *Spanisches Theater* (1803–9) and *Blumensträusse italienischer, spanischer und portugiesischer Poesie* (1804). On the other hand, his own poems (*Gedichte*, 1800) met with little success.

Between 1816 and 1826 Schubert set some of Schlegel's original verse in 'Abendlied für die Entfernte' (D856), 'Die gefangenen Sänger' (D712), 'Die verfehlte Stunde' (D409), 'Lebensmelodien' (D395), 'Lob der Tränen' (D711), 'Sprache der Liebe' (D410), and 'Wiedersehn' (D855). He also set translations by Schlegel of Petrarch* (D628–9) and Shakespeare (D889). (*See also* Gries* and Schütz.*)

Settings: D395, 409–10, 628–9, 711–12, 855–6, 889.
(Menhennet)

Schlegel, (Karl Wilhelm) Friedrich von (b. Hanover, 10 March 1772; d. Dresden, 12 January 1829). Poet and critic; brother of August Wilhelm von Schlegel.* Though the son of a pastor, he became a Roman Catholic in 1808; thereafter he frequently lectured in support of his new church. He had studied at the universities of Göttingen and Leipzig (1790–4), at first law, then philosophy and classical literature. With his brother, whom he joined at Jena in 1796, he was one of the principal founders and promoters of Romantic literature. Subsequently he lived for a time in Berlin, lectured at Jena (1801), and from 1802 spent several years in Paris, where he studied oriental languages. He then moved to Cologne and eventually settled in 1808 in Vienna, where he joined the Austrian civil service. He had married the novelist and translator Dorothea Veit (1763–1839), a daughter of Moses Mendels-sohn,* in 1804, and the couple's apartment became a centre for Vienna's intellectual and cultural life, attracting both residents such as Karoline Pichler,* and foreign visitors. Schlegel published some original works—poems, the first part of a novel, *Lucinde*, a tragedy, *Alarcos*—but it was his critical and aphoristic writings which, together with his lectures, made the greatest impact.

There is no evidence that Schubert ever met Schlegel, although the latter had contacts with certain members of his circle. Schlegel maintained a fairly intimate relationship with Franz von Bruchmann,* as evidenced by the fact that he was a witness at Bruchmann's wedding to Juliana von Weyrother on 25 June 1827. Franz von Schober* is also likely to have known him personally, for in a letter to Schubert's nephew Heinrich Schubert on 2 November 1876 he mentioned that Schlegel had greatly praised his libretto for *Alfonso und Estrella* (D732).

Schubert composed sixteen songs to poems by Schlegel between 1818 and 1825; ten of the texts were taken from the cycle *Abendröte*. The songs include 'Das Mädchen' (D652), 'Der Fluss' (D693), 'Der Knabe' (D692), 'Der Schiffer' (D694), 'Der Wanderer' (D649), 'Die Gebüsche' (D646), 'Die Rose' (D745), 'Die Sterne' (D684), 'Die Vögel' (D691), and 'Im Walde' (D708). The last-named song has been called 'assuredly one of Schubert's greatest inspirations' (R. Capell, *Schubert's Songs*).

Settings: D631–4, 646, 649, 652, 684, 690–4, 708, 745, 854.
(Capell, Hörisch, Porhansl², Weissberg)

Schlösser, Louis (b. Darmstadt, 17 November 1800; d. Darmstadt, 17 November 1886). Composer, violinist, Kapellmeister, and teacher. From spring 1822 to May 1823 he lived in Vienna where he studied with Josef Mayseder, Salieri,* and Ignaz von Seyfried. He also received instruction from Jean-François Le Sueur and Rodolphe Kreutzer in Paris. In 1846 he became Konzertmeister of the court Kapelle at Darmstadt, and in 1858 its Kapellmeister. He wrote several operas, including *Das Leben ein Traum* (1839) and *Die Braut des Herzogs* (1847), as well as a considerable amount of orchestral works, chamber music, and compositions for the violin. His son Carl William Adolph (1830–1913) became a well-known composer and piano teacher; he was on the staff of the Royal Academy of Music in London from *c*.1855 until 1903.

During his stay in Vienna, Schlösser very probably became acquainted with Schubert. In his recollections of Schubert which he published in the Leipzig *Neue Zeitschrift für Musik* on 10 and 17 August 1883, he even laid claim to a certain intimacy. While there may well have been contacts between them, his account of the concert at which he allegedly first saw and heard Schubert is manifestly false, since he describes Schubert as playing, among other items, 'the first of his two trios' and 'one of his delightful Impromptus'. In reality, the piano trios and the Im-promptus were not composed until several years later.

What is certain, on the other hand, is that Schlösser met Beethoven* while he was in Vienna. When he left for Paris, Beethoven even presented him with the canon 'Edel sei der Mensch' and gave him letters of introduction to Cherubini and the music publisher Maurice Schlesinger. In the Hildburghausen periodical *Halleluja*, in 1885, Schlösser related how he first caught sight of Beethoven after a performance of *Fidelio* which he had attended with 'his very good friend Franz Schubert' on 4 November 1822. (The date may be a mistake for '3 November', which was the opening night of a new production of the opera at the Kärntnertor-Theater.) It was Schubert who had drawn his attention to Beethoven: 'At that moment, Schubert gently tugged at my arm, while pointing with his finger at the man in the middle who was just then turning his head, so that the bright light of the lamps fell on his face . . .'. (Beethoven was accompanied by Anton Schindler* and Stefan von Breuning.) It should be added that Schlösser's account of his contacts with Beethoven is viewed with no less suspicion by some modern scholars than his published memories of Schubert.

(Noack)

Schmidt, Georg Philipp [called 'Schmidt von Lübeck'] (b. Lübeck, 1 January 1766; d. Altona, near Hamburg, 28 October 1849). Physician, civil servant; poet. The son of a prominent Lübeck merchant, he studied law and public finance at the universities of Jena and Göttingen (1786–90); later he switched to medicine, qualifying at Kiel University in 1797. He practised for some time as a doctor in Kiel, Lübeck, and Warsaw, but before long entered the Danish government service, in which, until his retirement in 1829, he engaged in financial and commercial activities.

He knew personally many leading contemporary writers, including Goethe,* Herder,* Schiller,* and Wieland. He himself wrote occasional verse, mainly influenced by the Göttinger Hainbund and the rhapsodic and nationalistic style of poetry known as 'Bardendichtung'. Many of his poems first appeared in *W. G. Beckers Taschenbuch zum geselligen Vergnügen* (Leipzig). A collection of them, *Lieder*, was published at Altona in 1821 (augmented editions in 1826 and 1847). Some of his poems were set by contemporary composers, including Schubert.

The latter's song 'Der Wanderer' (D489) was inspired by a poem by Schmidt which had been published in different versions, with different titles, and even ascribed to a different author. Called 'Des Fremdlings Abschied', it appeared, over Schmidt's name, in *W. G. Beckers Taschenbuch zum geselligen Vergnügen* in 1808. It was also printed, in a largely identical version, but entitled 'Der Unglückliche' and attributed to Zacharias Werner,* in *Dichtungen für Kunstredner*, edited by Johann Ludwig Deinhardstein* (Vienna, Trieste, 1815). This was the text used by Schubert for his song, to which he himself gave the title 'Der Wanderer'. According to Kreissle,* his attention had been drawn to the poem by a Viennese clergyman by the name of Horni. He made three versions of his setting, all of them probably in or about October 1816. It was the third one which was published by Cappi & Diabelli* in May 1821, the poet being correctly identified as Schmidt von Lübeck.

Anselm Hüttenbrenner* informed Liszt* in 1854 that Schubert himself 'sang and played' the song for the first time at a soirée at Matthäus von Collin's* which took place in *c*.1820. Johann Ladislaus Pyrker von Felsö-Eör,* to whom 'Der Wanderer' was later dedicated, was present on that occasion. The song helped to establish the composer's reputation and was repeatedly performed at private as well as public concerts. Thus it is known to have been sung by August von Gymnich* at Ignaz von Sonnleithner's* on 19 January 1821; by an unidentified singer at a concert at the 'Zum römischen Kaiser' inn on 18 November 1821; and by Johann Hoffmann at 'evening entertainments' of the Gesellschaft der Musikfreunde on 2 December 1824 and 30 March 1826. Moreover, several contemporaries later remembered with great admiration Johann Michael Vogl's* numerous renditions of the song. It also made Schubert's name better known outside Vienna: when Jakob Wilhelm Rauscher sang it at a concert of the Steiermärkischer Musikverein (Styrian Music Society) at Graz on 19 April 1826, it was so enthusiastically applauded that it had to be repeated; and at a concert at Linz on 23 July of that same year it was 'received with the applause it merited' (*Wiener allgemeine Theaterzeitung*, 19 August 1826). In the *Wiener Zeitung* of 30 May 1828, in a puff for the newly published song 'Auf der Bruck' (D853), the publisher Tobias Haslinger* claimed that it was as original a composition as 'Erlkönig' (D328) and 'Der Wanderer', and could well 'rival those two favourite songs in excellence'. During the first decades after Schubert's death, 'Der Wanderer' continued to enjoy very great popularity. The song even became the subject of poems, panegyrics, and short stories. (*See also* Nestroy* and Staudigl.*)

In 1822, Schubert used bars 23–30 as the theme for the variations in the Adagio section of the so-called 'Wanderer' Fantasia (D760).

Setting: D489.

(Hackenberg, Hilmar/Brusatti, Kreissle, Schwarz)

Schneller, Julius Franz Borgias [pseud. Julius Velox] (b. Strasburg, 3 March 1777; d. Freiburg im Breisgau, 12 May 1833). Historian, philosopher, and poet. After studying philosophy, history, and law at the University of Freiburg, where his father taught Roman law, he completed his law studies in Vienna (1796–8). He was employed as a private tutor and subsequently (1804–5) in the censorship office. In 1804 he had two plays produced at the Burgtheater, the tragedy *Vitellia* and the comedy *Gefangenschaft aus Liebe* (based on Louis Dupaty's *La Prison militaire*). In the spring of that year he was introduced to Karoline Pichler* and soon became a popular member of her circle.

In 1805 he was appointed an instructor in history at the Lyzeum at Linz, where Josef von Spaun* was among his pupils; the following year he took up a similar post at the Lyzeum at Graz. He was revered by his pupils, but his influence extended beyond the confines of the school, and he became, in Faust Pachler's* phrase, 'the soul of Graz'. His circle included at least two persons whose names are closely associated with Schubert: Faust's mother Marie Pachler* and Johann Baptist Jenger.* In 1815 he married a widow, Anna Prokesch, and as a result became stepfather to Anton Prokesch (later Count Anton Prokesch von Osten*).

Although Schneller established a solid reputation as a scholarly writer, particularly as a result of several important works on historical subjects, his repeated attempts to obtain a teaching post in Vienna were blocked by the authorities because of his liberal political views which brought him into conflict with the censors. He left Graz in 1823 to take up a professorship in philosophy and history at the University of Freiburg.

On 7 October 1826 the *Wiener Zeitschrift für Kunst, Literatur, Theater und Mode* published his poem 'An Franz Schubert vom Rheinstrome', in which he expressed admiration for Schubert's songs, the titles of several of which he worked, somewhat laboriously, into the text. His invitation to Schubert ('thou, son of the great Danube') to visit the Rhine was not taken up by the composer.

(*ÖBL*, Pachler, Pichler, Wurzbach[1])

Schnorr von Karolsfeld, Ludwig Ferdinand (b. Königsberg, Prussia [Kaliningrad, Russia], 11 October 1788; d. Vienna, 13 April 1853). Painter, etcher, and lithographer; son of the well-known painter Johann Veit Schnorr von Karolsfeld (1764–1841). Trained in Vienna and resident there throughout most of his life, he was appointed assistant custodian of paintings at Belvedere Palace in 1841, advancing to principal custodian two years later. In the 1820s he painted predominantly religious pictures and subjects taken from literature, history, and legend. In 1821 he converted to Catholicism. After the death in 1829 of his friend Friedrich von Schlegel,* whose religious ideas had profoundly influenced him, the mystical strain disappeared from his work and he turned towards landscapes.

It was probably through Moritz von Schwind,* who studied privately with him (1821–3), that Schnorr von Karolsfeld came into contact with Schubert's circle. In 1822 he was among those who attended the reading parties and Schubertiads at Franz von Schober's.* In 1825 Schubert dedicated 'to his friend L. F. Schnorr von Karolsfeld' his Op. 37, consisting of the songs 'Der Alpenjäger' (D588) and 'Der Pilgrim' (D794). These are the only documented contacts between the two men, but C. Bodenstein, in *Hundert Jahre Kunstgeschichte Wiens 1788–1888* (Vienna, 1888), mentions a portrait by Schnorr showing Schubert in the company of several friends, among them Eduard von Bauernfeld,* Moritz von Schwind, and Schnorr himself. The portrait, if it ever existed, is lost.

(*ALBK, ÖBL*)

Schober, Franz (Adolf Friedrich) von (b. Torup Castle, near Malmö, Sweden, 17 May 1796; d. Dresden, 13 September 1882). Son of Franz von Schober (1760–1802) and his wife Katharina, née Dörf(f)el [Derffel] (1764–1833). The couple, who had married in Vienna in 1786, had three other children: Axel (1789–1817), who became a lieutenant in the Austrian army; Ludwiga, who married the Italian tenor Giuseppe Siboni in Vienna in 1810 and was accidentally shot by him in 1812; and Sophie, who married Johann Ignaz Zechenter, a land surveyor, in 1823 and died in 1825.

The father, who was ennobled in 1801, had been employed as manager of Baron Alexius Stierblad's estate at Torup since *c.*1780. After his death, the rest of the family moved to Germany, where, from 1803 to 1806, Schober attended the school run by the well-known educationist and theologian Christian Gotthilf Salzmann at Schnepfental, near Gotha. In 1807 he attended the Akademisches Gymnasium in Vienna, and, from 1808 to 1815, Kremsmünster School, in Upper Austria. In 1815 he enrolled at the University of Vienna, where, from 1816, he studied law. He did not, however, complete the course. His mother had lost a substantial part of the fortune she had brought back with her to Vienna, yet still seems to have been quite comfortably off, and Schober spent most of his life dabbling at a variety of activities, without ever settling down seriously to any of them. He was highly intelligent and well read, wrote poetry, had artistic leanings, entertained liberal political views and tepid religious ones, and generally led a life of considerable self-indulgence. He was likely to be a prominent, and even dominant, figure in any group, admired by some, distrusted by others; and such, indeed, was the position which he came to occupy in Schubert's circle.

It may be assumed that when he was introduced to Schubert by Josef von Spaun* in Vienna in 1815, he had not yet heard any of the former's compositions. Kreissle* suggested that Schober was eager to meet the young composer, having heard performances of his songs at Spaun's home in Linz in 1813. But this notion was subsequently rejected by Spaun himself, who stated that Schubert's songs could not yet have been known in Linz at that time. On the other hand, Schober was certainly, by early 1813, i.e. well before he left Kremsmünster, in close contact with Josef von Spaun's circle, in particular with Spaun's brother Anton, Josef Kenner,* Johann Mayrhofer,* and Anton Ottenwalt.* In fact, over the next several years, they all engaged, much of the time by letter, in a sometimes heated debate about matters of aesthetics and morality.

Once he had settled in Vienna, Schober soon gathered around him a group of young people interested in cultural subjects, whom he regularly entertained at the apartment which he shared with his mother and his sister Sophie [26 Tuchlauben]. Spaun later spoke of the exceptionally hospitable manner in which he and his brother Franz were received there. Among the visitors was Schubert, and before long the Schobers offered him highly practical encouragement in the form of free accommodation in their home, thereby releasing him from the hated drudgery of a schoolmaster's existence, and enabling him to devote himself entirely to composing. (At any rate, it seems highly probable that he gave up teaching at this time.) Thus the Schobers' generosity undoubtedly had a significant influence on his life. Schubert lived in their apartment from autumn 1816 until August 1817. It was during this period (probably in February or March 1817), that Schober introduced him to Johann Michael Vogl*.

Schubert was to benefit from Schober's support and hospitality on several further occasions. In 1820–2, he was among the guests whom Schober entertained for a short time during the summer at Atzenbrugg Castle in Lower Austria, a property owned by Klosterneuburg Monastery and administered by Schober's uncle Josef Derffel (*see also* Leopold Kupelwieser* and Ludwig Mohn*). Moreover, Schubert and Schober spent a month together, in the autumn of 1821, at and near St Pölten, in Lower Austria, as guests of the bishop, Johann Nepomuk von Dankesreither,* who was a relative of Schober's. During their stay they worked on the text and music of the opera *Alfonso und Estrella* (D732).

In 1822 Schubert once more moved in with the Schobers, who were now living at the Göttweigerhof [9 Spiegelgasse], and he remained their guest until the summer of 1823 (except for a period between late 1822 and spring 1823). His hosts regularly arranged Schubertiads, and Schober also held reading parties; these considerably widened Schubert's knowledge of contemporary literature. When Schober left Vienna in August 1823 for Breslau [Wrocław], with the apparent intention of making a name for himself as an actor, the reading sessions continued for a while at Ludwig Mohn's, but were suspended in the spring of 1824. Evidently Schubert was not alone in feeling that 'our circle, as I had indeed expected, has lost its guiding force with your departure' (letter to Schober, 30 November 1823). While in Germany, Schober remained in contact with several members of the group, notably with Moritz von Schwind,* who felt profound admiration and affection for him and very frequently corresponded with him. Schwind acted, moreover, as go-between for Schober and Justina von Bruchmann, to whom Schober was secretly engaged. When the secret was discovered and Justina was forced by her parents and by her brother, Franz von Bruchmann,* to break off the engagement in late 1824, a split occurred within the group, with Schwind and Schubert firmly siding with the absent Schober and against Bruchmann.

Little is known about Schober's activities at Breslau, other than that his acquaintances there included the writer Karl von Holtei and the philosopher Henrik Steffens, and that he met with little success on the theatrical stage, where he appeared under the name 'Torupson'. Back in Vienna in the summer of 1825, he soon re-established a certain ascendancy over those of his former friends who had remained loyal to him. New acquaintances tended, however, to be rather critical, like Eduard von Bauernfeld* who wrote in his diary on 8 March 1826: 'Schober surpasses all of us in intellect, and still more in conversation! Yet there is much in him that is artificial, and his best qualities risk being suffocated by idleness'; and in August he recorded: 'Schober idle, as usual'.

During the last three years of his life, Schubert was more than ever in Schober's company, for in addition to regularly wining and dining with him and others at various taverns, he was his house guest, or possibly lodger, during much of that period (for details, *see* 'A Chronicle of Schubert's Life', pp. xxii–xxiv above). When he moved to his brother Ferdinand's* lodgings at the beginning of September 1828, he did so only in the hope of recovering his health at Neu-Wieden where the air was supposedly better for his health, and with the evident intention of subsequently returning to Schober's apartment, where he had enjoyed the luxury of having at his disposal a music room and two other rooms, and where he had left nearly all his manuscripts.

In 1826 Schober acquired the Lithographisches Institut in Vienna, which had been founded in 1817 by Count Adolf Pötting und Persing. In the spring and summer of 1828, the Institut published Schubert's Opp. 96 and 106, containing first editions of the songs 'Das Weinen' (D926), 'Die Sterne' (D939), 'Fischerweise' (D881), 'Gesang: Was ist Silvia' (D891), 'Heimliches Lieben' (D922), 'Jägers Liebes-lied' (D909), and 'Vor meiner Wiege' (D927). Schober sold the Institut not long after Schubert's death, by which time it was close to bankruptcy.

It is evident that Schubert remained on the best of terms with Schober until the end, and that he had indeed good reason to do so. After his death, his relatives asked Schober to write new words to his poem 'Pax vobiscum', which Schubert had set to music in 1817 (D551), and the new text was sung during the funeral service at St Josef's Church in the Margareten suburb on 21 November. Schober reportedly also designed the funeral monument at Währing district cemetery, with Ludwig Förster's* help.

Schober's later life appears to have been as unfocused as his earlier years. He lived for a while at Pest [Budapest], visited Schwind in Munich, and devoted some of his time to managing the family estate near Vienna. After his mother's death in 1833, the estate was sold and Schober travelled in Italy, France, and Belgium. He was back in Hungary in time to witness Liszt's* triumphant return to his native land in December 1839. (He was to relate the events in *Briefe über F. Liszt's Aufenthalt in Ungarn* in 1843.) In Vienna, in 1840, Schober became very friendly with Liszt, who, in a letter to Count Leo Festetics, described him as 'un noble cœur et un noble esprit'. Liszt subsequently invited Schober to accompany him on his concert tours as his secretary, but nothing came of the proposal. Some time later, Schober went to Weimar, where he held the titles of chamberlain and legation counsellor. While in Weimar, he helped to bring about a performance of *Alfonso und Estrella* under Liszt's direction (for some details of the production, *see* Liszt*).

Schober next moved to Dresden, and there, in 1856, he married the writer Thekla von Gumpert (1810–97), with whom he had reportedly been acquainted in his youth and who was now well known for her *Töchter-Album*, an annual publication for teenage girls. The marriage lasted barely four years. Thereafter Schober resided, for the most part, in Hungary, Munich (1769–74), and Dresden. Unfortunately, he could never be induced to write down his recollections of Schubert. 'I would very much have liked to write a small book about him and our life together, but have never managed to do so,' he confessed in a letter to Bauernfeld in 1869. 'How could

I ever make you, who writes so easily and so excellently, understand the insurmountable incapacity to write which has, to my despair, afflicted me throughout my life and has been a veritable misfortune for me?' He did, however, write some poetry: in 1826 he published a small collection, *Paligenesien aus den heiligen Büchern des alten Bundes*, at Breslau, and these poems were later included in *Gedichte* (Stuttgart, 1842), of which a further edition appeared at Leipzig in 1865.

Schober remains the most enigmatic member of Schubert's circle. As already indicated, reactions to his character and behaviour varied considerably. In July 1816, when Schober was barely 20, Anton Ottenwalt, in a letter to Josef von Spaun, expressed strong criticism of his character and serious doubts about the likelihood of any future improvement: 'The blossom is blighted; where shall the fruit come from?' And Spaun's mother put an end to the deep attachment which her daughter Marie had formed for Schober, because, as Spaun later explained, Schober 'was not a religious man'; but the break was made gently, and the two families remained on amicable terms. Such was not the case when Schober's secret engagement to Justina von Bruchmann was discovered in 1824 (see above). On that occasion, Franz von Bruchmann, who was then still battling against his own spiritual demons (he would not recover his Christian faith for two more years), wrote a violently abusive letter to Schober; and in his later autobiography (not intended for publication) he recalled with satisfaction how he had driven away a man who 'had had the outrageous temerity to seek to sully one of the most precious jewels of my family'.

But the fiercest denunciation of Schober's morals was pronounced by Josef Kenner, whose condemnation is all the more remarkable for having been made, not in the heat of the moment but several decades later, in letters to Ferdinand Luib* on 10 and 22 May 1858; moreover, by his own account, Kenner had had little contact with Schober after 1816. Kenner described Schober as an exceptionally charming and highly gifted young man, but one entirely lacking in moral principles, vain, jealous, a veritable Mephistopheles who ensnared and corrupted innocent souls, a false prophet who craved total domination over his disciples. Kenner stated, moreover, that he had been informed (for he rarely saw Schubert either after 1816) that Schober's dazzling but perverse personality had exercised a disastrous and lasting influence on the impressionable Schubert. Perhaps, in accusing Schober of corrupting Schubert, Kenner was holding him responsible for the circumstances which led to Schubert contracting syphilis, probably through contact with prostitutes. Schober himself appears to have been similarly infected; and there may have been a connection between his venereal disease and the decision to leave Vienna in 1823.

Whatever truth there may be in Kenner's allegations of moral corruption, his wholly negative assessment of the influence which Schober is likely to have had on Schubert needs to be set against Josef von Spaun's statement that the relationship was undoubtedly beneficial to Schubert from an artistic point of view. Like Kenner, Spaun met Schober and Schubert when they were still quite young, but he was linked with both in an intimate association for many more years than Kenner. In his remarks about Schober which appear among his comments on Kreissle's* Schubert biography (*see* Spaun*), he makes no reference to the moral dimension, but writes: 'Contact with a young man as passionately interested in the arts and as well educated as Schober, and who, moreover, was himself a skilful poet, is bound to have had an extremely stimulating and beneficial influence on Schubert. Schober's friends became also Schubert's friends, and I am convinced that his very close contact with this circle was of far greater benefit to Schubert than if he had lived within a group of musicians and other composers, whom, in any case, he did not neglect.'

In 1822 Schubert dedicated his Op. 14 to Schober; it consisted of the songs 'Geheimes' (D719) and 'Suleika I' (D720). Between 1815 and 1827, he set sixteen poems by Schober, mostly for single voice. The songs include 'Am Bach im Frühlinge' (D361), 'An die Musik' (D547), 'Pilgerweise' (D789), 'Schatzgräbers Begehr' (D761), 'Schiffers Scheidelied' (D910), and 'Todesmusik' (D758). Furthermore, Schober provided the libretto for the opera *Alfonso und Estrella* (see above) which Schubert composed between September 1821 and February 1822. The text of the second-act aria 'Der Jäger ruhte' also appeared as a separate poem entitled 'Die Wolkenbraut' in Schober's *Gedichte*; in that incarnation it has been given the work-number D683.

Settings: D143, 361, 546–7, 551, 683, 709, 732, 740, 758, 761, 786, 789, 792, 875, 909–10, 930, 990B. (Bruchmann, Gramit[1,2], Hilmar[2], Holland, Liszt[3], Neumayr, *ÖBL*, Steblin[1,3], Weiss)

Schoberlechner, Johann Karl (bapt. Vienna, 30 May 1800; d. Vienna, 26 April 1879). Singer (bass-baritone). Son of Josef Schoberlechner (b. 1767), a haberdasher; from 1813 he worked in his father's shop 'Zur schönen Wienerin'. At the same time, he studied singing with Josef Mozatti. From the early 1820s he participated in numerous concerts, at which he sang primarily in arias and ensembles from Italian operas, especially those by Rossini. Thus, while he regularly performed at 'evening entertainments' of the Gesellschaft der Musikfreunde which also featured vocal compositions by Schubert, it was not until 21 December 1826 that he sang in one of them himself, namely 'Der Zwerg' (D771). Thereafter he sang Schubert's songs more frequently at these evening concerts. In particular, he gave the first performances of 'An Schwager Kronos' (D369), on 11 January 1827; 'Lied des gefangenen Jägers' (D843), on 8 February 1827; 'Der Kampf' (D594), on 6 December 1827; and 'Der Lindenbaum' (D911/5) and 'Im Dorfe' (D911/17), on 22 January 1829. He sang 'Der Zwerg' again on 13 December 1827 and at a concert by the pianist Franziska Sallamon on 2 February 1829; on the latter occasion, his rendition was rated by the critic of the *Wiener allgemeine Theaterzeitung* as 'excellent, entirely in the spirit of the composer'. He did not take part in Schubert's own concert on 26 March 1828, but he was among the artists appearing at the memorial concerts on 30 January and 5 March 1829, when he sang 'Die Allmacht' (D852) and in the first-act finale from *Don Giovanni*.

Between 1836 and 1845 he was a member of the court Opera company, specializing in the baritone roles of Rossini, Bellini, and Donizetti operas; but he also appeared in German opera, e.g. as the Prince Regent in Conradin Kreutzer's *Das Nachtlager in Granada* in 1837, and as Peter the Great at the Viennese première of Lortzing's *Zar und Zimmermann* on 22 October 1842. In 1837 he sang in Italy with great success. From 1851 to 1870 he was in charge of productions at the Opera. He used the stage name 'Schober'.

He was the cousin of the pianist and composer Franz de Paula Jakob Schoberlechner (1797–1843), and brother-in-law of the soprano Sophie Schoberlechner (1825–92) who sang under the name 'Cittadini'.

(*ÖBL*)

Schönstein, Karl, Baron (b. Ofen [Budapest], 27 June 1797; d. Aussee [Bad Aussee, Styria], 19 July 1876). Civil servant; singer. Son of Baron Franz Xaver Schönstein (*c*.1747–1827), a senior official at the Hungarian ministry of finance. A lawyer by training, he moved to Vienna in 1816, and subsequently held various posts in government service. He became a court secretary in 1831 and Regierungsrat in 1839. He retired from his senior post at the ministry of finance in 1856.

He was an extremely gifted amateur singer who performed to great acclaim at private musical parties, especially those given by the Viennese aristocracy. A fervent admirer of Italian music, it was not until he met Schubert in 1818, through his friend Count Johann Karl Esterházy,* that he began to appreciate German Lieder. Thereafter he devoted himself almost entirely to them, and he became, after Johann Michael Vogl,* the most admired Schubert singer of his time. Schubert enjoyed accompanying him and held him in the highest regard: 'I always very much enjoy hearing Baron Schönstein sing,' he wrote, on 25 September 1828, to Johann Baptist Jenger* (who himself frequently partnered Schönstein, as did Irene von Kiesewetter*). Indeed, Schönstein later claimed that Schubert had repeatedly told him that he composed most of his songs with his [Schönstein's] vocal range in mind. According to Leopold von Sonnleithner,* he possessed a 'noble-sounding tenor-baritone voice'.

Schubert dedicated *Die schöne Müllerin* (D795) to Schönstein in 1824. In addition, the publishers Anton Diabelli & Co.* dedicated the first edition of the vocal quartet 'Gebet' (D815) to him in 1840. Schönstein described (first to Ferdinand Luib* and later to Kreissle*) the circumstances in which the latter composition came to be written, while both he and Schubert were staying at Zseliz in September 1824. They maintained their professional and personal relationship until the end of Schubert's life. (However, Schönstein's statement to Ferdinand Luib in 1857 that Schubert had dined and consumed much wine at his house some ten days before his death 'in high spirits, even boisterously merry' and feeling 'completely well' must be incorrect, in view of Schubert's plaintive remark, in his note to Franz von Schober* on 12 November, that he had not eaten or drunk anything for the past eleven days.)

During the following years, Schönstein continued to give great pleasure with his performances of Schubert's Lieder. Sonnleithner, whose remark about the noble quality of his voice has already been quoted, also praised his 'sound vocal training, grasp of aesthetic and intellectual aspects, and sensitivity and vivacity'. In short, he judged Schönstein to be 'one of the best, if not the best Schubert singer' he had heard. Anselm Hüttenbrenner* likewise admired his 'exceptionally beautiful' renditions of Schubert's songs, which 'frequently moved one to tears', a response also experienced by Liszt* who, in a letter to his friend Lambert Massart in May 1838, wrote of listening to Schönstein's performances of Schubert with great delight and frequently with tears in his eyes. And Josef von Spaun,* at whose house Vogl and Schönstein had on several occasions performed those 'marvellous songs', linked their names in an eloquent tribute: 'Anyone who has heard Vogl sing *Winterreise*, "Fragment aus dem Aeschylus", "Der entsühnte Orest", "Der Zwerg", "Der Wanderer an den Mond", "Die Sterne", "Fülle der Liebe", "Dithyrambe" by Schiller, "An Sylvia" ["Gesang: Was ist Silvia"], "Das Zügenglöcklein", "Die junge Nonne", "Der Mönch" [i.e. "Der Kreuzzug"], "Der Pilgrim", and "Der Alpenjäger" by Schiller, the deeply moving, splendid, and yet so simple song "Allerseelen" ["Am Tage Aller Seelen"], etc., and Baron Schönstein sing the "Müller songs" [*Die schöne Müllerin*], "Die zürnende Diana" ["Der zürnenden Diana"], "Im Grünen" ["Das Lied im Grünen"], "[Der] Winterabend", "Ständchen" by Shakespeare, "An die Musik", etc., has known enough delight to last him all his life and will never hear anything more beautiful.' Spaun stated that Schönstein modelled his interpretations of Schubert's songs on Vogl's.

In 1845 Schönstein married Rosalie von Kleyle (*c*.1817–46), a daughter of Franz Joachim von Kleyle, estate manager of archduke Karl, who had received Schubert in his house at Penzing, near Vienna [14 Beckmanngasse]. In 1849 Schönstein married Maria Amalia von Winther (1826–60).

(*ÖBL, Schubert: Erinnerungen*)

Schopenhauer, Johanna (Henriette), née Trosiener (b. Danzig [Gdansk, Poland], 9 July 1766; d. Jena, 16 April 1838). Writer; mother of the philosopher Arthur Schopenhauer (1788–1860) and of the poetess and novelist Adele Schopenhauer (1797–1848). In 1785 she married the much older merchant Heinrich Floris Schopenhauer, with whom she moved to Hamburg in 1803. After his death in 1805 she lived at Weimar (1806–29) where she associated with Goethe* and his circle, later at Bonn, and finally from 1837 at Jena. She published a number of novels, including *Gabriele* (1819–20), *Die Tante* (1823), *Sidonia* (1827–8), and *Richard Wood* (1837), as well as some travels books and a partial autobiography.

Schubert took the text of his song 'Hippolits Lied' (D890) from *Gabriele*, and although Johanna Schopenhauer had indicated in the preface to the novel that the author of the poem was Friedrich von Gerstenberg,* it was mistakenly attributed to her in the first edition published by Anton Diabelli & Co.* in 1830.

(Sagarra)

Schreiber, Aloys Wilhelm (b. Bühl, near Baden-Baden, 12 October 1761; d. Baden-Baden, 21 October 1841). Poet, narrative writer, and historian. He taught aesthetics at the Gymnasium at Baden-Baden (1784–8) and subsequently earned his living as a private tutor, playwright, and dramatic critic at Mainz until 1797, when he moved to Rastatt; there he worked as a journalist and editor. Later, he held a chair of aesthetics and history at the University of Heidelberg (1805–13) and then became historiographer at the court of Grand Duke Karl Ludwig Friedrich of Baden, at Karlsruhe. He retired in 1826.

Schreiber enjoyed his most productive period as a writer around the turn of the century, when he published, among other works, numerous tales and novellas (*Romantische Erzählungen*, 2 vols., 1795), the novel *Wollmar* (1794), poetry (*Rhapsodien*, 1791; *Gedichte*, 1801), plays, and dramatic criticism, as well as travel books and guides, including *Streifereien durch einige Gegenden Deutschlands* (1795). Later, while at Karlsruhe, he published several works on the history of the grand duchy of Baden.

In 1818 Schubert composed the following four songs to texts by Schreiber: 'An den Mond in einer Herbstnacht' (D614), 'Das Abendrot' (D627), 'Das Marienbild' (D623), and 'Der Blumenbrief' (D622).

Settings: D614, 622–3, 627.
(Biehler, Häntzschel[2], Porhansl[1])

Schubart, Christian (Friedrich Daniel) (b. Obersontheim, Württemberg, 24 March 1739; d. Stuttgart, 10 October 1791). Poet, composer, and pianist; son of the pastor, cantor, and schoolmaster Johann Jacob Schubart (1711–74). He was brought up at Aalen, where his father moved in 1840. He then attended school at Nördlingen and later read theology at the University at Erlangen, but his studies were terminated by his parents in 1760 because of his undisciplined behaviour. His musical gifts—he was already an excellent pianist and a promising composer—led to appointments as organist at Geisslingen (1763) and at the court of Württemberg at Ludwigsburg (1769). However, he was dismissed from the latter post for unsatisfactory conduct by Duke Karl Eugen in 1773. At Augsburg, and later at Ulm, he published a newspaper, *Die deutsche Chronik*, in which he wrote about politics, literature, and music. In 1777 he was lured from the free imperial town of Ulm to Württemberg territory, where he was incarcerated without trial for ten years in the fortress of Hohenasperg, mainly, it is believed, as vindictive punishment for having printed disparaging remarks in his newspaper about the notoriously tyrannical and dissolute Karl Eugen and his mistress, Franziska von Hohenheim. It was while he was in prison that he wrote some of his finest poems, as well as an interesting essay on music, *Ideen zu einer Ästhetik der Tonkunst*. On his release in 1787 he was appointed court and theatre poet at Stuttgart.

His poetic output was considerable and extremely varied, ranging from political poems ('Die Fürstengruft', 'Kaplied') and religious verse in the manner of Klopstock* to poems inspired by his own experiences and to others akin to folk-songs. He furthermore composed music for the piano and at least eighty songs, about fifty of which were settings of his own texts. In this connection, it is rather ironical that 'Die Forelle', which inspired one of Schubert's most celebrated songs, had previously been set by Schubart himself to music which is utterly forgotten today. His *Sämmtliche Gedichte* appeared, in two volumes, in 1785–6; an edition of his collected works was published in eight volumes in 1839–40.

Between *c.*1816 and 1821 Schubert composed four songs to poems written by Schubart: 'An den Tod' (D518), 'An mein Klavier' (D342), 'Die Forelle' (D550), and 'Grablied auf einen Soldaten' (D454). Of 'Die Forelle' he made no fewer than five different versions, the first two between late 1816 and July 1817, the last one in October 1821. Only the fourth version (made in autumn 1820) was published in his lifetime; it was first printed in the *Wiener Zeitschrift für Kunst, Literatur, Theater und Mode* on 9 December 1820.

Settings: D342, 454, 518, 550.
(Hammerstein, Hartkopf, Honolka, Porhansl[8])

Schubert, Ferdinand (Lukas) (b. Vienna, 18 October 1794; d. Vienna, 26 February 1859). Teacher, composer, violinist, and organist; older brother of Franz Schubert. He was initially taught to play the violin by his father,* the piano by his brother Ignaz, and singing by Michael Holzer,* choirmaster at Lichtental parish church. He then studied the violin and organ with Holzer, who also gave him tuition in thoroughbass and composition. At the string quartet sessions arranged by his father he took the first violin part. Eventually, when he was already a qualified teacher, he completed his musical education under Josef Drechsler, later Kapellmeister at St Stephen's Cathedral.

In 1810, while training to become a teacher, he worked as an assistant at his father's school. At the end of that year, he became an assistant teacher at the school attached to the imperial orphanage in the Alsergrund suburb; in 1816 he was made a full teacher there. From 1820 to 1824 he held the combined posts of teacher and choirmaster at a boys' school in the Alt-Lerchenfeld suburb. Finally, he was appointed in 1824 to a teaching position at the St Anna Normalhauptschule [3–3a Annagasse], which comprised a secondary school as well as a teachers' training college, both of which establishments he had himself attended. In 1851 he became its director. He also served as an inspector of schools, and wrote a number of introductory textbooks on arithmetic, geometry, and geography.

At the same time, he came to be regarded as a highly competent musician. He played among the first violins in Otto Hatwig's* orchestra, and developed into a sufficiently good organist to apply in 1822 (as it turned out, unsuccessfully) for the post of second court organist. In 1827 he played the organ at the religious ceremony at Währing parish church, during which Beethoven's* coffin received the final blessing. He was among the fifty elected representatives (Repräsentanten) of the

Gesellschaft der Musikfreunde, and in 1834 was appointed to the committee responsible for organizing the society's concerts. From 1838 he gave organ lessons at the Conservatory.

Throughout his life, his careers as schoolteacher and musician were closely intertwined. He taught piano, violin, and singing, played the organ at school services, and wrote various compositions for the pupils. Altogether, his musical output ran to more than ninety works. These included four Masses, a Requiem (which was sung in Schubert's presence at Hernals parish church on 3 November 1828), and several other sacred compositions, as well as two Singspiels for children, twenty-nine choruses, and a large number of songs for use in schools. However, some of the music which he publicly claimed to have composed (and even published under his own name) had, in fact, been written by his brother Franz. The most celebrated example is the so-called *Deutsches Requiem* (D621), which Franz composed at Zseliz in 1818 at Ferdinand's request. The latter conducted it in September of that year at the orphanage as his own composition, subsequently used it in December 1819 at an examination in musical theory (as a result of which he managed to secure the post at Alt-Lerchenfeld), and eventually arranged to have it published by Anton Diabelli & Co.* under his own name in 1826. Other pseudo-Ferdinand, *recte* Franz, compositions include: *Namensfeier* (D294), performed at the orphanage in honour of its director, Franz Michael Vierthaler, on 29 September 1815 and of which a copy, written out by Ferdinand, bore a dedication to Vierthaler (however, in the account which he wrote of his brother's life in 1839, he cites this cantata as one of the works composed for him by Franz); *Salve Regina* (D386), published by Ferdinand as his Op. 12 in 1833; important parts of the *Hirtenmesse*, Ferdinand's 'Pastoral Mass' published in 1846, which not only uses his brother's Kyrie (D45), but also borrows extensively from his minuets D41 and various other works; and certain pieces in *Der kleine Sänger*, a collection of vocal duets published by Ferdinand in 1853.

The above deceptions, in so far as they occurred in his lifetime, undoubtedly had the approval of his brother, who was eager to further Ferdinand's career. Their extant correspondence provides ample proof of the profound affection which they felt for one another. 'You surely know how dear every moment spent in your company is to me,' Ferdinand wrote to Franz on 4 August 1825. At the beginning of September 1828, on the advice of his doctor, Ernst Rinna von Sarenbach,* Schubert moved to Ferdinand's lodgings [6 Kettenbrückengasse] in the supposedly more salubrious Neu-Wieden suburb, and there he resided during the remaining eleven weeks of his life, except for a three-day excursion which he made in early October, together with Ferdinand and two friends (perhaps Josef Mayssen* and Johann Rieder, the brother of the painter Wilhelm August Rieder*) to Eisenstadt, where they visited Haydn's grave. Ferdinand looked devotedly after him during the final illness. 'My brother [is] conscientiousness itself,' Schubert wrote to Franz von Schober* on 12 November. It was Ferdinand who proposed that he be buried at Währing district cemetery, near Beethoven.

After Schubert's death, Ferdinand, although not legally the sole heir to his property (certain documents bear the signatures of other heirs as well as his own), appears to have been recognized by the others, for all practical purposes, as the proprietor of the very numerous musical autographs left by his brother—for the most part, of course, of as yet unpublished works. It was Ferdinand, at any rate, who applied himself, for the remainder of his life, to finding publishers for them. He also tried to derive some income from performances of the still unpublished compositions. Thus, in 1835, notices appeared in the Vienna *Allgemeiner musikalischer Anzeiger* (5 March), Leipzig *Neue Zeitschrift für Musik* (3 April), and Paris *Gazette musicale* (26 April), offering, in his name, performing rights 'at modest fees' for a number of operas, symphonies, and Masses. That he shared any money received from publishers or musicians with other members of the family seems unlikely, in the light of Robert Schumann's* letter to Breitkopf & Härtel* of 6 January 1839, in which he tried to persuade the firm to acquire some of the Schubert autographs he had found in Ferdinand's possession: 'As far as payments are concerned, you would encounter modest demands ... At the same time, Schubert's brother cannot forgo payment altogether, for he is entirely without means, he is the father of eight children, and Schubert's estate constitutes his sole property.' (On the sale of the 'Great' C major Symphony *see* Breitkopf & Härtel,* Felix Mendelssohn,* and Schumann.*)

In addition to his efforts to arrange for the publication of Schubert's music, Ferdinand was instrumental in keeping his name before the Viennese public by conducting a number of concerts consisting entirely or mainly of his works, some of which were receiving their first public performance. Thus, at his concert at the Landhaus on 30 March 1830, the Overture in B flat major (D470), the *Kantata zu Ehren von Josef Spendou* (D472), and the final chorus from the Singspiel *Fernando* (D220) were all played for the first time in public. Ferdinand furthermore made arrangements of a number of Schubert's compositions for public performance, in some cases augmenting the existing orchestration, in others replacing the instrumental accompaniment by a piano reduction, elsewhere changing the vocal parts. As Liszt* was to do later, he orchestrated the piano accompaniment in several of the songs, e.g. 'Der Taucher' (D77), 'Die junge Nonne' (D828), and 'Erlkönig' (D328). His tinkering with the original music did not always meet with the approval of the critics. After his arrangement of 'Erlkönig' for three voices, chorus, and orchestra had been performed at a Schubert memorial concert on 15 February 1835, H. Adami wrote in the *Allgemeine Theaterzeitung*: 'The trio consisted of the Erlking, the father, and the son, and the chorus took, as it were, the place of an audience joining in the performance. Such an arrangement is completely unacceptable.'

Following Schumann's visit to Vienna, Ferdinand published a biographical sketch of his brother ('Aus Franz Schuberts Leben') in Schumann's *Neue Zeitschrift für Musik* (23 April–3 May 1839). At his death, he still possessed numerous unpublished Schubert manuscripts, some of which were reportedly acquired by the Gesellschaft der Musikfreunde in 1862. The remainder passed into the care of Eduard Schneider, a barrister and the son of Ferdinand's and Franz's sister Maria Theresia. Schneider showed the music to George Grove* and Arthur Sullivan* when they visited Vienna in 1867. He subsequently (1881–3) sold the manuscripts to Nikolaus Dumba,* who later presented some of them to the Gesellschaft der Musikfreunde and bequeathed the rest to the city of Vienna.

Ferdinand Schubert married twice, on 7 January 1816 Anna Schülle (1794–1831), and on 2 August 1831 Therese Spazierer (1803–82). The two marriages produced more than twenty children. His daughter Emma (b. 1846) lived until April 1927.

(Brusatti, Hilmar[1], Van Hoorickx[3,4], Weinmann[10])

Schubert, Franz Anton (b. Dresden, 20 July 1768; d. Dresden, 5 March 1827). Double-bass player and composer. He was a member of the Dresden orchestra from 1786, was appointed director of Italian opera at Dresden in 1808, and became royal composer of church music in 1814. He is remembered in musical history mainly for his caustic comments on our Schubert's 'Erlkönig' (D328), of which a copy had been sent to him by mistake by Breitkopf & Härtel,* to whom it had been submitted either by Schubert himself or by Josef von Spaun.* In his letter of 18 April 1817, he informed the publishers that he was most certainly not the composer of that 'cantata', and that he would retain the copy 'in order to ascertain, if possible, who has so impertinently sent you such trash, and also to discover the wretched fellow who has thus misused my name'. Breitkopf & Härtel asked him to return the manuscript, but did not publish the song. They did, however, in that very same year, publish a setting of Goethe's* poem by Peter Grønland [Grönland]. Schubert's composition was eventually published in Vienna in 1821 (*see* Leopold von Sonnleithner*).

By a curious coincidence, *W. G. Beckers Taschenbuch zum geselligen Vergnügen* for the year 1821 (Leipzig, 1820) offered among its musical supplements Schubert's 'Widerschein' (D639) and Franz Anton Schubert's setting of 'Die Lebensgefährten', a poem by Arthur Nordstern [pseud. of Gottlob Adolf Ernst von Nostiz und Jänkerdorf]. A writer in the *Conversationsblatt* (Vienna) of 28 September 1820 declared that the Dresden Schubert 'cannot bear comparison with his Viennese namesake'.

Franz Anton Schubert was not the only musician in his family. His brother Anton (1766–1853) played the double-bass in the Dresden orchestra for fifty years from 1790, and his son Franz (1808–78) was a composer and violinist who became deputy Konzertmeister of the same orchestra in 1837 and its Konzertmeister in 1861. He was on friendly terms with Franz von Schober,* which accounts for the Dresden Schubert family coming into possession of certain of the Viennese Schubert's musical autographs; these were eventually acquired by the Saxon State Library.

(Laux, Warrack[4])

Schubert, Franz Theodor Florian, (b. Neudorf, near Mährisch-Schönberg [Nová Ves, near Šumperk, Czech Republic], 11 July 1763; d. Vienna, 9 July 1830). Schubert's father. Son of Karl Schubert (1723–87), a peasant living at Neudorf, and his wife Susanne, née Mück (1733–1806). He worked as a teaching assistant in Moravia for three years before moving to Vienna in late 1783. There, in 1784, he became an assistant to his brother Karl (1755–1804) at a school in the Leopoldstadt suburb. (Karl, who was to be Franz Schubert's godfather, had arrived in Vienna several years earlier.) In 1786 Franz Theodor was appointed to a teaching position in the suburb of Himmelpfortgrund, in the parish of Lichtental.

On 17 January 1785, he married Maria Elisabeth Katharina Vietz (*see* the next article; his brother Karl was to marry her sister Magdalene in 1792.) The couple had fourteen children: Ignaz Franz (b. 8 March 1785, d. 30 November 1844), Elisabeth (b. 1 March 1786, d. 12 August 1788), Karl (b. 23 April 1787, d. 6 February 1788), Franziska Magdalena (b. 6 June 1788, d. 13 August 1788), Magdalena (b. 5 July 1789, d. 1 January 1792), Franz (b. 11 August 1790, d. 10 September 1790), Anna Karolina (b. 11 July 1791, d. 29 July 1791), Peter (b. 29 June 1792, d. 14 January 1793), Josef (b. 16 September 1793, d. 18 October 1798), Ferdinand Lucas* (b. 18 October 1794, d. 26 February 1859), Karl (b. 6 November 1795, d. 20 March 1855), Franz Peter (b. 31 January 1797, d. 19 November 1828), Aloysia Magdalena (17 December 1799, d. 18 December 1799), and Maria Theresia (b. 17 September 1801, d. 7 August 1878).

Franz Theodor's school was located in a house named 'Zum roten Krebsen' in Obere Hauptstrasse [54 Nussdorferstrasse] and the family occupied rooms in the same building. It is there that Franz Schubert was born. The house was acquired by the City of Vienna in 1908, and a Schubert Museum opened there on 18 June 1912. In the spring of 1801, Franz Theodor and his wife jointly bought the house 'Zum schwarzen Rössl' [3 Säulengasse], situated diagonally opposite their previous residence, and there they removed with their children and the school in the autumn of that year.

After his wife died on 28 May 1812, Franz Theodor remarried on 25 April 1813. His second wife, Anna Kleinböck [Kleyenböck] (b. 1 June 1783, d. 25 January 1860), bore him five more children: Maria Barbara Anna (b. 23 January 1814, d. 5 August 1835), Josefa Theresia (b. 9 April 1815, d. 27 May 1861), Theodor Cajetan Anton (b. 15 December 1816, d. 30 July 1817), Andreas Theodor (b. 7 November 1823, d. 20 April 1893), and Anton Eduard (b. 3 February 1826, d. 7 September 1892). After several unsuccessful attempts to find employment in other Viennese schools, Franz Theodor finally obtained a transfer to one located in the Rossau suburb [11 Grünetorgassse] for the beginning of 1818. He took up residence with his family at the schoolhouse in Rossau, but did not sell the house in Säulengasse until 1826.

Our future composer was educated at his father's school from 1803 until 1808, when he was admitted to the Stadtkonvikt as a boy chorister. After leaving it in 1813, he trained as a teacher at the St Anna Normalhauptschule [3–3a Annagasse].

Thereafter he was employed as an assistant to his father from 1814 to 1816, and during the school year 1817/18. Even after he had given up teaching in order to devote all his time to music, he still occasionally stayed at the Rossau schoolhouse.

For his father's name-day on 4 October 1813, he wrote the words and music of the trio *Zur Namensfeier meines Vaters* (D80); it is the only one of his vocal compositions in which the guitar is used as the accompanying instrument. The following year, after his Mass in F major (D105) had been performed at Lichtental parish church on 16 October, his proud father reportedly presented him with a five-octave piano built by the well-known piano maker Conrad Graf. The father was himself a fairly competent amateur musician. It was he who gave Franz his first instruction on the violin. In addition, there were string quartet sessions at his house, at which he was the cellist, while Ferdinand played first violin, Ignaz second violin, and Franz viola. They formed the origin of the private concerts which were later held at the apartments of Franz Frischling, Otto Hatwig,* and Anton von Pettenkoffer.*

(Ronge, Schöny²)

Schubert, Maria Elisabeth Katharina, née Vietz (b. Zuckmantel, Austrian Silesia [Cukmantl, Czech Republic], 30 October 1756; d. Vienna, 28 May 1812). Schubert's mother. Daughter of Franz Johann Vietz (1720–72), a metalworker and gunsmith, and his wife Maria Elisabeth Konstanze, née Riedl (1724–?72). Maria Elisabeth Katharina married Franz Theodor Florian Schubert* in Vienna on 17 January 1785. She bore him fourteen children, of whom our composer was the twelfth (and the fourth of five to reach adulthood). She died of typhus.

(Ronge, Schöny²)

Schücking, Clemens August (1759–90). Poet, born at Münster. His long poem 'Hagars Klage in der Wüste Bersaba', inspired by *Genesis*, 21: 14–16, was printed in the *Göttinger Musenalmanach* for 1781. A musical setting by Zumsteeg* was published in Leipzig in 1797.

The young Schubert, who was greatly influenced by Zumsteeg, used the poem in what is his earliest known complete setting of a text. The extant (partial) autograph is dated 30 March 1811. 'Hagars Klage' first appeared in print in the *Gesamtausgabe* of 1884–97.

Setting: D5.

Schulze, Ernst (Konrad Friedrich) (b. Celle, 22 March 1789; d. Celle, 29 June 1817). Poet. From 1806 to 1812 he studied theology, philology, and aesthetics at the University of Göttingen. The death of his fiancée Cäcilie Tychsen in 1812 profoundly affected him and inspired an important part of his poetry. In 1814 he served briefly as a volunteer in the Wars of Liberation against Napoleon. His last years were marked by his unrequited love for Cäcilie's older sister Adelheid.

His major work was the epic *Cäcilie: Ein romantisches Gedicht* (published post-humously in 1818–19) which tells the story of Cäcilie and her minstrel Reinald, set within the context of the Christianization of Denmark. His most popular poem, however, was the far shorter 'Die bezauberte Rose' (1818), which describes the transformation of princess Klothilde into a rose and her eventual restoration to her original form. Other poems appeared in *Gedichte* (1813), and in the posthum-ously printed cycles *Poetisches Tagebuch, vom 29sten Junius 1813 bis 17ten Februar 1817* and *Reise durch das Weserthal 1814*, in which he expressed, in a formalized manner, his unhappy love for Adelheid. A four-volume edition of his collected verse appeared in Leipzig in 1818–20.

Schulze's poems attracted many composers, most of whom are largely forgotten today. Among them was King Georg V of Hanover who made no fewer than thirty-seven settings for single voice and twenty-five for male chorus. In 1825–6, Schubert used poems from the *Poetisches Tagebuch* in the partsong 'Ewige Liebe' (D825A) and the following ten songs: 'An mein Herz' (D860), 'Auf der Bruck' (D853), 'Der liebliche Stern' (D861), 'Im Frühling' (D882), 'Im Jänner 1817' (D876), 'Im Walde' (D834), 'Lebensmut' (D883), 'O Quell, was strömst du rasch und wild' (D874), 'Über Wildemann' (D884), and 'Um Mitternacht' (D862).

In addition, Schubert contemplated writing an opera based on 'Die bezauberte Rose'. According to a letter from Moritz von Schwind* to Leopold Kupelwieser,* he took a libretto written by his doctor J. Bernhardt* with him to Zseliz in 1824; but he evidently did not feel sufficiently inspired by the text, for in March 1825 he invited Eduard von Bauernfeld* to prepare another libretto on the same subject. However, Bauernfeld wrote instead the libretto *Der Graf von Gleichen*, and Schubert later made some sketches for that opera (D918). At the same time, he did not definitely abandon the project of turning Schulze's poem into a stage work until he learned in 1826 that he had been forestalled by Josef Maria Wolfram, whose opera *Maja und Alpino, oder Die bezauberte Rose* had received its première in Prague on 24 May of that year.

Settings: D825A, 834, 853, 860–2, 874, 876, 882–4.
(Müller, Pfeiffer-Belli, Ricklefs)

Schumann, Robert (Alexander) (b. Zwickau, Saxony, 8 June 1810; d. Endenich, near Bonn, 29 July 1856). Composer; one of the earliest Schubertians (O. E. Deutsch* called him 'one of the first and most enthusiastic champions of Schubert's art'). His diary for the year 1828 contains admiring remarks, couched in character-istically Romantic language, about the 'Wanderer' Fantasia (D760) and Schubert's Polonaises for piano duet (D599 and/or D824). He even wrote a letter to Schubert, but did not send it; regrettably, its text is not known. In August and September 1828 he composed eight Polonaises for piano duet in imitation of Schubert's similar compositions. After news had reached him of Schubert's death, his friend Emil Flechsig, with whom he was sharing lodgings, heard him sob bitterly all night.

Schumann's growing enthusiasm for Schubert's music was partly inspired by his increasing admiration for the writings of Jean Paul. From Heidelberg, where he was supposedly learning to become a lawyer but was in reality devoting nearly all his time to music, he wrote on 6 November 1829 to his future father-in-law Friedrich Wieck, with whom he had begun to study the piano the previous year: 'Schubert is still my "one and only Schubert", all the more so since he has everything in common with my "one and only Jean Paul". To play his compositions is for me like reading one of Jean Paul's novels ... Just as others record their fleeting emotions in their diaries, so Schubert confided his passing moods to his music paper. His soul was so steeped in music that he wrote notes where others use words ...' In 1833 Schumann worked on (but did not complete) a set of variations on Schubert's so-called *Trauerwalzer* (D365/2).

His strong interest in Schubert's music was to produce unexpected and memorable results a few years later. He had decided to spend the winter of 1838/9 in Vienna, a city to which he had long been attracted for artistic reasons ('Don't you know that it is one of my oldest and dearest wishes that circumstances may one day allow me to live for a number of years in the city ... in which Beethoven* and Schubert lived?' he had written to his future wife Clara Wieck on 17 March 1838). Now he was hoping to establish himself professionally in Vienna, to publish there the journal *Neue Zeitschrift für Musik* (which he had founded with some friends in Leipzig in 1834 and of which he had been editor almost from the beginning), and perhaps even to make his home there with Clara. He arrived in Vienna on 3 October 1838 and remained until 5 April 1839. Although he was unable to realize any of his hopes, the visit was significant for other reasons.

He had been in contact with Ferdinand Schubert* already prior to this trip, for in its issue of 3 April 1835 the *Neue Zeitschrift für Musik* had printed a statement by Ferdinand inviting theatre managements and musicians to apply for the performing rights 'at modest fees' for a number of as yet unpublished major works, namely several operas, six symphonies, and five Masses, left by his brother and which were now in his possession. (A similar announcement appeared in the Vienna *Allgemeiner musikalischer Anzeiger* and, in French, in the Paris *Gazette musicale*.) Schumann was now able to examine these compositions in Vienna and he was amazed at their high quality. He hastened to inform Breitkopf & Härtel* on 6 January 1839 of the treasures he had discovered, and offered to arrange the symphonies for piano duet, if the firm was prepared to publish them in that form. When Breitkopf & Härtel expressed their willingness to examine some of the scores, Ferdinand sent them the autograph and a set of orchestral parts of the Symphony in C (D589), together with a copy he had himself made of the 'Symphony No. 7', i.e. the 'Great' C major Symphony (D944). The latter work subsequently received its first performance at the Gewandhaus in Leipzig under the direction of Felix Mendelssohn* on 21 March 1839.

Schumann missed that performance since he was still in Vienna, but he was in Leipzig when the symphony was again played there on 12 December 1839. After attending a rehearsal the previous day, he wrote to his friend Ernst Adolf Becker: 'It realized all the ideals of my life. It is the greatest achievement in instrumental music since Beethoven, not excepting even Spohr and Mendelssohn.' And to Clara he wrote on the same day: 'Today I was blissfully happy. At rehearsal they played a symphony by Franz Schubert. If only you had been there. I cannot describe it to you; all the instruments are like so many human voices, it is full of ingenuity, and what instrumentation ... and the length, that heavenly length, like a novel in four volumes, longer than the ninth symphony [of Beethoven]. I was utterly enraptured and only wished that you were my wife and that I could also write such symphonies.' In 1840, in an article devoted to the same symphony in the *Neue Zeitschrift für Musik* (No. 12, pp. 81–3), Schumann again praised its 'heavenly length'; the expression has ever since been associated with that work. He also affirmed that 'he who does not know this symphony knows as yet little of Schubert'. Breitkopf & Härtel printed the orchestral parts of the symphony that same year and the full score in 1849.

Schumann also wrote in the *Neue Zeitschrift für Musik* about other Schubert works, always sympathetically and with admiration. He furthermore published first editions of the following three compositions in supplements to the periodical: 'Chor der Engel' (D440) on 18 June 1839, the Andante from the Piano Sonata in C major (D840) on 10 December 1839, and the Aria with Chorus (No. 21) from *Fierrabras* (D796) in 1840. In addition, he printed in the periodical an extended account by Ferdinand of Schubert's life and works ('Aus Franz Schuberts Leben') in April–May 1839, and also, in that same year, several letters written by Schubert, his poem 'Der Geist der Welt', and his allegorical story 'Mein Traum'. All these texts, which he had received from Ferdinand, were being published for the first time.

Schumann's devotion to Schubert ultimately produced a rather eerie incident which was recorded in the diary of Ruppert Becker, a son of the aforementioned Ernst Adolf Becker and a member of the Düsseldorf orchestra, who visited Schumann on 24 February 1854, three days before he tried to commit suicide by throwing himself into the Rhine: 'During the hour I spent with him, he talked quite sensibly, except when he told me that Franz Schubert had appeared to him and had played him an exquisite melody. He had, he further assured me, written it down and composed variations on it.'

Schumann must have been gratified when Anton Diabelli & Co.* dedicated to him the first edition of Schubert's last three piano sonatas (D958–60) in 1839. (Schubert had intended to dedicate them to Johann Nepomuk Hummel.*)

(Platinga, Schumann[1,2,3])

Schuppanzigh, Ignaz (b. Vienna, 20 November 1776; d. Vienna, 2 March 1830). Violinist and conductor. He learned to play the viola before the violin, but made the latter his principal instrument when he decided to become a professional musician. From 1794 to 1799 he played first violin in a quartet which performed regularly at the residence of Prince Karl Lichnowsky. In addition, he became associated, as conductor and from *c.*1798 also as manager, with the popular concerts given in the Augarten.

In the winter of 1804/5 he began to give public concerts with a new quartet. In 1808 he formed the so-called 'Razumovsky Quartet', for the purpose of providing chamber music for Lichnowsky's brother-in-law, Count [later Prince] Andreas Kirillovich Razumovsky; the other members, chosen by Schuppanzigh, were Josef Linke,* Louis Sina, and Franz Weiss. Some time after the count's palace was destroyed by fire in 1814 the group was dissolved, and during the following years Schuppanzigh performed in Germany, Poland, and St Petersburg. He returned to Vienna in 1823 and almost immediately resumed his career as a chamber-music player, replacing Josef Böhm,* in the latter's absence, in a series of concerts with the quartet which Böhm had formed in 1821 with Karl Holz,* Linke, and Weiss. He also became a member of the court Kapelle, and later conductor of the court Opera orchestra.

Schuppanzigh won great praise for the performances he directed of the quartets of Haydn, Mozart, and Beethoven.* He also played an important role in Schubert's career. He presented, or took part in, the first performances of the following compositions: the Quartet in A minor (D804), on 14 March 1824 (this was also the first public performance of any of Schubert's quartets, and Schubert dedicated the work to Schuppanzigh when it was published in September of that year); the Octet (D803), on 16 April 1827 (he had also played at the private run-through at Count Troyer's* shortly before); the Piano Trio in E flat major (D929), on 26 December 1827 ('It was splendidly executed by Bo[c]klet,* Schuppanzigh, and Linke', Schubert informed Anselm Hüttenbrenner* on 18 January 1828); and the overture to *Fierrabras* (D796) on 6 January 1829.

On the above evidence, there seems no reason to doubt Schuppanzigh's interest in Schubert's chamber music and his support for the composer. Yet, if Franz Paul Lachner* is to be believed ('Erinnerungen an Schubert und Beethoven', *Die Presse* [Vienna], 1 November 1881), he did not always show understanding for Schubert's music or offer encouragement. Thus, after he had taken part (in or around February 1826) in a run-through of the Quartet in D minor ('Death and the Maiden', D810) at Lachner's apartment, he reportedly told Schubert that the work was without any merit and that he should stick to writing songs. In another version of this incident, Ludwig Speidel, basing himself on a conversation he had had with Lachner, stated that the players found the music so difficult that they gave up the struggle well before the end of the first movement, whereupon Schuppanzigh assured Schubert that the movement was 'unplayable' ('Noch ein Schubert-Denkmal', *Die Presse*, 10 October 1867).

(Forbes⁴, Jancik⁴, Moser¹)

Schütz [Schütz-Lacrimas], (**Christian**) **Wilhelm von** (b. Berlin, 13 April 1776; d. Leipzig, 9 August 1847). Dramatist and poet. The son of a senior Prussian official, he studied law before himself entering government service. In 1807 he was appointed Landrat at Ziebingen, near Frankfurt an der Oder, but, as a member of the aristocratic faction opposed to the state reforms instituted by King Friedrich Wilhelm III, he was suspended from his post in 1811. His wife Barnime (née Countess Finckenstein), whom he had married in 1809, died in 1812. Apart from various travels, he appears to have lived at Ziebingen for the remainder of his life, except for a period of several years from 1820 on, during which he pursued various literary activities at Dresden. He converted to the Catholic faith in *c.*1830.

In his twenties, Schütz was among the early Romantic writers who associated with Ludwig Tieck* and August Wilhelm von Schlegel.* His verse tragedy *Lacrimas* (1803) made him well known; his later plays included *Karl der Kühne, Der Graf und die Gräfin von Gleichen, Graf von Schwarzenberg*, and *Niobe*. He also wrote some poems.

In 1825 Schubert set two passages from *Lacrimas* in 'Lied der Delphine' and 'Lied des Florio' (D857/1–2). The two songs were first published by Anton Pennauer* in 1829 as *Zwey Scenen aus dem Schauspiele 'Lacrimas' von A. W. Schlegel.* The erroneous attribution to Schlegel resulted from the fact that the title-page of the first edition of the play (Berlin, 1803) did not mention the author's name, but bore the indication 'Herausgegeben von August Wilhelm Schlegel'.

Setting: D857.

(Grawe, Sempdner)

Schwarzenberg, Mathilde Theresia (Walpurgis Franciska), Princess (b. Krumau [Český Krumlov, Czech Republic], 1 April 1804; d. Vienna, 3 November 1886). Daughter of Prince Josef Johann Nepomuk Schwarzenberg (1769–1833) and his wife Pauline Karolina, née Princess Arenberg (1774–1810). The father was a noted music lover who maintained his own orchestra and regularly arranged performances of oratorios and chamber music at his palace in Mehlmarkt [Neuer Markt] in Vienna. It was there that Haydn's *The Creation* was first performed, as was the Septet Op. 20 by Beethoven,* who dedicated his Piano Quintet Op. 16 to the prince. Mathilde's brother Felix (1800–52) was prime minister of Austria from 1848 until his death. Another brother, Friedrich (1809–85), became archbishop of Salzburg in 1836 and archbishop of Prague in 1850; he was created a cardinal in 1842.

Mathilde suffered throughout her childhood from a deformation of the spine which left her unable to walk and even, at times, to rise unaided from a sitting position. For several years she was in the care of the celebrated French surgeon Antoine Dubois in Paris, and from November 1819 until June 1821 she was a patient at the well-known orthopaedic clinic run by Johann Georg Heine at Würzburg. None of the treatments improved her condition. However, on 20 June 1821, while still at Würzburg, she was 'miraculously' cured by Prince Alexander Hohenlohe-Waldenburg-Schillingsfürst, a controversial priest whose aggressive proselytizing methods and claims of being a wonder healer brought him into conflict with other churchmen and theologians. (He was the son of Prince Karl Albrecht II of Hohenlohe-Waldenburg-Schillingsfürst; his sister Maria Theresia Josefa married Count Moritz Fries.*) According to his biographer L. Sebastian, an undated document preserved in the Schwarzenberg archives confirms that Mathilde was completely and permanently cured of her paralysis.

In 1827 Schubert dedicated to her his Op. 62, which, under the title 'Gesänge aus *Wilhelm Meister*' (D877), presented settings for single voice of the three Goethe* poems 'Heiss mich nicht reden', 'Nur wer die Sehnsucht kennt', and 'So lasst mich scheinen', as well as a setting of the second text for duet. Schubert may have been brought into contact with the princess by the tenor Josef Barth* who had been employed in her father's household since 1807. She was among the subscribers to *Schwanengesang* (D957) in 1829.

Not much is known about Mathilde's later activities, but C. von Wurzbach states that she was a 'true and selfless friend and companion' to her brother Felix until the end of his life.

(Berger¹, *ÖBL*, Sebastian, Taddey, Wurzbach¹)

Schwind, Moritz von (b. Vienna, 21 January 1804; d. Munich, 8 February 1871). Painter. Son of court secretary Johann Franz von Schwind (1752–1818) and his second wife Franziska, née von Holzmeister. After attending the Schottengymnasium (1818–21), he began to study philosophy at the University of Vienna before deciding to become an artist. He received instruction from Ludwig Ferdinand Schnorr von Karolsfeld* and Johann Peter Krafft at the Vienna Academy of FineArts, and later in Munich from Peter Cornelius, but he was in large measure self-taught and developed a highly individualistic style. He is best known for his wall-paintings and book illustrations, and for his representation of legends and fairy-tales, notably in the three great series *Cinderella* (1852–4), *The Seven Ravens* (1857–8), and *Melusine* (1868–9).

Through Josef von Spaun* he made Schubert's acquaintance in 1821. Intelligent, amusing, good-looking and flirtatious, he soon became a popular member of the Schubert circle. He was nicknamed 'Cherubin', after the young page in Mozart's *Le nozze di Figaro*. He himself was particularly impressed by Franz von Schober* and corresponded regularly with him after Schober moved to Breslau in 1823. 'I realize more and more that my whole life is a conversation with you,' he wrote on 9 April 1824, and Eduard von Bauernfeld* noted in his diary on 18 July 1825, shortly before Schober's return to Vienna: 'Moritz reveres him like a god.' Despite periodic strains, the friendship endured for well over thirty years. In the end, however, there was a complete break between them.

Schwind was also on intimate terms with Bauernfeld who had been a fellow pupil at the Gymnasium, and whom he introduced to Schubert in 1825. But none of the relationships enjoyed by Schwind in the 1820s appears to have been closer than his friendship with Schubert. 'I go to see him nearly every evening,' he informed

Schober on 6 March 1824. And on 14 February 1825, after Schubert had moved into a house [9 Technikerstrasse] close to the one in which he was living with his mother near St Charles's Church, Schwind wrote to Schober: 'We meet every day, and as far as I can I share his entire life with him.' In addition to his warm personal feelings for Schubert, he greatly admired his music.

Schubert, for his part, not only felt great affection for Schwind whom he jokingly called his 'beloved', he also respected his musical judgement and, according to Bauernfeld, 'every new song or composition for the piano was first communicated to his young friend'. Music certainly played an important role in Schwind's life ('I cannot live without music,' he wrote to Schober on 20 July 1833). He was himself an accomplished amateur performer. 'Schubert and Schwind sang the most beautiful Schubert songs,' Franz von Hartmann* noted in his diary on 8 December 1826, after an evening spent at Spaun's. And his brother Fritz von Hartmann recorded on 4 March 1827 that, at Schober's, Schwind had sung some of Schubert's earlier songs 'which enchanted us'. Schwind also played the violin and was an excellent pianist. 'Schwind and my brother Ludwig played some splendid four-handed pieces by Schubert [in Linz, at the Ottenwalts'*],' Fritz wrote in his diary on 18 October 1827. Forty years later, after a reunion with Schwind, Franz von Hartmann noted: 'He was just as he used to be, and played Schubert waltzes enchantingly on the piano.'

Schwind remained greatly attached to Schubert until the latter's death, and thereafter cherished his memory. When news of Schubert's death reached him in Munich where he had been pursuing his art studies since the previous month, he wrote to Schober (25 November 1828): 'You know how much I loved him, so you will understand that I can hardly bear the thought that I have lost him. We still have some dear and kindly disposed friends, but no longer anyone who lived through those beautiful, unforgettable times with us and has not forgotten them...I wept for him, as I would for one of my brothers...The more I now appreciate what he was, the more I understand what he suffered. You are still here, and you still love me with the same love which in those unforgettable times bound us to our beloved Schubert. To you I offer all the love which has not been buried with him ...' Schwind lived in Munich until 1840, and subsequently at Karlsruhe (1840–4) and Frankfurt am Main (1844–7). In 1847 he returned to Munich, which was to remain the main centre of his activities until his death.

Music constituted one of the principal sources of inspiration for Schwind's paintings. His early works included vignettes for the title-pages of various piano arrangements of famous operatic arias (1823), as well as the series *Der Hochzeitszug des Figaro* (1825), thirty drawings prompted by the third-act finale in *Le nozze di Figaro*. Among the most successful artistic achievements of his maturity were *Symphonie* (1852), a large oil-painting in four 'movements' based on Beethoven's* Choral Fantasy, Op. 80; the frescoes depicting scenes from Mozart's *Die Zauberflöte* in the loggia of the new Vienna opera-house (1866–7); and, in the foyer of the same building, the ceiling decorations and the lunettes illustrating well-known operas

(1867). (In the execution of the frescoes he was assisted by his pupils Karl Mossdorf and Otto Donner von Richter; the paintings in the foyer were done by another pupil, Franz Xaver Barth, from his cartoons.)

Schwind's association with Schubert is reflected in several of his works, from the earliest period to the very last one. His drawing of Schubert's room in the Wipplingerstrasse (1821) is often invoked to disprove the allegation that the composer chronically lacked access to a piano in his youth. Another drawing by Schwind, showing Schubert at the piano, was auctioned at Sotheby's in London in December 1992 (it had been in the possession of the pianist Wilhelm Kempff). While the sale catalogue ascribed the sketch to the 1860s, it may, in fact, have been made in Schubert's lifetime (*see* R. Steblin in *Schubert durch die Brille*, No. 10, 1993).

Nor did Schwind forget Schubert after his death. As early as 1835, he conceived the idea of a 'Schubert Room', destined for performances of his works, the walls of which would be decorated with illustrations of his songs; but although he made some preliminary sketches while in Rome that year, nothing came of the project— nor of a later one to instal a Schubert Room in a new house [51 Kärntnerstrasse] being built for the banker Eduard von Todesco in 1863.

Schubert is, however, present in a number of other works by Schwind. Thus, in 'The Rehearsal', the first 'movement' of *Symphonie*, Schubert and Johann Michael Vogl* are portrayed among the audience. Both reappear in 1862 in the so-called *Lachner-Rolle*, a series of drawings done on a single roll of paper, which humorously depicts several episodes from the life of Franz Paul Lachner* who was celebrating the twenty-fifth anniversary of his appointment as conductor of the Munich court Opera. And among the lunettes in the foyer of the Vienna opera-house is one devoted to Schubert. It presents, in the centre, a scene from the Singspiel *Die Verschworenen* [*Der häusliche Krieg*] (D787), and, to the right and left of it, illustrations of the songs 'Der Fischer' (D225), 'Der Wanderer' (D489), 'Der zürnenden Diana' (D707), and 'Erlkönig' (D328).

But the grandest memorial devised by Schwind for his former friend is without doubt the celebrated sepia drawing *A Schubert Evening at Josef von Spaun's* (1868) which shows Vogl, accompanied by Schubert at the piano, singing to a group of more than forty rapt listeners. 'Among other projects, I have undertaken the representation of a Schubertiad, in which our whole group is portrayed,' he informed Ferdinand von Mayerhofer.* 'It is not quite as beautiful as it was, but rather in the nature of an old gentleman chattering about events at which he was present in his youth and to which he still remains attached in his heart.' It is generally assumed that the drawing is based on the first big Schubertiad held at Spaun's on 15 December 1826 (at which, according to Franz von Hartmann's diary, 'there was a huge gathering'). Countess Karoline von Esterházy,* who was not present on that occasion (nor, as far as is known, at any other Schubertiad), looks out on the assembled guests from a portrait on the wall, which reproduces a painting done of her by Josef Teltscher* (for Schubert's relations with the countess, *see* the article devoted to her). The group apparently includes also a few later admirers of the composer, such as Eleonore Strotzberg, née Stohl, a well-known Schubert singer who was not born until 1832. Schwind commenced a sketch in oils of the drawing in 1871, but did not complete it.

In March 1828, in Vienna, Schwind became engaged to Anna Hönig,* but the engagement was broken off in October 1829, largely on account of religious differences, for she was considerably more pious than he was; during a quarrel he had once tartly advised her to 'fall in love with the Pope.' In September 1842, at Baden-Baden, he married Louise Sachs, the daughter of an army officer; they had a son and four daughters.

(*ALBK*, Brown[4], Göltl, Porhansl[7], Schwind[1,2], Steblin[5], Weigmann)

Scott, Sir Walter (b. Edinburgh, 15 August 1771; d. Abbotsford, 21 September 1832). Poet and novelist. The earliest evidence of Schubert's interest in Scott dates from the year 1823. Writing from Steyr on 14 August, he informed Franz von Schober* that he was 'reading Walter Scott'. According to Karoline Pichler,* Johann Michael Vogl,* who was Schubert's companion on that journey, counted Scott among his favourite writers, so he may well have had some influence on Schubert's choice of reading matter.

Altogether, Schubert was to set ten verse passages from Scott's novels, eight for single voice and two as partsongs. The composition of the two earliest songs, 'Gesang der Norna' (D831) from *The Pirate*, and 'Lied der Anne Lyle' (D830) from *A Legend of Montrose*, is ascribed to the beginning of 1825. In the spring or early summer of 1825 he composed the five songs 'Ellens Gesänge I–III' (D837–9), 'Lied des gefangenen Jägers' (D843), and 'Normans Gesang' (D846), and the two partsongs 'Bootgesang' (D835) and 'Coronach' (D836), all to texts from 'The Lady of the Lake.' Finally, perhaps in March 1826, he composed the 'Romanze des Richard Löwenherz' (D907) from *Ivanhoe*. By far the most famous of his Scott songs is 'Ellens Gesang III', more generally known by its opening words, 'Ave Maria'. (*See also* MacDonald,* and Scott's translators Mayer,* K. L. M. Müller,* Spiker,* and Storck.*)

Settings: D830–1, 835–9, 843, 846, 907.
(Deutsch[4], Fiske)

Sechter, Simon (b. Friedberg [Frymburk, Czech Republic], 11 October 1788; d. Vienna, 10 September 1867). Theorist, composer, pianist, and organist. He moved to Vienna in 1804 and, after completing his musical education there, was employed as a teacher of piano and singing at the School for the Blind (1810–25). At the same time, he established a solid reputation as a theorist, and after the death of Johann Georg Albrechtsberger he was regarded as the leading musical theorist in Vienna. In 1824 he was appointed assistant court organist, and the following year succeeded Jan Václav Voříšek* as principal organist. He was much sought after as a teacher and in

1851 was engaged as professor of thoroughbass and counterpoint at the Vienna Conservatory, a post which he occupied until his death. Among his pupils were Anton Bruckner, Franz Grillparzer,* Gustav Nottebohm,* Sigismond Thalberg, Johann Vesque von Püttlingen,* and Henry Vieuxtemps.

A startlingly prolific composer, Sechter is believed to have written some 8,000 works; he reportedly composed at least one fugue each day. However, only a small part of his music appeared in print. His opera *Ali Hitsch-Hatsch* was produced in Vienna in 1844. Of his theoretical writings, the three-volume *Die Grundsätze der musikalischen Komposition* (Leipzig, 1853–4) attracted the greatest attention.

According to Anton Schindler,* Schubert considered taking instruction in counterpoint from Sechter in 1824, but was dissuaded by Karl Pinterics,* who warned about the possibly adverse effect which the imposition of strict rules at so late a stage might have on his compositional style. This statement, like so many others made by Schindler, has been treated with caution. What is certain is that late in 1828 Schubert, who during the last year of his life evinced an interest in problems of musical theory, did arrange to take some lessons in counterpoint and fugue with Sechter, possibly at the suggestion of Gottfried von Preyer, who himself studied with Sechter from 1828 to 1834. Schubert went for his first, and only, lesson, on 4 November 1828, together with Josef Lanz.*

Leopold von Sonnleithner,* in referring to the tuition given to Schubert by Sechter, described the latter as Schubert's 'friend'. Sechter himself no doubt defined the nature of their contacts more accurately, when he wrote to Ferdinand Luib* in 1857: 'Regarding your question about my relations with Schubert, I can merely report that we felt respect for one another, but did not meet frequently.' After Schubert's death, Sechter published a fugue for the organ or piano in his memory.

(Brown[9])

Seidl, Johann Gabriel (b. Vienna, 21 June 1804; d. Vienna, 18 July 1875). Poet; son of the lawyer Johann Gabriel Seidl (d. 1823). After studying philosophy and law at Vienna University, he worked from 1829 until 1840 as a schoolmaster at Cilli in Styria [Celje, Slovenia]. In 1840 he returned to Vienna as assistant custodian of the collection of coins and antiquities. In addition, he held the post of keeper of the imperial treasure (1856–71).

The author of numerous scientific studies, especially in the areas of numismatics and archaeology, he was admitted in 1851 to the Academy of Sciences, of which he had been a corresponding member since 1848. He furthermore won recognition as an accomplished poet and, to a lesser extent, as a dramatist. His *Dichtungen* (three parts, 1826–8) first made him known to the general reading public. The poems in *Bifolien* (1836) are considered his best, but he also had considerable success with his dialect poetry (*Flinserln*, 1828, etc.). 'He is rightly very popular and highly regarded as a poet,' C. Cerri wrote in the Graz periodical *Iris* in 1850. 'Especially his lyrical poems are deeply felt, warm-hearted, gemütlich, and tremendously musical.' A modern critic, S. Lechner, has described his poetry as 'the perfect incarnation of the Biedermeier style'. C. von Wurzbach cites more than thirty nineteenth-century composers who set his poems to music. Seidl also edited the literary almanach *Aurora* from 1828 to 1858.

He was in contact with Schubert by June 1824 at the very latest, for in a letter dated 1 July he urged him to get on with composing the music for the dramatic fairy-tale *Der kurze Mantel,* since the producer Friedrich Demmer had promised to open the next season at the Theater an der Wien with Seidl's work. However, it was not Schubert, but a trio of other composers—Josef von Blumenthal, Philipp Jakob Riotte, and Ignaz von Seyfried—who eventually provided the music for the choruses, songs, and dances which formed an integral part of that spectacle (produced on 6 November 1824).

Between 1826 and 1828, Schubert set a number of Seidl's poems. In 1827 he published the songs 'Das Zügenglöcklein' (D871), 'Der Wanderer an den Mond' (D870), and 'Im Freien (D880)'; the partsong 'Grab und Mond' (D893) also appeared in print that year. The summer of 1828 saw the publication of the Refrainlieder 'Bei dir allein', 'Die Männer sind méchant', 'Die Unterscheidung', and 'Irdisches Glück' (D866/1–4), which he dedicated to Seidl.

The other Seidl settings appeared posthumously. Publication of Op. 105, comprising 'Am Fenster' (D878), 'Sehnsucht' (D879), 'Widerspruch' (D865), and 'Wiegenlied' (D867) was announced by Josef Czerny* on 21 November 1828, the day of Schubert's funeral. His last Seidl song, 'Die Taubenpost' (D965A), composed in October 1828, was included in *Schwanengesang* (D957), which was published in the spring of 1829. (The song was first performed by Johann Michael Vogl* at the memorial concert on 30 January 1829.) The partsongs 'Nachthelle' (D892) and 'Nachtgesang im Walde' (D913) were not published until 1839 and 1846 respectively. It is not known which poems Schubert returned to Seidl on 4 August 1828, because, as he explained, he 'could not discover in them any poetic qualities whatsoever or anything suitable for setting to music'.

Schubert's death prompted Seidl to write a poem, 'Meinem Freunde Franz Schubert! Am Vortage seines Begräbnisses. (Den 20. November 1828.)', which was printed in the *Wiener Zeitschrift für Kunst, Literatur, Theater und Mode* on 6 December. In the portrait which Josef Teltscher* painted of Seidl the following year one can see, displayed on the piano, the music of some of the songs Schubert had set.

Seidl was married in 1829 to Therese Schlesinger (d. 1854). They had two children: a daughter, Wilhelmine (b. 1833); and a son, Karl (1830–61), who married Karoline Schubert, one of the daughters of Ferdinand Schubert.*

Settings: D865–7, 870–1, 878–80, 892–3, 913, 965A (975/14).
(Hilmar-Voit, Lebensaft, Wurzbach[1,2])

Senn, Johann Chrysostomus (b. Pfunds, Tyrol, 1 April 1795; d. Innsbruck, 30 September 1857). Poet. He was educated at the Stadkonvikt in Vienna (1808–13). He was strongly influenced in his political views by his father, Franz Michael Senn (1762–1813), a judge who actively supported the Tyrolean movement for independence from Bavaria in 1809. Josef Kenner* later described him as 'a splendid and warm-hearted youth ... candid with his friends, reserved with others, forthright, vehement, hating all constraint.'

He must have known Schubert at the Konvikt, and when he subsequently studied at the university and then earned his living as a private tutor he remained in contact with him. Their relations were quite intimate in 1818, for he was one of the four persons whom Schubert addressed as 'best and dearest friends' in a letter from Zseliz on 3 August of that year, adding: 'How could I ever forget you, you who are everything to me! Spaun,* Schober,* Mayrhofer,* Senn—are you well?' He and Senn used to drink together at Achatius Lenkay's wine shop [6 Singerstrasse].

It was through his close acquaintance with Senn that Schubert got into trouble with the authorities in March 1820. The police, having become aware of Senn's presence at what they considered suspicious gatherings at a Viennese inn, raided his rooms and confiscated his private papers. In an official account of what happened on that occasion, the high commissioner of police, Leopold Ferstl [later Ferstl von Förstenau], condemned Senn's 'defiant and offensive behaviour' and then continued: 'His friends who were present, the school assistant Schubert from Rossau and the law student St[r]einsberg,* as well as the two students who arrived later, the privately educated Zechenter from Cilli [Celje, Slovenia] and the son of the merchant Bruchmann,* a fourth-year law student, are reported to have adopted a similar attitude and to have verbally abused and insulted the official conducting the inquiry. The High Commissioner of Police is officially reporting this matter, so that the outrageous and criminal behaviour of these persons may be appropriately punished.' In the event, Schubert appears to have been let off with a caution, but Senn was arrested and kept in custody for some fourteen months before being deported to Tyrol. From there he kept in touch with some of his old friends, mainly through Franz von Bruchmann who regularly corresponded with him and even visited him at Innsbruck in September 1822, and also, together with Senn's former pupil Baron Doblhoff-Dier,* at Trient [Trento] in the autumn of 1823. (In 1827–8 Bruchmann was to try, unsuccessfully, to draw Senn back to the Christian faith, and in that connection composed and sent to him a detailed account of his own spiritual odyssey.) Moritz von Schwind,* who met Senn at Innsbruck in 1830, later included him in his group portrait *A Schubert Evening at Josef von Spaun's.** But Senn never saw Schubert again. He did, however, write a sonnet about him.

Unable to find gainful employment as a civilian, Senn enlisted in the army in 1823; he was commissioned in 1828, took part in the Italian campaign of 1831, and resigned the following year. After working for some time in the law office of his cousin Alois Fischer in Salzburg, he returned to Innsbruck. There he eked out a modest living with clerical work, grew increasingly lonely and embittered in his later years, and died in poverty.

A volume of his poems, *Gedichte*, appeared in 1838, but the censor prevented the publication of much of his political verse. The patriotic poem 'Der rote Tiroler Adler' became extremely popular. Schubert set two of his poems in 'Schwanen-gesang' (D744) and 'Selige Welt' (D743), perhaps in the autumn of 1822.

Settings: D743–4.

(Dürhammer, Enzinger, Fischer[9], Leitgeb, Wurzbach[1])

Shakespeare, William (bapt. Stratford-on-Avon, 26 April 1564; d. Stratford-on-Avon, 23 April [new style: 3 May] 1616). In July 1826 Schubert set three songs from his plays in 'Gesang: Was ist Silvia' (D891) from *The Two Gentlemen of Verona*, 'Ständchen: Horch, horch! die Lerch im Ätherblau' (D889) from *Cymbeline*, and 'Trinklied: Bacchus, feister Fürst des Weins' (D888) from *Antony and Cleopatra*. The first text ('Who is Sylvia? What is she?') had been translated by Eduard von Bauernfeld,* the second ('Hark, hark, the lark at heaven gate sings') by August Wilhelm von Schlegel,* and the third ('Come, thou monarch of the vine') by Bauernfeld and Ferdinand Mayerhofer von Grünbühel.* The translations appeared in the German-language edition of Shakespeare published in Vienna in 1824–6 by Josef Trentsensky, which presented partly new translations (by Bauernfeld and others) and partly earlier German versions (by Schlegel and others).

Settings: D888–9, 891.

(Porhansl[7])

Silbert, Johann Petrus (b. Colmar, 29 March 1772/7; d. Vienna, 27 December 1844). Poet and translator. Following studies at the University of Mainz he appears to have led an unsettled existence, during which he temporarily resided in Vienna. Later he taught at schools at Klausenburg and Kronstadt in Transylvania [now Cluj and Brasov, Romania], before returning to Vienna where he became an instructor in French language and literature at the Polytechnic Institute. He retired in 1835 in order to concentrate on the preparation of devotional works, of which he produced an astonishing number. According to C. von Wurzbach, 'seventy-four works comprising well over 100 volumes, all of an equally edifying and ascetic content, flowed from this single pen'. They include translations from Saint Augustine, Saint Bernard, Fénélon, Saint François de Sales, Fray Luis de Granada, and Thomas à Kempis.

Many of his works were published in Vienna, among them a volume of poetry, *Die heilige Lyra*, in 1819. From it Schubert took the text for the two songs 'Abendbilder' (D650) and 'Himmelsfunken' (D651), composed that same year.

Settings: D650–1.

(Wurzbach[1])

Slavík [Slawik], **Josef** (b. Jinetz [Jince, near Přibram, Czech Republic], 26 March 1806; d. Pest [Budapest], 30 May 1833). Violinist and composer. After studying the violin at the Prague Conservatory (1816–23) with Friedrich Wilhelm Pixis, he played in the Estates Theatre orchestra in Prague for the next three years, and also at concerts in Prague and other Czech cities. In 1826 he moved to Vienna where he performed at concerts, played (without pay) in the court Kapelle, and gave lessons. His first concert, on 9 April 1826, was a huge success, prompting critics to compare him with the famous Polish violinist Karol Józef Lipiński and with Paganini, who was his foremost model. His admiration for Paganini was heightened when the latter gave a series of concerts in Vienna in 1828. Slavík left for Paris in October 1828, but returned to Vienna after a few months to take up a paid appointment with the court Kapelle. He died of typhus while staying at Pest at the beginning of a concert tour.

He was admired above all for his dazzling virtuosity, but his playing must have possessed other qualities than mere technical mastery, for Chopin, who heard him and became friendly with him in Vienna in 1830, described him in letters to his family as 'a great and truly inspired violinist' and 'a second Paganini', even predicting that he would surpass the original one, and adding: 'He also knows how to enchant the listener, how to move men to tears.'

While in Vienna, Slavík became acquainted with Schubert. His performance with Karl Maria von Bocklet* of the Rondeau in B minor (D895) at a party given by Domenico Artaria (perhaps early in 1827) and attended by Schubert was probably the first of that work. At his concert at the Landhaus on 20 January 1828 he gave the first public performance, together with the same pianist, of the Fantasia in C major (D934) which Schubert is believed to have composed for him.

Slavík's compositions, not all of which have survived, were mostly bravura pieces for his instrument. At the above-mentioned concert in 1828 he played his 'new' *Variations* for violin and the first movement of a 'new' violin concerto.

(Chopin, Němcová, Výborný², Wurzbach¹)

Smetana, Rudolf von (b. Vienna, 7 September 1802; d. Gars am Inn, Bavaria, 2 September 1871). Lawyer; Redemptorist. In 1823 he joined the reading parties held in Ludwig Mohn's* rooms. He also attended various social functions of Schubert's circle, such as the New Year's Eve party at Mohn's that year and the ball given by Franz von Schober's* mother on 24 March 1824. A week later, Baron Doblhoff-Dier* informed Schober that Smetana came every day to Leopold Wasserburger's café [14 Seilerstätte/22 Weihburggasse], where he himself and Schubert were faithful clients. Smetana was thus in regular contact with Schubert during this period, but there is no evidence that their relations ever became intimate.

Smetana qualified as a lawyer in 1827. On 19 November 1828, the day of Schubert's death, he married Franz von Bruchmann's* sister Justina (1805–29), who had previously been engaged to Schober. After her death in childbirth he joined the Redemptorist order, of which he eventually became vicar-general; he relinquished his duties in 1857.

(Dilgskron)

Sonnleithner, Ignaz von (b. Vienna, 30 July 1770; d. Vienna, 27 November 1831). Son of Christoph Sonnleithner (1734–86), a lawyer and composer (of church music, symphonies, quartets), and his wife Maria Anna, née Doppler; brother of Josef Sonnleithner,* and father of Leopold von Sonnleithner.* Having qualified in 1794, he practised successfully as a lawyer and notary. He furthermore lectured on law at different educational institutions (from 1814 at Vienna University), and wrote several textbooks. He was also active in humanitarian causes. He was ennobled in 1828.

Sonnleithner was a great music lover, as was his wife Anna (née Putz). He was personally acquainted with all the leading Viennese composers of his time and knew their works well. Though not formally trained, he was a popular amateur singer, thanks to his pleasing bass voice. He reportedly acquitted himself very creditably in a broad range of parts, both serious and comic. He was a soloist in various oratorios (including Handel's *Messiah* and *Samson* and Abbé Maximilian Stadler's* *Die Befreiung von Jerusalem*), and sang leading roles in operas by Mozart (Figaro, Leporello, Don Alfonso), Paisiello, and other composers. He was also frequently invited to join in performances given by church choirs.

His ten children (three others died in infancy) thus grew up in a household where they heard a great amount of music. The oldest, Leopold, showed himself to be particularly musical and became the moving spirit behind the private concerts with which his father's name is associated, and which brought together professional as well as fine amateur performers. The first of these concerts took place on 26 May 1815. The family had recently moved from a first-floor apartment at the Gundelhof [4 Bauernmarkt/5 Brandstätte] to a much larger one on the third, where there was a sizeable drawing-room which, together with the adjacent rooms, could accommodate more than 120 persons. It was there that the concerts were held, always on Fridays, in the first year weekly, thereafter once a fortnight during the six winter months only, and eventually at a less frequent rate. The final concert of the 1823–4 season, held on 20 February 1824, turned out to have been the last, for Anna Sonnleithner died that autumn, after which no further concerts were arranged.

The music presented during those nine years included much chamber music, works for the piano (sonatas and concertos), virtuoso pieces for different instruments, and a wide range of vocal music: arias, duets, and ensembles from various operas, songs for solo voice, male-voice quartets, and even some larger works such as Haydn's *Die Schöpfung* (15 November 1816) and *Die sieben letzten Worte unseres Erlösers am Kreuze* (4 April 1817), Schubert's cantata *Prometheus* (D451, 8 January 1819, with Ignaz von Sonnleithner singing the title part), and Leopold von Sonnleithner's cantata *Hoffnung und Glaube* (14 January 1820).

As a result of the growing admiration which Leopold, who was responsible for choosing the programmes and the artists, felt for Schubert's Lieder and partsongs, these musical soirées played a highly significant role in the composer's career. Thus, the quartet 'Das Dörfchen' (D598) received its first performance at the Sonnleithners' on 19 November 1819, and 'Erlkönig' (D328) was also first sung there, on 1 December 1820 (by August von Gymnich,* accompanied by Anna Fröhlich*). The great impression made by 'Erlkönig' on that occasion led directly to its publication, as well as to that of certain other Schubert songs. (Regarding these editions, and also the genesis of the whole concert series, *see* Leopold von Sonnleithner.*) Other vocal compositions by Schubert performed at these soirées included 'Der Wanderer' (D489) on 19 January 1821, 'Gretchen am Spinnrade' (D118) on 2 March 1821, 'Der Jüngling auf dem Hügel' (D702) and the octet 'Gesang der Geister über den Wassern' (D714) on 30 March 1821, and Psalm 23 (D706) on 9 June 1822.

Ignaz von Sonnleithner's sister Anna Maria (1767–1819) married Wenzel Grillparzer and was the mother of Franz Grillparzer.* His brother Christoph Heinrich (1773–1841) became a distinguished civil servant and was ennobled in 1831. Another brother, Franz Xaver (1759–1832), who likewise reached a senior position in government service, was the author of numerous books on legal subjects.

(Jancik⁵, Sonnleithner, Wurzbach¹)

Sonnleithner, Josef (b. Vienna, 3 March 1766; d. Vienna, 26 December 1835). Lawyer, librettist, and translator; brother of Ignaz von Sonnleithner,* and uncle of Leopold von Sonnleithner.* He was employed at court from 1787, at first in Emperor Josef II's private office, later in the chancellery. At the same time, he gave early proof of his interest in the theatre by publishing the *Wiener Theater-Almanach* (1794–6). In 1812 he brought out a three-volume edition of the plays of Philipp Hafner, the dramatist who had played such a pivotal role in the development of Viennese theatre in the mid-eighteenth century. From March 1802, Sonnleithner was also a partner in the Kunst- und Industrie-Comptoir which published first editions of many of Beethoven's* works.

His interest in music and the stage were soon accorded public recognition. For a short period (February–August 1804) he was artistic director of the Theater an der Wien under Baron Braun; more importantly, he served as secretary of the court theatres from 1804 until 1814. During that time, he prepared German versions of a number of French plays by such authors as Charles Guillaume Étienne and Pigault-Lebrun, as well as opera librettos, again mostly adapted from French models. The libretto for which he is best remembered is that used by Beethoven in the original (1805) version of *Fidelio*, based on Jean-Nicolas Bouilly's *Léonore, ou L' Amour conjugal*, it was later revised by Stefan von Breuning (1806) and Georg Friedrich Treitschke (1814).

It was through Sonnleithner's efforts that the Gesellschaft adeliger Frauen zur Beförderung des Guten und Nützlichen (Society of Ladies of the Nobility for the

Promotion of Good and Useful Works) was founded in 1811. The following year, the society arranged a charity concert in aid of the blind in the rooms of the piano manufacturer Johann Andreas Streicher (12 April 1812), and subsequently undertook, with Sonnleithner's assistance, the far more ambitious project of presenting two performances of Handel's oratorio *Alexander's Feast* (which in Vienna was then known as *Timotheus*), with almost 600 participants, at the imperial winter riding school (29 November and 3 December 1812); the receipts were to provide assistance for Austrian victims of the Napoleonic wars. The artistic and financial success of the latter venture encouraged Sonnleithner to propose the establishment of a permanent musical society in Vienna. The result was the foundation, in 1814, of the Gesellschaft der Musikfreunde, for which Sonnleithner acted as (unpaid) secretary until his death twenty-one years later. He eventually bequeathed to the society a large corpus of material which he had assembled on the history of music, as well as his collections of instruments and portraits of musicians. Among the latter was one of Schubert, which he had commissioned in *c*.1827. The painting used to be attributed to Josef Mähler, but may be the work of Franz Eybl.

Nothing is known about Sonnleithner's personal relations with Schubert, but he is certain to have been well acquainted with him, if only through meeting him at his brother's musical soirées and as a result of contacts made on behalf of the Gesellschaft. He showed his admiration for Schubert's music by placing the song 'Erlkönig' (D328), the quartet 'Das Dörfchen' (D598), and the octet 'Gesang der Geister über den Wassern' (D714) on the programme of a concert which, in his capacity as secretary of the above-mentioned Society of Ladies of the Nobility, he organized at the Kärntnertor-Theater on 7 March 1821. Later that same year the literary annual *Aglaja*, which he had founded in 1815, printed the poem 'Als sie, zuhörend, am Klavier sass' by his nephew Franz Grillparzer,* in which the latter expresses his love for Katharina Fröhlich;* she is described as listening in utter delight to a pianist, whom tradition has identified as Schubert. When, in October 1826, the Gesellschaft decided to award a sum of 100 gulden to Schubert, Sonnleithner offered to advance the money, if the society's current funds should prove insufficient for such a payment.

(Jancik⁵, Pohl¹, Slezak, Wurzbach¹)

Sonnleithner, Leopold von (b. Vienna, 15 November 1797; d. Vienna, 4 March 1873); oldest son of Ignaz von Sonnleithner,* and nephew of Josef Sonnleithner.* He studied law, like his father, qualifying in 1819, and became a prominent member of his profession; from 1848 he also served for some years on the city council.

He is remembered above all for his great contribution to the musical life of Vienna. He was himself an accomplished musician, having studied composition and theory with Josef Preindl, who also gave him instruction in piano, organ, and string instruments. In fact, Preindl encouraged him to devote all his time to music, but, as Sonnleithner's friend Wilhelm Böcking later explained, 'the young man already possessed a mature enough judgement not to overestimate his own talent, and preferred to become a competent jurist rather than a mediocre musician.' However, music was to remain the favourite occupation of his leisure hours. Starting in 1813, he held regular Sunday string quartet sessions with schoolfriends at his family's apartment at the Gundelhof [4 Bauernmarkt/5 Brandstätte], thereby gaining a thorough knowledge, not merely of chamber but also of much orchestral and operatic music, which, in those days, was frequently available in arrangements for small ensembles. In addition, the group, which was on occasion augmented by other instruments, accompanied at private choral practices likewise organized by Leopold von Sonnleithner. On those occasions he would arrange the score, copy out the parts, and direct the rehearsals. Gradually, these performances reached a high enough standard to attract an audience of family friends. They thus formed the origin of the celebrated musical soirées given by Ignaz von Sonnleithner between 1815 and 1824, but which, as far as all arrangements were concerned, including the choice of music and performers, remained throughout his son's responsibility.

As a result, Leopold von Sonnleithner's growing interest in Schubert's compositions was to be of great consequence for the latter's career. He met Schubert when, as a law student, he took part in the performance of the cantata *Prometheus* (D451) at Professor Heinrich Josef Watteroth's* house in July 1816. Even before he became more closely acquainted with the composer, he came to know and admire his songs, thanks to fellow students who had been given copies of them by Schubert's friends at the Stadtkonvikt. Sonnleithner told Ferdinand Luib* in 1857 that he had been particularly impressed by the Goethe* songs and, foremost among them, by 'Erlkönig' (D328), and that he had thereupon decided to present Schubert's vocal compositions at his father's concerts. The first of Schubert's works to be performed at Ignaz von Sonnleithner's soirées appears to have been the above-mentioned cantata *Prometheus*, which was sung on 8 January 1819, with the host himself taking the title part. The quartet 'Das Dörfchen' (D598) was performed on 19 November of the same year, and 'Erlkönig' on 1 December 1820. The singer on the latter occasion was August von Gymnich* and the accompanist Anna Fröhlich.* Leopold von Sonnleithner had first presented Schubert's music and then the composer himself to Anna and her sisters, and it was through them that Gymnich had come to know his songs. (For details, *see* Fröhlich.*)

The effect produced by this first performance of 'Erlkönig' was such that Sonnleithner and some of his friends took steps to have at least a number of Schubert's songs published. When efforts to interest Viennese publishers in 'Erlkönig' met with no success, Sonnleithner, Josef Hüttenbrenner,* and two other music lovers (Johann Schönauer and Johann Nepomuk Schönpichler) decided to cover the costs of publication themselves. 'Erlkönig' was put on sale in April 1821, with Cappi & Diabelli* acting as agents on commission; the edition is believed to have had a first printing of 225 copies. The response was all that could have been hoped for. The benefactors soon disposed of sufficient funds to enable them to underwrite further publications. Altogether, Schubert's Opp. 1–7 and 12–14 were issued in this manner between April 1821 and December 1822, comprising a total of twenty-eight songs. Schubert's acceptance, in late 1822 or early 1823, of offers privately made to him by Anton Diabelli* to acquire all future rights to these compositions in return for cash payments was deplored by Sonnleithner and his friends, who believed that he would eventually have reaped far greater financial benefits if he had retained ownership of the songs. None the less, Sonnleithner wrote to Luib in 1857, 'this, essentially ungrateful, action by Schubert did not in any way cause us to turn away from him; we regretted his weakness, but continued to promote the performance and dissemination of his works.'

Sonnleithner was closely associated with the Gesellschaft der Musikfreunde, the musical society established through the efforts of his uncle Josef. He even conducted three of its concerts (18 November 1821, 3 March 1822, and 15 December 1822). The first concert included the first performance of Schubert's Overture in E minor (D648), the second the male-voice quartet 'Geist der Liebe' (D747). (Two of Sonnleithner's own compositions had been played in earlier concerts of the society: an overture on 29 March 1818, and an anthem for vocal quartet, 'Lob Gottes im Frühling', on 30 April 1820.) Sonnleithner also conducted the concert given at the Theresian Academy on 11 February 1822 in celebration of the birthday, on the following day, of Emperor Francis I of Austria. The concert opened with the overture to Mozart's opera *La clemenza di Tito* and closed with Schubert's setting (*Am Geburtstage des Kaisers*, D748) of a text specially written for the occasion by Johann Ludwig Ferdinand Deinhardstein;* the programme also included 'Erlkönig'.

Leopold wrote extensively on musical matters, and repeatedly about Schubert, always sympathically and with discernment. Particularly worthy of attention are the following texts: (1) a brief biography ('Biographische Skizze') published anonymously in the monthly report of the Gesellschaft der Musikfreunde for February 1829; (2) three statements (dated 1 November 1857, 4 December 1857, and 5 March 1858) prepared in response to Ferdinand Luib's request for information, from which the above account of his relations with Schubert is in large measure derived and which provide, in addition, a wealth of interesting observations on Schubert's appearance, his compositions, and the proper manner of singing his Lieder, with recollections of Schubert's own interpretations; (3) an article entitled 'Über den Vortrag des Liedes, mit besonderer Beziehung auf Franz Schubert', which appeared in *Rezensionen und Mitteilungen über Theater und Musik* (Vienna) on 7 November 1860 and treated at greater length the question of how Schubert's Lieder should be sung.

Furthermore, Sonnleithner published, in *Rezensionen* ... (1861–3), a series of fascinating articles on the musical salons of the early nineteenth century, under the overall title 'Musikalische Skizzen aus Alt-Wien' (reprinted in *Österreichische*

Musikzeitschrift in 1961). Of particular interest to Schubertians is Sonnleithner's account of how the modest musical sessions held at the house of Schubert's father* eventually led to the private concerts at Otto Hatwig's* and Anton von Petten-koffer's.* The very informative section on Ignaz von Sonnleithner's concerts, which contains some brief remarks on their importance to Schubert's career, was written by Wilhelm Böcking, evidently with the help of material supplied by Leopold.

Finally, mention should be made of the comprehensive manuscript notes made by Sonnleithner on the history of opera and ballet in Vienna, which are now preserved in the archives of the Gesellschaft der Musikfreunde.

(Gibbs, Perger/Hirschfeld, Sonnleithner, Wurzbach[1])

Spaun, Josef von [later Baron] (b. Linz, 11 November 1788; d. Linz, 25 November 1865). Civil servant; oldest child of Franz Xaver von Spaun (1756–1804), a lawyer, and his wife Josefa, née von Steyrer (1757–1835). The mother was fond of music and particularly enjoyed singing Zumsteeg's* songs, and later those of Schubert.

Spaun attended the Lyzeum at Linz, where one of his teachers was Julius Schneller.* During his law studies in Vienna, where he moved in 1805, he boarded at the Stadtkonvikt. There he was made responsible for running the school orchestra, in which he led the second violins. He helped to build up its repertoire by acquiring additional scores; on one occasion, he was forced to return to Linz on foot, because he had spent the money for his fare on the purchase of two Beethoven* symphonies. It was through his participation in the nightly music sessions that he became acquainted, in November 1808, with Schubert, who had recently been admitted to the Konvikt. His interest piqued by the boy's evident talent, Spaun befriended Schubert, who discussed music with him and, on one occasion, shyly played a minuet of his own composition. Generally withdrawn and solitary, the boy came to look upon Spaun as his best friend at the Konvikt.

In early September 1809, his studies completed, Spaun left Vienna to take up his first post in government service at Linz. He did not return to Vienna until March 1811, upon his transfer to the ministry of finance; two years later he was attached to the office of the state lottery. He remained in Vienna until the autumn of 1821, and during those years he was to prove himself a most devoted friend to Schubert, whose early efforts at composition he actively encouraged. His support and his social connections were of the utmost significance for Schubert's career (*see* especially Matthäus von Collin*). While Schubert was still at the Konvikt, Spaun supplied him with music paper, which he could not otherwise have afforded, and, no less importantly, took him to the opera, where Schubert came to know a number of works, beginning with Josef Weigl's* *Das Waisenhaus* and *Die Schwei-zerfamilie*. The opera which made the greatest impression on him was Gluck's *Iphigenie in Tauris* [*Iphigénie en Tauride*]. In addition to admiring the music (Gluck was to remain one of his favourite composers), he was profoundly moved by the performances of the principal singers, Anna Milder* and Johann Michael Vogl.*

Among the various persons whom he met through Spaun were Matthäus von Collin (Spaun's cousin), Karl von Enderes,* Josef von Gahy,* Josef Kenner,* Theodor Körner,* Leopold Kupelwieser,* Johann Baptist Mayrhofer* (Spaun's oldest friend), Franz von Schober,* Moritz von Schwind,* and Josef Wilhelm Witteczek.* Several of them became close friends. In 1816 Spaun shared Witteczek's rooms at the house of Heinrich Josef Watteroth,* one of his former law professors at the university; Schubert also stayed at the house for a brief time that year. It was for a ceremony in Watteroth's honour that he composed the cantata *Prometheus* (D451).

In April 1816 Spaun tried unsuccessfully to arouse Goethe's* interest in Schubert's songs (*see* Goethe*). The following spring either Spaun or, this time, Schubert himself offered 'Erlkönig' (D328) to Breitkopf & Härtel,* with no better results. Schubert set a poem by Spaun himself in 1817 in the song 'Der Jüngling und der Tod' (D545); it was not published in either the composer's or the poet's lifetime.

In September 1821 Spaun was transferred to the customs office at Linz. In January 1822 Schubert set, in the form of a parody of an Italian operatic aria, complete with recitative, a humorous epistle by Matthäus von Collin reproaching Spaun for not writing ('Herrn Josef Spaun, Assessor in Linz', D749). During the following years Schubert's reputation grew considerably in Linz, primarily thanks to Albert Stadler* and to Spaun and his family and friends. It was at the suggestion of Stadler and Spaun's brother Anton, who were both serving on the committee of the Linz Gesellschaft der Musikfreunde, that Schubert was made an honorary member of that society in 1823. In July of that year, when Schubert visited Linz with Vogl, he was introduced by Josef von Spaun and Stadler to Friedrich Ludwig von Hartmann* and his family, who all became fervent Schubertians. Thus, although, as far as is known, Schubert and Spaun did not correspond during that period, they kept in touch through friends and met occasionally (Spaun spent several weeks in Vienna in the winter of 1824/5). In December 1822 Schubert dedicated to Spaun his Op. 13, which consisted of the songs 'Der Alpenjäger' (D524), 'Der Schäfer und der Reiter' (D517), and 'Lob der Tränen' (D711).

In May 1825 Spaun was posted to Lemberg [Lvov]. During much of the year he spent there, still attached to the customs service, he was a frequent visitor to the house of Count Revertera and his wife, the former Anna von Hartmann, who both arrived there in late August 1825. He was also on friendly terms with Mozart's son Franz Xaver Wolfgang, as well as with Ludwig Kajetan and Josefine Baroni von Cavalcabò, two prominent music lovers. (Later, after his return to Vienna, Spaun sent a number of Schubert songs to Countess Revertera, and also some marches for piano duet—probably D859 and 885—to the Baronis.)

In Vienna, where he arrived back on 1 July 1826, Spaun was once again employed in the office of the state lottery, of which he was to become director in 1841. His long connection with that office is not without irony, since he strongly disapproved of lotteries and never bought a ticket himself. However, he carried out his duties conscientiously and to the evident satisfaction of his superiors. As for his friendship with Schubert, it flourished during the two years following his return; they met constantly, in private houses (Spaun himself hosted several splendid Schubertiads) or at the taverns 'Zum [Grünen] Anker' [10 Grünangergasse] and 'Zum Schloss Eisenstadt' [6 Naglergasse] and other establishments. In April 1827 Schubert dedicated the Piano Sonata in G major (D894) to Spaun.

The last great Schubertiad at Spaun's in the composer's lifetime took place on 28 January 1828 (for particulars, *see* Bocklet*). It was given in honour of Franziska Roner von Ehrenwerth (1795–1890), to whom Spaun had become engaged earlier that month. The 19-year-old Franz von Hartmann described her as being 'thirty years old, but very nice, cultivated, and pretty' (she was, in fact, 32, seven years younger than her husband). They were married on 14 April 1828, and had five children: Heinrich (b. and d. 1829); Josef (1830–49), who, as an army lieutenant, was fatally wounded at the battle of Novara (Piedmont) in March 1849; Constanze (1831–1919); Hermann (1833–1919), who became an admiral; and Marie (1837–1920). Schubert is believed to have composed the four 'Canzonen' (D688) for Franziska Roner von Ehrenwerth in 1820.

Spaun last saw Schubert in mid-November 1828, when he visited him at his brother Ferdinand's* lodgings; he did not realize that his friend was then so close to death. On 23 December, the day on which the memorial service was held, the Spauns gave a soirée devoted to Schubert's music. Spaun also prepared a lengthy obituary, which, after it had at his request been edited by his brother-in-law Anton Ottenwalt,* was published under the title 'Über Franz Schubert' in the *Öster-reichisches Bürgerblatt für Verstand, Herz und gute Laune* (Linz) in three instalments on 27 March, 30 March, and 3 April 1829. The full text of Spaun's original draft was published by G. Schünemann in 1936; it was also extensively reproduced in *Schubert: Erinnerungen*. The text, as edited by Ottenwalt, appears, translated into English, in *Schubert: Biography*.

Spaun left recollections of Schubert and his circle in three further documents, none of which was printed in his lifetime. In 1858, prompted by Ferdinand Luib's* enquiries (to which, however, he does not appear to have directly responded), he wrote down another account of Schubert's life, 'Aufzeichnungen über meinen Verkehr mit Franz Schubert', which contains additional information, especially about their personal contacts. Also of interest are the notes on his family and friends, including Schubert, which are contained in the family chronicle which Spaun completed in March 1864. Finally, and of considerable value to Schubertians, are the critical comments which Spaun wrote down after reading Kreissle's* comprehensive two-volume biography of the composer. In these he corrects certain factual errors, as well as certain aspects of the physical and moral portrait drawn by Kreissle, whom he reproaches, in particular, for having produced a book which 'contains too little light and too much shade about Schubert the man'. Of interest, too, are his very favourable remarks about Schober, which contrast strikingly with those made by certain other contemporaries, and the long and detailed discussion of Vogl's outstanding merits as a Schubert singer. In *Schubert: Erinnerungen* the first and third of the above texts are reproduced integrally, and the relevant passages are quoted from the family chronicle.

Spaun was made a baron in 1859. Two years later he retired from government service, in which he had spent fifty-two years of his life. He died on 25 November 1865 while staying with his daughter Constanze at Linz; three days later he was buried at Traunkirchen, where he had owned an estate. (Regarding the Pinterics*-Witteczek Schubert collection, which Spaun inherited in 1859 and bequeathed to the Gesellschaft der Musikfreunde in Vienna, *see* Witteczek.*)

Spaun possessed a highly attractive personality and was held in affection by all who came into contact with him. No one benefited from his generosity and enjoyed his company more than Schubert, who wrote to him from Linz on 21 July 1825, when Spaun was already at Lemberg: 'Linz without you is like a body without its soul, or a horseman without his head, or a soup without salt.' After Spaun's death, Moritz von Schwind wrote to Spaun's niece Henriette: 'If any one of [Schubert's] friends can be called the best and noblest, it has to be our old friend Spaun.' Ludwig von Köchel likewise paid a deeply felt tribute to Spaun's exceptional character in an obituary in the *Wiener Zeitung* (9 March 1866): 'One can say of him with full justification: he was a true friend, and therefore he had friends himself.'

Spaun's brothers Anton, Franz, and Max had all met Schubert by 1816. Anton (1790–1849), a lawyer, took a profound interest in literature and history. He was the author of *Heinrich von Ofterdingen und das Nibelungenlied* (1840), and published a collection of Austrian folk-songs (1845). He was also the founder of the Ober-österreichisches Landesmuseum [Provincial Museum of Upper Austria] at Linz. In 1818 he married Henriette von Vogelsang. In October 1825, Schubert and Vogl performed some of Schubert's latest songs at their apartment in Linz.

Franz (1792–1829) married Louise Wanderer, the daughter of a surgeon resident at Nussdorf, near Vienna, in 1824. At the time of his death, he was district commissioner for Steyr. The youngest, Max (1797–1844), became a boarder at the Stadtkonvikt in Vienna in 1813. While there, he played the cello in the student orchestra. In the later 1820s, when Josef was again living in Vienna, Max stayed in the capital on at least two occasions (December 1826 and April 1828), and during those visits he was present at several Schubertiads and other gatherings of Schubert's circle. He is frequently mentioned in Franz von Hartmann's diary, usually under the nickname 'Spax'. Eventually he became secretary of the court treasury in Vienna. He married Marie Zach, who came from Laibach [Ljubljana], in 1833. Concerning Josef's sister Marie (1795–1847), *see* Ottenwalt* and Schober.*

Setting: D545.
(Litschauer³, Schünemann, Wurzbach¹)

Spendou, Josef (b. Möschnach [Mošnje, Slovenia], 1757; d. Kirnberg, 16 January 1840). Ecclesiastic and educator. Orphaned at an early age, he was educated in

Vienna from 1769. Later he studied law, but soon switched to theology. In 1782 he was appointed catechist at the teachers' training college, in 1785 deputy director of the Vienna general seminary; from 1788 until 1816 he served as chief inspector of elementary schools. He was greatly respected for his frequently novel pedagogical ideas. In 1816 he became dean of the chapter of St Stephen's Cathedral.

When Schubert applied for the position of music master at a teachers' training college at Laibach [Ljubljana] in April 1816, Spendou provided a (now lost) statement affirming Schubert's competence as a teacher. The application was, however, unsuccessful. In September of that year, Schubert composed a cantata, to a text by Johann Baptist Hoheisel, in Spendou's honour (*Kantate zu Ehren von Josef Spendou*, D472). The cantata, which comprised four numbers for soloists and different groups of voices and probably also an overture (D470), is believed to have been first performed on 22 January 1817, at a ceremony celebrating the twentieth anniversary of the establishment of the institute for the widows of Viennese schoolteachers, which Spendou had founded and of which he was president. The first public performance, directed by Ferdinand Schubert,* was given at the Landhaus on 21 March 1830. In the latter year, the cantata was published by Anton Diabelli & Co.* in an arrangement made by Ferdinand, in which the original instruments were replaced by the piano.

Spendou's brother Anton (1739–1813) was a canon at St Stephen's Cathedral.

(Wurzbach[1])

Spiker, Samuel Heinrich (b. Berlin, 24 December 1786; d. Berlin, 24 May 1858). Translator, journalist, editor, and librarian (at the Royal Prussian Library). His interest in British affairs—he travelled through England and Scotland in 1816, and translated Shakespeare* and Walter Scott*—earned him the nickname 'Lord Spiker'. The sobriquet probably also owed something to his flamboyant life-style. He edited the *Journal für Land- und Seereisen* from 1819 to 1827, and in the latter year acquired the leading Berlin newspaper *Berlinische Nachrichten von Staats- und gelehrten Sachen*, which he ran successfully until his death.

Schubert took the text for his 'Gesang der Norna' from Spiker's translation (Berlin, 1822) of Scott's novel *The Pirate*. The song, composed early in 1825, had not yet appeared in print when Spiker arrived in Vienna in the autumn of 1826 to receive the presentation copy of Beethoven's* Ninth Symphony which was dedicated to King Friedrich Wilhelm III of Prussia. Schubert's song was published by Anton Diabelli & Co.* in March 1828.

Setting: D831.

(Pröhle)

Spina, C. A. (publishing firm). Music publishing business directed by Carl Spina (b. Vienna, 23 January 1827; d. Vienna, 5 July 1906) from late 1851 until 1872. He had become a partner in the firm Anton Diabelli & Co.* in December 1850, and, following the retirement of Anton Diabelli* in January 1851 and of his own father Anton Spina (1790–1857) later that same year, he assumed sole charge of the business, which he renamed 'C. A. Spina'. In 1872 the firm was acquired by Friedrich Schreiber, who himself merged with the Hamburg publishing house August Cranz in 1876.

Spina published first editions of a considerable number of works by Schubert, including sixteen songs, among them 'An die Nachtigall' (D196), 'Das Abendrot' (D627), 'Das Geheimnis' (D793), 'Das Sehnen' (D231), 'Der Traum' (D213), 'Die Blumensprache' (D519), 'Die Sternennächte' (D670), and 'Die Vögel' (D691); some partsongs, among them 'Gesang der Geister über den Wassern' (D714); the Piano Sonata in A minor (D537), *Thirteen Variations on a Theme by Anselm Hüttenbrenner** (D576), and piano arrangements of the oratorio *Lazarus* (D689) and of the overtures to several of Schubert's stage works; the String Quartet in B flat major (D112), the String Quintet (D956), and the Octet (D803, but omitting the fourth and fifth movements); and the 'Unfinished' Symphony (D759).

Spina took over the 'Schubert Salon' which had been established by Anton Diabelli & Co. [at 2 Seilerstätte], close to the 'Zur ungarischen Krone' restaurant [14 Himmelpfortgasse] where Schubert and his friends had frequently met from *c.*1821 on, and not far from the Café Wasserburg [14 Seilerstätte/22 Weihburggasse] which had also been popular with the group. The opening ceremony on 28 February 1851 had begun with a prologue written by Bauernfeld.* The twenty-fifth anniversary of Schubert's death was commemorated at the salon on 25 November 1853. The salon closed in 1860, when the house was demolished.

First editions: D112, 155, 177, 195–6, 213–14, 231, 283, 331, 337, 404, 406, 519, 537, 576, 591, 627, 644, 670, 689, 691, 714, 732, 759, 787, 790, 793, 796–7, 803, 923, 956.
(Slezak, Weinmann/Warrack)

Stadler, Albert (b. Steyr, Upper Austria, 4 April 1794; d. Vienna, 5 December 1888). Composer and pianist; occasional poet. He attended Kremsmünster School from 1806 until 1812, and in the autumn of the latter year moved to Vienna to study law at the university. He was a boarder at the Stadtkonvikt, where, he informed Ferdinand Luib* in 1858, his great love of music soon drew him to Schubert. They became good friends, and since Schubert regularly visited the school even after he had ceased to be a pupil there, Stadler was familiar with most of the music which Schubert wrote between 1813 and 1817 (in this connection, *see also* Holzapfel*). More importantly for future musicologists, he made copies of all the compositions to which he had access. These copies later proved of great importance in the preparation of the collected edition of Schubert's works. In 1817 Stadler started a long and successful career as a civil servant in his native Steyr, from where he moved to Linz in 1821 and thence to Salzburg in 1845. According to O. E. Deutsch* (*Schubert: Erinnerungen*), he later worked in the Lower Austrian administration, from which he did not retire until 1876. His wife (see below) had died in 1863.

During his stay in Vienna he provided Schubert with the libretto for the Singspiel *Fernando* (D220) and with the text for the song 'Lieb Minna' (D222), both composed by Schubert in 1815. He may also be the author of the poem set in 'Der Strom' (D565), the autograph of which bears a dedication to him (but O. E. Deutsch suggests that the text may have been written by Schubert himself). After leaving Vienna, Stadler did not maintain his intimate contact with Schubert, who was a notoriously bad correspondent, but they met again in Steyr and Linz.

During his visit to Steyr with Johann Michael Vogl* in the summer of 1819, Schubert stayed with Stadler's uncle Albert Schellmann;* Stadler was then living in the same house, as was his future wife, Antonie Weilnböck. While Schubert was there, Stadler wrote a poem in celebration of Vogl's birthday on 10 August, which was set as a trio by Schubert (*Kantate zum Geburtstag des Sängers Johann Michael Vogl*, D666) and duly sung on the birthday by Schubert, Josefine von Koller,* and a certain Bernhard Benedict, with Stadler accompanying. That same year, Stadler adapted for string quartet and sextet the arrangement which Schubert had made for piano duet (D592) of the Overture in D major 'in the Italian Style' (D590). In 1820, in Vienna, Schubert set in 'Namenstagslied' (D695) another poem by Stadler, written for the name day of their mutual friend Josef von Koller. Also in 1820, Schubert sent an inscribed autograph of his 'Morgenlied' (D685) to Stadler and Josefine von Koller.

After he had settled at Linz, Stadler played an active role in the local Gesellschaft der Musikfreunde, which was established in late 1821 and as whose secretary he served for some eight years (1823–31). Moved by his profound admiration for Schubert's works, he did his best, both in and outside the Gesellschaft, to make Schubert's name better known in Linz. In 1823, he was at least partly responsible for the society awarding honorary membership to Schubert. Stadler was also in close contact with other Schubertians at Linz, in particular the Hartmann,* Ottenwalt,* Spaun,* and Weissenwolff* families, and often took part in music-making at their homes. He seems to have been especially friendly with the Hartmanns, whom he had already previously met on a visit to Salzburg in 1819. He often played duets with Anna von Hartmann, and later gave piano lessons to her sister Therese; his name frequently appears in Franz von Hartmann's chronicle of his family. On 28 July 1823, he and Josef von Spaun introduced Schubert to the Hartmanns (*see* the article on the Hartmann family).

Stadler had further opportunities to renew his friendship with Schubert in 1825, as the latter stayed at Linz more than once in the course of that year. Around 1 October, he and Stadler spent at least one night as guests at Castle Steyregg, the Weissenwolffs' country residence, on which occasion they shared a room. Schubert left soon afterwards for Vienna and they did not meet again, but Stadler continued to cherish his friend's music. On 17 October 1826, Franz von Hartmann recorded in his diary that Stadler and Josef von Gahy* had played 'glorious Schubert marches' and Schubert's overture to *Alfonso und Estrella* (D773) at the

Hartmanns', and three days later they performed duets, mainly by Schubert, at the Ottenwalts'.

Only a few of Stadler's own compositions appeared in print; among them were settings of poems by Heine,* Theodor Körner,* and Karl Gottfried von Leitner.*

Settings: D220, 222, ?565, 666, 695.

(Hilmar[6], Litschauer[3], Wurzbach[1])

Stadler, Maximilian [Abbé] [baptismal names: Johann Karl Dominik] (b. Melk, Lower Austria, 4 August 1748; d. Vienna, 8 November 1833). Composer, music historian, and keyboard performer. He was educated at Lilienfeld Monastery and in Vienna, became a novice at Melk Monastery in 1766, and celebrated his first Mass there in 1772. After teaching at Melk (1775–82), he held ecclesiastic appointments in Lower and Upper Austria until 1796, when he went to live in Vienna in a private capacity. There he devoted much of his time to music, for, in addition to being a composer, he was an accomplished performer on the violin, piano, and organ. From 1803 until 1815 he was in charge of parishes at Alt-Lerchenfeld, a suburb of Vienna, and Böhmisch Krut [Grosskrut] in Lower Austria. In 1815 he retired on a pension and moved to Vienna, where he applied himself to gathering material for a history of Austrian music; the manuscript, long thought to have been lost, was discovered in Vienna in 1969 and published by K. Wagner (Kassel, 1974). As a composer, Stadler wrote much church music, as well as instrumental works, songs, and music for plays. As a choirboy in the court Kapelle, Schubert probably sang in two performances of some of Stadler's choruses for Heinrich von Collin's* play *Polyxena* on 15 December 1811 (at the university) and 24 December 1811 (at the Burgtheater).

Schubert is said to have expressed great admiration for Stadler's music. While no record exists of any personal contacts between them, it is possible that Stadler, notwithstanding the great difference in their ages, maintained a friendly relationship with Schubert, as R. N. Freeman has stated. They are, at any rate, linked by musical association. Schubert, while staying with Johann Michael Vogl* at Steyr in August 1823, made an arrangement (D.Anh.II,4) of Stadler's setting of Psalm 8, adding various instruments to the original piano (or organ) accompaniment and making certain alterations in the vocal part, which 'Vogl performed in his then still powerful baritone to the edification and admiration of all' at Steyr parish church (letter from Albert Stadler* to Ferdinand Luib* in 1858). For his part, Stadler composed a fugue on Schubert's name in his memory.

(Brown[5], Freeman, Hellmann[2])

Staudigl, Josef (b. Wöllersdorf, Lower Austria, 14 April 1807; d. Döbling, near Vienna, 28 March 1861). Bass. He began to study theology at Zwettl Monastery in 1823, and in 1825 he became a novice at Melk, but he left two years later intending to study medicine in Vienna. Short of money, he joined the chorus at the Kärntnertor-Theater instead. He soon assumed small roles, but it was not until he replaced an indisposed singer in the role of Pietro in Auber's *Masaniello* [*La Muette de Portici*] in 1836 that he really made his mark. He subsequently had an outstanding career as an operatic and oratorio singer; from 1845 to 1848 he appeared at the Theater an der Wien.

He was equally successful during his frequent engagements abroad; in particular, he paid several triumphant visits to England during the 1840s. Following his appearance as Caspar in *Der Freischütz* at Covent Garden on 2 May 1842, he was complimented in the *Morning Post* on having displayed 'a combination of voice and feeling that most of his predecessors might envy and none of his contemporaries could surpass or perhaps even equal'. Among other roles which he sang to great acclaim during that season as a member of a visiting German opera company were Figaro, Leporello, Sarastro, Pizarro, and Marcel (in *Les Huguenots*); he was, *The Times* music critic declared at the end of the two-month season, 'unapproachable as a bass singer, with a voice sonorous and of amazing scope'. On 26 August 1846, at Birmingham, he created the part of the Prophet in Felix Mendelssohn's* oratorio *Elijah*.

He was also very popular as a Schubert singer and especially celebrated for his renditions of 'Erlkönig' (D328) and 'Der Wanderer' (D489), both of which he sang countless times in public. The Viennese critic K. Gross wrote in the *Allgemeine Wiener Musikzeitung* after a performance of 'Der Wanderer' in September 1841: 'The manner in which Staudigl sings this "most beautiful song" by our national bard Schubert is well known, and not only to us, for his rendition of it is already famous throughout Europe and has never so far been heard anywhere without his being obliged to repeat it, which was again the case today.' A review in the journal *Der Wanderer* of yet another performance of the same song the following month was more pithy but no less enthusiastic: ' "Der Wanderer" by Schubert and Staudigl! Need I say more?'

It is all the more interesting, then, that two persons who had been closely associated with Schubert were not greatly impressed by Staudigl. Josef von Spaun,* while praising the beauty of his voice, considered that his interpretations of Schubert Lieder 'did not stand comparison' with those of Johann Michael Vogl,* who, in his opinion, showed a far more profound understanding of the text; and Leopold von Sonnleithner* expressed the view that Staudigl's readings were all too frequently capricious and excessively dramatic, and would not have met with the composer's unqualified approval.

Staudigl, who was also a talented composer and painter, retired from the stage in 1856. The following year he was interned in a mental asylum near Vienna. One of his sons, likewise called Josef (1850–1916), became a well-known baritone who sang at Karlsruhe (1874–84), as well as in other German cities and European countries, and also in the United States (1884–6, 1898). He enjoyed a certain reputation as a Schubert singer, but it did not rival his father's.

(Brusatti, Charlton[1,2], Kutsch/Riemens, Rosenthal)

Stauffer [Staufer], **Johann Georg** (b. Vienna, 26 January 1778; d. Vienna, 24 January 1853). Guitar, lute, and violin maker. He was a pupil of the well-known violin maker Franz Geissendorf who had moved to Vienna from Bavaria some time before 1779 and had in 1781 taken over the workshop of the late Johann Georg Thir.

Stauffer came to be regarded as the finest guitar maker in Vienna. Later he turned increasingly to the production of violins, but without achieving the same excellence. In 1813, and again in 1814, he applied unsuccessfully for the position of violin maker to the court. Later he took charge of the firm of the instrument maker Ignaz Christian Bartl [Partl], after the latter had died childless in 1819. Around 1843 he resided for a time with his son Johann Anton at Kaschau [Kassa] in Hungary [now Košice, Slovak Republic] and may have established a workshop there. He died in poverty.

In *c.*1823 Stauffer invented the 'guitare d'amour' or 'arpeggione', a cross between the guitar and the cello. In 1824 Schubert wrote his Sonata for arpeggione and piano (D821) for Vincenz Schuster who, according to the preface to the first edition of the sonata (J. P. Gotthard,* 1871), performed it 'soon afterwards'. In 1825 Schuster published a tutor for the new instrument, *Anleitung zur Erlernung des von Herrn Georg Staufer neu erfundenen Guitarre-Violoncells*. The arpeggione remained in use for little more than ten years. In modern times Schubert's sonata is usually played on the cello; in fact, the first edition was already entitled 'Sonata for arpeggione or violoncello and pianoforte'.

(Geiringer, Lütgendorff)

Stockhausen, Julius (Christian) (b. Paris, 22 July 1826; d. Frankfurt am Main, 22 September 1906). Baritone, conductor, and teacher, of Alsatian descent. Son of the harpist and composer Franz (Anton Adam) Stockhausen (1789–1868) and the soprano Margarethe Stockhausen, née Schmuck (1803–77). In addition to singing, he studied the piano, organ, violin, and cello. His instructors included his own parents, and later, for singing, the younger García. Starting in 1848, he performed in all the important European musical centres. While he did not neglect the operatic stage, he concentrated on oratorios and Lieder, and he became particularly celebrated as an interpreter of the songs of Schubert and Schumann. Brahms,* whom he met at Düsseldorf in 1856, later accompanied him at a number of recitals and wrote his *Magelone Lieder* for him. From 1863 to 1867 Stockhausen was conductor of the Hamburg Philharmonische Konzertgesellschaft and of the Singakademie. At his first concert in Hamburg (6 March 1863) he conducted Schubert's 'Great' C major Symphony (D944). From 1874 to 1878 he was director of the Sternscher Gesangverein in Berlin. Subsequently he settled in Frankfurt am Main where, in 1880, he established his own school of singing.

Stockhausen was generally regarded as the best Schubert singer of his time. His repertoire covered more than thirty Lieder, in addition to the cycles *Die schöne Müllerin* (D795) and *Winterreise* (D911). He was, moreover, the first to sing the complete *Die schöne Müllerin* at a concert—on 4 May 1856, in Vienna. He repeated this, for him strenuous but deeply satisfying, feat on several later occasions, including at Cologne on 28 October 1862 before an audience of two thousand. George Grove* wrote of his performance of Schubert's and Schumann's Lieder in his *Dictionary of Music and Musicians* (London, 1879–89): 'The rich beauty of the voice, the nobility of the style, the perfect phrasing, the intimate sympathy, and, not least, the intelligible way in which the words were given ... all combined to make his singing of songs a wonderful event.' Other critics, like Eduard Hanslick, were equally warm in their praise. It is, however, interesting to note that surviving members of Schubert's own circle were less dazzled by Stockhausen's singing. While Leopold von Sonnleithner,* writing in 1857, was prepared to recognize Stock-hausen's supremacy ('his rendition comes closest to the noble and unaffected interpretation which Schubert himself desired'), he did not do so without qualifica-tion. And Josef von Spaun* was even less enthusiastic: 'The much acclaimed Stockhausen ... did not even come within reach of Vogl's* deeply felt interpreta-tion. I heard him perform the beautiful song "Der Zwerg" [D771] at a private gathering. His reading was vastly inferior to Vogl's intensely moving one, which brought out the full richness of this marvellous song.'

Several of Stockhausen's pupils made names for themselves as Schubert singers. One was Karl Scheidemantel, the famous Wagnerian baritone who was also the first Faninal in Richard Strauss's *Der Rosenkavalier.* Another was Raimund von Zur Mühlen; yet another was Johannes (Martinus) Messchaert.

(Lafite, Pascall, Wirt)

Stolberg[-Stolberg], **Friedrich** [Fritz] **Leopold**, Count (b. Bramstedt, Holstein, 7 November 1750; d. Sondermühlen, near Osnabrück, 5 December 1819). Poet, novelist, dramatist, and translator. Son of Count Christian Günther Stolberg-Stolberg (1714–65), chamberlain to Queen Sophie Magdalene, widow of King Christian VI of Denmark. Together with his brother Christian (1748–1821) he studied law and literature at the universities at Halle (1770–2) and Göttingen (1772–3). In 1777 the brothers' paths diverged: Christian settled as a magistrate at Tremsbüttel in Holstein, whilst Friedrich moved to Copenhagen as envoy of Friedrich August, prince-bishop of Lübeck and duke of Oldenburg. He subse-quently held a variety of administrative and diplomatic posts in the service of the bishopric and of the Danish government and travelled extensively. In 1793 he was appointed to a senior administrative position at Eutin, the place of residence of the bishops of Lübeck. A religious crisis, which prompted him to resign all his offices, led to his conversion to Catholicism in 1800. Thereafter he lived for a time at Münster in Westphalia, from 1812 at Tatenhausen Castle, near Bielefeld, and finally, from 1816, at Sondermühlen Castle.

The brothers' literary works were repeatedly published together. However, Fried-rich is generally considered the more gifted writer and translator of the two.

Among the Greek works he rendered into German were Homer's *Iliad* (1778), a number of Plato's dialogues (1796–7), and several of Aeschylus's* tragedies (1802). His original works include several neo-classical tragedies with chorus (*Theseus, Servius Tullius, Timoleon*), the novel *Die Insel* (1788), and poems. After his conversion he was preoccupied with religious matters, as is evidenced by his fifteen-volume *Geschichte der Religion Jesu Christi* (1806–18).

Schubert composed the following nine songs to poems by Stolberg: in 1815, 'Abendlied' (D276) and 'Morgenlied' (D266); in 1816, 'An die Natur' (D372), 'Daphne am Bach' (D411), 'Lied in der Abwesenheit' (D416), 'Romanze' (D144), 'Stimme der Liebe' (D412); and in 1823, 'Auf dem Wasser zu singen' (D774) and 'Lied' ['Die Mutter Erde'] (D788). Of these, only 'Auf dem Wasser zu singen', which is based on a poem inspired by Stolberg's love for his first wife, Agnes von Witzleben (1761–88), was published in Schubert's lifetime. It is one of his most admired compositions. To quote Dietrich Fischer-Dieskau: 'This song displays the most entrancing qualities of Schubert's lyricism, inasmuch as it combines a typically Austrian sensuous delight in melody with the instrumental excellence of the piano works which he was composing at the same period, such as the Impromptus and *Moments musicaux*.'

Settings: D144, 266, 276, 372, 411–12, 416, 774, 788.
(Fischer-Dieskau, Mix[1,2])

Stoll, Josef Ludwig (b. Vienna, 1778; d. Vienna, 22 June 1815). Poet and dramatist; son of a prominent physician, Maximilian Stoll (1742–88). In 1801, after extensive travels in Europe, he settled at Weimar where he wrote comedies for the court theatre (*Das Bild Amors, Scherz und Ernst, Streit und Liebe*). In 1807, on Goethe's* recommendation, he was appointed resident poet at the Burgtheater in Vienna. There, in 1808, he founded with Baron Leo Seckendorf the magazine *Prometheus*, which printed poems by Goethe, August Wilhelm von Schlegel,* Friedrich von Schlegel,* and Wieland, among others; it ran to six issues. In 1811 the first part of his *Poetische Schriften* was published at Heidelberg; the planned second part never appeared. During his final years Stoll lived in increasing poverty, having lost his post at the theatre and squandered a not inconsiderable inheritance.

His poems inspired three Schubert songs, all composed in 1815: 'An die Geliebte' (D303), 'Labetrank der Liebe' (D302), and 'Lambertine' (D301). Beethoven,* who was in contact with Stoll from 1807, had already published his own setting of 'An die Geliebte' in 1811, and a revised version in 1814.

Settings: D301–3.
(Fischer[10], Sauer[3], Wurzbach[1])

Storck, D. Adam (d. 1822). Teacher; translator. In 1819, at Essen, he published 'Das Fräulein vom See', a German version of Sir Walter Scott's* poem 'The Lady of the Lake'. On the title-page he is described as a professor at Bremen.

Between April and July 1825, Schubert composed five songs to texts taken from Storck's translation: 'Lied des gefangenen Jägers' (D843), 'Normans Gesang' (D846), and 'Ellen's *Gesänge*' (D837–9). In addition, he set two further passages from Scott's poem in the partsongs 'Bootgesang' (D835) and 'Coronach: Totengesang der Frauen und Mädchen' (D836). When the seven settings were published together in April 1826, the original English text was printed in addition to the German one for all except 'Normans Gesang'.

In a letter to his father* and stepmother from Steyr on 25 [?28] July 1825, Schubert, who had recently spent several weeks at Gmunden as the guest of Ferdinand Traweger,* wrote that of the various songs which he and Johann Michael Vogl* had performed at the Trawegers' and at the house of Franz Ferdinand von Schiller [later Baron Schiller*], it was his new Scott songs which had pleased the most. He added: 'They also wondered greatly at the piety which I expressed in a hymn to the Holy Virgin [i.e. 'Ave Maria', D839] and which, it appears, grips the heart and incites it to devotion. I believe this is because I have never strained to feel devout, and have never composed hymns or prayers of this kind unless I have been spontaneously moved by devotion; but then the devotion is usually genuine and true.' According to Anton Ottenwalt,* Schubert regarded 'Normans Gesang' as 'the best of the Scott songs'.

The first semi-public performance of 'Lied des gefangenen Jägers' was given by Johann Karl Schoberlechner at an 'evening entertainment' of the Gesellschaft der Musikfreunde on 8 February 1827, that of 'Normans Gesang' by Ludwig Titze* at another such concert on 8 March of the same year. On 31 January 1828, again at an 'evening entertainment', Theresia Josephi performed 'Ellens Gesang' (probably 'Ave Maria').

Settings: D835–9, 843, 846.

Streinsberg, Josef Ludwig von (1798–1862). Civil servant; son of Josef von Streinsberg, a court secretary. A fellow pupil of Schubert at the Stadtkonvikt, he reportedly became a close friend in 1812–13. He went on to study law and then entered government service.

He remained on intimate terms with Schubert, as is shown by the fact that he was among the seven friends to whom Schubert addressed a letter from Zseliz in September 1818. A few weeks earlier, Schubert had composed 'Grablied für die Mutter' (D616, to a text by an unknown poet) on the occasion of the death of Streinsberg's mother Maria Anna on 26 June. In March 1820 Streinsberg was present, as was Schubert, when the police searched Johann Senn's* lodgings. According to the police report, Streinsberg joined the rest of Senn's friends in 'verbally abusing and insulting' the official concerned. Some time later he found employment in the customs office at Linz. In August 1823 he visited Schubert and Johann Michael Vogl* during their stay at Steyr. The following year he moved back to Vienna, having been appointed to a position at the court treasury, and eventually he became head of department in one of the ministries. On 7 January 1826 he married Isabella Josefa von Bruchmann (1801–36), a sister of Franz von Bruchmann.*

In a letter to Ferdinand Luib* on 29 May 1858, Streinsberg wrote: 'I remained in constant contact with [Schubert] until 1823.' One may deduce from this statement that they did not renew their former intimacy after Streinsberg had returned to Vienna. This conclusion is borne out by the absence of any record of contacts subsequent to the above-mentioned meeting at Steyr.

Sullivan, Sir **Arthur (Seymour)** (b. Lambeth, London, 13 May 1842; d. London, 22 November 1900). Composer and conductor; the musical half of the Gilbert and Sullivan partnership. He began his studies at the Royal College of Music in 1856 and continued them at the Leipzig Conservatory in 1858, returning to London in the spring of 1861. Shortly afterwards he made the acquaintance of George Grove.* A warm relationship quickly developed between them.

Grove was a devoted Schubertian, and Sullivan had come back from Leipzig full of enthusiasm for Schubert's music. When Grove set out for Vienna in 1867, on his journey of exploration into Schubert's manuscripts, the companion he chose was Sullivan. The latter's presence in Vienna was to be of invaluable assistance to him, especially since he had himself had no formal musical training. In his remarks on Schubert's symphonies, which were printed in the appendix to the English translation of Kreissle's* biography, Grove observed, regarding certain features of the autograph of the 'Great' C major Symphony (D944): 'These were noted by Mr. Sullivan, when we looked through the manuscript together in the library of the Musik-Verein on the 8th October 1867, and they may therefore be received with perfect confidence.' Sullivan's pianistic skills also proved useful, for Grove was only an indifferent performer. In a letter to Olga von Glehn on 9 October, he described what had happened when the publisher Carl Spina had handed them 'a pile of MS music about as big as a portmanteau' for their examination: 'First we spend an hour in incoherent raptures, then we get more reasonable and part it all into lots and begin to go through it thoroughly. Then we take the things we like into the other room, and Arthur plays, and we decide to have or not to have.'

Their friendship continued throughout the rest of their lives (they were to die within six months of each other).

(Graves, Jacobs, Young)

Sulzer, Salomon (b. Hohenems, Vorarlberg, 30 March 1804; d. Vienna, 17 January 1890). Cantor and composer. The family had changed its name from Levy to Sulzer after moving to Hohenems from nearby Sulz in the mid-eighteenth century. Highly musical and endowed with a beautiful voice, Sulzer was designated to become cantor at Hohenems when he was only 13, but he did not take up the appointment until 1820. In the intervening years he studied theory, conducting, and composition at Karlsruhe, and also travelled through Switzerland, France, and Swabia as an apprentice to several different cantors. After being appointed cantor at the new synagogue in Vienna in 1826, he received further tuition from Ignaz von Seyfried, whose numerous compositions included a number of biblical music dramas.

Sulzer's arrival in Vienna coincided with the opening of a new Jewish temple [Seitenstettengasse]. As part of the overall reform of the religious services instituted by Rabbi Isaak Noah Mannheimer, Sulzer was entrusted with the reorganization of the musical side of the liturgy. In this connection, he compiled a collection of models for the different sections of the service, as well as for functions such as weddings, funerals, and special festivals. The first volume of this collection appeared in 1839[?] under the title *Schir Zion* [*The Harp of Zion*]. Of the 159 items, Sulzer supplied 122, a number of which were based on traditional synagogue melodies which he had harmonized; among the other composers represented— for Sulzer had requested contributions from several Viennese musicians—were Josef Drechsler, Josef Fischhof, Seyfried, Michael Umlauf, and Schubert. In 1860 Sulzer published a collection of religious songs, *Dudaim* [*Mandrakes*], for use in school and at home, and in 1865 a second volume of *Schir Zion*.

With his magnificent baritone voice and his deeply felt and often impassioned interpretations, Sulzer made an unforgettable impression on his listeners. Liszt* was among those who paid eloquent tribute to him. Schubert was reportedly so impressed by Sulzer's singing that, on one occasion, he asked him to sing 'Der Wanderer' (D489) three times in succession. He is also said to have regarded him as the ideal interpreter of 'Die Allmacht' (D852) and of his other religious songs. The journalist F. Uhl wrote: 'He who has not heard, or rather experienced, Sulzer sing "Die Allmacht", has little idea of the power of music.'

Sulzer may have been introduced to Schubert by Seyfried who was Kapellmeister at the Theater an der Wien from 1801 until 1826 and later wrote the articles on Schubert and Ferdinand Schubert* for the *Enzyklopädie der gesamten musikalischen Wissenschaften, oder Universal-Lexikon der Tonkunst* published by Gustav Schilling in 1838. Schubert's contribution to *Schir Zion* was an a cappella setting of the Hebrew text of Psalm 92, for solo baritone, quartet, and chorus. This work (D953) was first performed at the Vienna synagogue, with Sulzer assuming the solo part, shortly after Schubert had completed it in July 1828. In 1870, it was published separately by J. P. Gotthard* in Vienna with Moses Mendelssohn's* German translation of the text.

From 1844 until 1847 Sulzer taught singing at the Conservatory of the Gesellschaft der Musikfreunde. He did not retire as chief cantor until 1881, when he was already approaching 80. He and his wife Fanni, née Hirschfeld, had fourteen children. Three of the daughters became professional singers; his son Josef (*c.*1850–1926) was a composer and cellist, and choirmaster of the Viennese Jewish community; another son, Julius (d. 1891), was a composer and conductor.

(Brody, Mandell, Werner[1], Wurzbach[1])

Suppé, Franz (von) (b. Spalato, Dalmatia [Split, Croatia], 18 April 1819; d. Vienna, 21 May 1895). Composer and conductor, of Belgian descent. Having studied law at Padua, he went to Vienna after his father's death in 1835 and thereafter devoted himself to music. He became Kapellmeister at the Theater an der Wien in 1845, transferred to the Kaitheater in 1862, and in 1865 moved to the Carltheater where he remained until 1882. He wrote numerous scores for the stage. Among the most successful of his operettas were *Die schöne Galatea* (Berlin, Meysels-Theater, 30 June 1865), *Fatinitza* (Carltheater, 5 January 1876), and *Boccaccio* (Carltheater, 1 February 1879).

On 10 September 1864 the Carltheater presented his one-act Liederspiel *Franz Schubert*, in which he made use of Schubert's own melodies. The libretto was furnished by Hans Max [pseud. of Baron Johann Päumann]. Originally, the action was to take place at Weidling am Bach, north of Vienna, but this locality was subsequently replaced by the Höldrichsmühle [Höldrich Mill] near Mödling, to the south of Vienna. As Päumann was to explain in a letter to the secretary of the Wiener Männergesangverein on 9 March 1874, the change resulted from the decision to create a role for the celebrated comic actor Alois [Louis] Grois and to model his part on Liberatus Starker, a musician and well-known eccentric who had spent the last years of his life in Mödling and had died there in 1845.

In *Franz Schubert*, the mill and its setting are portrayed as the source of inspiration for the songs of the cycle *Die schöne Müllerin* (D795). This figment of the librettist's imagination subsequently gave rise to the widely accepted myth that Schubert had actually stayed at the Höldrichsmühle, and to this legend was eventually attached the conclusion (not suggested in the Singspiel) that the songs had in fact been inspired by Schubert's love for a local 'maid of the mill'. In due course, a plaque was affixed to the building commemorating Schubert's supposed visit.

In the original production of Suppé's Liederspiel, the part of Schubert was taken by the popular actor and singer Karl Treumann. At its revival at the Opera in 1886, it was entrusted to Fritz Schrödter, an excellent tenor who would come out of retirement in 1916 to star, once again as Schubert, in Berté's* *Das Dreimäderlhaus*.

(Branscombe[9], Keller, Werba, Wurzbach[1])

Széchényi, Louis [Ludwig], Count (b. Horpács, Hungary, 6 November 1781; d. ?Vienna, 7 February 1855). Poet; son of Count Ferenc [Franz] Széchényi (1754–1820), a prominent Hungarian statesman and founder of the Hungarian National Museum, who, after his retirement from public life, settled in Vienna in 1811.

In November 1821 Schubert dedicated to Széchényi his Op. 7, which contained the songs 'Der Flug der Zeit' (D515) and 'Die abgeblühte Linde' (D514), both settings of poems written by Széchényi himself, together with 'Der Tod und das Mädchen' (D531). Nothing is known about any personal contacts between Schubert and the count. Since 'Der Tod und das Mädchen' was composed in February 1817, it is thought that the Széchényi songs may date from the same period. The tenor Franz Ruess gave the first performance of 'Die abgeblühte Linde' at an 'evening entertainment' of the Gesellschaft der Musikfreunde on 6 March 1823.

Széchényi was later appointed chief steward to Archduchess Sophie, wife of Archduke Franz Karl and mother of the future emperor Franz Josef. He married twice: in 1801 Countess Aloisia Clam-Gallas (d. 1822), and in 1824 Countess Franciska de Paula Wurmbrand.

Settings: D514–15.
(Werba, Wurzbach[1])

Teltscher, Josef Eduard (b. Prague, 15 January 1801; d. near Athens, 7 July 1837). Portraitist, lithographer, and painter on ivory. In *c*.1820 he moved to Vienna where his uncle Franz Teltscher kept a shop; in 1823 he enrolled as a student at the Academy of Fine Arts. In 1829 he visited Graz, apparently intending to remain only a short while, but in fact he lived there for the next three years, during which he painted many of the local notables. For some of that time he stayed with Karl and Marie Leopoldine Pachler,* to whom he had been introduced by his friend Johann Baptist Jenger.* The latter was his companion on the journey to Greece in 1837, during which Teltscher drowned while bathing in the harbour of Piraeus.

It may also have been Jenger who introduced him to Schubert. The earliest known evidence of his friendship with Schubert is provided by an entry in Sophie Müller's* diary on 11 January 1826, which records that among her visitors that day was Teltscher, who 'brought Schubert *lithographed*'. The portrait in question (which is lost) is therefore likely to have been executed shortly before that date. Teltscher's name appears in Sophie Müller's diary repeatedly during the following months, especially in February and March, at which time he executed lithographs of the actress and her father. Jenger was present on several occasions, as was Schubert. On 13 May 1826 Sophie mentions that 'both Hüttenbrenners [Anselm* and Josef*], Teltscher, and Schubert dined here'. Another indication of the increasing intimacy between Teltscher, Schubert, and Jenger in the course of 1826 is Jenger's statement in a letter to Marie Pachler on 1 August 1826 that, even if he himself should be unable to travel to Graz that autumn, 'my friend Schubert and the painter Teltscher will certainly come'. In the event, none of them did, but in May 1827 Jenger announced a visit by all three for September; however, only he and Schubert made the journey (*see* Pachler*).

It was perhaps for Baron Schönstein* that Teltscher made his charming triple portrait of Schubert, Jenger, and Anselm Hüttenbrenner in 1827 [?1828]; the original water-colour is lost and the painting is known only through a colour print. In April 1829 a lithographed portrait of Schubert executed by Teltscher and printed by the firm Mansfeld & Co. was offered for sale in Vienna. The receipts were to help defray the costs of the funeral monument which it was proposed to erect at Schubert's grave at Währing district cemetery. This portrait was assumed by O. E.

Deutsch* to have been identical with that referred to in the above-mentioned entry in Sophie Müller's diary in January 1826. However, it now appears that it was probably newly lithographed by Teltscher for the occasion and was based on a separate drawing which he had made (in ?1826) in preparation for the triple portrait. A writer in the Vienna *Allgemeine Theaterzeitung* on 23 April 1829 praised the lithograph for showing 'Schubert's true character, that of a guileless, childlike, pious, and upright nature'.

Apart from Anselm Hüttenbrenner, Jenger, and Sophie Müller, Teltscher drew or painted several other persons associated with Schubert and listed in this dictionary, including Countess Karoline Esterházy, Marie Pachler, Schönstein, and Ignaz von Sonnleithner. The portrait of Karoline Esterházy was acquired by Schönstein, and presented by him in April 1863 to Moritz von Schwind* who already possessed a copy of it; Schwind incorporated the portrait in 1868 in *A Schubert Evening at Josef von Spaun's.* Teltscher also made two very moving drawings of Beethoven* on his death-bed.

(*ALBK*, Hilmar[4], Jestremski[1], Pachler, Steblin[4])

Tieck, (Johann) Ludwig (b. Berlin, 31 May 1773; d. Berlin, 28 April 1853). Poet, novelist, translator, and critic. He studied theology and especially literature at the universities at Halle, Göttingen, and Erlangen (1792–4), and thereafter made his living as a writer, in Berlin and elsewhere, for he moved around a great deal and also travelled abroad. It was not until 1819 that he settled permanently at Dresden; in 1825 he was appointed literary adviser to the court theatre there. In 1841 he returned to Berlin at the invitation of King Friedrich Wilhelm IV. One of the most prominent members of the Romantic movement in Germany, he was an exceptionally fertile writer who made his mark in several literary genres, including poetry. An edition of his collected works (Berlin, 1828–54) ran to twenty-eight volumes.

In early 1819, Schubert set his poem 'Abend', but only a sketch of the song (D645) has survived. In 1825 Franz von Schober* tried to persuade Tieck to produce at Dresden Schubert's opera *Alfonso und Estrella* (D732), for which Schober had written the libretto. Schubert, who was then in Upper Austria, was informed of Schober's efforts by Moritz von Schwind* (letter of 1–6 August 1825) and urged by him to send news of the whereabouts of the score ('You must write at once whether it is still in Dresden or where else, Tieck is waiting for the information'). Nothing further is known about the matter, other than that no performance took place at Dresden. (*See also* Liszt* and Weber.*)

Setting: D645.
(Neumann[1])

Tiedge, Christoph August (b. Gardelegen, 14 December 1752; d. Dresden, 8 March 1841). Poet. He attended school at Magdeburg and from 1770 studied law at Halle. From 1777 he worked as a translator and clerk at Magdeburg; between 1781 and

1797 he earned his living as a secretary and tutor. He spent the years 1799–1802 in Berlin; in 1819 he settled at Dresden.

His best-known work is the philosophical poem *Urania: Über Gott, Unsterblichkeit und Freiheit* (Halle, 1801), which, in its rationalism, shows the influence of Kant and Schiller.* Other publications include *Elegien und vermischte Gedichte* (2 vols., Halle, 1803–7) and the cycle *Das Echo, oder Alexis und Ida* (1812). His collected works appeared in eight volumes at Halle between 1823 and 1829. In August 1815, Schubert set one of his poems in the song 'An die Sonne'.

Setting: D272.
(Biesterfeld, Porhansl[9])

Titze [Tietze, Tieze], **Ludwig** (b. Braunau [Broumov, Czech Republic], 1 April 1797; d. Vienna, 11 January 1850). Tenor. He studied law in Prague and in Vienna, where he settled in *c.*1821. From 1824 until his death, he was employed as an assistant proctor at the University. At the same time, he soon became a familiar performer at private and public concerts. He had a beautiful voice and was especially admired as an interpreter of Schubert's songs. 'Herr Tietze once again enthralled the audience with his velvety voice which reaches the very depths of one's heart,' S. Saphir wrote in the *Wiener allgemeine Theaterzeitung* on 1 April 1824 after a performance of 'Erlkönig' (D328). And Leopold von Sonnleithner* later warmly praised his simple and unaffected manner of singing Schubert's Lieder, which he considered infinitely preferable to the subtle and declamatory interpretation favoured by certain persons 'who are forever searching behind the musical idea (which they do not comprehend and accordingly disdain) for another, poetic or philosophical, idea'.

The earliest documented occasion on which Titze sang in one of Schubert's compositions in Vienna was a concert given by the cellist Josef Merk at the Landhaus on 15 April 1822, at which he took one of the two tenor parts in 'Geist der Liebe' (D747). However, he may already have sung in the first performance of that quartet, which had taken place at the Grosser Redoutensaal on 3 March of that year. Thereafter he was frequently heard in Schubert Lieder and partsongs, sometimes accompanied by the composer.

He gave the first performances of the following Lieder during Schubert's lifetime: 'Rastlose Liebe' (D138) on 29 January 1824, 'Der Einsame' (D800) on 23 November 1826, 'Normans Gesang' (D846) on 8 March 1827, 'Im Freien' (D880) on 6 May 1827, 'Gute Nacht' (D911/1) on 10 January 1828, all at 'evening entertainments' of the Gesellschaft der Musikfreunde; 'Romanze des Richard Löwenherz' (D907) on 2 February 1828, at the Landhaus; and 'Auf dem Strom' (D943), at Schubert's concert at the Musikverein on 26 March 1828. In addition, he sang the solo tenor part at the first performance of 'Nachthelle' (D892) at another 'evening entertainment' on 25 January 1827. In 1825 Schubert dedicated the Offertory in C major (D136) 'to his friend Ludwig Titze'.

Writing in March 1868 to an unidentified correspondent who had sent him portraits of Titze and his wife (in Titze's case, at any rate, probably a lithograph by Albert Decker), Josef Hüttenbrenner* declared that Titze had been 'Schubert's greatest enemy'. He alleged that Titze had objected to the performances of Mozart's Requiem at St Ulrich's (Maria Trost) Church on 27 November 1828 and Anselm Hüttenbrenner's* Requiem at St Augustine's Church on 23 December, on the grounds that Schubert, while a good writer of songs, was not a great composer, and only great composers merited a Requiem. It should be added, however, that Josef Hüttenbrenner is not always a very reliable witness.

What is certain, on the other hand, is that Titze continued to provide proof of his great interest in Schubert's music after the latter's death. Not only did he subscribe to *Schwanengesang* (D957) in 1829, but he continued actively to promote Schubert's music. Thus he sang in some more first performances: of 'Der blinde Knabe' (D833) on 8 January 1829; *Mirjams Siegesgesang* (D942) at the memorial concert on 30 January 1829; 'Drang in die Ferne' (D770) on 19 February 1829; and 'An mein Herz' (D860) on 7 February 1833. On one notable occasion (29 April 1838), he sang 'Erlkönig' and 'Liebesbotschaft' (D957/1) to Liszt's* accompaniment. In the *Wiener allgemeine Theaterzeitung* on 1 May, H. Adami specially praised their rendition of 'Erlkönig': 'I do not believe that this accompaniment has ever been played so brilliantly. It is to Herr Titze's credit that he held his own so successfully against such a splendid performance.'

He was engaged as a tenor in the court Kapelle in 1832, and was a member of the organizing committee of the Concerts spirituels. His name is variously spelt in contemporary documents; he himself always signed 'Titze'.

(Brusatti, Liszt[4]. For some of the biographical information at the beginning of this article I am indebted to Regierungsrat C. Hösler, Vienna.)

Traweger, Ferdinand (b. Gmunden, Upper Austria, 26 October 1787; d. Gmunden, 6 April 1832). Merchant; patron of music. Schubert stayed at his house [2 Badgasse/ 8 Theatergasse] from 4 June to 15 July 1825. Johann Michael Vogl,* who accompanied Schubert on this trip, also stayed there for at least part of that time. Schubert (who may already have met Traweger on an earlier occasion) greatly enjoyed his visit: 'We lodged at Traweger's who owns a splendid piano and is, as you know, a great admirer of my humble self,' he wrote to Josef von Spaun* on 21 July. 'I lived there very comfortably and at my ease.' And to his father* and stepmother, he reported: 'I ... have spent six weeks at Gmunden, the surroundings of which are truly heavenly and most deeply moved and benefited me, as did the inhabitants, especially the excellent Traweger. I lived at Traweger's very free and easy, like one of the family.' There was much music-making at Traweger's house during Schubert's stay. Traweger was especially fond of male-voice quartets, and it was probably for him that Schubert composed the Latin drinking-song 'Edit Nonna' ('Trinklied aus dem 16. Jahrhundert', D847) at Gmunden that July. Albert Stadler* compared

Traweger's role in the musical life of Gmunden to that of Sylvester Paumgartner* at Steyr.

Traweger and his wife Elisabeth (?1787–1846) had two daughters and a son, Eduard (1820–1909). Schubert took a great liking to the boy. He taught him the song 'Morgengruss' (D795/8), and also presented him with a silver toothpick after Eduard had bravely allowed Schubert to apply leeches to his neck, as ordered by his doctor.

Schubert considered a further visit to the Trawegers in the summer of 1828, but nothing came of the idea. According to Eduard's later recollections, when news of Schubert's death reached the family, 'my father and mother wept much, and we children wept with them'. When Eduard, who became a captain in the police force, died in 1909, he was believed to have been the last person who had known Schubert.

Troyer, Ferdinand, Count (b. Brünn [Brno], 1 February 1780; d. Vienna, 23 July 1851). Clarinettist. Son of Count Ferdinand Johann Nepomuk Troyer (1749–89) and his wife Ernestine, née Countess Wallis. The father, who was fond of music and a competent horn player, gave parties, at which both he and Ferdinand performed. Another son, Franz Anton (1783–1854), played the cor anglais. In 1813 the two brothers moved to Vienna, where Ferdinand studied with the well-known clarinet-tist Josef Friedlowsky. From 1816 he performed at concerts of the Gesellschaft der Musikfreunde. When, at a concert at the Grosser Redoutensaal on 2 March 1817, he played the clarinet obbligato to Sextus's aria 'Parto, parto' from Mozart's *La clemenza di Tito*, his 'sensitive, extremely tender handling' of the instrument won praise. At a concert of the Gesellschaft der Musikfreunde on 1 March 1818, he performed two movements of a clarinet concerto by Bernhard Henrik Crusell.

Troyer became chamberlain and later chief steward to Archduke Rudolf,* who dedicated a sonata for clarinet and piano of his own composition to him. In 1824 Troyer commissioned Schubert to write the Octet (D803). It was completed on 1 March and received its first performance that spring at Troyer's apartment [13 Graben], with Troyer himself taking the clarinet part. (Franz Paul Lachner's* statement, in his 'Erinnerungen an Schubert und Beethoven' in *Die Presse* of 1 November 1881, that the octet was played for the first time at his own lodgings is regarded as incorrect.) The first public performance, in which the Schuppanzigh* Quartet took part, was given at the Musikverein on 16 April 1827.

(Danhelovsky, Pohl[1], Weston[1,2], Wurzbach[1])

Uhland, (Johann) Ludwig (b. Tübingen, 26 April 1787; d. Tübingen, 13 November 1862). Poet, dramatist, scholar, and politician; grandson of a professor of theology at the University of Tübingen and son of the university's secretary. A lawyer by training, he was initially employed in the Württemberg ministry of justice, but in 1814 set up in private practice at Stuttgart. At the same time, he developed a deep and abiding interest in medieval literature, and from 1829 until 1832 he held an appointment as professor of German language and literature at Tübingen University. He was also, for many years, a liberal member of the Württemberg parliament and, in 1848–9, a member of the short-lived Frankfurt National Assembly.

In 1815 he brought out a collection of verse (*Gedichte*) which was enormously successful. It included, among other pieces, his two most famous ballads, 'Die Rache' and 'Des Sängers Fluch'. His *Vaterländische Gedichte* (1817) were inspired by his political ideas, which were also reflected in the two verse tragedies, *Ernst, Herzog von Schwaben* (1818) and *Ludwig der Baier* (1819). Lastly, his enthusiasm for medieval poetry led to such scholarly publications as *Über das altfranzösische Epos* (1812) and *Alte hoch- und niederdeutsche Volkslieder* (1844–5).

His poetry has attracted many composers, among them Schumann*, Brahms*, and Richard Strauss. Rather surprisingly, Schubert set only one poem, 'Frühlingsglaube', but between 1820 and 1822 he made three versions of it before he was satisfied. In R. Capell's words, 'there was never another music so innocent at once and so pathetically sensitive'. The song was published by Sauer & Leidesdorf* in April 1823.

Setting: D686.

(Capell, Fröschle, Schneider)

Umlauff von Frankwell, Johann Baptist Carl (b. Mährisch-Schönberg [Šumperk, Czech Republic], 23 December 1796; d. Vienna, 8 March 1861). Lawyer and judge; poet and translator. Son of Vinzenz Umlauff, a teacher and choirmaster. He studied at Olmütz [Olomouc] and later in Vienna, where he became a pupil of Heinrich Josef Watteroth.* After completing his law studies in 1818, he was employed on the staff of the Vienna city council; in 1821 he was posted to Suczawa in Bukovina [Suceava, Romania]. During the next thirty years he held increasingly important legal appointments, mostly at Czernowitz [Chernovtsy, Ukraine], the principal city of the district (from 1849, duchy) of Bukovina. In 1853 he was appointed president of the higher district court at Pressburg [Bratislava], and from 1857 he occupied a similar position at Pest [Budapest]. On his retirement in 1860 he moved back to Vienna. He was ennobled for his distinguished services and took the title 'von Frankwell'.

Most of the information available about his career comes from the biography published by his son Viktor in 1861. The book also contains some interesting remarks about Umlauff's relations with Schubert during his early years in Vienna, but they need to be viewed with caution, being evidently based on recollections communicated to Viktor by his father towards the end of his life, long after the events described.

According to the biography, Umlauff made Schubert's acquaintance in 1818 and took to calling on him in the mornings, on the way to the office. (From late 1818 until the end of 1820 Schubert shared a room with Johann Mayrhofer* at a location corresponding to today's 2 Wipplingerstrasse.) During these visits, Umlauff would try out Schubert's latest songs. He had a good tenor voice and is said to have taken lessons with Johann Michael Vogl.* On 7 March 1821 he participated in the first public performances of the partsongs 'Das Dörfchen' (D598) and 'Gesang der Geister über den Wassern' (D714) at the Kärntnertor-Theater. He also sang in a performance of the latter work at Ignaz von Sonnleithner's* on 30 March of that year. At another concert at the Kärntnertor-Theater, on 22 April 1821, he took part in the first performance of 'Die Nachtigall' (D724). He was reportedly so highly regarded as a singer that he was offered an attractive contract at the Kärntnertor-Theater, but he respected his parents' wish that he should make the law his career.

Umlauff was a man of considerable culture, with a profound interest in literature as well as music. Among the papers which he left at his death were several poems, partial translations of Tasso's *Gerusalemme liberata* and Ariosto's *Orlando furioso*, and a lengthy fragment, dating from 1821, of a satirical epic poem entitled *Hans Dampf, oder Die seltene Heirat*. His enthusiasm for music led him to organize numerous amateur performances of well-known orchestral works and operas at his house at Czernowitz. His son claimed, furthermore, that 'he was the first to make known Schubert's songs, with French and Moldavian texts, in this furthermost corner of the monarchy, whence they were soon introduced into Moldavia and Bessarabia'.

(Umlauff, Wurzbach[1])

Unger, Johann Karl (b. Rissdorf, Zips, Hungary [Ruskinova, Slovak Republic], 13 April 1771; d. Vienna, c.1836). Teacher, writer, and amateur singer; father of Karoline Unger.* He at first studied theology at Neutra [Nitra, Slovak Republic] and in Vienna, but subsequently turned to law. In 1796 he was appointed professor in the history of law at the Theresian Academy, Vienna. He left his post three years later to become tutor to the son of Baron Ignaz Forgács and in 1810 entered the service of Baron Rudolf Josef Hackelberg-Landau as financial adviser. His literary achievements included contributions to various periodicals and almanacs, as well as several books ranging from moral tracts and primers for young persons to a biography of the French soprano Joséphine Fodor-Mainvielle. He also published a volume of poems (*Gedichte*, Vienna, 1797).

Unger was a friend of Count Johann Karl Esterházy* and is believed to have introduced Schubert to the count when the latter was looking for a music teacher for his daughters. Schubert wrote two partsongs to texts by Unger: in January 1818 'Die Geselligkeit' (D609), and in April 1821 an earlier 'Die Nachtigall' (D724). The latter was encored at its first performance at the Kärntnertor-Theater on 22 April 1821. Its reappearance on the programme of several other concerts during the following years testifies to its popularity.

Settings: D609, 724.
(Wurzbach[1])

Unger [Ungher, Unger-Sabatier], **Karoline** [Caroline, Carolina, Carlotta] (b. Stuhlweissenburg [Székesfehérvár, Hungary], 28 October 1803; d. Florence, 23 March
1877). Contralto; daughter of Johann Karl Unger.* She studied with Mozart's sister-
in-law Aloisia Lange, Antonio Salieri,* and Johann Michael Vogl.* She was engaged
at the Kärntnertor-Theater in January 1821, having already made a certain name for
herself in concerts; on 19 November 1819, for instance, she sang a duet from
Rossini's *Aureliano in Palmira* with Sophie Linhart at an 'evening entertainment'
of the Gesellschaft der Musikfreunde. On 7 May 1824, at the Kärntnertor-Theater,
she took part in the first performance of Beethoven's* Ninth Symphony.

In 1825 she left for Italy, where she performed for several years, at Naples, Milan,
and various other cities. In 1833–4 she sang in Paris, in 1837–40 in Vienna, and in
1840–2 at Dresden. She was as much admired for the beauty of her voice as for the
artistry with which she used it. In 1843, two years after her marriage to the French
writer François Sabatier, she retired from the stage and thereafter resided at
Florence.

She has the distinction of being the only singer known to have been coached by
Schubert, namely in 1821 for the role of Isabella [Dorabella] which she was to
assume in the opera *Mädchentreue*, a German version by Georg Friedrich Treitschke
of Mozart's *Così fan tutte*, at the court theatre; for his efforts Schubert received 50
gulden. Later Unger became an outstanding interpreter of his Lieder. The poet
Nikolaus Lenau, to whom she was briefly engaged, described her performances of
'Gretchen am Spinnrade' (D118) and 'Der Wanderer' (D489) as 'a vocal storm of
passion'. The French tenor Adolphe Nourrit,* who met her in Venice in 1838, told
his wife that she was 'a distinguished artist, lacking neither in wit nor education'
and a person 'who had been brought up to revere Schubert'.

(Hellmann-Stojan[3], *New Opera Grove*, Quichérat)

Uz, Johann Peter (b. Ansbach, 3 October 1720; d. Ansbach, 12 May 1796). Civil
servant; poet. Having studied law at Halle (1739–43), he later held various legal
posts in the civil service at Ansbach and Nuremberg, reaching the rank of Geheimer
Justizrat.

Like his fellow students at Halle, Johann Wilhelm Ludwig Gleim and Johann
Nikolaus Götz, Uz became best known for his Anacreontic poetry in praise of wine,
women, and song. His first volume of poems, *Lyrische Gedichte* (1749), was reissued
in an augmented edition (*Lyrische und andere Gedichte*) in 1755; later collections
appeared under the titles *Poetische Werke* (1768) and *Sämmtliche Poetische Werke*
(1772). A man of very wide interests which embraced history, philosophy, theology,
literary history, and philology, in addition to poetry and the law, he assembled a
personal library of some 5,000 books.

In 1816, Schubert set six of his poems in the songs 'An Chloen' (D363), 'Der gute
Hirt' (D449), 'Die Liebesgötter' (D446), 'Die Nacht' (D358), and 'Gott im Frühlinge' (D448), and the partsong 'An die Sonne' (D439). Later (?1827) he composed

the partsongs 'Gott im Ungewitter' (D985) and 'Gott der Weltschöpfer' (D986) to two other poems by Uz.

Settings: D358, 363, 439, 446, 448–9, 985–6.
(Porhansl[5], Verweyen/Witting)

Vering, Josef von (b. 1793; d. Vienna, 24 March 1862). Physician. Son of Dr Gerhard von Vering (1755–1823), who was born at Oesede (near Osnabrück), moved to Vienna not later than 1775, and enjoyed a long and distinguished career as a senior medical officer in the Austrian army; he retired in 1822. Josef qualified as a doctor in Vienna in 1816. He became a specialist in the treatment of syphilis, ear ailments, scrofula, and gout. His publications include *Über die Heilung der Lust-seuche durch Quecksilbereinreibungen* (1821), *Syphilo-Therapie* (1826), *Heilung der Skrophelkrankheit* (1829), and *Heilart der Gicht* (1832).

Vering took over as Schubert's doctor in mid-November 1828 from Dr Rinna von Sarenbach,* who had fallen ill. On 16 November he examined the composer together with Dr Johann Baptist Wisgrill, a professor of surgery who had been a court choirboy with Schubert at the Stadtkonvikt in 1808–11. As a result of the consultation, the treatment appears to have been slightly modified, but to no avail. Schubert died three days later.

Vering's sister Julie married Beethoven's* childhood friend Stefan von Breuning. After her death in 1809 Breuning married Konstanze Ruschowitz. Their son Gerhard published, in the Vienna *Neue freie Presse* on 19 and 20 November 1884, an account of conversations he had had with Anna Fröhlich* and Katharina Fröhlich* about Grillparzer* and Schubert ('Aus Grillparzers Wohnung'). His article 'Die Schädel Beethovens und Schuberts', in which he discussed the findings made on the occasion of the exhumation of their remains in 1863 (*see* Hellmesberger*), appeared in the same newspaper on 17 September 1886.

(*Lexikon der Ärzte*, Wurzbach[1])

Vesque von Püttlingen, Johann, Baron [pseud. J. Hoven] (b. Opole, Poland, 23 July 1803; d. Vienna, 30 October 1883). Civil servant; composer. Like his father, also named Johann (1760–1829), who became director of the court library, he studied law and spent his life in government service, rising to the rank of head of depart-ment in the foreign ministry. He was accorded the title Hofrat in 1847 and made a baron in 1866; he retired in 1872.

His music teachers included Moscheles, Sechter,* and Voříšek.* As a composer, he concentrated almost entirely on operas and songs, writing nine of the former and some three hundred of the latter. While he had only very limited success with his operas, he won general praise as a composer of Lieder: 'His name surpasses almost all others in this category,' a Viennese critic, J. N. Hofzinser, declared in 1841, placing him among the very few contemporary musicians who approached Schu-bert's excellence in that genre. His reputation has endured to this day and he is generally considered the outstanding Austrian composer of Lieder between Schubert and Hugo Wolf. In 1851 he published *Die Heimkehr*, a collection of settings of poems from Heine's* *Reisebilder*. He also contributed to Vienna's musical life in other ways; in 1862–3 he served as vice-president of the Gesellschaft der Musikfreunde.

Vesque was on friendly terms with Schubert. In a letter to C. von Wurzbach on 15 November 1876, he recalled that in the summer of 1827 he would, on Tuesday afternoons, accompany Schubert to Johann Michael Vogl's* lodgings in the Wieden suburb. On these occasions Vogl used to sing Schubert songs, and Vesque would sometimes perform one of them himself, accompanied by Schubert. He was still in contact with both men the following year, for he wrote in his diary on 5 March 1828: 'Evening party with Vogl, Schubert, and Grillparzer*', but did not indicate where the soirée had taken place (perhaps, as O. E. Deutsch* suggests, in his father's rooms in the imperial palace). Vesque admired Schubert's songs and was influenced by them in his own Lieder. His twin interests in music and the law led him to write a book on musical copyright, *Das musikalische Autorrecht* (1864).

(Brusatti, Sietz[1,2], Wurzbach[1])

Vitrorelli, Jacopo Andrea (b. Bassano, Venetia, 10 November 1749; d. Bassano [?Milan], 12 June 1835). Poet. He lived for some years in Venice (1787–97) and later at Padua (1809–14), where he was in charge of the Ginnasio di S. Giustina. From 1816 he was employed as a book censor by the Austrian government.

He wrote a great deal of occasional verse, much of it in a burlesque or satirical vein, and, in his later years, some devotional poetry; but his greatest success came with the publication of the *Anacreontiche a Irene* in 1815. No fewer than twenty-nine editions were printed by 1825, and the poems were translated into German (by Franz Sachse) and Latin (by Francesco Filippi and Giuseppe Trivellato). They attracted a number of composers, among them the young Giuseppe Verdi who set 'Non t'accostar all'urna' in 1830, and Schubert who, in 1820, set the same poem and also 'Guarda, che bianca luna', probably for Franziska Roner von Ehrenwerth (*see* Spaun*). The two songs (D688/1–2) were first published by J. P. Gotthard* in 1871. Since the autograph in which they appear also contains settings of two texts known to have been written by Metastasio (D688/3–4), the words of D688/1–2 used likewise to be attributed to that poet until Vittorelli was identified as their author by the Norwegian bass and Schubert scholar Odd Udbye (see *Schubert: Thematisches Verzeichnis*, p. 401).

Settings: D688/1–2.
(*GDEU*, Wurzbach[1])

Vogl, Johann Michael (b. Ennsdorf, near Steyr, Upper Austria, 10 August 1768; d. Vienna, 20 November 1840). Baritone. Nothing is known about his family other than that his father was a grocer and also had some (ill-defined) connection with ships. Vogl lost both parents at an early age and was brought up by an uncle. The exceptional quality of his voice attracted attention when he was still a boy, and, as a result, he sang in the choir of his parish church and received some musical training. At Kremsmünster School, which he attended from 1781, he became friendly with his fellow pupil Franz Xaver Süssmayr, the future composer and friend of Mozart. It was Süssmayr who, several years later when both had moved to Vienna and Vogl had completed his law studies at the university, encouraged him to switch to a musical career. On 1 May 1794 Vogl took up an engagement with the court Opera company, of which he was to remain a member for twenty-eight years.

He reportedly made his operatic début as Korporal Hagel in the comic opera *Die gute Mutter* by Paul Wranitzky. This work was first produced at the Kärntnertor-Theater on 11 May 1795 and received five more performances over the following four weeks. Even if it should be true that he thus had to wait more than a year for his first solo role, it is worth noting that he sang the part of Publio in a concert performance of *La clemenza di Tito* which was arranged by Constanze Mozart in Vienna on 31 March 1795. (It is not known whether he had already sung the part in the concert performance of the same opera at the Kärntnertor-Theater on 29 December 1794.) Intelligent, well educated, endowed with a beautiful voice, and possessing an impressive stage presence, he soon established himself as a leading singer who excelled equally in German and Italian opera. Among his most successful roles were Mikély in Cherubini's *Les Deux Journées* [*Der Wasserträger*], Oreste in Gluck's *Iphigénie en Tauride*, Dr Berg in Gyrowetz's *Der Augenarzt*, Jacob in Méhul's *Joseph*, Count Almaviva in Mozart's *Le nozze di Figaro*, Télasco in Spontini's *Fernand Cortez*, Sternberg in Josef Weigl's* *Das Waisenhaus*, and Jakob Friburg in the same composer's *Die Schweizerfamilie*. He also sang Pizarro at the première of the 1814 version of *Fidelio*. He retired on a pension in late 1822.

Today he is most famous for his association with Schubert, which was of crucial importance to the latter's career and, at the same time, opened an exciting new chapter in his own. Schubert had been profoundly moved by Vogl's performances when Josef von Spaun* took him to the opera while he was still a pupil at the Stadtkonvikt (in this connection, *see* Milder-Hauptmann* and Spaun*). He finally had an opportunity to make Vogl's personal acquaintance in February or March 1817, when the singer agreed to meet him at Franz von Schober's* apartment [26 Tuchlauben] where Schubert was living at the time. Schober had probably met Vogl through the singer Giuseppe Siboni who had married his sister Ludwiga. Vogl arrived expecting to be unimpressed, but he was quickly captivated by the beauty and originality of Schubert's songs. Within a short time he came to admire them greatly.

The prominent position which he occupied in Viennese musical life enabled him to further Schubert's career significantly by singing his songs at the private functions at which he was always a welcome and admired guest. One important such occasion was a soirée given by Matthäus von Collin* in *c.*1820. In addition, Vogl obtained for

Schubert a commission to write the opera *Die Zwillingsbrüder* (D647) for the Kärntnertor-Theater, and he himself took the parts of the two brothers at the première on 14 June 1820.

While he only very rarely sang Schubert's songs before a wider public, he did so at two important moments in the composer's career, in 1821 and 1828. On 7 March 1821, at the Kärntnertor-Theater, he gave the first public performance of 'Erlkönig' (D328), at a concert arranged by Josef Sonnleithner.* His performance that day undoubtedly helped to establish Schubert's reputation as an exceptionally gifted song composer outside the more limited circle of music lovers who had already come to admire him at private gatherings. The critic of *Der Sammler* reported on 27 March: 'Herr Vogl sang "Erlkönig", a composition by Herr Schubert, which, as a result of earlier performances by Herr Vogl, had been greatly acclaimed and much applauded in private circles. Herr Vogl excels at this kind of musical declamation, and he earned great applause.' Indeed, the song, for which Anselm Hüttenbrenner* played the accompaniment, was encored. And at Schubert's own concert on 26 March 1828, Vogl sang no fewer than five songs, all of them in first performances: 'Der Kreuzzug' (D932), 'Die Allmacht' (D852), 'Die Sterne' (D939), 'Fischerweise' (D881)—apparently substituted for the previously announced 'Der Wanderer an den Mond' (D870)—and 'Fragment aus dem Aeschylus' (D450).

At the same time, there is evidence that Vogl continued throughout most of the 1820s to sing Schubert songs at private gatherings; in particular, he took part in various Schubertiads given by Karl von Enderes,* Spaun, Josef Wilhelm Witteczek,* and other members of Schubert's circle. 'Vogl is here, and has sung once at Bruchmann's* and once at Witzeck's [Witteczek's],' Schubert wrote to Schober from Vienna on 30 November 1823. 'He spends almost all his time studying my songs, writes out the voice-part for himself, and his whole life revolves, as it were, around them.' Vogl was invited to lunch, together with Schubert, by Sophie Müller* on 24 February 1825 and afterwards sang Schubert songs, as he also did on later visits; and at Spaun's, on 15 December 1826, he performed close to thirty of them. After Schubert's death, he gave first performances of 'Aufenthalt' (D957/5) and 'Die Taubenpost' (D965A) at the memorial concert on 30 January 1829. In 1834, when already well into his sixties, he sang 'Erlkönig' at a public concert; and a year before his death, at Enderes's, he sang the entire *Winterreise* (D911).

Vogl was still in his prime as a singer when he met Schubert, and revered in Vienna as 'our master of declamatory singing' (*Allgemeine musikalische Zeitung*, 21 March 1821). Spaun wrote in 1864: 'There are only a few persons still living who enjoyed the experience of hearing Vogl sing, but those few will never forget the impression he made. They have not heard anything like it since.' (For a further eloquent tribute by Spaun, *see* Schönstein.*) But if most of Vogl's contemporaries were full of praise for his performances of Schubert songs, some found his renditions excessively dramatic, and later writers tended to be more critical of his use of embellishments (which he recorded in his notebooks, of which a copy has survived); it was even alleged that he exercised a harmful influence in this respect on Schubert's compositional style.

However, Spaun, for one, firmly rejected the first charge, declaring that the theatrical manner of Vogl's performance produced a more powerful effect in the case of many songs, and that, moreover, thanks to his very sensitive and intelligent interpretation of the text, Vogl was able to arouse interest not only in the music, but also in the words. As far as Vogl's embellishments are concerned, it has been convincingly demonstrated by Walther Dürr (in the periodical *19th Century Music* in 1979) that a singer's recourse to 'non-essential' ornamentation (i.e. that not prescribed by the composer) was a practice widely adopted and generally accepted in Schubert's day, and that the convention thus constitutes one of those 'forgotten rules of performance, without which our understanding of what a Schubert song meant in his lifetime remains incomplete'. (For that reason, Vogl's versions of the songs have been printed in the appendices to the Lieder in the new collected edition.) Schubert himself evidently liked Vogl's interpretations of his songs, since he wrote to his brother Ferdinand* on 12 September 1825, following a visit with Vogl to Salzburg: 'The manner in which Vogl sings and I accompany, the way in which we seem, at such a moment, to become *one*, is something quite new and unheard of for these people.' Lastly, regarding the allegation that Vogl may have influenced Schubert's style of composition, Spaun dismissed it as 'completely false': 'No one ever exercised the slightest influence on his manner of composing... At the most he may have made a few concessions out of consideration for Vogl's vocal range, but even those only rarely and reluctantly.'

Later, however, particularly during the final period of his life, Vogl sought to compensate for the declining power and quality of his voice by resorting to less musical means such as cries and falsetto, and his performances were increasingly characterized by a certain affectation. Writing to Ferdinand Luib* in 1857, Leopold von Sonnleithner* remarked that Schubert would certainly not have approved of Vogl's singing during the last years of his life.

There is every indication that, on a personal level, Schubert enjoyed a very pleasant relationship with Vogl, which is especially remarkable in view of the latter's thirty-year seniority and the great difference in their artistic and social standing in Vienna at the time they met. On three occasions—in 1819, 1823, and 1825—Schubert spent vacations in Upper Austria in Vogl's company. During the first journey, while staying at Steyr, he composed a cantata (D666) to celebrate Vogl's birthday and joined in its performance (*see* Koller* and Albert Stadler*). In August 1821 he dedicated to Vogl his Op. 6, consisting of the songs 'Am Grabe Anselmos' (D504), 'Antigone und Oedip' (D542), and 'Memnon' (D541). Only in 1822 was there a period of strain between them, which was apparently related to Schubert's unsuccessful efforts to secure a production at the court Opera of *Alfonso und Estrella* (D732), for which Schober had written the libretto. On 20 July 1822 Anton von Spaun, Josef's brother, wrote to his wife from Vienna: 'Vogl is very incensed at

Schober, for whose sake Schubert has behaved most ungratefully towards Vogl...
Vogl also says that Schober's libretto is bad and a complete failure, and that
Schubert is altogether on the wrong track.' However, by December Schubert was
able to inform Josef von Spaun that he was once more on amicable terms with Vogl
'now that he has left the theatre and I no longer feel embarrassed in that respect'.

Vogl was extremely well read. During the last years of his life, when he suffered
from gout, he derived considerable comfort from Montaigne's *Essays*; other favourite authors were Epictetus and Marcus Aurelius. He was also a composer, with at
least three Masses and a number of songs and arias to his credit.

In 1826, shortly before his fifty-eighth birthday, he married Kunigunde Rosa (b.
1795; d. after May 1868), whose father, the painter Josef Rosa [Roos], had been
custodian of paintings at Belvedere Palace. The couple had a daughter, Henriette.

(Dürr¹, Hadamowsky, Liess, Michtner)

Voříšek, Jan Václav [Worzischek, Johann Hugo] (b. Wamberg [Vamberk, Czech
Republic], 11 May 1791; d. Vienna, 19 November 1825). Composer, pianist, and
violinist. Taught by his father, Václav Voříšek (*c.*1749–1815), a schoolmaster and
organist, he became a child virtuoso on the piano. Later he studied philosophy
and law at the University of Prague (1810–13), while continuing to give concerts and
studying composition with Václav Jan Křtitel Tomášek.

In 1813 he moved to Vienna where he later completed his law studies and briefly
worked as a clerk in the navy department of the war office under Raphael Georg
Kiesewetter,* in whose salon he was able to satisfy his love of music by directing
some of the amateur concerts regularly held there. He also became a frequent visitor
to Ignaz von Sonnleithner's* salon, and it was apparently there that he met
Schubert. In addition, he performed repeatedly in public as pianist and violinist,
and in 1819 he conducted two concerts of the Gesellschaft der Musikfreunde. In
1822 he was appointed assistant court organist, and in 1823 succeeded Wenzel
Růžička* as court organist. When it became apparent in the late summer of 1825
that he did not have long to live, Moritz von Schwind* urged Schubert to apply for
the post as soon as it was declared vacant. In the event, there was no public
announcement; the position was filled internally, by the promotion of the assistant
organist Simon Sechter.*

In addition to church music, Voříšek composed a number of orchestral pieces, all
of which included a part for the piano, with the exception of the Symphony, Op. 24
(performed at concerts of the Gesellschaft der Musikfreunde on 23 February 1823
and 13 December 1829). He also wrote works for the solo piano, some chamber
music, and sixteen songs which were heavily indebted to Schubert. On the other
hand, Schubert himself was influenced by Voříšek, and through him also by
Tomášek, in the shorter lyrical piano pieces in ternary form which he entitled
'Impromptus' and '*Moments musicaux*'. By 1827, the year in which Schubert
composed his Impromptus (D899, D935), Tomášek had published some ten sets

of Eclogues, Rhapsodies, and Dithyrambs; Voříšek's Impromptus, Op. 7, had appeared in Vienna in 1822.

(Simpson, Stedron)

Walcher von Uysdael, Ferdinand (1799–1873). Civil servant. He was born at Waidhofen an der Ybbs, Lower Austria, qualified as a lawyer, and was subsequently employed in the navy section of the war office. He joined Schubert's circle in *c.*1826, probably as a result of his friendship with Franz and Fritz von Hartmann;* by early 1827 he was on intimate terms with Schubert. He was himself a fine singer, with a low tenor voice. Franz von Hartmann recalled in his family chronicle that when he and his brother had visited Walcher at his lodgings on 12 January 1827, he 'sang for us Schubert's "Drang in die Ferne" (D770) and "Auf dem Wasser zu singen" (D774) most beautifully'.

When Walcher was posted to Venice in May 1827, Schubert wrote the Allegretto in C minor for piano (D915) in his album, with the accompanying words 'To my dear friend Walcher, for remembrance'. Since this is the only known autograph of the work, which was not published in Schubert's lifetime, it may be assumed that it was specially composed for Walcher. The latter does not appear to have remained in Venice very long, for, according to Anna Fröhlich's* later recollections, he was present at the first semi-public performance of 'Ständchen' (D920) at an 'evening entertainment' of the Gesellschaft der Musikfreunde on 24 January 1828, and even had to fetch Schubert, who had forgotten all about the concert, from a nearby beer cellar.

Walcher later had a distinguished career, holding senior administrative positions under Archduke Karl, and subsequently under his son, Archduke Albrecht. For his services, he was granted the title Hofrat.

Waldmüller, Ferdinand Georg (b. Vienna, 15 January 1793; d. Hinterbrühl, near Mödling, Lower Austria, 23 August 1865). Painter, often called the greatest exponent of Viennese Biedermeier. His enormous output comprises above all landscapes, genre paintings, and portraits, including famous ones of Beethoven* (1823) and Grillparzer* (1844).

In his book *Hundert Jahre Kunstgeschichte Wiens 1788–1888* (Vienna, 1888), C. Bodenstein stated that Waldmüller had been in contact with Schubert and his circle. However, firm evidence of this association only came to light in the late 1970s, as a result of the discovery of a drawing in a sketchbook used by the painter in 1827 and now preserved in the Albertina collection of graphic art in Vienna. The drawing shows Schubert and Josefine Fröhlich* seated at the piano (it is not clear whether only Josefine or both are actually playing), with Johann Michael Vogl* standing behind them. All three are singing; three other persons are shown listening to them. Since the drawing appears among the last pages of the sketchbook and was therefore probably executed in late 1827, O. Biba has suggested (*Österreichische Musikzeitung*, 1978) that it may depict the first or a later performance of 'Der

Hochzeitsbraten' (D930), a trio for soprano, tenor, and bass, which Schubert composed in November 1827 to a text by Franz von Schober.* The three listeners have been tentatively identified as Grillparzer, Franz Paul Lachner,* and the landscape painter and violinist Ludwig Kraissl. The drawing was shown at the Schubert exhibition arranged by the Gesellschaft der Musikfreunde in Vienna in 1978 and is described and reproduced in the catalogue.

(*ALBK*, Biba¹, Bodenstock, Hilmar/Brusatti)

Watteroth, Heinrich Josef (b. Worbis, near Kassel, 17 November 1756; d. Vienna, 13 August 1819). He studied law at Erfurt and Göttingen, before settling in Vienna in 1777. After taking courses on a variety of subjects at the university and obtaining his doctorate in law, he taught statistics at the Theresian Academy (1783–6). Subsequently he lectured at Vienna University on history, statistics, political science, and law, eventually concentrating in his teaching on the last two subjects. He wrote extensively on various topics, but his enlightened ideas were viewed with some suspicion by the church. His students included Ignaz Franz Castelli,* Franz Grillparzer,* Anselm Hüttenbrenner,* Johann Mayrhofer,* Baron Schlechta,* Leopold von Sonnleithner,* Josef von Spaun,* Albert Stadler,* and Josef Wilhelm Witteczek.* Spaun later described him as a 'very popular teacher', and Castelli wrote in his memoirs of the 'unforgettable Professor Watteroth, the friend, the father of us all'. He and his wife Anna occupied a spacious house, with a fine garden, in the Landstrasse suburb [17 Erdbergstrasse]. Mayrhofer, Spaun, and Witteczek (who later married Watteroth's daughter Wilhelmine) lived there for a time, as Schubert may have done, briefly, in the spring of 1816. He is believed to have composed the six Écossaises (D421) there.

Watteroth was a great music lover and gave musical soirées, at which Schubert was a frequent guest. Schubert also owed his first commission indirectly to Watteroth, as he recorded in his diary on 17 June 1816: 'Today I have for the first time composed for money.' He had been asked to provide the music for a cantata, *Prometheus*, which some students of Watteroth's wished to perform in honour of his name day on 12 July; the text was supplied by one of them, Philipp Dräxler [later Dräxler von Carin]. Rehearsals were held in the consistorial hall at the university. Owing to inclement weather, the performance of the cantata (D451), which was to be given in Watteroth's garden, had to be postponed until 24 July, when Schubert himself conducted.

All that is known about *Prometheus*, about its performance at Watteroth's, and about the history of the autograph (of which all trace has been lost since 1828) derives from the following sources: an appeal for information regarding the whereabouts of the autograph, published by Aloys Fuchs* in the *Allgemeine Wiener Musikzeitung* on 14 July 1842; two letters from Leopold von Sonnleithner to Ferdinand Luib,* dated 1 November 1857 and 5 March 1858 (these formed the basis for Kreissle's* remarks about the work in his Schubert biography); and an appeal for news of the autograph published by Leopold von Sonnleithner in Leopold Alexander Zellner's *Blätter für Theater, Musik und bildende Kunst* in Vienna on 5 March 1867 (this appeal was also issued separately). All the above texts are printed in *Schubert: Erinnerungen.*

(Deutsch[1], Wurzbach[1])

Weber, Carl Maria (Friedrich Ernst) von (b. Eutin, ?18 November 1786; d. London, 5 June 1826). Composer, conductor, and pianist. He arrived in Vienna in mid-February 1822 to conduct some performances of *Der Freischütz,* which had been in the repertoire of the Kärntnertor-Theater since the previous November. During his stay he met Schubert, who, according to Josef von Spaun,* felt great admiration for that work.

Since Schubert is known to have completed his opera *Alfonso und Estrella* (D732) on 27 February, it is more than likely that he spoke about it to Weber, perhaps with a view to having it performed at Dresden where Weber was then music director, even though Schubert's main hope at this time was for a production in Vienna. There was some correspondence about the opera the following autumn between Schubert (or Josef Hüttenbrenner,* acting on his behalf) and Weber, and on 7 December 1822 Schubert was able to inform Spaun that Weber had sent 'a very promising letter'. When Wilhelmine Schröder, who had been appearing at the Kärntnertor-Theater (and had sung Agathe there under Weber in March 1822), arrived in Dresden early in 1823 to take up a contract at the court theatre, she is reported to have delivered the libretto of *Alfonso und Estrella* to Weber; the score was to follow later (*see also* Mosel*).

These various efforts had still not borne fruit when Weber returned to Vienna in September 1823 to prepare the première of *Euryanthe* (25 October). The opera appears to have been the cause of a cooling-off in Weber's relations with Schubert, although there are differing accounts of what passed between them. Max Maria von Weber states in his biography of his father that Schubert launched into a lengthy and violent criticism of the opera before others in Sigmund Anton Steiner's art and music shop, and that his remarks, when repeated to Weber, led to a rift in their relations. This account was rejected by Spaun as alleging behaviour incompatible with Schubert's modest and retiring nature. Spaun's own account is probably more trustworthy, for his recollections of Schubert's activities are generally reliable; moreover, in this particular instance, he stresses that he was told the details by Schubert himself. In his version of the events, Schubert called on Weber on the day after the première, and, when asked for his opinion, replied that while he liked much of *Euryanthe,* he preferred *Der Freischütz,* since the new opera seemed to him lacking in tunefulness. To this honest, if hardly diplomatic, reply Weber is said to have reacted coldly.

On the other hand, O. E. Deutsch* doubts all the accounts of a supposed falling-out between the two composers over *Euryanthe,* since both are known to have been in a small group of persons who went to inspect a new type of piano on 28 October, three days after the première. Deutsch's argument hardly seems conclusive, and Spaun's account reads persuasively enough. In any case, whatever the accuracy of the various stories, it is certain that Schubert did not think very highly of the opera, for he wrote to Franz von Schober* on 30 November: 'Weber's *Euryanthe* turned out wretchedly and its poor reception was, in my view, quite justified.' (*See also* Keppen.*)

Alfonso und Estrella was not produced in Dresden and had to wait for its première until 24 June 1854, when it was conducted by Liszt* at Weimar.

Weigl, Josef (b. Eisenstadt, 28 March 1766; d. Vienna, 3 February 1846). Composer. Son of the cellist Josef (Franz) Weigl (1740–1820) and the soprano (Anna Maria) Josefa Weigl, née Scheffstoss; brother of Thaddäus Weigl.* A pupil of Antonio Salieri,* Weigl wrote more than thirty operas and composed music for several ballets, cantatas, and sacred works. He was appointed deputy Kapellmeister at the court theatre in 1790, and Kapellmeister two years later. In 1804 he became director of music for both German and Italian opera.

Josef von Spaun,* who took Schubert to hear his first operas while he was still at the Stadtkonvikt, later recalled that Schubert had been greatly impressed by Weigl's *Das Waisenhaus* and *Die Schweizerfamilie.* When Schubert learned in January 1827 that the post of deputy court Kapellmeister, for which he had applied, had been assigned to Weigl, he remarked (according to his brother Ferdinand*): 'Since it has been given to as worthy a man as Weigl, I have no reason to complain.' It is true that, in a letter to Anselm Hüttenbrenner* on 19 May 1819, Schubert, disappointed in his hopes for an early production of his recently completed opera *Die Zwillings-brüder* (D647), had put the blame for his failure on the 'scoundrels' ('Canaillen') Weigl and Georg Friedrich Treitschke (a librettist and producer at the Kärntnertor-Theater). But Spaun was no doubt right in his later explanation that this was no more than the expression of intense, but passing, frustration, and that Schubert really had a very high regard for Weigl. (Schubert's opera was produced at the Kärntnertor-Theater on 14 June of the following year.)

(Angermüller[1])

Weigl, Thaddäus (b. Vienna, 8 April 1776; d. Vienna, 29 February 1844). Composer, conductor, and publisher; brother of Josef Weigl.* A pupil of Johann Georg Albrechtsberger, he worked from 1795 as an arranger for the new music publishing house established at the court theatre. In 1803 he became deputy Kapellmeister at the Kärntnertor-Theater and in 1806 he was appointed resident composer at that theatre. Between 1799 and 1805, he had five operettas and fifteen ballets performed there. Later he decided to devote all his time to the publishing firm he had founded in 1803, which specialized in music of his Viennese contemporaries. The firm went bankrupt in 1831. It was taken over by Anton Diabelli & Co.*

Between April 1826 and August 1828, Weigl published first editions of fourteen songs and the *Divertissement sur des motifs originaux français* for piano duet (D823) by Schubert. The songs included 'An den Mond' (D193), 'An die Musik' (D547), 'Des Mädchens Klage' (D191), 'Um Mitternacht' (D862), and the four Refrainlieder 'Bei dir allein', 'Die Männer sind méchant', 'Die Unterscheidung', and 'Irdisches Glück' (D866/1–4). After Schubert's death, Weigl issued the first edition of 'Das Echo' (D990C), in July 1830.

First editions: D191, 193, 312, 547, 595, 633–4, 823, 856, 862, 866, 990C.

(Angermüller[2])

Weintridt, Vincentius (1778–1849). Professor of theology at the University of Vienna. Among his students were Moritz von Schwind* and Eduard von Bauernfeld,* who both had great respect and affection for him. A somewhat unorthodox but inspiring teacher—Bauernfeld described him as 'a secular priest, but also a man of the world'—he was regarded with suspicion by his Catholic superiors, who accused him of expounding radical ideas in his lectures and exercising a bad moral influence on his students. As a result, he was relieved of his post in 1820. Four years later he became a deacon in the small town of Retz, some 80 km. north-west of Vienna. In 1843 he was given another eccleciastical appointment at Nikolsburg [Mikulov, Czech Republic]. He died there a few years later.

On 22 January 1822 Schwind took Schubert to a party at Weintridt's, who was then living in Schenkenstrasse [8 Bankgasse] in Vienna. At the party, Schubert sang some of his songs. The event is of interest since Bauernfeld was among the guests; however, they did not become close friends until some years later. In April 1825, Bauernfeld and Schwind went to stay with Weintridt for a week at Retz. According to Bauernfeld, the 'witty *bon vivant*' was feeling out of his element in that '*ultima Thule* on the Moravian border'. A grand Schubertiad was held in celebration of their visit, which was attended by 'friends, musicians, and painters'.

(Bauernfeld[2], Wurzbach[1])

Weisse, Maximilian von (b. Ladendorf, Lower Austria, 16 October 1798; d. Wels, Upper Austria, 10 October 1863). He was admitted to the Stadtkonvikt, Vienna, as an alto boy chorister in 1808, at the same time as Schubert was accepted as a soprano. During his studies there he was repeatedly reprimanded for lack of application, but he evidently made up for it later, for he became a distinguished scientist. Although he qualified as a lawyer in 1822, he opted for a career in astronomy. After working as an assistant at the Vienna observatory (1823–5), he was appointed professor of astronomy and director of the observatory at Cracow. He published a number of scientific studies in German, Latin, and Polish, and became a corresponding member of the Royal Astronomical Society in London (1848) and of the Academy of Sciences in Vienna (1849); he was ennobled in 1855. He retired in 1861.

In a letter to Ferdinand Luib* on 13 December 1857, he mentioned that while they were both at the Konvikt, Schubert had composed an overture for him, and that, at a later date, Schubert had asked to borrow the manuscript, so that he could orchestrate what was evidently a piano score. According to Weisse, Schubert never returned the autograph, which is lost. The overture has been assigned the work-number D14.

(Günther, Wurzbach[1])

Weissenwolff, Johann Nepomuk Ungnad, Count (b. Vienna, 11 May 1779; d. Linz, 27 April 1855). He served in the army until 1819, was later active in politics, and proved a generous patron of the arts. In 1815 he had married Countess Sophie Gabriele Augusta Breunner-Enkevoirt (b. Copenhagen, 2 May 1794; d. Linz, 23 April 1847). The couple lived at Linz during the winter, and at Castle Steyregg, some 7 km. east of the city, in the summer. They were both highy musical, gave private concerts at their house, and were members of the Linz Gesellschaft der Musikfreunde; from 1837 until his death the count served as the society's president.

Schubert may have been presented to the Weissenwolffs during his stay at Linz in the summer of 1823, for two of his most devoted friends, Albert Stadler* and Josef von Spaun*, were among their acquaintances. They were, in any case, familiar with his music a few months later, for Franz von Hartmann* mentions in his family chronicle, in reference to his sister Anna's frequent visits to the Weissenwolffs in early 1824, that Schubert's music 'flourished' at their house. And Karl Haas, a friend of the countess, wrote in a letter to Max Clodi* on 18 June 1824 that he had recently heard her sing 'Schubert's "Müllerlieder" [i.e. *Die schöne Müllerin* (D795)] and his very newest, fantastically beautiful, compositions' so splendidly that 'I believe that only now do I understand the full significance of the Schubertian song'.

Schubert stayed at Steyregg several times in the summer and early autumn of 1825, by himself and together with Johann Michael Vogl* or Stadler. On 25 [?28] July he wrote to his father* and stepmother from Steyr: 'The countess ... is a great admirer of my humble self, has all my songs, and sings some of them quite prettily. The Walter Scott*, songs made such a favourable impression on her that she even made it clear that it would by no means displease her if I were to dedicate them to her.' And Schubert did indeed dedicate the seven Scott settings (D835–9, 843, 846) to the countess when they were published in April 1826.

(Litschauer[3], Weinmann[10], Wurzbach[1])

Werner, [Friedrich Ludwig] **Zacharias** (b. Königsberg, Prussia [Kaliningrad, Russia], 18 November 1768; d. Vienna, 17 January 1823). Dramatist and poet; son of Jacob Friedrich Werner, a highly esteemed professor of history and rhetoric at Königsberg University. He himself studied law at that university and also attended lectures on philosophy given by Immanuel Kant. In 1793 he joined the Prussian civil service, for which he worked in South Prussia, Warsaw, and Berlin until 1806. Thereafter he travelled for several years in Germany and abroad. In April 1810, in the course of a lengthy stay in Rome, he converted to Roman Catholicism, and in June 1814 he was ordained at Aschaffenburg. He subsequently settled in Vienna, where his fiery sermons made a great impression during the Congress. On Sunday, 9 October 1814, he preached at Lichtental parish church (where Schubert's Mass in F major (D105) was performed a week later).

At the beginning of his literary career, Werner published a volume of poetry, *Vermischte Gedichte* (1789). It was, however, as a playwright that he made his mark in the German Romantic movement. He developed a novel kind of historical play in *Die Söhne des Tales* (published in 2 parts, 1803–4), *Das Kreuz an der Ostsee* (1806), and the controversial *Martin Luther, oder Die Weihe der Kraft* (1807). His other historical dramas include *Attila, König der Hunnen* (1808), *Wanda, Königin der Sarmaten* (1810), and *Cunegunde die Heilige, römisch-deutsche Kaiserin* (1815). In *Der vierundzwanzigste Februar* (produced 1810, published 1815) he created a new type of tragedy which came to be known in literary history as 'Schicksalstragödie' ('fate tragedy').

Schubert composed two songs to texts taken from Werner's plays: in January 1817, 'Jagdlied' (D521) from *Wanda, Königin der Sarmaten*, and in 1820, 'Morgenlied' (D685) from *Die Templer auf Zypern*, the first part of *Die Söhne des Tales*. In addition, he set Werner's poem 'Impromptu. In Tharants Ruinen geschrieben', which had been printed in the Leipzig periodical *Die Harfe* in 1815. Of this song (D513A), which opens with the words 'Nur wer die Liebe kennt', only a fragment survives, which has been completed by Reinhard van Hoorickx and was published by him in that form in the July–September 1974 issue of *Mitteilungen des Steirischen Tonkünstlerbundes*.

Settings: D513A, 521, 685.

(Fried, Wurzbach[1])

Willemer, Maria Anna [Marianne] **Katharina Therese von**, née Pirngruber [known as Jung] (b. near Linz, 20 November 1784; d. Frankfurt am Main, 16 December 1860). Actress and poetess; illegitimate daughter of the actress Maria Anna Elisabeth Pirngruber by the actor Georg Wilhelm Jung (d. 1796). In 1798 mother and daughter arrived in Frankfurt as members of a troupe directed by the ballet-master Traub. In *c*.1800 the twice-widowed Johann Jakob Willemer (1760–1838), a banker, Prussian Geheimrat (he was to be ennobled in 1816), and former Frankfurt senator, took Marianne into his house where she was educated with his own children. As part of her education, she received instruction in singing, piano, and guitar. On 27 September 1814 she became Willemer's third wife.

Marianne had been introduced to Goethe* at Wiesbaden in August 1814, and the following summer he spent several weeks at the Willemers' summer residence 'Gerbermühle', outside Frankfurt. During his visit, the 66-year-old poet conceived a profound affection for Marianne, which she returned. He left Frankfurt on 18 September, and later that same month the Willemers called on him briefly at Heidelberg. This was to be Marianne's last meeting with Goethe, but they subsequently corresponded until his death in 1832. Goethe's feelings for Marianne found expression in *Buch Suleika* in his *West-östlicher Divan* (published in 1819), into which, moreover, he inserted several poems from her pen, without, however, identifying their true author. Their mutual love and her role in the composition of the *Divan* were revealed by H. Grimm in his article 'Goethe und Suleika' in the *Preussische Jahrbücher* in 1869; Marianne had told him her secret in 1851.

The two Suleika poems by 'Goethe' which Schubert set in 1821 were among those written by Marianne von Willemer. They form a pair, inasmuch as 'Suleika I' (D720) invokes the East Wind and 'Suleika II' (D717) the West Wind, both of which act as messengers between the lovers. 'Suleika II' ('Ach um deine feuchten Schwingen') was first sung in public in Berlin on 9 June 1825 by Anna Milder-Hauptmann,* to whom the song was dedicated when it was published by Anton Pennauer* in Vienna two months later.

Settings: D717, 720.

(Friedrichs, Kahn, Pyritz, Willemer)

Winkler, Karl Gottfried Theodor [pseud. Theodor Hell] (b. Waldenburg, 9 February 1775; d. Dresden, 24 September 1856). Poet, translator, impresario, and editor. He studied law at Wittenberg, where he met Novalis.* Later he worked for several years as archivist and secretary in the civil service at Dresden. From 1814, he held various posts in the theatre administration of that city. He was supervisor of Italian opera from 1825 to 1832, and in 1841 was appointed deputy director of the court theatre.

His range of literary interests and command of languages are illustrated by the fact that among the works which he translated into German were Byron's poem *Mazeppa*, Camoëns's epic *Os Lusíadas*, and Eugène Scribe's play *Un verre d'eau*. In addition, he published the annuals *Penelope* (1811–48) and *Dramatisches Vergissmein-nicht* (1824–49), and edited the Dresden *Abendzeitung* (1817–43). In 1821 he published a volume of poetry under the title *Lyratöne*. He was a close friend of Weber* and wrote the libretto for the latter's (uncompleted) opera *Die drei Pintos*.

In July 1816, Schubert set one of his poems in the song 'Das Heimweh'.

Setting: D456.

(Hüttel)

Witteczek, Josef Wilhelm (b. 1787; d. Vienna, 10 April 1859). Civil servant. Schubert met him through Josef von Spaun* who shared Witteczek's rooms at Heinrich Josef Watteroth's* house in 1816. Witteczek studied law and subsequently had a successful career in government service; he was accorded the title Hofrat in 1828. He married Watteroth's daughter Wilhelmine (1800–47) in 1819.

He became a fervent admirer of Schubert's music, regularly attended the Schubertiads at Spaun's and also hosted many himself, both before and after the composer's death. Johann Michael Vogl* and Baron Schönstein* regularly performed at his musical soirées. In May 1827 Schubert dedicated to Witteczek his Op. 80, consisting of the songs 'Das Zügenglöcklein' (D871), 'Der Wanderer an den Mond' (D870), and 'Im Freien' (D880).

After Karl Pinterics's* death in 1831, Witteczek acquired his large collection of manuscript copies of Schubert songs. Witteczek very considerably extended the range of the material assembled by Pinterics by collecting printed (mostly first) editions of all Schubert compositions (except symphonies, Masses, and operas) published up to the year 1850, and copies of as yet unpublished ones. In addition, he collected critical reviews of Schubert's works and portraits of his friends and of the interpreters of his music. At his death, he left this splendid collection to Spaun, who, in due course, bequeathed it to the Gesellschaft der Musikfreunde, as Witteczek had desired. It was to prove extremely useful in the preparation of the *Gesamtausgabe* published by Breitkopf & Härtel.*

(Wurzbach¹)

Wolf, Anna [Nanette] **Rosina** (b. Hallstatt, 13 July 1808; d. Gmunden, 16 January 1878). She was the daughter of Johann Nepomuk Wolf (1777–1842) and his wife Therese, née Eigl (1783–1837). The father came from Bohemia, taught at Hallstatt from 1807 to 1811, and then took up a teaching post at Gmunden. In 1842 Nanette married Albert Franziskus Böhm (1818–86), who was likewise a schoolmaster and later became district inspector of schools. Their only child, Albert (1846–1921), had a successful career in the civil service as a lawyer and judge, rising to the rank of Oberlandesgerichtsrat.

Johann Nepomuk Wolf was greatly interested in music and possessed, among other scores, editions of Haydn's oratorios *Die Jahreszeiten* and *Die Schöpfung*. Nanette was a good pianist and sang contralto. During his stay at Gmunden in the summer of 1825 Schubert visited the family several times and played duets with Nanette both at her house and at Baron Schiller's.* Nanette also accompanied Johann Michael Vogl* in Schubert songs and occasionally sang some herself, to her own accompaniment.

Her son left some interesting notes about her contacts with Schubert among his papers; these W. Pauker printed in his book *Lenaus Freundin Nanette Wolf in Gmunden* (Vienna, Leipzig, 1923).

(Pauker)

Zettler, Alois (b. Brünn [Brno], 1778; d. Vienna, 7 November 1828). Civil servant; poet. After studying philosophy at Prague University he was admitted to the Holy Cross order, but left at the end of his probationary year. In 1799 he moved to Vienna. There, from 1801 to 1808, he was employed as instructor at the Oriental

Academy. Subsequently he entered government service, in which he eventually reached the rank of court secretary in the police and censorship department.

Zettler's poems appeared in various Austrian periodicals betweeen 1811 and 1816; they were published in volume form by his friend Christoph Kuffner* in 1836. Schubert set one of them in 'Trinklied: Ihr Freunde und du gold'ner Wein' in April 1815.

Setting: D183.
(Wurzbach[1])

Zumsteeg [Zum Steeg], **Johann Rudolf** (b. Sachsenflur, near Mergentheim, 10 January 1760; d. Stuttgart, 27 January 1802). Composer and conductor. He was educated at the Carlsschule at Stuttgart, studied the cello with Eberhard Malterre and Agostino Poli, and in 1781 became solo cellist in the court orchestra; from 1785 to 1794 he taught music at the Carlsschule. In 1791 he assumed responsibility for German music at the court theatre, and in 1793 succeeded Poli as court Konzertmeister. Unlike his predecessor, he was a great admirer of Mozart and directed the first Stuttgart performances of *Così fan tutte*, *Die Zauberflöte*, and *Don Giovanni*.

His own early operas show the still powerful influence of Nicolò Jommelli, who had reigned over music at Stuttgart from 1754 to 1768, whilst in *Tamira* (1788) he followed the fashion set by Georg Benda's melodramas. In his last three operas, *Die Geisterinsel* (1798), *Das Pfauenfest* (1801), and *Elbondocani* (1803), he ploughed a more independent furrow. He also wrote some instrumental music, as well as sacred works. But he is known above all for his Lieder and ballads, of which he wrote close to three hundred and which were very highly regarded by his contemporaries.

Several of Schubert's friends later recalled the delight which he took in singing Zumsteeg's songs in his youth. He told Josef von Spaun* in 1811 that he found them deeply moving and could 'revel in those songs for days at a time'. Inevitably, he was influenced by them in some of his own early songs, especially when setting poems previously used by Zumsteeg, such as 'Die Erwartung' (D159), 'Hagars Klage' (D5), 'Lied der Liebe' (D109), and 'Ritter Toggenburg' (D397), in all of which 'besides some instances of melodic correspondence, the close connection is traceable in their formal similarities and the choice of key and metre' (G. Maier). However, Schubert's individual style and independent conception of the relation of words and music soon asserted themselves. In a wider sense, though, his early admiration for Zumsteeg is likely to have played a significant part in forming his enduring attachment to the German song.

(Kindermann, Maier)

Bibliography and Abbreviations

❧

Adametz   Adametz, K., *Franz Schubert in der Geschichte des Wiener Männergesang-Vereines* (Vienna, [1938]).

ADB   *Allgemeine deutsche Biographie* (56 vols., Munich, 1875–1912; repr. Berlin, 1967–71).

ALBK   *Allgemeines Lexikon der bildenden Künstler von der Antike bis zur Gegenwart*, begründet von U. Thieme und F. Becker (37 vols., Leipzig, 1907–50; repr. Leipzig, 1970–1).

Alth/Obzyna   Alth, M. von, and Obzyna, G., *Burgtheater 1776–1976: Aufführungen und Besetzungen von zweihundert Jahren* (2 vols., Vienna, n.d.).

Angermüller[1]   Angermüller, R., 'Weigl, Joseph', in *New Grove*.

Angermüller[2]   —— 'Weigl, Thaddäus', in *New Grove*.

Angermüller[3]   —— *Das Salzburger Mozart-Denkmal: Eine Dokumentation (bis 1845) zur 150-Jahre-Enthüllungsfeier* (Salzburg, 1992).

Antonicek[1]   Antonicek, S., 'Assmayr', in *MGG*.

Antonicek[2]   Antonicek, T., 'Castelli', in *MGG*.

Antonicek[3]   —— 'Dietrichstein-Proskau-Leslie', in *MGG*.

Arneth   Arneth, A. von, *Aus meinem Leben* (2 vols., Vienna, 1891–2).

Bach   Bach, A. B., *The Art Ballad: Loewe and Schubert* (Edinburgh, 1890).

Badstüber   Badstüber, H., *Christoph Kuffner, ein vergessener Poet des Vormärz: Ein Beitrag zur österreichischen Literaturgeschichte* (Leipzig, 1907).

Badura-Skoda Badura-Skoda, E., 'Zum Charakterbild Anton Schindlers', *ÖMZ*, 32 (1977), 241–6.

Bauer   Bauer, A., *150 Jahre Theater an der Wien* (Vienna, 1952).

Bauernfeld[1]   Bauernfeld, E. von, *Gesammelte Schriften* (12 vols., Vienna, 1871–3).

Bauernfeld[2]   'Aus Bauernfelds Tagebüchern: I. (1819–1848)', mitgeteilt von C. Glossy, *Jahrbuch der Grillparzer-Gesellschaft*, 5 (1895), pp. vii–217.

Baumann   Baumann, C. C., *Wilhelm Müller, the Poet of the Schubert Song Cycles: His Life and Works* (University Park, Pennsylvania, 1981).

Baumert/Grüll Baumert, H. E., and Grüll, G., *Burgen und Schlösser in Oberösterreich: Salzkammergut und Alpenland* (2nd edn., Vienna, 1983).

Bayne   B[ayne], T[homas Wilson], 'Macdonald, Andrew', *The Dictionary of National Biography*, xii (London, 1893), 474.

Becker   Becker K., *Johann Baptist Jenger (1793–1856): Ein Breisgauer Freund Franz Schuberts* (Bühl, 1978).

Berger[1]   Berger, A., *Das Fürstenhaus Schwarzenberg* (Vienna, 1866).

Berger[2]   Berger, K., *Theodor Körner* (Bielefeld, 1912).

Biba[1]	Biba, O., 'Einige neue und wichtige Schubertiana im Archiv der Gesellschaft der Musikfreunde', *ÖMZ*, 33 (1978), 604–10.
Biba[2]	—— 'Franz Schubert in den musikalischen Abendunterhaltungen der Gesellschaft der Musikfreunde', in *Schubert-Studien*, herausgegeben von F. Grasberger und O. Wessely (Vienna, 1978), 7–31.
Biba[3]	—— *Franz Schubert und seine Zeit: Ausstellung, Archiv der Gesellschaft der Musikfreunde in Wien, 17. Oktober bis 22. Dezember 1978. Katalog* (Vienna, 1978).
Biba[4]	—— 'Franz Schubert und die Gesellschaft der Musikfreunde in Wien', in *Schubert-Kongress Wien 1978: Bericht*, herausgegeben von O. Brusatti (Graz, 1979), 23–36.
Biehler	Biehler, O., 'Aloys Schreiber, 1761–1841: Sein Leben und seine Werke', *Zeitschrift für die Geschichte des Oberrheins*, 55 (1942), 598–675.
Biesterfeld	Biesterfeld, W., 'Tiedge', in *LL*.
Bodendorff[1]	Bodendorff, W., 'Zur Genealogie Michael Holzers', *Schubert Brille*, 9 (1992), 85–9.
Bodendorff[2]	—— 'Friedrich Anton Franz Bertrand: Ein fast vergessener Balladen-Dichter', *Schubert Brille*, 16/17 (1996), 53–8.
Bodenstein	Bodenstein, C., *Hundert Jahre Kunstgeschichte Wiens 1788–1888* (Vienna, 1888).
Branscombe[1]	Branscombe , P., 'Heine', in *New Grove*.
Branscombe[2]	—— 'Kanne', in *New Grove*.
Branscombe[3]	—— 'Klopstock', in *New Grove*.
Branscombe[4]	—— 'Körner', in *New Grove*.
Branscombe[5]	—— 'Kotzebue', in *New Grove*.
Branscombe[6]	—— 'Müller, Wenzel', in *New Grove*.
Branscombe[7]	—— 'Nestroy', in *New Grove*.
Branscombe[8]	—— 'Rückert', in *New Grove*.
Branscombe[9]	—— 'Suppé', in *New Grove*.
Brody	Brody, E., 'Schubert and Sulzer Revisited: A Recapitulation of the Events Leading to Schubert's Setting in Hebrew of Psalm 92, D953', in *Schubert Studies: Problems of Style and Chronology*, ed. E. Badura-Skoda and P. Branscombe (Cambridge, 1982), 47–60.
Brown[1]	Brown, M. J. E., 'A Schubert Text', *Music and Letters*, 33 (1952), 282–4.
Brown[2]	—— 'Some Unpublished Schubert Songs and Song Fragments', *Music Review*, 15 (1954), 93–102.
Brown[3]	—— 'Schubert's Settings of the *Salve Regina*', *Music and Letters*, 37 (1956), 234–49.
Brown[4]	—— *Schubert: A Critical Biography* (London, 1958).
Brown[5]	—— 'Schubert: Discoveries of the Last Decade', *Musical Quarterly*, 47 (1961), 293–314.
Brown[6]	—— *Essays on Schubert* (London, 1966).
Brown[7]	—— 'The Therese Grob Collection of Songs by Schubert', *Music and Letters*, 49 (1968), 122–34.
Brown[8]	—— 'Randhartinger', in *New Grove*.
Brown[9]	—— 'Sechter', in *New Grove*.

Bruchmann	*Franz v. Bruchmann, der Freund J. Ch. Senns und des Grafen Aug. v. Platen: Eine Selbstbiographie aus dem Wiener Schubertkreise, nebst Briefen*, eingeleitet und herausgegeben von M. Enzinger, *Veröffentlichungen des Museum Ferdinandeum* (Innsbruck), 10 (1930), 119–379.
Brusatti	Brusatti, O., *Schubert im Wiener Vormärz: Dokumente 1829–1848* (Graz, 1978).
Budde	Budde, E., 'Berlin und die *Schöne Müllerin*', *ÖMZ*, 46 (1991), 649–58.
Budden	Budden, J., 'Barbaia', in *New Opera Grove*.
Burkhart	Burkhart, F., 'Franz Schubert's *Deutsche Messe*: Schicksale eines berühmten Messliedes', *ÖMZ*, 31 (1976), 565–73.
Capell	Capell, R. *Schubert's Songs* (2nd, rev. edn., London, 1957).
Carner	Carner, M., 'Lanner', in *New Grove*.
Charlton[1]	Charlton, D., 'Staudigl, Joseph (i)', in *New Grove*.
Charlton[2]	—— 'Staudigl, Joseph (ii)', in *New Grove*.
Chézy	*Unvergessenes: Denkwürdigkeiten aus dem Leben der Helmina von Chézy, von ihr selbst erzählt* (2 pts., Leipzig, 1858).
Chochlow	Chochlow, J., 'Neues über Schubert: Aus den Wiener Aufzeichnungen von P. J. Köppen', *Schweizer musikpädagogische Blätter*, 72/3 (Sept. 1984), 93–9.
Chopin	*Frédéric Chopin: Lettres*, recueillies par H. Opienski et traduites par S. Danysz (Paris, 1933).
Clercq[1]	Clercq, R. O. de, 'Skizze des kurzen, überaus fruchtbaren Lebens eines Vergessenen, des einst berühmten und vielgesungenen Dichters und Literaten Wilhelm "Griechen"-Müller . . .', *Vom Pasqualatihaus* (Vienna), 4 (1994), 5–17.
Clercq[2]	—— ' "Tout vous est déjà dédié, pourtant!" Ou l'histoire possible de Franz Schubert et de la comtesse Caroline Esterházy', *Cahiers F. Schubert* (Paris), 4 (1994), 15–33.
Cloeter	Cloeter, H., *Häuser und Menschen von Wien* (Vienna, 1915).
Collin	Collin, M. von, *Nachgelassene Gedichte*, ausgewählt und mit einem biographischen Vorworte begleitet von J. von Hammer (2 vols., Vienna, 1827).
Cone	Cone, E. T., 'Schubert's Beethoven', *Musical Quarterly*, 56 (1970), 779–93.
Cooper	Cooper, B. (ed.), *The Beethoven Compendium: A Guide to Beethoven's Life and Music* (London, 1991).
Cysarz	Cysarz, V., 'Mandyczewski', in *MGG*.
Czeike	Czeike, F., *Historisches Lexikon Wien* (5 vols., Vienna, 1992–6).
Danhelovsky	Danhelovsky, K., 'Graf Ferdinand Troyer, der Schubertmäzen', in *Bericht über den internationalen Kongress für Schubertforschung, Wien, 25. bis 29. November 1928* (Augsburg, 1929), 239–40.
Daunicht	Daunicht, R., 'Chézy', in *MGG*.
Davis	Davis, S., 'Rellstab', in *New Grove*.
Deissinger	Deissinger, H., *Ferdinand Sauter: Sein Leben und Dichten*, herausgegeben, ergänzt . . . von O. Pfeiffer (Vienna, 1926).
Denny	Denny, T. A., 'Wo haben Kupelwieser und Schober ihre Sujets für Schubert gefunden? Eine Neubewertung (*Fierrabras*) und ein Zwischenbericht (*Alfonso und Estrella*)', *Schubert Brille*, 5 (1990), 32–7.

Deutsch[1]   Deutsch, O. E., 'Ein Schuberthaus in Erdberg: Die Wiege der *Prometheus-Kantate*. Mit zum Teil ungedruckten Erinnerungen', *Der Merker*, 10 (1919), 478–89.

Deutsch[2]   —— 'Das k.k. Stadtkonvikt zu Schuberts Zeit', *Die Quelle*, 78 (1928), 477–90.

Deutsch[3]   —— 'Schuberts Verleger', *Der Bär*, 5 (1928), 13–30.

Deutsch[4]   —— 'The Walter Scott Songs', *Music and Letters*, 9 (1928), 330–5.

Deutsch[5]   —— 'Der Liederdichter Reissig', *Neues Beethoven-Jahrbuch*, 6 (1935), 59–65.

Deutsch[6]   —— 'Beethovens Textdichter Reissig', *Anspruch*, 1936/4, 69–71.

Deutsch[7]   —— 'The Riddle of Schubert's Unfinished Symphony', *Music Review*, 1 (1940), 36–53.

Deutsch[8]   —— *Schubert und Grillparzer: Ein Vortrag* (Vienna, 1949). Repr., with some differences, in *ÖMZ*, 32 (1977), 497–505.

Deutsch[9]   —— 'Schubert: The Collected Works', *Music and Letters*, 32 (1951), 226–34.

Deutsch[10] —— 'Rieders Schubert-Bildnis', *ÖMZ*, 14 (1959), 1–3.

Dilgskron   Dilgskron, K., *P. Rudolf v. Smetana: Ein Beitrag zur Geschichte der Congregation des allerheiligsten Erlösers* (Vienna, 1902).

Dove[1]   Dove, R., 'Platen', in *LL*.

Dove[2]   —— 'Rückert', in *LL*.

Dürhammer   Dürhammer, I., 'Schlegel, Schelling und Schubert: Romantische Beziehungen und Bezüge in Schuberts Freundeskreis', *Schubert Brille*, 16/17 (1996), 59–93.

Dürr[1]   Dürr, W., 'Schubert and Johann Michael Vogl: A Reappraisal', *19th Century Music*, 3 (1979–80), 126–40.

Dürr[2]   —— '"Die Grenzen der Kunst möglichst zu erweitern": Beethoven und Schubert', *Schubertiade Hohenems 1988* (programme), 10–30.

EB   *Encyclopaedia Britannica* (24 vols., London, 1960).

Eder   Eder, G., 'Schubert und Caroline Esterházy', *Schubert Brille*, 11 (1993), 6–20.

Ehinger   Ehinger, H., 'Rochlitz', in *MGG*.

Einstein   Einstein, A., *Schubert*, trans. D. Ascoli (London, 1951).

Eisenberg   Eisenberg, L., *Grosses biographisches Lexikon der deutschen Bühne im XIX. Jahrhundert* (Leipzig, 1903).

Eisenhardt   Eisenhardt, G., 'Wilhelm Müllers Komponisten', *Vom Pasqualatihaus* (Vienna), 4 (1994), 27–38.

Enzinger   Enzinger, M., *Die deutsche Tiroler Literatur bis 1900: Ein Abriss* (Vienna, 1929).

Evidon   Evidon, R., 'Hellmesberger', in *New Grove*.

Fechner·   Fechner, J.-U., 'Claudius', in *LL*.

Federhofer   Federhofer, H., 'Hüttenbrenner', in *MGG*.

Feitzinger   Feitzinger-Wolf, A., 'Faust Pachler (C. Paul) als Mensch und als Dichter', *Österreichisches Jahrbuch* (1897), 286–313.

Fellinger   Fellinger, I., 'Kanne', in *MGG*.

Feuchtmüller Feuchtmüller, R., *Leopold Kupelwieser und die Kunst der österreichischen Spätromantik* (Vienna, 1970).

Fischer[1]   Fischer, C., 'Castelli', in *LL*.

Fischer[2] —— 'Craigher de Jachelutta', in *LL*.
Fischer[3] —— 'Deinhardstein', in *LL*.
Fischer[4] —— 'Kuffner', in *LL*.
Fischer[5] —— 'Leitner', in *LL*.
Fischer[6] —— 'Mailáth', in *LL*.
Fischer[7] —— 'Pyrker', in *LL*.
Fischer[8] —— 'Schlechta von Wssehrd', in *LL*.
Fischer[9] —— 'Senn', in *LL*.
Fischer[10] —— 'Stoll', in *LL*.
Fischer-Dieskau Fischer-Dieskau, D., *Auf den Spuren der Schubert-Lieder: Werden, Wesen, Wirkung* (Wiesbaden, 1974).
Fiske Fiske, R., 'Scott, Sir Walter', in *New Grove*.
Forbes[1] Forbes, Elizabeth, 'Milder-Hauptmann', in *New Opera Grove*.
Forbes[2] Forbes, Elliot, 'Rudolph', in *New Grove*.
Forbes[3] —— 'Schindler', in *New Grove*.
Forbes[4] —— 'Schuppanzigh', in *New Grove*.
Franken Franken, F. H., *Die Krankheiten grosser Komponisten* (2 vols., Wilhelms-haven, 1989).
Freeman Freeman, R. N., 'Stadler, Maximilian', in *New Grove*.
Fried Fried, J., 'Werner', in *LL*.
Friedrichs Friedrichs, E., *Die deutschsprachigen Schriftstellerinnen des 18. und 19. Jahr-hunderts: Ein Lexikon* (Stuttgart, 1981).
Fries Fries, A., *Die Grafen von Fries: Eine genealogische Studie* (Dresden, 1903).
Fröhlich 'Briefe von Katharina Fröhlich an ihre Schwestern', mitgeteilt von A. Sauer, *Jahrbuch der Grillparzer-Gesellschaft*, 4 (1894), 81–118.
Fröschle Fröschle, H., 'Uhland', in *LL*.
Fürstenau Fürstenau, 'Lewy', in *ADB*.
Gänzl/Lamb Gänzl, K., and Lamb, A., *Gänzl's Book of the Musical Theatre* (London, 1988).
Garland Garland, H., and Garland, M., *The Oxford Companion to German Literature* (Oxford, 1976).
GDEU *Grande dizionario enciclopedico Utet* (20 vols., Turin, 1966).
Geiringer Geiringer, K., 'Schubert's Arpeggione Sonata and the "Super Arpeggio"', *Musical Quarterly*, 65 (1979), 513–23.
Gibbs Gibbs, C. H., 'Einige Bemerkungen zur Veröffentlichung und zu den frühen Ausgaben von Schuberts "Erlkönig"', *Schubert Brille*, 12 (1994), 33–48.
Goldmann Goldmann, B., 'Gries', in *LL*.
Göltl Göltl, R., *Franz Schubert und Moritz von Schwind: Freundschaft im Bieder-meier* (Munich, 1989).
Gramit[1] Gramit, D., 'The Intellectual and Aesthetic Tenets of Franz Schubert's Circle: Their Development and Their Influence on His Music', Ph.D. diss. (Duke University, NC, 1987).
Gramit[2] —— 'Schuberts "Bildender Umgang": Denken und Ästhetik bei Schuberts Jugendfreunden', *Schubert Brille*, 8 (1992), 5–21.

Grasberger	Grasberger, F., 'Gustav Nottebohm: Verdienste und Schicksal eines Musikgelehrten', *ÖMZ*, 22 (1967), 739–41.
Graves	Graves, C. L., *The Life and Letters of Sir George Grove* (London, 1903).
Grawe	Grawe, C., 'Schütz', in *LL*.
Grillparzer¹	'Aus dem Grillparzer-Archiv: Briefe von und an Grillparzer', herausgegeben von C. Glossy, *Jahrbuch der Grillparzer-Gesellschaft*, 1 (1890), pp. xvii–396.
Grillparzer²	*Briefe und Dokumente*, in *Franz Grillparzer: Sämtliche Werke*, herausgegeben von A. Sauer, fortgeführt von R. Backmann (43 vols., Vienna, 1909–48).
Gruber	Gruber, C. M., *Nicht nur Mozarts Rivalinnen* (Vienna, 1990).
Grun	Grun, B., *Die leichte Muse: Kulturgeschichte der Operette* (Munich, 1961).
Gualerzi	Gualerzi, G., 'Barbaja', in *MGG*.
Guhde	Guhde, E., *Gottlieb Konrad Pfeffel: Ein Beitrag zur Kulturgeschichte des Elsass* (Winterthur, 1964).
Günther	Günther, 'Weisse', in *ADB*.
Haberland	Haberland, D., 'Körner', in *LL*.
Habisreutinger	Habisreutinger, J. M., 'Willemer', in *LL*.
Hackenberg	Hackenberg, J., *Georg Philipp Schmidt von Lübeck: Ein volkstümlicher Lyriker aus der klassischen Zeit* (Hildesheim, 1911).
Hadamowsky	Hadamowsky, F., *Die Wiener Hoftheater (Staatstheater)* ... (2 pts., Vienna, 1966–75).
Haderer	Haderer, F., 'Martin Joseph Prandstetter (1760–1798). Magistratsrat, Freimaurer, Dichter und Jakobiner', Doctoral diss. (University of Vienna, 1968).
Haefs	Haefs, W., 'Kalchberg', in *LL*.
Hamann	Hamann, B., *Die Habsburger: Ein biographisches Lexikon* (Vienna, 1988).
Hammerstein	Hammerstein, R., 'Schubart', in *MGG*.
Hanslick	Hanslick, E., *Geschichte des Concertwesens in Wien* (2 vols., Vienna, 1869–70).
Häntzschel¹	Häntzschel, G., 'Bürger', in *LL*.
Häntzschel²	—— 'Schreiber', in *LL*.
Hartkopf	Hartkopf, W., 'Schubart', in *LL*.
Harvey	Harvey, P., *The Oxford Companion to English Literature* (4th edn., rev. D. Eagle, Oxford, 1967).
Hascher	Hascher, X. A., 'Franz Schubert et la France', *Cahiers F. Schubert* (Paris), 1 (1992), 27–46; 2 (1993), 48–67; 6 (1995), 25–70; 8 (1996), 29–73, 101–2. *See also* Clerco, R. O. de, 'Addendà et corrigenda', 8 (1996), 91–100.
Hase	Hase, O. von, *Breitkopf & Härtel: Gedenkschrift und Arbeitsbericht* (4th edn., 2 vols., Leipzig, 1917–19).
Heck	Heck, T. F., 'Matiegka', in *New Grove*.
Heers	Heers, A., *Das Leben Friedrich von Matthissons* (Leipzig, 1913).
Heiderich	Heiderich, M., 'Kosegarten', in *LL*.
Heim	Heim, K., 'Müller, Wilhelm', in *MGG*.
Hellmann-Stojan¹	Hellmann-Stojan, H., 'Bocklet', in *MGG*.
Hellmann-Stojan²	—— 'Stadler, Maximilian', in *MGG*.
Hellmann-Stojan³	—— 'Unger, Karoline', in *MGG*.
Hellmann-Stojan⁴	—— 'Vogl', in *MGG*.

Herbeck Herbeck, L., *Johann Herbeck: Ein Lebensbild von seinem Sohne Ludwig* (Vienna, 1885).

Hettner Hettner, 'Bürger', in *ADB*.

Heuberger Heuberger, R., *Franz Schubert* (3rd edn., Berlin, 1920).

Heussner Heussner, H., 'Rellstab', in *MGG*.

Hilmar[1] Hilmar, E., 'Ferdinand Schuberts Skizze zu einer Autobiographie', in *Schubert-Studien*, herausgegeben von F. Grasberger und O. Wessely (Vienna, 1978), 85–117.

Hilmar[2] —— 'Eine Wiener Schubert-Gesellschaft und ihre Zielsetzung', in *Studien zur Musikwissenschaft: Beihefte der Denkmäler der Tonkunst in Österreich*, 32 (Tutzing, 1981), 205–14.

Hilmar[3] —— 'Eine unbekannte Komposition von Franz Schubert' *ÖMZ*, 44 (1989), 160–1.

Hilmar[4] —— *Schubert* (Graz, 1989).

Hilmar[5] —— 'Eine Quelle zur Schubert-Sammlung von Nikolaus v. Dumba', *Schubert Brille*, 4 (1990), 18–20.

Hilmar[6] —— 'Kompositionen von Albert Stadler, Schubert-Abschriften u. a. in der Sammlung Leopold Cornaro in Wien', *Schubert Brille*, 5 (1990), 26–30.

Hilmar[7] —— 'Eine Schubert-Miniatur', *Schubert Brille*, 7 (1991), 42–3.

Hilmar[8] —— 'Ein "Geheimes Programm" in den drei wiederentdeckten Manuskripten zum Zyklus *Die schöne Müllerin*?', *Schubert Brille*, 11 (1993), 35–47.

Hilmar[9] —— 'Die musikalischen Vorlagen in Bertés *Dreimäderlhaus*', *Schubert Brille*, 13 (1994), 129–32.

Hilmar[10] —— 'Anmerkungen zu August Wilhelm Rieders Schuber-Portraits', *Schubert Brille*, 15 (1995), 135–6.

Hilmar[11] —— 'Karl Goldmark über den Schubert-Sänger Anton Haizinger d. J.', *Schubert Brille*, 15 (1995), 100–2.

Hilmar/Brusatti *Franz Schubert: Ausstellung der Wiener Stadt-und Landesbibliothek zum 150. Todestag des Komponisten. Katalog* (Vienna, 1978).

Hilmar-Voit Hilmar-Voit, R., 'Zu Schuberts "Letzten Liedern": Einige Zweifel an überlieferten Daten und Fakten', *Schubert Brille*, 6 (1991), 48–55.

Hinske Hinske, N., 'Mendelssohn, Moses', in *LL*.

Holland Holland, H., 'Schober', in *ADB*.

Honolka Honolka, K., *Schubart: Dichter und Musiker, Journalist und Rebell. Sein Leben, sein Werk* (Stuttgart, 1985).

Hoorickx[1] Hoorickx, R. van, 'Schubert's Guitar Quartet', *Revue belge de musicologie*, 31 (1977), 111–35.

Hoorickx[2] —— 'Further Schubert Discoveries', *Music Review*, 39 (1978), 95–9.

Hoorickx[3] —— 'Ferdinand Schuberts "Entlehnungen" aus Werken seines Bruders Franz', *Schubert Brille*, 3 (1989), 13–16.

Hoorickx[4] —— 'Franz und Ferdinand Schubert', *ÖMZ*, 45 (1990), 691–8.

Hörisch Hörisch, J., 'Schlegel, Friedrich von', in *LL*.

Höslinger Höslinger, C., 'Aus den Aufzeichnungen des Freiherrn von Pratobevera', in *Schubert-Studien*, herausgegeben von F. Grasberger und O. Wessely (Vienna, 1978), 119–29.

Huber Huber, M., 'Kind', in *LL*.

Hüttel   Hüttel, W., 'Winkler', in *New Grove*.
Hüttenbrenner   Hüttenbrenner, F., 'Anselm Hüttenbrenner und Schuberts H-moll-Symphonie', *Zeitschrift des historischen Vereines für Steiermark*, 52 (1961), 122–37.
Jackman[1]   Jackmann, J. L., 'Galuppi', in *New Grove*.
Jackman[2]   —— 'Goldoni', in *New Grove*.
Jacobs   Jacobs, A., *Arthur Sullivan: A Victorian Musician* (3rd edn., Oxford, 1992).
Jancik[1]   Jancik, H., 'Blahetka', in *MGG*.
Jancik[2]   —— 'Mosel', in *MGG*.
Jancik[3]   —— 'Rieder, Ambros', in *MGG*.
Jancik[4]   —— 'Schuppanzigh', in *MGG*.
Jancik[5]   —— 'Sonnleitner', in *MGG*.
Jancik/Kahl   ——, and Kahl, W., 'Kreissle von Hellborn', in *MGG*.
Janecka-Jary   Janecka-Jary, F., 'Schubert im österreichischen Stumm- und Tonfilm', *Schubert Brille*, 13 (1994), 109–28.
Jestremski[1]   Jestremski, M., 'Unveröffentliche Dokumente aus dem Nachlass Anselm Hüttenbrenners', *Schubert Brille*, 15 (1995), 94–9.
Jestremski[2]   —— 'Josef Kriehubers Schubert-Lithographien', *Schubert Brille*, 16/17 (1996), 172—80.
Johnson   Johnson, D., 'Nottebohm', in *New Grove*.
Joost[1]   Joost, U., 'Kleist, Ewald Christian von', in *LL*.
Joost[2]   —— 'Matthisson', in *LL*.
Kahl   Kahl, W., 'Diabelli', in *MGG*.
Kahn   Kahn-Wallerstein, C., *Marianne von Willemer: Goethes Suleika und ihre Welt* (Berne, 1961).
Kantner   Kantner, L., 'Anton Diabelli: Ein Salzburger Komponist der Biedermeierzeit', *Mitteilungen der Gesellschaft für Salzburger Landeskunde*, 98 (1958), 51–88.
Keller   Keller, O., *Franz von Suppé: Der Schöpfer der deutschen Operette* (Leipzig, 1905).
Keppen   Keppen, F. P., *Biografija P. I. Keppena* (St Petersburg, 1911).
Kiener   Kiener, H., 'Jaëll', in *MGG*.
Kier   Kier, H., *Raphael Georg Kiesewetter (1773–1850): Wegbereiter des musikalischen Historismus* (Regensburg, 1968).
Kindermann   Kindermann, J., 'Zumsteeg', in *MGG*.
King   King, A. H., 'Deutsch', in *New Grove*.
Kinsey   Kinsey, B., 'Schubert and the Poems of Ossian', *Music Review*, 34 (1973), 22–9.
Klein[1]   Klein, R., 'Schuberts "Kupelwieser-Walzer": Informationen zu einer Überlieferung', *ÖMZ*, 23 (1968), 79–81.
Klein[2]   —— *Schubert-Stätten* (Vienna, 1972).
Klein[3]   —— 'Sensationelle Enthüllung beim Ost-Berliner Beethoven-Kongress', *ÖMZ*, 32 (1977), 202–3.
Köchel   Köchel, L. von, 'Nachruf: Joseph, Freiherr von Spaun, k.k. Hofrath in Pension', *Wiener Zeitung*, 9 Mar. 1866.
Költzsch   Költzsch, H., *Franz Schubert in seinen Klaviersonaten* (Leipzig, 1927).

Konold   Konold, W., *Felix Mendelssohn Bartholdy und seine Zeit* (Laaber, 1984).
Kosch   Kosch, W., *Deutsches Theater-Lexikon: Biographisches und bibliographisches Handbuch* (Klagenfurt, 1953-).
Krackowizer   Krackowizer, F., *Geschichte der Stadt Gmunden in Ober-Österreich* (3 vols., Gmunden, 1898–1900).
Kramer   Kramer, R., 'Schubert's Heine', *19th Century Music*, 8 (1984–5), 213–25.
Kranefuss   Kranefuss, A., 'Hölty', in *LL*.
Krause   Krause, P., 'Unbekannte Dokumente zur Uraufführung von Franz Schuberts grosser C-Dur-Sinfonie durch Felix Mendelssohn Bartholdy', *Beiträge zur Musikwissenschaft* (Berlin), 1987, 240–50.
Kreissle   Kreissle von Hellborn, H., *Franz Schubert* (2 vols., Vienna, 1865).
Kriegleder   Kriegleder, W., 'Ratschky', in *LL*.
Krüger   Krüger, H. A., *Deutsches Literatur-Lexikon: Biographisches und bibliographisches Handbuch mit Motivübersichten und Quellennachweisen* (Munich, 1914).
Kupelwieser   Kupelwieser de Brioni, M. L., *Une grande amitié: F. Schubert et L. Kupelwieser* (Paris, n.d.).
Kupferberg   Kupferberg, H., *The Mendelssohns: Three Generations of Genius* (New York, 1972).
Kürschner   Kürschner, J., 'Haizinger', in *ADB*.
Kusche   Kusche, L., *Franz Schubert* (Munich, 1962).
Kutsch/Riemens   Kutsch, K. J., and Riemens, L., *Grosses Sängerlexikon* (2 vols., Berne, 1987). Supplements in 1991 and 1994.
Lafite   Lafite, C., *Das Schubertlied und seine Sänger* (Vienna, 1928).
La Mara   *Musikerbriefe aus fünf Jahrhunderten* ... herausgegeben von La Mara [Lipsius, Marie] (2 vols., Leipzig, 1886).
Landon   Landon, C., 'Neue Schubert-Funde: Unbekannte Manuskripte im Archiv des Wiener Männergesang-Vereines', *ÖMZ*, 24 (1969), 299–323. Published in English as 'New Schubert Finds', *Music Review*, 31 (1970), 215–31.
Laux   Laux, K., 'Schubert, Dresdner Musiker...', in *MGG*.
Lebensaft   Lebensaft, E., 'Seidl', in *LL*.
Legouvé   Legouvé, E., *Soixante ans de souvenirs* (3 vols., Paris, 1885–7)
Leitgeb   Leitgeb, J., 'Johann Senn (1795–1857)', in *Wort im Gebirge: Schrifttum aus Tirol*, iv (Innsbruck, 1952), 183–214.
Leuchtmann[1]   Leuchtmann, H., 'Lachner', in *New Grove*.
Leuchtmann[2]   —— 'Rochlitz', in *New Grove*.
Lexikon der Ärzte   *Biographisches Lexikon der hervorragenden Ärzte aller Zeiten und Völker*, herausgegeben von A. Hirsch. Zweite Auflage durchgesehen und ergänzt von W. Haberling, F. Hübotter, H. Vierordt (5 vols., Berlin, 1929–34; Supplement, 1935).
Liess   Liess, A., *Johann Michael Vogl: Hofoperist und Schubertsänger* (Graz, 1954).
Linnemann   Linnemann, R., *Fr. Kistner 1823/1923* (Leipzig, 1923).
Liszt[1]   *Franz Liszt's Briefe*, gesammelt und herausgegeben von La Mara [Lipsius, Marie] (8 vols., Leipzig, 1893–1905).
Liszt[2]   *Correspondance de Liszt et de la comtesse d'Agoult*, publiée par D. Ollivier (2 vols., Paris, 1933–4).

Liszt[3]   *Franz Liszt: Briefe aus ungarischen Sammlungen, 1835–1886*, gesammelt und erläutert von M. Prahács (Basle, 1966).

Liszt[4]   *Franz Liszt: Unbekannte Presse und Briefe aus Wien, 1822–1886*, herausgegeben von D. Legány (Vienna, 1984).

Litschauer[1]   Litschauer, W., 'Mayrhofer', in *LL*.

Litschauer[2]   —— (ed.) *Neue Dokumente zum Schubert-Kreis: Aus Briefen und Tagebüchern seiner Freunde* (Vienna, 1986).

Litschauer[3]   —— (ed.) *Dokumente zum Leben der Anna von Revertera, Neue Dokumente zum Schubert-Kreis*, ii (Vienna, 1993).

Little   Little, W. A., *Gottfried August Bürger* (New York, 1974).

LL   *Literatur Lexikon: Autoren und Werke deutscher Sprache*, herausgegeben von W. Killy (15 vols., Gütersloh, 1988–93).

Lohberger   Lohberger, H., 'Marie Pachler', *Blätter für Heimatkunde* (Graz), 36 (1962), 81–4.

Lorenz   Lorenz, S., 'Kotzebue', in *LL*.

Lorenzen   Lorenzen, K., 'Claudius', in *MGG*.

Lütgendorff   Lütgendorff, W. L., Freiherr von, *Die Geigen- und Lautenmacher vom Mittelalter bis zur Gegenwart* (6th edn., 2 vols., repr. Tutzing, 1975). Supplement by T. Drescher (Tutzing, 1990).

MacArdle[1]   MacArdle, D., 'Anton Felix Schindler, Friend of Beethoven', *Music Review*, 24 (1963), 50–74.

MacArdle[2]   —— 'Beethoven und Karl Holz', *Die Musikforschung*, 20 (1967), 19–29.

McCorkle   McCorkle, M. L., *Johannes Brahms: Thematisch-bibliographisches Werkverzeichnis* (Munich, 1984).

Macdonald   Macdonald, M., *Brahms* (London, 1990).

McKay   McKay, E. N., *Franz Schubert's Music for the Theatre* (Tutzing, 1991).

Maier   Maier, G., 'Zumsteeg', in *New Grove*.

Mailáth   Mailáth, Johann, *Leben der Sophie Müller, weiland k.k. Hofschauspielerinn...* (Vienna, 1832).

Mandell   Mandell, E., 'Salomon Sulzer, 1804–1890', in *The Jews of Austria: Essays on their Life, History and Destruction*, ed. J. Fraenkel (2nd edn., London, 1970), 221–9.

Männergesangverein[1]   *Jahresbericht des Wiener Männer-Gesang-Vereines über das 29. Vereinsjahr vom 1. Oktober 1871 bis zum 30. September 1872* (Vienna, 1872).

Männergesangverein[2]   *Jahresbericht des Wiener Männer-Gesang-Vereines über das 45. Vereinsjahr vom 1. Oktober 1887 bis zum 30. September 1888* (Vienna, 1888).

Mansfeld   Mansfeld, H. A., 'Wiener Theaterleute auf Wanderschaft: Passanweisungen des Wiener Magistrates, Konskriptionsamtes in den Jahren 1792–1850', *Jahrbuch der Gesellschaft für Wiener Theaterforschung*, 11 (1959), 72–172.

Marshall/Warrack   Marshall, J., and Warrack, J., 'Haizinger', in *New Grove*.

May   May, F., *The Life of Johannes Brahms* (2nd edn., London, 1948).

Menhennet   Menhennet, A., 'Schlegel, August Wilhelm von', in *LL*.

MGG   *Die Musik in Geschichte und Gegenwart: Allgemeine Enzyklopädie der Musik.* Herausgegeben von F. Blume (14 vols., Kassel, 1949–68); Supplement (2 vols., Kassel, 1973–9); *Register* (Kassel, 1986).

Michtner   Michtner, O., *Das alte Burgtheater als Opernbühne, von der Einführung des deutschen Singspiels (1778) bis zum Tod Kaiser Leopolds II. (1792)* (Vienna, 1970).

Mikoletzky[1]   Mikoletzky, H. L., 'Schweizer Händler und Bankiers in Österreich (vom 17. bis zur Mitte des 19. Jahrhunderts)', in *Österreich und Europa: Festgabe für Hugo Hantsch zum 70. Geburtstag* (Graz, 1965), 149–81.

Mikoletzky[2]   —— *Österreich: Das entscheidende 19. Jahrhundert. Geschichte, Kultur und Wissenschaft* (Vienna, 1972).

Mix[1]   Mix, Y.-G., 'Stolberg Stolberg, Christian Graf zu', in *LL*.

Mix[2]   —— 'Stolberg Stolberg, Friedrich Leopold Graf zu', in *LL*.

Moser[1]   Moser, A., *Geschichte des Violinspiels* (2nd edn. by H.-J. Nösselt, 2 vols., Tutzing, 1966–7).

Moser[2]   Moser, H. J., *Goethe und die Musik* (Leipzig, 1949).

Müller   Müller, H., 'Ernst Schulzes Werk in Vertonungen: Zur Wirkungsgeschichte des Celler Dichters in der Musik', *Celler Chronik*, 1 (1983), 112–59.

Najmájer   Najmájer, M. von, 'Bei den Schwestern Fröhlich', *Jahrbuch der Grillparzer-Gesellschaft*, 14 (1904), 141–8.

Němcová   Němcová, A., 'Slavík', in *New Grove*.

Nettheim   Nettheim, N., 'How the Young Schubert Borrowed from Beethoven', *Musical Times*, 132 (1991), 330–1.

Neumann[1]   Neumann, M., 'Tieck', in *LL*.

Neumann[2]   Neumann, W., 'Kistner & Siegel', in *MGG*.

Neumayr   Neumayr, A., *Musik und Medizin* (6th edn., 3 vols., Vienna, 1995).

New Grove   *The New Grove Dictionary of Music and Musicians*, ed. S. Sadie (20 vols., London, 1980).

New Opera Grove   *The New Grove Dictionary of Opera*, ed. S. Sadie (4 vols., London, 1992).

Noack   Noack, E., 'Schlösser', in *MGG*.

Nohl   Nohl, L., *Beethovens Leben* (3 vols., Vienna, Leipzig, 1864–1906).

Obermaier   Obermaier, W., 'Neues zu Schuberts Lebensdokumenten', *Schubert Brille*, 5 (1990), 38–41.

ÖBL   *Österreichisches Biographisches Lexikon 1815–1950* (Vienna, 1957–).

ÖMZ   *Österreichische Musikzeitschrift* (Vienna).

Orel   Orel, A., 'Fröhlich', in *MGG*.

Ottich   Ottich, M., 'Rückert', in *MGG*.

Pachler   Pachler, F., *Beethoven und Marie Pachler-Koschak: Beiträge und Berichtigungen* (Berlin, 1866).

Pascall   Pascall, R. J., 'Stockhausen, Julius (Christian)', in *New Grove*.

Pauker   Pauker, W., *Lenaus Freundin Nanette Wolf in Gmunden* (Vienna, 1923).

Perger/Hirschfeld   Perger, R. von, and Hirschfeld, R., *Geschichte der k.k. Gesellschaft der Musikfreunde in Wien* (Vienna, 1912). Perger is responsible for pt. 1: '1812–1870'.

Pfannkuch   Pfannkuch, W., 'Kind', in *MGG*.

Pfeiffer-Belli Pfeiffer-Belli, W., 'Ernst Schulze, Dichter der Rose, Minnesänger der Romantik', in *Marginalien zur poetischen Welt: Festschrift für Robert Mühlher zum 60. Geburtstag*. Herausgegeben von A. Eder, H. Himmel, A. Kracher (Berlin, 1971), 219–31.

Pichler   Pichler, C., *Denkwürdigkeiten aus meinem Leben* ... Herausgegeben von
                 E. K. Blümml (2 vols., Munich, 1914).
Platen   Platen, A. Graf von, *Der Briefwechsel.* Herausgegeben von L. von
                 Scheffler und P. Bornstein (4 vols., Munich, 1911–31; repr. Hildesheim,
                 1973).
Platinga   Platinga, L. B., *Schumann as Critic* (New Haven, 1967).
Plesske   Plesske, H.-M., 'Breitkopf & Härtel', in *New Grove.*
Pohl[1]   Pohl, C. F., *Die Gesellschaft der Musikfreunde des österreichischen Kaiserstaates
                 und ihr Conservatorium* (Vienna, 1871).
Pohl[2]   —— 'Lincke, Joseph', in *New Grove.*
Porhansl[1]   Porhansl, L., 'Bemerkung zu Franz Schuberts Textvorlagen nach Johann
                 Mayrhofer und Aloys Schreiber', *Schubert Brille*, 2 (1989), 12–14.
Porhansl[2]   —— 'Zu Franz Schuberts Textvorlagen nach Theodor Körner und Fried-
                 rich v. Schlegel', *Schubert Brille*, 3 (1989), 22–5.
Porhansl[3]   —— 'Schuberts Textvorlagen nach Salis-Seewis und Kleist: Einige Bemer-
                 kungen', *Schubert Brille*, 4 (1990), 11–13.
Porhansl[4]   —— 'Schuberts Textvorlagen nach Friedrich Baron de la Motte Fouqué
                 und Gottfried August Bürger', *Schubert Brille*, 5 (1990), 22–5.
Porhansl[5]   —— 'Die Textvorlagen zu Schuberts Liedern nach Friedrich Kind und
                 Johann Peter Uz', *Schubert Brille*, 6 (1991), 34–6.
Porhansl[6]   —— 'Ferdinand Sauter: Ein Aussenseiter im Schubert-Kreis', *Schubert
                 Brille*, 7 (1991), 109–15.
Porhansl[7]   —— 'Zu Schuberts Textvorlagen: Die Wiener Shakespeare-Ausgabe und
                 die Beiträge seiner Freunde', *Schubert Brille*, 9 (1992), 113–24.
Porhansl[8]   —— 'Schuberts Textvorlagen nach Friedrich Wilhelm Gotter und Chri-
                 stian Friedrich Daniel Schubart', *Schubert Brille*, 10 (1993), 69–74.
Porhansl[9]   —— 'Schuberts Textvorlagen nach Pfeffel, Ratschky und Tiedge', *Schubert
                 Brille*, 13 (1994), 106–8.
Porhansl[10]   —— ' "Der Liedler": Zu Kenners Textvorlage und zu Schwinds Illustratio-
                 nen', *Schubert Brille*, 16/17 (1996), 110–16.
Prod'homme   Prod'homme, J. G., 'Les Œuvres de Schubert en France', in *Bericht über den
                 internationalen Kongress für Schubertforschung, Wien, 25. bis 29. November
                 1928* (Augsburg, 1929), 87–110.
Pröhle   Pröhle, H., 'Spiker, Samuel Heinrich', in *ADB.*
Prosl   Prosl, R. M., *Die Hellmesberger: Hundert Jahre aus dem Leben einer Wiener
                 Musikerfamilie* (Vienna, 1947).
Pross   Pross, W., 'Herder', in *LL.*
Pyritz   Pyritz, H., *Goethe und Marianne von Willemer: Eine biographische Studie*
                 (3rd edn., Stuttgart, 1948).
Pyrker   Pyrker, J. L., *Mein Leben, 1772–1847,* herausgegeben von A. P. Czigler
                 (Vienna, 1966).
Quicherat   Quicherat, L., *Adolphe Nourrit* (3 vols., Paris, 1867).
Raab   Raab, L., *Wenzel Müller: Ein Tonkünstler Altwiens* (Baden, 1928).
Raabe   Raabe, P., *Liszts Schaffen* (2nd edn., Tutzing, 1968).
Rector   Rector, M., 'Pfeffel', in *LL.*
Redlich   Redlich, H. F., 'Deutsch', in *MGG.*

Reed[1]   Reed, J., *The Schubert Song Companion*, with prose translations by N. Deane and C. Larner (Manchester, 1985).

Reed[2]   —— *Schubert* (London, 1987).

Reed[3]   —— 'Die Rezeptionsgeschichte der Werke Schuberts in England während des 19. Jahrhunderts', *Schubert Brille*, 5 (1990), 43–50.

Reinalter   Reinalter, H., *Aufgeklärter Absolutismus und Revolution: Zur Geschichte des Jakobinertums und der frühdemokratischen Bestrebungen in der Habsburgermonarchie* (Vienna, 1980).

Ricklefs   Ricklefs, J., and Ricklefs, U., 'Schulze', in *LL*.

Riedl   Riedl, G., 'Klenke', in *LL*.

Riege   Riege, H., 'Köpken', in *LL*.

Riley   Riley, H. M. K., 'Chézy', in *LL*.

Robinson[1]   Robinson, M. F., 'Metastasio', in *New Grove*.

Robinson[2]   Robinson, P., 'Lablache', in *New Opera Grove*.

Robinson[3]   —— 'Nourrit, Adolphe', in *New Grove*.

Roedl   Roedl, U. [Adler, B.], *Matthias Claudius: Sein Weg und seine Welt* (3rd edn., Hamburg, 1969).

Ronge   Ronge, P., 'Franz Schubert, der Mensch: Geschwister, Vorfahren, Lebenslauf', *Genealogie*, 16 (1967), 721–36.

Rosenthal   Rosenthal, H., *Two Centuries of Opera at Covent Garden* (London, 1958).

Ross   Ross, M., 'Cibber', in *EB*.

Rowland   Rowland, H., *Matthias Claudius* (Boston, 1983).

Sagarra   Sagarra, E., 'Schopenhauer, Johanna (Henriette)', in *LL*.

St Pölten   *Jubileums-Catalog des Bisthums St. Pölten: Festschrift zum hundertjährigen Jubileum dieses Bisthums, 1784–1884* (St. Pölten, 1884).

Sauder[1]   Sauder, G., 'Jacobi', in *LL*.

Sauder[2]   —— 'Klopstock', in *LL*.

Sauer[1]   Sauer, A., 'Grillparzer und Katharina Fröhlich', *Jahrbuch der Grillparzer-Gesellschaft*, 5 (1895), 219–92.

Sauer[2]   —— 'Zur Biographie der Schwestern Fröhlich', in *Grillparzer-Studien*, herausgegeben von O. Katann (Vienna, 1924), 254–77.

Sauer[3]   Sauer, E., 'Joseph Ludwig Stoll', *Germanisch-romanische Monatsschrift*, 9 (1921), 313–19.

Saul   Saul, N., 'Novalis', in *LL*.

Schaal   Schaal, R., 'Fuchs, Alois', in *MGG*.

Scheit/Partsch Scheit, K., and Partsch, E. W., 'Ein unbekanntes Schubertlied in einer Sammlung aus dem Wiener Vormärz', *Schubert Brille*, 2 (1989), 15–18.

Schimpf   Schimpf, W., 'Gotter', in *LL*.

Schletterer   Schletterer, [H. M.], 'Schechner', in *ADB*.

Schlösser   Schlösser, R., *Friedrich Wilhelm Gotter: Sein Leben und seine Werke …* (Hamburg, 1894).

Schmidt   Schmidt, A., *Fouqué und einige seiner Zeitgenossen: Biographischer Versuch* (Zurich, 1988).

Schmidt-Görg Schmidt-Görg, J., 'Holz', in *MGG*.

Schmutzenhofer Schmutzenhofer, W., 'Leidesdorf', in *MGG*.

Schneider   Schneider, H., *Uhland: Leben, Dichtung, Forschung* (Berlin, 1920).

Schober   Schober, U., *Johann Georg Jacobis dichterische Entwicklung* (Breslau, 1938).

Schochow   *Franz Schubert: Die Texte seiner einstimmig komponierten Lieder und ihre Dichter*, vollständig gesammelt und kritisch herausgegehen von M. und L. Schochow (2 vols., Hildesheim, 1974).

Schönherr   Schönherr, M., 'Berté', in *MGG*.

Schöny[1]   Schöny, H., 'Die Vorfahren des Malers Leopold Kupelwieser', *Adler*, 7 (1967), 241–5.

Schöny[2]   —— 'Notizen zur Genealogie um Franz Schubert', *Genealogie*, 18 (1969), 534–7.

Schrader   Schrader, G. W., *Biographisch-literarisches Lexicon der Thierärzte aller Zeiten und Länder* . . ., vervollständigt von E. Hering (Stuttgart, 1863).

Schubert: Biography O. E. Deutsch, *Schubert: A Documentary Biography*, trans. E. Blom (London, 1946).

Schubert Brille Schubert durch die Brille (Vienna).

Schubert: Die Dokumente Schubert: Die Dokumente seines Lebens. Gesammelt und erläutert von O. E. Deutsch (Kassel, 1964).

Schubert: Dokumente Franz Schubert: Dokumente 1817–1830, vol. i: *Texte* . . . Herausgegeben von T. G. Waidelich (Tutzing, 1993).

Schubert: Erinnerungen Schubert: Die Erinnerungen seiner Freunde, gesammelt und herausgegeben von O. E. Deutsch (Leipzig, 1957).

Schubert: Thematisches Verzeichnis Deutsch, O. E., *Franz Schubert: Thematisches Verzeichnis seiner Werke in chronologischer Folge.* Neuausgabe in deutscher Sprache bearbeitet und herausgegeben von der Editionsleitung der Neuen Schubert-Ausgabe und W. Aderhold (Kassel, 1978).

Schulz   Schulz, G., 'Fouqué', in *LL*.

Schumann[1]   Schumann, R., *Gesammelte Schriften über Musik und Musiker.* Herausgegeben von M. Kreisig (5th edn., 2 vols., Leipzig, 1914).

Schumann[2]   *Briefe und Gedichte aus dem Album Robert und Clara Schumanns.* Herausgegeben von W. Boetticher (Leipzig, 1979).

Schumann[3]   *Robert und Clara Schumann: Briefe einer Liebe.* Herausgegeben von H.-J. Ortheil (Königstein, 1982).

Schünemann   Schünemann, G., *Erinnerungen an Schubert: Josef von Spauns erste Lebensbeschreibung* (Berlin, 1936).

Schütz   Schütz, R., *Stephen Heller: Ein Künstlerleben* (Leipzig, 1911).

Schwarz   Schwarz, C., 'Schmidt, Georg Philipp', in *LL*.

Schwarze   Schwarze, R., 'Kleist, Ewald Christian von', in *ADB*.

Schwind[1]   Schwind, M. von, *Briefe.* Herausgegeben und erläutert von O. Stoessl (Leipzig, 1924).

Schwind[2]   —— *Briefe 1822–1870.* Herausgegeben von H. Gärtner (Leipzig, 1986).

Searle   Searle, H., 'Liszt', in *New Grove*.

Sebastian   Sebastian, L., *Fürst Alexander von Hohenlohe-Schillingsfürst, 1794 bis 1849, und seine Gebets-Heilungen* (Kempten, 1918).

Sembdner   Sembdner, H., *Schütz-Lacrimas: Das Leben des Romantikerfreundes, Poeten und Literaturkritikers Wilhelm von Schütz (1776–1847)* (Berlin, 1974).

Siegert   Siegert, R., 'Sauter, Samuel Friedrich', in *LL*.

Sietz[1]	Sietz, R., 'Vesque von Püttlingen', in *MGG*.
Sietz[2]	—— 'Vesque von Püttlingen', in *New Grove*.
Simmer	Simmer, N., 'Aus dem Leben des Waldviertelentdeckers J. F. A. Reil', *Das Waldviertel*, 18 (1969), 301–8.
Simpson	Simpson, A., 'Voříšek', in *New Grove*.
Skrine[1]	Skrine, P., 'Collin, Heinrich Joseph von', in *LL*.
Skrine[2]	—— 'Collin, Matthäus von', in *LL*.
Slezak	Slezak, F., *Beethovens Wiener Originalverleger* (Vienna, 1987).
Solomon[1]	Solomon, M., 'Franz Schubert and the Peacocks of Benvenuto Cellini', *19th Century Music*, 12 (1988–9), 193–206.
Solomon[2]	—— 'Schubert: Some Consequences of Nostalgia', *19th Century Music*, 17 (1993–4), 34–46.
Sonnleithner	Sonnleithner, L. von, 'Musikalische Skizzen aus Alt-Wien', eingeleitet von O. E. Deutsch, *ÖMZ*, 16 (1961), 49–62, 97–110, 145–57.
Spiel	*Der Wiener Kongress in Augenzeugenberichten*. Herausgegeben und eingeleitet von H. Spiel, (2nd edn., Düsseldorf, 1965).
Stadlen[1]	Stadlen, P. 'Zu Schindlers Fälschungen in Beethovens Konversationsheften', *ÖMZ*, 32 (1977), 246–52.
Stadlen[2]	—— 'Schindler und die Konversationshefte', *ÖMZ*, 34 (1979), 2–18.
StadtChronik	*StadtChronik Wien: 2000 Jahre in Daten, Dokumenten und Bildern* (Vienna, 1986).
Steblin[1]	Steblin, R., 'Die Atzenbrugger Gäste-Listen neu entdeckt: Ein wichtiger Beitrag zur Schubert-Ikonographie', *Schubert Brille*, 9 (1992), 65–80.
Steblin[2]	—— 'Neue Forschungsaspekte zu Caroline Esterházy', *Schubert Brille*, 11 (1993), 21–33.
Steblin[3]	—— 'Nochmals die Atzenbrugger Gäste-Liste', *Schubert Brille*, 10 (1993), 35–41.
Steblin[4]	—— 'Schwinds Portraitskizze "Schubert am Klavier": Ein Gewinn für Österreich', *Schubert Brille*, 10 (1993), 45–52.
Steblin[5]	—— 'The Peacock's Tale: Schubert's Sexuality Reconsidered', *19th Century Music*, 17 (1993–4), 5–33.
Steblin[6]	—— 'Le Mariage malheureux de Caroline Esterházy: Une histoire authentique, telle qu'elle est retracée dans les lettres de la famille Crenneville', *Cahiers F. Schubert* (Paris), 5 (1994), 17–34.
Steblin[7]	—— 'Wilhelm Müllers Aufenthalt in Wien im Jahre 1817: Eine Verbindung zu Schubert durch Schlechta', *Vom Pasqualatihaus* (Vienna), 4 (1994), 19–26.
Štědroň	Štědroň, B., 'Voříšek', in *MGG*.
Stekl	Stekl, K., 'Zur Richtigstellung des Aufenthaltes Josef Kupelwiesers in Graz', *Mitteilungen des Steirischen Tonkünstlerbundes*, 47–8 (1971), 10–13.
Suppan	Suppan, W., *Steirisches Musiklexikon* (Graz, 1962–6).
Taddey	Taddey, G. (ed.), *Lexikon der deutschen Geschichte: Personen, Ereignisse, Institutionen, von der Zeitwende bis zum Ausgang des 2. Weltkrieges* (2nd, rev. edn., Stuttgart, 1983).
Thomas	Thomas, W., 'Schillergedicht und Schubertlied', in his *Schubert-Studien* (Frankfurt am Main, 1990), 7–79.

Tovey¹   Tovey, D. F., *Essays in Musical Analysis* (6 vols., London, 1935–9).
Tovey²   —— 'Tonality in Schubert', in his *Essays and Lectures in Music* (London, 1949), 134–59.
Traubner   Traubner, R., *Operetta: A Theatrical History* (Oxford, 1983).
Tyrrell   Tyrrell, J., 'Pazdírek', in *New Grove*.
Ullrich   Ullrich, H., 'Karl Holz und Franz Schubert', *ÖMZ*, 33 (1978), 595–8.
Ulrich   Ulrich, P. S., *Theater, Tanz und Musik im 'Deutschen Bühnenjahrbuch': Ein Fundstellennachweis von biographischen Eintragungen, Abbildungen und Aufsätzen . . .* (2 vols., Berlin, 1985).
Umlauff   Umlauff, Ritter von Frankwell, V., *Leben und Wirken eines österreichischen Justizmannes: Ein biographisches Denkmal zur Erinnerung an den jub. k.k. Oberlandesgerichts-Präsidenten Johann Karl Ritter Umlauff von Frankwell* (Vienna, 1861).
Verweyen/Witting   Verweyen, T., and Witting, G., 'Uz', in *LL*.
Výborný¹   Výborný, Z., 'Pazdírek', in *MGG*.
Výborný²   —— 'Slavík', in *MGG*.
Waidelich¹   Waidelich, T. G., 'Die Weimarer Uraufführung von *Alfonso und Estrella* unter Franz Liszt', *Schubert Brille*, 6 (1991), 5–21.
Waidelich²   —— *Franz Schubert, 'Alfonso und Estrella': Eine frühe durchkomponierte deutsche Oper. Geschichte und Analyse* (Tutzing, 1991).
Waidelich³   —— 'Weitere Addenda zur neuen Ausgabe der Dokumente', *Schubert Brille*, 15 (1995), 5–45.
Waidelich⁴   —— ' "Vielleicht hielt er sich zu streng an das französische Original": Ein Plagiat Kotzebues als Libretto für Walter, Reichardt und Schubert', *Schubert Brille*, 16/17 (1996), 94–109.
Wallmoden   Wallmoden, T. von, 'Leon', in *LL*.
Walker¹   Walker, A., 'Liszt and the Schubert Song Transcriptions', *Musical Quarterly*, 67 (1981), 50–63.
Walker²   ——*Franz Liszt* (3 vols., Ithaca, New York, 1987–96).
Walker³   Walker, E., 'Mystical Songs', *Music and Letters*, 9 (1928), 324–9.
Walton   Walton, G., 'Cowley', in *EB*.
Warrack¹   Warrack, J., 'Kind', in *New Grove*.
Warrack²   —— 'Müller, Wilhelm', in *New Grove*.
Warrack³   —— 'Schechner', in *New Grove*.
Warrack⁴   —— 'Schubert: German family of musicians active in Dresden . . .', in *New Grove*.
Weber   Weber, W., 'Salis-Seewis', in *LL*.
Weigmann   Weigmann, O., *Schwind: Des Meisters Werke in 1265 Abbildungen* (Stuttgart, n.d.).
Weinmann¹   Weinmann, A., 'Haslinger', in *MGG*.
Weinmann²   —— 'Pennauer', in *MGG*.
Weinmann³   —— 'Eine österreichische Volkshymne von Franz Schubert', *ÖMZ*, 27 (1972), 430–4.
Weinmann⁴   ——*J. P. Gotthard als später Originalverleger Franz Schuberts* (Vienna, 1979).
Weinmann⁵   —— 'Cappi', in *New Grove*.

Weinmann[6] —— 'Cappi, Pietro', in *New Grove*.

Weinmann[7] —— 'Haslinger', in *New Grove*.

Weinmann[8] —— 'Sauer', in *New Grove*.

Weinmann[9] —— *Verzeichnis der Verlagswerke J. P. Gotthard* (Vienna, 1981).

Weinmann[10] Weinmann, I., 'Schubert, Ferdinand Lukas', in *MGG*.

Weinmann[11] —— 'Franz Schuberts Beziehungen zu Zseliz: Eine Zusammenfassung der einschlägigen Literatur und der neuesten Forschungsergebnisse' (Vienna, 1975). Unpublished typescript at the Nationalbibliothek, Vienna.

Weinmann/Warrack Weinmann, A., and Warrack, J., 'Diabelli', in *New Grove*.

Weiss Weiss, A., *Franz von Schober: Lebensbild eines Freundes Franz Schuberts* (Vienna, 1907).

Weissberg Weissberg, L., 'Schlegel, Dorothea von', in *LL*.

Werba Werba, R., *Schubert und die Wiener: Der volkstümliche Unbekannte* (Vienna, 1978).

Werner[1] Werner, E., 'Sulzer', in *MGG*.

Werner[2] —— *Mendelssohn: Leben und Werk in neuer Sicht* (Zurich, 1980).

Wessely[1] Wessely, O., 'Kiesewetter, Raphael Georg', in *MGG*.

Wessely[2] —— 'Das Linzer Musikleben in der ersten Hälfte des 19. Jahrhunderts', *Jahrbuch der Stadt Linz* (1953), 283–442.

Wessely[3] —— 'Fuchs, Aloys', in *New Grove*.

Wessely[4] —— 'Herbeck', in *New Grove*.

Wessely[5] —— 'Kiesewetter, Raphael Georg', in *New Grove*.

Weston[1] Weston, P., *Clarinet Virtuosi of the Past* (London, 1971).

Weston[2] —— *More Clarinet Virtuosi of the Past* (London, 1977).

Willemer *Im Namen Goethes: Der Briefwechsel Marianne von Willemer und Hermann Grimm.* Herausgegeben und eingeleitet von H. J. Mey (Frankfurt am Main, 1988).

Willfort Willfort, M., 'Das Urbild des Andante aus Schuberts Klaviertrio Es-Dur, D929', *ÖMZ*, 33 (1978), 277–83.

Wilpert Wilpert, G. von, *Deutsches Dichterlexikon: Biographisch-bibliographisches Handwörterbuch zur deutschen Literaturgeschichte* (Stuttgart, 1963).

Wirth Wirth, J., *Julius Stockhausen, der Sänger des deutschen Liedes...* (Frankfurt am Main, 1927).

Wodtke[1] Wodtke, F. W., 'Kotzebue', in *MGG*.

Wodtke[2] —— 'Matthisson', in *MGG*.

Worgull Worgull, E., 'Zwei Fehlzuschreibungen in der Schubert-Ikonographie', *Schubert Brille*, 16/17 (1996), 158–71.

Würz[1] Würz, A., 'Lachner', in *MGG*.

Würz[2] —— 'Müller, Wenzel', in *MGG*.

Wurzbach[1] Wurzbach, C. von, *Biographisches Lexikon des Kaiserthums Oesterreich, enthaltend die Lebensskizzen der denkwürdigen Personen, welche 1750 bis 1850 im Kaiserstaate und in seinen Kronländern gelebt haben* (60 vols., Vienna, 1856–91).

Wurzbach[2] Wurzbach, W. von, 'Johann Gabriel Seidls Leben und Werke', in *Johann Gabriel Seidls ausgewählte Werke ...*, herausgegeben von W. von Wurzbach (4 vols., Leipzig, n.d.), vol. i, pp. v–lxxx.

Youens[1]   Youens, S., 'Schubert and the Poetry of Graf August von Platen-
                Hallermünde', *Music Review,* 46 (1985), 19–34.
Youens[2]   —— 'Behind the Scenes: *Die schöne Müllerin* before Schubert', *19th Century
                Music,* 15 (1991–2), 3–22.
Youens[3]   —— *Schubert: 'Die schöne Müllerin'* (Cambridge, 1992).
Young   Young, P. M., *George Grove, 1820–1900: A Biography* (London, 1980).
Zenger   Zenger, M., *Geschichte der Münchener Oper.* Nachgelassenes Werk heraus-
                gegeben von T. Kroyer (Munich, 1923).
Zimmer   Zimmer, H., *Theodor Körners Braut: Ein Lebens- und Charakterbild Antonie
                Adambergers* (2nd edn., Stuttgart, 1918).

Index of Schubert's Works[1]

‹⁜›

---

[1] This index lists all references contained in the chronicle of Schubert's life and in the dictionary, except for those which appear at the end of certain articles under the headings 'Settings' and 'First Editions' and which identify compositions by work-numbers alone.

Index of Names

ఌఝఌ